Phelps' Mills, Pine Creek, Pa. From the High Hill on the North, looking South.

OTZINACHSON;

OR,

A HISTORY OF THE

WEST BRANCH VALLEY

OF THE

SUSQUEHANNA:

EMBRACING

A FULL ACCOUNT OF ITS SETTLEMENT—TRIALS AND PRIVATIONS ENDURED BY THE FIRST PIONEERS—FULL ACCOUNTS OF THE INDIAN WARS, PREDATORY INCURSIONS, ABDUCTIONS, MASSACRES, &c.,

TOGETHER WITH

AN ACCOUNT OF THE FAIR PLAY SYSTEM;

AND THE

Trying Scenes of the Big Runaway;

INTERSPERSED WITH

BIOGRAPHICAL SKETCHES OF SOME OF THE LEADING SETTLERS, FAMILIES, ETC., TOGETHER WITH PERTINENT ANECDOTES, STATISTICS, AND MUCH VALUABLE MATTER ENTIRELY NEW.

BY J. F. MEGINNESS.

PHILADELPHIA:
PUBLISHED BY HENRY B. ASHMEAD,
GEORGE STREET ABOVE ELEVENTH.
1857.

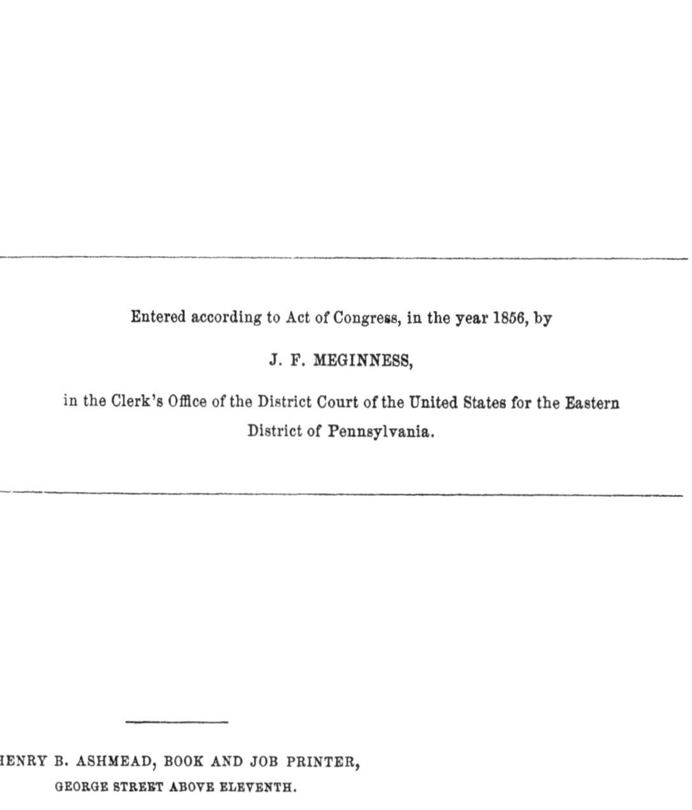

HENRY B. ASHMEAD, BOOK AND JOB PRINTER,
GEORGE STREET ABOVE ELEVENTH.

TO

COL. ROBERT CRANE,

OF

JERSEY SHORE, LYCOMING COUNTY, PA.,

THIS WORK IS RESPECTFULLY

Dedicated,

BY THE AUTHOR,

AS A TOKEN OF RESPECT AND ESTEEM.

PREFACE.

The design of this work is to lay before the people of the West Branch Valley, and adjacent country, as full and accurate a history of the difficulties and privations endured by the early settlers, as we possibly can at this late day. It is to be regretted that the work was not undertaken years ago, when the old pioneers were living, and in the full enjoyment of their intellectual faculties; when *all* the facts could have been collected and arranged with comparative ease and accuracy. But the enterprise has been neglected, till all, with two or three exceptions, of the survivors of the Revolutionary period, have been consigned to the tomb.

Few people now living in this beautiful and romantic vale, are aware that it has been the scene of some of the most thrilling and bloody events in the early history of Pennsylvania; and that it is a fruitful field for the researches of the historian, and possessed of sufficient material to make an exciting and entertaining work.

The vale of Wyoming has been immortalized in song and story—the poet and the historian have given it a world-wide notoriety: the Valley of the blue Juniata, "where wild roved an Indian girl," has been the theme of polished pens, and is known throughout the Union; but the picturesque Valley of the Otzinachson, as prolific as any of them in material, has been neglected, and is comparatively unknown.

Much labor and expense have been devoted to the preparation of this work, and although every available effort has been made, and the co-operation of numerous well-informed persons been secured, it is acknowledged that many errors will undoubtedly be detected. But upon the whole, it is believed that a greater amount of matter has been collected, and presented to the people, than has ever been published before respecting this Valley. The dates of surveys, early settlements, &c., may be implicity relied upon, as they have been taken from the official documents; the accounts of the massacres, captivities, &c., are as correct as they can well be found at this late period. In fact, everything entering into the composition of the work, has been carefully digested, and the authorities sifted with care.

Much valuable matter has been contributed by literary gentleman—residents of the Valley—who have manifested a lively interest in the work, and to whom I acknowledge myself deeply indebted. The assistance derived from the following gentleman, I cannot appreciate too highly: James F. Linn, Esq., Mr. O. N. Worden, J. F. Wolfinger, Esq., Geo. A. Snyder, Esq., Mr. Thomas Wood, A. H. McHenry, and H. L. Dieffenbach, Esqrs. All of my information in reference to land titles, names of early settlers, boundaries of treaties, &c., is derived from Mr. McHenry, who, probably, is in possession of more facts of this kind, than any other man living in Northern Pennsylvania. Having devoted more than twenty years of his life to surveying, the study of land titles, and the acquisition of historical facts, he now possesses a vast fund of valuable information. With the assistance of these gentlemen, and numerous others, and all the available documents of the State, Pennsylvania Historical Society, Philadelphia Library, &c., I feel that I have succeeded as well, at least, as any that have preceded me.

But, notwithstanding all the care and research, as I have already observed, many errors will no doubt be detected by the careful reader. It is my desire that those who may discover errors, of any kind whatever, will inform me of them immediately, so that if a future edition should be put to press, they may be corrected.

It has been the constant aim of the writer to preserve a plain, concise, and unostentatious style, without any attempt at fine writing or rhetorical flourishes, confidently believing that the people would be better pleased with such an effort, than if it was done up in the style of romance and the garb of fiction. This work is historical—nothing but *facts* have been narrated; and whenever a *doubt* arose about an event or circumstance, such an intimation has been given.

J. F. Meginness.

Jersey Shore, Pa., Nov. 1, 1856.

CONTENTS.

CHAPTER VII.

CHAPTER VIII.

CHAPTER IX.

CHAPTER X.

CHAPTER XI.

CHAPTER XII.

CHAPTER XIX.

CHAPTER XX.

CHAPTER XXI.

CHAPTER XXII.

CHAPTER XXIII.

CHAPTER XXIV.

CHAPTER XXV.

CHAPTER XXVI.

CHAPTER XXVII.

CHAPTER XXVIII.

CHAPTER XXIX.

CHAPTER XXXV.

CHAPTER XXXVI.

CHAPTER XXXVII.

CHAPTER XXXVIII.

CHAPTER XXXIX.

CHAPTER XL.

CHAPTER XLI.

CHAPTER XLII.

CHAPTER XLIII.

CHAPTER XLIV.

CHAPTER XLV.

CHAPTER XLVI.

CHAPTER XLVII.

CHAPTER XLVIII.

CHAPTER XLIX.

CHAPTER L.

CHAPTER LI.

CHAPTER LII.

CHAPTER LIII.

APPENDIX.

Residence of Capt. P. Jarrett, Lock Haven, Pa.

HISTORY

OF THE

WEST BRANCH VALLEY.

CHAPTER I.

THE WEST BRANCH VALLEY—INDIAN NAME OF THE RIVER—REFLECTIONS—THE CLIMATE.

ON taking up this volume, the reader will probably ask, "Where is the West Branch Valley?" Anticipating such an interrogatory, it is thought advisable to define its geographical position, previous to entering upon a history of its first settlement.

The Susquehanna river flows through the interior of Pennsylvania. Two large streams running in opposite directions, unite at Northumberland, and form the main river. They are called the North and West Branches. The North Branch has its source in Otsego Lake; the West Branch rises near the head waters of the Alleghany river, in the mountains of the same name. It flows almost in an easterly direction till opposite Muncy, when it sweeps around Bald Eagle Mountain, and runs directly

2

south to its confluence with the other stream. The length of this branch is about two hundred miles. The Aborigines called it the OTZINACHSON—hence the title of this book.

The Valley of the West Branch begins at Northumberland, and properly ends at Lock Haven. At this point the river bursts through a bold ridge of the Alleghanies, which rises from the water's edge to a great height.

The Valley is not wide. Several smaller ones put into it at various points, the most extensive of which is Buffalo. The spurs of the Appalachian chain are visible on every hand, lending an additional charm of beauty to the receding landscape. The scenery is varied, wild and picturesque; and it is impossible to form a correct idea of its variegated beauties without visiting the spot. The Valley is in a high state of cultivation, containing some of the finest farms and most flourishing towns in the interior of the State. It is embraced in the counties of Northumberland, Union, Lycoming and Clinton.

What a contrast does the beautiful vale of the Otzinachson now present, to the time when it was inhabited by the Aborigines? Let us, in imagination, look back to the period when the red man dwelt on the banks of the stream—roamed in the forest, or hunted the deer and the elk on the declivities of the surrounding mountains: when he built his humble wigwam in some shady dell, beneath the wide-spreading branches of the mighty oak. It was indeed a happy scene—his young papooses gamboled in their rude simplicity on the banks of the murmuring rivulet—the squaws cultivated their patches of corn and chanted songs of the spirit-land—and the dusky warrior plied his birch-bark canoe over the crystal waves of the beautiful Otzinachson. Happy scene!

This Valley was then a fairy land—an Indian paradise—the cherished home of the rude, yet *noble*, children of the forest. But mighty changes were destined to occur—tragedies calculated to cause a thrill of horror to run through the frame, *must* transpire before their cup of destiny is filled.

The Valley has entirely changed, and the last red man has long since been gathered to his fathers. Highly cultivated farms occupy the spot where the Indian village stood, and the busy hum of enterprise is heard on every hand. In summer time the luxuriant grain waves over the graves that contain the cherished remains of their ancestors, and the *rude* hand of civilization has defaced the last mementoes reared to perpetuate their memory.

The climate of the Valley is truthfully portrayed in the following lines:—

"Beneath the temperate zone this vale doth lie,
Where heat and cold a grateful change supply.
To fifteen hours extends the longest day,
When Sol in cancer points his fervid ray.
Yet here the winter season is severe;
And summer's heat is difficult to bear:
But western winds oft cool the scorching ray,
And southern breezes warm the winter's day.
Yet oft tho' warm and fair the day begun,
Cold storms arise before the setting sun,
Nay oft so quick the change, so great its pow'r,
As summer's heat, and winter, in an hour!"

CHAPTER II.

THE ABORIGINES OF THE VALLEY—THEIR NAMES, CHARACTER AND DISPOSITION.

FROM the most reliable accounts we have of the Aborigines of the Valley, it appears that various tribes inhabited it at different periods; and from traces of fortifications found at various points, it is evident that it was once peopled by a superior race, of whom we have not the least account.

The earliest tribes of which we have any account, that dwelt among the forests of New Jersey, Pennsylvania and Delaware, called themselves the Lenni Lenape, meaning the original people. This was a general name comprehending a number of tribes, quite distinct in their character, yet speaking the same language and meeting around the same council fire. The dialect spoken by them was termed the Algonquin. Their grand council-house extended from the eastern bank of the Hudson river to the Potomac in Virginia.

The Lenni Lenape nation was divided into three principal tribes, embracing in its subdivisions the Unamis, or Turtle tribes; the Unalachtgos, or Turkeys, and the Monseys, or Wolf tribes. The former occupied the country along the coast, between the sea and the Kittatinny or Blue Mountain. They were generally known among the whites as the Delaware Indians. The Monseys or Wolf tribes, the most active and warlike of the whole, occupied the mountainous country between the Kittatinny mountain and the sources of the Susquehanna and Delaware rivers, kindling their great council fire at the Minisink flats. These three principal tribes were again subdivided into a variety of subordinate clans, assuming names suited to their character or station. The Lenni Lenape were afterwards conquered by the Six Nations, and became subject to them.

Another great tribe, called by the French the Iroquois, but calling themselves the Aquanuschioni, or "united people," deserve particular attention, as they afterwards became identified to some extent with the history of this valley. They were called Mengwe by the Delawares; Maquas, by the Dutch; Mingoes, by the English and Americans. They were a confederate nation, consisting of Mohawks, Oneida, Onondago, Cayuga, and Seneca. They were originally known by the title of the Five Nations. In 1712, the Tuscarora tribe was forcibly expelled from the interior of North Carolina, and flying northward was taken in and adopted as the Sixth tribe, making what was afterwards known as the Six Nations.

The language of all these tribes, excepting the Tuscaroras, was radically the same, and different from the Lenni Lenape. Their domain stretched from the borders of Vermont to Lake Erie, and from Lake Ontario to the head waters of the Alleghany, Susquehanna, and Delaware rivers. This territory they styled their long house. The grand council fire was held in the Onondago valley. The Senecas guarded the western door of the house, the Mohawks the eastern, and the Cayugas the southern, or that which opened upon the Susquehanna. The Mohawk nation was the first in rank, and to it appertained the office of principal war chief; to the Onondagos, who guarded the grand council fire, appertained in like manner the office of principal civil chief, or chief sachem. The Senecas, in numbers and military energy, were the most powerful.

The Seneca tribe frequently inhabited the valley of the West Branch, and used it as a favorite hunting ground. The Cayugas also came here and dwelt for a time. It seemed that the beautiful vale in later years was set apart for hunting purposes, and when the whites commenced encroaching upon these lands, the wrath of the Indians was speedily aroused, and they committed those bloody tragedies which were of so frequent occurrence.

The Monsey tribe, distinguished for their warlike character, also dwelt in the valley of the Otzinachson, and their name is now perpetuated in the beautiful village of the same title. Above Lock Port a short distance, is a level spot of land, known at this day by the name of "Monseytown," where tradition has it that an Indian village belonging to this tribe was located. The remains of their corn-fields were pointed out for a long time after the white settlers came and took possession of the country.

But the Aborigines of the Valley have long since disappeared, and scarcely a trace remains to indicate their former existence. The last straggling relics of the various tribes, that frequently passed through this way, long after they had evacuated their favorite hunting grounds, to cast a last lingering glance upon the spot they loved so well, and drop a tear upon the little mound that enclosed the bones of their ancestors, are gone forever.

Notwithstanding the Indians were denominated savages, and possessed of much ferocity, they were a noble race. They were the unsophisticated children of nature, and a close examination of their character discloses noble traits that are worthy of emulation by the more refined nations of the world. They considered themselves created by an almighty, wise, and benevolent Spirit, to whom they looked for guidance and protection. Many of them were in the habit of seeking some high elevation, where they could commune with the "Great Spirit," and contemplate with awe and veneration the beauties of the surrounding landscape. While they paid their humble adorations at the shrine of the Great Manitou, they were not unmindful of their duties to one another. They looked upon the good things of the earth as a common stock, bestowed by the Great Spirit for the benefit of all. They held that the game of the forest, the fish of the rivers, and the grass or other articles of spontaneous growth, were free to all who chose to take them. They ridiculed the idea of fencing in a meadow or a pasture. This noble principle had a tendency to repress selfishness and foster generosity. Their hospitality was proverbial. The Indian considered it a duty to share his last morsel with a stranger.

When the first settlers arrived, the Indians received them with open arms, supplied them with food, and shared with them the rude comforts of their humble wigwams. They were actuated by the noblest impulses of the human heart, and considered it their duty to take the white strangers in and minister to their wants. But how was this noble spirit of generosity repaid? By treachery and deceit. They came to cheat the Indians, and when the latter became satisfied of their character, and that instead of being friends, they were insidious enemies—their vindictive passions were aroused, and terribly did they exhibit the ferocity of their nature.

CHAPTER III.

INDIAN TOWNS OF THE VALLEY—THEIR PLACES OF BURIAL—MOUNDS—REMAINS OF FORTIFICATIONS—DISCOVERY OF AN INDIAN POTTERY—CURIOSITIES—WAR PATHS.

THE most important Indian town of which we have any account, was located where Sunbury now stands, and was called Shamokin. Rev. David Brainerd who visited it in 1745, says: "This town, as I observed in my Diary of May last, lies partly on the east side of the river, partly on the west, and partly on a large island in it, and contains upwards of fifty houses, and nearly three hundred persons."

Shamokin was a place of great note among the Indians, from its central position, near the confluence of the two streams; and was the headquarters of distinguished chiefs who presided over the Six Nations.

Allumoppies, one of the Kings of the Delawares, dwelt here as early as 1728, as mention is made of him by Conrad Weiser, who visited the place in 1744, on a mission in reference to the murder of John Armstrong on the Juniata. The great and good chief, Shikellamy, also dwelt here.

A town called Ostanwackin stood a short distance up the West Branch, and was visited by Count Zinzendorf as early as 1742. It was inhabited by a number of

Europeans—French—who had adopted the Indian custom; and the celebrated Madame Montour. Its exact location is not known.

Shikellamy had a small town at, or near, the mouth of Warrior Run. The Monsey tribe also had a village on the beautiful flats near the present town of Muncy.

Conrad Weiser, the Indian interpreter and agent, mentions that he once made a journey to the town of Otstuagy, forty-five miles above Shamokin, for the purpose of assisting the Indians to fence in a cornfield. It was a town of some note, and stood on both sides of Loyal Sock Creek. The trading establishment in after years stood on the east side of the creek, between the village of Montoursville and the river. It was inhabited by the Delawares.

An Indian town also stood on the site now occupied by Dunnsburg. Another called "Patterson's town," was located opposite the mouth of Chatham's Run.

The next most important one was located on the level bottom a short distance above Lock Port, and belonged to the Monseys. They also cultivated corn here. Traces of their village were perceptible long after the arrival of the whites, and some of the oldest inhabitants remember the little hillocks where the corn grew. The place is known at this day by the name of the "Monsey Town Flats."

An extensive Indian burying ground was located at the upper end of Sunbury, where it seemed that hundreds, and for aught we know, thousands of Indians had been consigned to the grave from time immemorial. Years after the white settlers came they found large quantities of Indian relics and implements of war, consisting of stone hatchets, pipes, wampum, &c., that were displaced by the spring freshets in the river, which washed away the banks. Skeletons, too, in a perpendicular position, were thus exhumed in great numbers.

The hills around Shamokin, in various places, bear marks of having been excavated, but for what purpose it is now impossible to divine, and nothing is left but vague conjecture. It is alleged, by some, that the Indians were possessed of the knowledge of some kind of mineral which they used in considerable quantities.

P. B. Masser, Esq., of Sunbury, describes the remains of what appeared to have been a small furnace, covered by a mound, that was dicovered near the Bloody Spring. It was examined by him in 1854. The bed appeared to have been about six feet square, and constructed of stone. It bore every trace of having been subjected to the action of an intense fire, as the sand was baked and blackened in such a manner as not to be mistaken. On giving it a careful examination, several small particles of gold were discovered, which he still retains in his possession. A tradition is preserved that three Englishmen, at a very early period, came here and erected the furnace.

An extensive Indian burying ground existed on the farm of Mr. Nesbit, opposite the mouth of Buffalo Creek. It consisted of a large mound, twenty-five or thirty feet in diameter. Mr. Nesbit remembers when it was opened, and states that in the bottom was a floor of flat stones, on which the bodies appeared to have been placed in a sitting posture; which he inferred from the fact, that the skulls were all on the top of the other bones. When exposed to the air they soon crumbled into dust. The mound contained no implements of war, only a few stone pipes; and on the summit, an ash tree was growing, which was hollow, and outside of which the concentric circles indicated it to be seventy years old.

About 1833, or earlier, an oak was felled on the north side of Muncy mountain, the growths of which showed it to be four hundred and sixty years old; and to have been marked by a cutting instrument three hundred and ninety years ago.

The next most extensive deposit of the dead, was on the Muncy Farm, or what is now known as "Hall's Farms," a short distance below Williamsport. A mound had been thrown up, and apparently filled with hundreds of bodies. In 1835, Mr. Fowler, the Phrenologist, visited it and carried away a number of skulls.

Traces of extensive burying grounds were visible, till within a few years, on Pine Creek, on the farm of Mr. Harvey Bailey on one side, and that of Mr. S. Simmons on the other. From the most reliable accounts I can glean respecting them, it seems that unusually large numbers were deposited there. On one side of the creek, a large trench was evidently dug and filled with a great number of dead, thrown promiscuously together, from the appearance of their remains, when laid bare by the action of the waters. Those buried on Bailey's farm seemed to have been deposited with a great deal of care and affection.

A tradition is preserved, but in a very vague and unsatisfactory manner, that two hostile tribes met and fought a desperate battle at this point, which well nigh proved a war of extermination; and the few survivors buried the dead in the trenches, which the waves of Pine Creek in after years exposed to view. The manner in which they were buried, and the large number, would naturally lead us to such a conclusion, but still we have not the least authentic evidence that such was the fact.

On the high point of the mountain, not far from the residence of Mr. Jesse Vickers, on Pine Creek, is the remains of seven mounds, formed out of stone, and evidently placed there by human hands. They are about two hundred yards apart, and in a straight line up the ridge. They have been torn open for years. Nothing is known respecting them. The view from this point of the valley of Pine Creek, both up and down, is beautiful. Doubtless they were erected for burial purposes.

On digging the canal through the rocks near Liberty, several skeletons were discovered, with Indian camp kettles, in a tolerably good state of preservation. They were sent to Peale's Museum in Philadelphia.

A burying ground evidently existed where Lock Haven now stands, as the workmen in digging the canal, disinterred the remains of great numbers.

In 1854, James Wilson and A. H. McHenry, of Jersey Shore, discovered what was evidently an extensive Indian pottery, about five miles up Quinn's Run. A large detached rock stood at this point, underneath which was a cave sufficiently large to shelter thirty men. It contained a great quantity of muscle shells. From appearances around the rock, the people came to the conclusion that some kind of mineral had been taken out. These gentlemen examined the ground, and found great quantities of broken pottery buried in a heap, and unmistakable traces of a hearth, where they had been baked. A double curbing of stones was nicely set in the ground, in the form of an ellipsis, about ten feet in diameter, where the kiln was erected. Charcoal, and other remains of fire, were distinctly visible. The muscle shells were carried there, pulverized, and mixed in the clay, which formed their pots. On examining broken specimens, the pulverized shells can be perceived in the form of small glistening particles. Various specimens of their broken pottery was collected by Mr. McHenry, and are now in his possession. Doubtless this was the manufactory at which all the pots for the inhabitants of the Valley were made. The clay existed here also.

At another time Mr. Wilson discovered a number of crucibles, at a place called the "Rock Cavern," on Tangascootack Creek, that had evidently been used for smelting some kind of mineral.

That the Valley of the West Branch was inhabited by a superior race, of whom we have no account, appears to be evident. Traces of peculiar fortifications, resembling those found in some of the Western States, are yet to be pointed out. One of these existed on the farm of Mr. Shoemaker, on the north side of Muncy Creek. It was square, and consisted of embankments thrown up in regular order, covering about one-fourth of an acre. A similar one existed on the farm of Gov. Shultz, below Williamsport. On the other side of the river, nearly opposite the mouth of Lycoming Creek, was found another, resembling the one on Muncy Creek, traces of which can probably be seen to this day. Mr. Shoemaker of Muncy, now an old man, but with memory bright and mind unimpaired, informs me that years ago he made a personal examination of this latter fortification, and found all the embankments well defined. Large trees were growing upon them however, the concentric circles of which would indicate many hundred years' growth, and entirely preclude the idea of their having been thrown up by the Anglo Saxon race. Mr. S. also states that many years ago he made inquiry of an old Seneca chief concerning them, but all the information the old Indian could give, was that he had it from his ancestors that they were erected by the white Indians. Of them we have no definite knowledge whatever.

On Mr. Simmons' farm, where the extensive Indian burying ground existed, are the remains of an ancient circular fortification, more properly resembling those found near Circleville, Ohio. Nearly all trace of it is lost by the action of the elements and the plow of the industrious farmer. In a few years more it will not be visible.

Several years ago a singular curiosity was plowed up in Wayne township, Clinton county. It consisted of a female figure in a sitting posture on a pedestal, sculptured out of a very hard block of stone, about six inches in length, and highly polished. The work was neatly executed, and was evidently done by a superior workman. The figure was beautifully formed, and the tissue of a fine veil thrown over the face could be distinctly seen, traced in the hard stone. It passed into the hands of a gentleman of Jersey Shore, who deposited it in the Lancaster Museum. By whom was it made?

A sword was plowed up a year or two since on the farm of Mr. Callahan, on Pine Creek, which evidently is an old English blade. It was imbedded in the ground in nearly a perpendicular position. It was probably carried there by Indians, as we have no accounts of English troops passing that way at any time. It was very much corroded by rust, and had undoubtedly laid in the ground for a long time. It is now in the possession of Dr. Lyman of Jersey Shore.

The Indian War Paths, leading through the Valley, and out of it, ran as follows:

The Shamokin Path continued up the river by the mouth of Warrior Run, and Shikellamy's town, thence through the gap in the Muncy hills to the town of Muncy, where the main road now passes.

The Wyoming Path left Muncy and ran up Glade Run, then over to Fishing Creek, near where Millville now stands—crossed the creek and went through Huntingdon Valley, and Nescopeck Gap, up the river to Wyoming.

The Wyalusing Path continued up Muncy Creek to the head, then crossed to Loyal Sock, half a mile from where the Berwick turnpike now crosses, then passed near where Dushore now stands, and struck the Wyalusing Creek near the north-east corner of Sullivan county, thence up to the flats.

The path from Muncy up the river, crossed Loyal Sock at Montour's Island, near where the canal now runs, thence up to Bonser's Run, and on up along the river to Sinnemahoning.

The Great Sheshequin Path ran up Bonser's Run, then over to Lycoming Creek, near the mouth of Mill Creek, thence to the head of Lycoming at the Beaver dams, thence down Towanda to Sheshequin flats.

Another Great Path started from Shamokin and passed up through the ravine a few yards below the bridge at Blue Hill, and continued up along the river through Buffalo Valley, then passed around the rocks and entered White Deer Hole Valley; thence along the south branch of White Deer Hole Creek, near where Elamsport now stands, and over the mountain into Nippenose Valley. Then out of the head of the Valley through the mountains, and on via Bald Eagle's Nest, at Milesburg, to Kittanning.

These were the principal Paths of the Valley, and are laid down correctly.

Residence of Peter Dickinson, Lock Haven, Pa

CHAPTER IV.

INDIAN TREATIES—PURCHASES EMBRACING THE SUSQUEHANNA —BOUNDARY LINES—SURVEYS—MANOR OF POMFRET—MUNCY MANOR—SURVEYS AT LYCOMING CREEK—SPECIAL GRANTS TO THE OFFICERS OF THE FRENCH WAR, &C., &C.

I NOW come to speak of the various treaties and purchases made from the Indians by the Proprietary Government, which will be found to embody much new and valuable information, not given in works heretofore written.

On the 3d of September, 1700, the sachems of the Susquehanna Indians, deeded to William Penn, the said river Susquehanna, and all the islands therein, and all the lands lying on both sides of it, "and next adjoining to the same, to the utmost confines thereof." The sale was confirmed to Col. William Dongan, Earl of Limerick, and formerly Governor of the Province of New York, who acted as the agent for William Penn in this transaction. The deed may be seen in Book F., Vol. 8, page 242.

This was the first deed conveying lands about the forks of the Susquehanna. It does not appear to have been the design of William Penn, at the time of this purchase, to soon settle the land, but it was evident that his design in purchasing, was to secure the right of way by the river through the Province.

On the 11th of October, 1736, a conveyance was made to John Penn, Thomas Penn, and Richard Penn; and signed by twenty-three Indian Chiefs of the Onondago, Seneca, Oneida, and Tuscarora Nations, for all the said river Susquehanna, "with the lands lying on both sides thereof, to extend eastward as far as the head of the branches or springs which run into the said Susquehanna, and all the lands lying on the west side of said river to the setting of the sun, and to extend from the mouth of said river northward up the same to the hills or mountains called in the language of the said nations *Tayamenarachta*, and by the Delaware Indians the *Kakachtanamin* hills."

This purchase is from the hills at and opposite the town of Dauphin, nine miles above Harrisburg, and south to the boundary of the Province.

But notwithstanding the purchase reaching from the west side of the Susquehanna to the setting of the sun, a large portion of the same territory was included in another purchase, made on the 5th of November, 1768, at Fort Stanwix. This deed conveyed all the land beginning on the north boundary line of the Province, to the east side of the east branch of the Susquehanna at the place called Owegy, and running with the said boundary line down this branch till it came opposite the mouth of a creek, called by the Indians *Awandac*, (Towanda) then across the river, and up said creek on the south side thereof, and along the range of hills called Burnett's hills by the English, and by the Indians ——, on the north side of them to the head of a creek running into the West Branch, called *Tiadaghton*, and down it to the river; then crossing and running up the south side, to the forks which lie nearest a place called

Kittanning, on the Ohio; from thence down the Ohio to the western bounds of the Province; thence around the southern boundary to the east of the Alleghanies, to the line of the tract purchased in 1758, by the said Proprietary, and from thence along the line of a tract purchased in 1749, around to the place of beginning. Those who may have the curiosity to examine this deed in full, can find it recorded at Philadelphia, in the Roll Office, in Book of Deeds No. 3, page 23.

From the boundaries laid down, it included some sixteen miles in width of the Province of New York, from the Delaware to the Susquehanna.

On the 16th of June, 1786, David Rittenhouse and Andrew Ellicott were appointed Commissioners to run the northern boundary of this State. On the 11th of May, 1787, John Adlum was employed by order of Council, as a Surveyor, to attend the Commissioners appointed to run and mark out the line. In the spring of 1787, Mr. Rittenhouse resigned on account of ill health, which was much regretted, as he was a man of science. Col. Andrew Porter, the father of Ex-Gov. Porter, was appointed Commissioner in his place, on the 31st of May, 1787. In November of the same year they made their report to the Governor, that they had finished running the line. This line was run on the forty-second degree of north latitude, which intersected the Susquehanna, sixty-one miles from the Delaware, and five and a half north of Tioga Point.

From the head of Towanda along the north side of the hills called Burnett's Hills, would undoubtedly be the range now known as the Elk Mountains; and further west the Briar Hill, &c. This is an unbroken mountain, till it is pierced by the second fork of Pine Creek, the stream called Tiadaghton. This arrangement would harmonize the language used in the deed. No other stream would answer; the head of the main branch of Pine Creek being some thirty miles north-west of the head of the second fork, which could not be reached by following the range of hills mentioned above, from the head of Towanda. The range of mountains extending westward from the head of Towanda Creek, crosses the main branch of Pine Creek one mile below the Big Meadows, at the mouth of the third fork, and fifty-five miles from the river.

From this geographical arrangement of the country, I can come to no other conclusion, than that the stream described as the western boundary of the purchase of 1768, on the north side of the West Branch, was the small stream now known as Yarnell's Creek, and down the same to the second fork of Pine Creek, and thence to the river, a distance of about fifty-three miles. The boundary, then, according to the deed, passed up the south side of the river to the forks of the West Branch at the Canoe Place, which is now the corner of Clearfield, Cambria, and Indiana counties. The line from this to Kittanning was run by James Galbraith, according to orders of Surveyor-General Lukens, bearing date April 17, 1768.

Having disposed, for the present, of the Proprietaries' Purchase of the Indians at the treaty of Fort Stanwix in 1768, I now propose to speak of the surveys made within that purchase. The first surveys made for the Proprietaries were called Manors, and in accordance with the custom established by William Penn, and continued by his sons, till the close of the Proprietary Government. Commencing on the south side of the purchase, I find a warrant directed by John Lukens, Surveyor-General, to William Maclay, a deputy for the district immediately south of this, and within the Purchase of 1754. It was dated December 27, 1768, on which Mr. Maclay surveyed on the 18th of February, 1769, a tract of 1328 acres, about one mile above the mouth of Penn's Creek, adjoining, on the south, the line dividing the Purchase of 1754 from that of 1768, and extending up the Susquehanna, 966½ perches.

About the same time another survey was made at Shamokin, in pursuance of a warrant from John Penn, Lieutenant-Governor, for a tract embracing 1060 acres, and called the Manor of Pomfret. This tract was surveyed nearly in the form of a square, and included the land on which Sunbury now stands.

The next is the Manor of Muncy, which was recommended by Job Chilloway, a friendly Indian. It was the most important point on the West Branch to the Proprietaries, on account of the fine location, the richness of the soil, and the centre point of several great War Paths, leading east, west, north and south. The warrant was issued by John Penn the 25th of December, 1768, and a survey of 1615 acres was soon made, nearly in a square form.

On the 31st of January, 1769, a warrant for 1000 acres was issued by the same, and as a portion of it has been the subject of much litigation, I copy it verbatim:

{L. S.} "PENNSYLVANIA, *ss.*

BY THE PROPRIETARIES.

These are to authorize and require you to survey and lay out, or cause to be surveyed and laid out for our use, the quantity of one thousand acres of land, viz. :—Five hundred acres thereof at the mouth of a creek known by the name of Lycoming, and extending thence down and upon the river Susquehanna, and the other five hundred acres in any part of the purchase lately made at Fort Stanwix of the Six Nations, that shall not interfere with any previous warrant, and to make return of the same in our Secretary's Office; and for the so doing this shall be your sufficient warrant. Witness, John Penn, Esq., Lieutenant-Governor and Commissioner of Property of the said Province, who by virtue of certain powers from said Proprietaries, hath hereunto set his hand and caused the seal of the Land Office to be affixed at Philadelphia, this thirty-first day of January, one thousand seven hundred and sixty-nine.

To John Lukens, Esq., Surveyor-General.

JOHN PENN.

To William Scull, Deputy Surveyor.

Execute this warrant, and make return of survey into my office.

JOHN LUKENS, S. G.

N. B. The last above mentioned 500 acres may be surveyed in the forks of Susquehanna between two runs a little above the head of Shamokin Island, or at the place called the Narrows, running a mile or more along the river and back to the hill called Hence Michael's Place.

JOHN LUKENS, G. G.

February 3, 1769.

P. S. If the land at Lycoming should be found to belong to Andrew Montour, lay out on this warrant 500 acres at any place thereabouts not already appropriated."

This is a true copy of the warrant issued by the Surveyor-General to his Deputy, filed in the office of the County Surveyor of Lycoming.

On the 22d of February, 1769, there were surveyed on this warrant, 180 acres, including the mouth of Mahoning Creek, and the land where the town of Danville now stands, by William Scull, Surveyor-General. On the 28th of the same month, 320 acres were surveyed on the same warrant, at the mouth of Buffalo Creek, by William Maclay, Surveyor-General.

On the 20th of March, 1769, 579 acres were surveyed on this warrant at the mouth, and on the east side of Lycoming Creek, running down the river, which includes at the present time, the farms owned by Oliver Watson, Esq., and Judge Grier of the Supreme Court. Thus ended the surveys of Manors in 1768.

In relation to Manors it seems to have been a policy settled by William Penn, at an early period of the history of land affairs, to reserve out of each purchase from the Indians, one-tenth of the lands, to be selected and laid out before the Land Office was opened for the granting of applications or warrants to individuals, which was intended as the property of himself and successors. This is inferred from a warrant issued by William Penn on the 1st of September, 1700, to Edward Pennington, then Surveyor-General, to survey for the Proprietor, 500 acres of every township of 5000 acres. This practice was continued, with some variations, up to the period of the American Revolution.

At different times, between the confirmation of the Purchase of 1768, and the opening of the Land Office, a number of special grants to various individuals, for valuable services rendered the Proprietaries, were made; amongst which was one on the 29th of October, 1768, to Andrew Montour, who had proved himself trustworthy and of eminent service to the Government.

On the 4th of February, 1769, a special application was issued in favor of the Rev. Dr. Francis Allison, being No. 2, for 1500 acres, and a survey was speedily made, of 1620 acres, above the mouth of Bald Eagle Creek, on that beautiful flat land. An Indian town also stood there.

The next of these special grants, was the lands to the officers who had served in the French and Indian wars of 1755–8. This survey was made in the month of March, 1769, by John Lukens, commencing on the western boundary of Dr. Allison's tract, and embracing the land along the river and Bald Eagle Creek, for some distance. Ensign McMeens had a tract of 216 acres, Lieut. Hunseeker 282, including the site of the town of Flemington; Capt. Green, 524 acres, including the mouth of Fishing Creek.

After these special grants were disposed of, preparations were made for the opening of the Land Office. In order to give a better understanding how business was transacted at that day, and applications granted, I copy the advertisement of the Secretary of the Land Office as follows:

"The Land Office will be opened on the third day of April next, at 10 o'clock in the morning, to receive applications from all persons inclinable to take up lands in the New Purchase, upon terms of five pounds sterling per hundred acres, and one penny per acre per annum quit-rent. No person will be allowed to take up more than three hundred acres, without a special license from the Proprietaries or Governor. The surveys upon all applications are to be made and returned within six months, and the whole purchase-money paid at one payment, and patent taken out within twelve months from the date of the application, with interest and quit-rent from six months after the application. If there be a failure on the side of the party applying, in either proving his survey and return to be made, or in paying the purchase-money, and obtaining the patent, the application and survey will be utterly void, and the Proprietaries will be at liberty to dispose of the land to any other person whatever. And as these terms will be strictly adhered to by the Proprietaries, all persons are hereby warned and cautioned, not to apply for more land than they will be able to pay for, in the time hereby given for that purpose.

By order of the Governor.

JAMES TILGHMAN,
Secretary of the Land Office.

Philadelphia Land Office, Feb. 23, 1769.

Residence of Allison White, Lock Haven, Pa.

CHAPTER V.

LAND HISTORY CONTINUED—NOTICE—THE ACT OF 1835—COPY OF AN APPLICATION—SURVEYS ALONG THE RIVER—MISTAKES—HAWKINS BOONE—COMMENCEMENT OF THE WARRANT SYSTEM.

NOTWITHSTANDING the stringency of the conditions enjoined upon those taking up lands, it is satisfactorily ascertained that they never were altogether complied with. When the system became practical, and the conditions were not fully complied with, the Proprietaries did not insist upon forfeitures being made. The conclusions, however, are plain, from the following notice issued by the Surveyor-General in 1774:

"That as the several Deputy Surveyors propose giving due attendance in their respective districts throughout the Province the present summer, all persons who have entered applications for land, and have not got them surveyed, are hereby desired to attend the Deputy-Surveyor in whose district the land may be, show the same, pay the charges for surveying, in order that the same may be returned into the Surveyor-General and Secretary's Offices, in order for Patenting, (agreeable to an advertisement lately published by the Secretary of the Land Office,) by order of his honor the Governor.

JOHN LUKENS, S. G."

It may as well be remarked here that, in many instances, the conditions of the advertisement never have been, to this day, complied with, so far as relates to the patenting of lands. The various acts passed by the Legislature to bring about a compliance, were in a great measure unheeded, and never enforced. In 1835, an act was passed that it was supposed would induce persons holding unpatented lands to avail themselves of its lenient provisions at once, as an effort had been making for more than sixty years to urge landholders to comply with the conditions they had agreed to on taking out their warrants, knowing, as they did, what was required of them. The act constituted the Board, or a majority, of the County Commissioners to appraise all such unpatented lands; and they were directed to make a table of rates, numbered 1, 2, 3 and 4, and all lands valued at $10 per acre and upwards, should be rated No. 1,—all valued at more than $7, and less than $10, should be rated No. 2,—all valued at over $4, and not over $7, should be rated No. 3,—all valued at $4, or less, to be rated No. 4: provided, that in making the valuation of lands, the value of the buildings thereon should be deducted. The next section provided that all lands rated No. 1, shall pay the amount of the purchase-money, with 6 per cent. interest per annum thereon; No. 2, the purchase-money and 4½ per cent. interest; No. 3, the fee money, and 3 per cent.; and No. 4, the original purchase-money without interest. This act was to continue in force three years, but at the expiration of that time it was extended, and has been extended from year to year, up to the present time. Yet thousands of dollars are due the Commonwealth for purchase-money, interest and patent fees, in those counties that existed under the Proprietary Government.

In reference to the advertisement of the Secretary of the Land Office, the time having arrived, preparations were made for the commencement of business. Location books were opened, and the tract applied for, numbered and described. It being understood that great numbers would attend ready to give in their locations at the same time, it was decided by the Governor and his agents, that the most unexceptionable method of receiving the locations, would be to put them altogether —after being received from the people—into a box, mix them well together, then draw them therefrom and number them as they came; this plan it was thought would determine the preference, without any show of partiality.

Below I give a copy of an application, as they were then issued :—

"No. 1085.

GEORGE GRANT, hath made application for three hundred acres of land, on the north side of the West Branch of Susquehanna, joining and above the Honorable Proprietors land at Muncy Creek, including Wolf Run.

Dated at Philadelphia, this third day of April, 1769.

To William Scull, Deputy Surveyor; you are to survey the land mentioned in this application, and make return thereof into the Surveyor-General's Office, within six months from the above date; and thereof fail not.

JOHN LUKENS, S. G."

When the office was opened on the 3d of April, 1769, there was issued on that day, 2782 applications, directed to the Surveyor-Generals in their respective districts embraced in the purchase of 1768, including the territory from Lycoming to Pine Creek. But before the surveys were made, the Proprietaries issued an order prohibiting any surveys being made west of Lycoming Creek, on the north side of the river, as the Indians claimed that territory, and expressed much dissatisfaction.* A large number of applications had, however, been issued for lands between these two streams, and placed in the hands of the Deputy Surveyor, (the originals are now in the office of the Deputy Surveyor of Lycoming county,) but were not made in accordance with the order. There was no action taken upon them till after the treaty of 1784, when the dispute was settled, and which will be referred to in another part of this work.

Instructions were also issued by the Surveyor-General to the Deputy, accompanying the application. Four Surveyors were appointed by the Commissioners of Property, for the surveying of the lands embraced in the treaty of 1768. Their names were, William Gray, for the south-eastern part; Charles Stewart, for the north part, up the North Branch; William Scull, for the north side of the West Branch above Chilisquaque; and Charles Lukens, for the south side, bounded on the south by the treaty line of 1754, and east by Buffalo Creek. His district also extended to the head waters of Bald Eagle Creek, and embraced the following valleys: Bald Eagle, Nittany, Sugar, Nippenose, White Deer Hole, White Deer, and the upper part of Buffalo.

Surveys had, however, been made by Thomas Smith, Deputy Surveyor of Cumberland county, in what is now Clearfield, in June, 1769. As soon as the applications were issued, the Surveyors were put to work. In the same month and year they were in White Deer Hole Valley making surveys, and on the 1st of July, in Black Hole Bottom; on the 4th, 5th and 6th, in Nippenose. The first survey in this Bottom, was made on the application of Elizabeth Brown, numbered 44, and

* This will be explained in its proper place.

included the mouth of the Creek. It was made on the 4th of July, 1769.

On the 7th of the same month, the first survey was made in Nippenose Valley, on the application of Ralph Foster, and embraced the tract where Sanderson's Mill now stands. On the 8th and 9th, surveys were made along the river in what is now Wayne township, Clinton county, and so on up.

In the month of October, 1769, surveys were made along the river, in the vicinity of Mosquito Creek, and various other places. This was in Charles Lukens' district.

In William Scull's district, we find them making surveys on Muncy Creek, including the land adjoining the borough of Hughesburg. The other surveyors were progressing with their work in a proportionate degree.

Applications were issued until the 31st of August, 1769, when they amounted to 4000. Surveys were never made, probably, on half of the applications issued, but as often as four or five times on the same tract. Priority seems to have been given in these cases, according to the prescribed rule for the regulation of such errors, and the first application generally prevailed. There were some five or six applications for the lands of John Cox, three miles above the mouth of Buffalo Creek, including an Indian town, and those of Elizabeth Brown, in Nippenose Bottom. Many of these applications were surveyed on other tracts—several opposite the Long Island were surveyed in Nippenose Valley, and some of them in Buffalo Valley. A tract was generally found to suit the application. These applications only cost a dollar for office fees, and a trifling sum to the first explorer or guide to the land, who was generally an expert woodsman, who sought out the best locations. Some lines were run and marked in order to define their locations to a particular spot. Hawkins Boone was the principal explorer and woodsman in Bald Eagle, Nittany, and other valleys. In some of his notes taken at the time, he mentions the Bald Eagle's Nest, near Milesburg, and a settler there named Huff, who had cut logs to erect a cabin. He was one of those early adventurers from Cumberland county, mention of whom will be made in the proper place.

The application of Andrew Hackett, included "an old Indian cornfield, near a mile from where Bald Eagle Creek cuts through the hill, and where the Frankstown road leads through to the Great Island." What kind of a road existed at that time will afford some conjecture.

In many cases the tracts were described by letters cut on a tree, standing in a particular place, or deer licks included, by which means they could be identified.

Many of the surveys made on these applications were not found for many years afterwards, as the people were soon compelled to abandon the frontier, and in many cases never returned. The location of many of these surveys is not determined to this day.

The year 1769 closed the application system, and in 1770, the Proprietaries commenced the issuing of warrants, which was pretty much on the same principle. Conditions, however, were fully set forth in the warrants, signed by the Governor, with the seal of the Land Office affixed. The original was filed in the Surveyor-General's Office, and a copy directed to the Deputy in the district where the land was supposed to lie. When it was doubtful where the land was, they were in many cases directed thus: "To the proper Deputy Surveyor." I had intended to give a copy of a warrant herewith, but the limits of this work will not permit of it.

Here I shall close the remarks in reference to the original surveys, warrants, &c. Much more valuable information could be given, as the subject is not half exhausted. Allusion will be made again to the disputed territory, and the last treaty at Fort Stanwix.

CHAPTER VI.

FIRST ENGLISH IN THE VALLEY—THE FRENCH—COUNT ZINZENDORF—REV. DAVID BRAINERD—VISITORS TO LONG ISLAND IN 1745—THE INDIAN CHIEF—GETS DRUNK AND FALLS IN THE FIRE.

THE Valley of the West Branch was visited at a very early period by adventurers, and Indian traders. The government also sent special messengers on several occasions to confer with the heads of the various tribes. The earliest account on record that I have been able to find, that relates to the Susquehanna and Shamokin, dates back as early as 1728. Gov. Gordon lays down certain instructions to Smith and Petty, who were about to make a journey to Shamokin. In this letter of instructions, the Governor particularly requests them to call upon his Indian friends Alummopees, Opekassel, Shachalawlin, and Shikellemy, and give them his particular regards. The latter of these chiefs, it is known, resided at Shamokin.

It appears that the Governor esteemed these Indians very highly, and hoped to hear from them soon. He also stated that he had learned of some injury being done them by the whites, whom he intended to punish if found out, as he could not tolerate any violations of good faith.

The same month, September, Wright and Blunstone

reported to Gov. Gordon, that they had learned from an Indian, that one Timothy Higgins had been hanged at Shamokin, but for what cause was not stated. He was the servant of an Indian trader named Henry Smith, who, it appears, had penetrated into that region.

The report of the hanging, after being investigated by Smith and Petty, turned out to be incorrect.

In the following year, 1729, Gov. Gordon wrote a letter of condolence to Shickelemy, and other chiefs at Shamokin, on the death of Carundawana. He also spoke feelingly of the death of a son of Shickelemy, which took place about that time, and sent a shroud to bury him in.

In the year 1730, a letter was received by the Governor from a number of Delaware Indians, describing the manner in which a white man received serious injury. The report stated that John Fisher and John Hartt, two of the Shamokin traders, accompanied a number of their tribe down the river on a hunting excursion. After having proceeded over one hundred miles, the Indians proposed to fire-hunt, by making a ring. The white men would go along with them, although they tried to dissuade them from it, alleging that they did not understand it, and might receive some injury. But they persisted in going. In the excitement of the hunt, John Hartt was shot in the mouth, the bullet lodging in his neck, which killed him.

The French had penetrated into the valley of the West Branch in considerable numbers before the arrival of the English, having came through from the Lakes. Rev. David Brainerd speaks of a number of Europeans found by him at the town of Ostanwackin, who had adopted the Indian method of living; amongst whom was the celebrated Madame Montour, a French woman, who was married to Carundawana. She was previously married to Roland Montour, a chief of the Seneca tribe, by whom she had several sons, that figure conspicuously in the history of the Valley.

Loskiel, in his history of Moravian Missions, states that on the 28th of September, 1742, Count Zinzendorf, accompanied by Conrad Weiser, Martin Mack and his wife, and two Indians, named Joshua and David, after a long and tedious journey through the wilderness, arrived at the town of Shamokin. The chief, Shickelemy, stepped out and gave them a hearty welcome. A savage presented the Count with a fine melon, for which the latter gave him his fur cap. Zinzendorf immediately announced himself as a messenger of the living God, come to preach unto them grace and salvation. Shickelemy replied that he was happy to receive and entertain an ambassador from the Great Spirit, and would afford him all the assistance in his power. As a proof of his integrity, it is stated that on one occasion when these pious missionaries were about going to prayers, the Indians were making a terrible noise with drums and singing, the Count sent word to Shickelemy, who immediately ordered silence.

The Count, after remaining a short time in Shamokin, crossed the river with a part of his company, and proceeded to the town of Ostanwackin, on the West Branch, where they were kindly received and entertained for two days, by Madamo Montour.

Rev. David Brainerd visited Shamokin in 1745, for the first time. He endured much suffering, being in delicate health. He was kindly received, and entertained in true Indian style, but had little satisfaction on account of the heathenish dance that occurred in the hut where he was obliged to lodge. After preaching to them, he went down to Juniata Island.

He returned to Shamokin in August, 1746, and preached to the Indians. The following extract is from his journal:

"Sept. 1.—Set out on a journey towards a place called the Great Island, about fifty miles from Shaumoking, on the north-western branch of the Susquehanna. At night lodged in the woods.

Sept. 2.—Rode forward, but no faster than my people went on foot. Was very weak on this as well as the preceding days. I was so feeble and faint that I feared it would kill me to lie out in the open air; and some of my company being parted from us, so that we had now no axe with us. I had no way but to climb into a young pine tree, and with my knife to lop the branches, and so make a shelter from the dew. But the evening being cloudy, with a prospect of rain, I was still under fears of being extremely exposed; sweat much, so that my linen was almost wringing wet all night. I scarcely ever was more weak and weary than this evening, when I was able to sit up at all. This was a melancholy situation; but I endeavored to quiet myself with considerations of my being in much worse circumstances amongst enemies, &c.

Sept. 3.—Rode to the Delaware town; found many drinking and drunken. Discoursed with some of the Indians about Christianity; observed my interpreter much engaged, and assisted in his work. A few persons seemed to hear with great earnestness and engagement of soul. About noon rode to a small town of Shauwaunoes, about eight miles distant; spent an hour or two there, and returned to the Delaware town, and lodged there. Was scarce ever more confounded with a sense of my own unfruitfulness and unfitness for my work than now. O what a dead, heartless, barren, unprofitable wretch did I now see myself to be!

Sept. 5.—Got to Shaumoking towards night; felt somewhat of a spirit of thankfulness that God had so far returned me.

Sept. 8.—Left Shaumoking, and returned down the river a few miles. Had proposed to tarry a considerable time longer among the Indians upon the Susquehanna, but was hindered from pursuing my purpose from sickness that prevailed there, the feeble state of my own people that were with me, and especially my own extraordinary weakness, having been exercised with great nocturnal sweats, and a coughing up of blood, almost the whole of the journey. I was a great part of the time so feeble and faint, that it seemed as though I never should be able to reach home; and at the same time very destitute of the comforts, and even the necessaries of life."

In the year 1745, says Loskiel in his history of Moravian Missions, Bro. Martin Mack and his wife went to Shamokin, where they staid two months. During this time they not only suffered much illness, and troubles of various kinds, but frequently were eye-witnesses to the most horrible and diabolical abominations, practised by the savages more in this place than any other. Several times they were in danger of being murdered by drunken Indians. Yet their fervent desire to gain souls for Christ, inspired them with such consolation, that, according to Mack's own statement, their hard fare in an Indian cottage afforded them more real pleasure, than all the luxuries of the most sumptuous palace could have done. They spent a part of their time in assisting the Indians to cultivate their corn.

From Shamokin they went on a visit to Long Island, where they were received with much kindness, especially by the chief. His drunkenness seemed to the Missionaries to be the greatest obstacle in the way of the Gospel. He got so drunk one evening that he fell into the fire, and burnt the flesh off one of his hands. They then returned to Shamokin.

In 1748, Shamokin was visited by Bishop Camerhoff, and the pious Zeisberger, who came for the purpose of establishing a Moravian Mission. They also speak of making an excursion up the river as far as the Long

Island, opposite Jersey Shore, and the Great Island, a few miles above.

These were the principal English adventurers, of whom I have any account, that first penetrated the wilds of the beautiful Otzinachson Valley, previous to the first permanent settlements. It is to be regretted that some of them did not leave behind them a full account of the appearance of the country at that day, and the various Indian towns with which the valley abounded.

CHAPTER VII.

FIRST HOUSE BUILT BY WHITE MEN AT SHAMOKIN—ITS SIZE—FIRST SETTLERS—MURDER OF ARMSTRONG—SHICKELEMY—HIS DEATH AND CHARACTER—CONRAD WEISER SENT TO CONDOLE WITH HIS FAMILY.

THE first house erected at Shamokin was by Conrad Weiser, for the Indian Chief Shickelemy, who employed him to build it. In Mr. Weiser's letter to James Logan, dated September 29th, 1744, he says:

"Sir:—The day before yesterday I came back from Shohomokin, where I have been with eight young men of my country people, whom Shickalemy hired to make a locke house for him, and I went with them to direct them. We finished the house in 17 days; it is 49½ foot long, and 17½ wide, and covered with singels."

This was unquestionably the first building, after the English plan, that was erected at that place—one hundred and twelve years ago. It was no doubt built of rough logs notched together, and the shingles with which it was covered, were probably what would be denominated at this day, clapboards.

For what purpose such a building was designed by Shickelemy, is not stated, further than it was a "*locke house*," in which, it is inferred, he intended to incarcerate some of his refractory subjects.

At the time Mr. Weiser was building the house, the fever was very bad among the Indians, and five or six were carried off whilst he was there. Alumoppees, the Delaware King, was prostrated for a long time previous, but finally recovered.

The first settlement made at Shamokin, was in the spring of 1747, by Martin Mack and his wife, who had visited the place in 1745. They were from the Moravian settlements below. Previous to their arrival, John Hagin and Joseph Powell, of the Mission, had built a house there, which, I presume, was the second one erected.

As Shamokin was an important point for the Indians, and used as a depot, or tarrying-place, for their war parties against the Catawbas of the south, they were very anxious to have a blacksmith to save them the trouble of long journeys to Tulpehocken or Philadelphia, to get their implements of war repaired. On application to the Provincial Government, their request was granted, on condition that he should remain with them no longer than they proved friendly to the English. As all was peace and harmony among the two nations at that time, of course they assented to the proposition, and a gentleman named Anthony Schmidt, from the mission at Bethlehem, had the honor of being the first representative of Vulcan at Shamokin.

In the spring of 1744, the first aggravated case of murder occurred on the Juniata. When John Armstrong, an Indian trader, and his two servants, James Smith and Woodworth Arnold, were inhumanly and barbarously murdered by an Indian of the Delaware tribe, named Musemeelin. The atrocity of this murder was so aggravating, that a Provincial Council was held to take the matter into consideration, and it was finally resolved that Conrad Weiser should be sent to Shamokin to make demands, in the name of the Governor, for those concerned in the affair.

Mr. Weiser arrived at Shamokin on the second day of May, 1744, and delivered the Governor's message to Alumoppees, the Delaware Chief, and the rest of the Delaware Indians, in presence of Shickelemy, and a few more of the Six Nations.

Alumoppees replied that it was true, that the evil spirit had influenced some of his tribe to commit the murder, and that he was very sorry it had occurred; they had taken the murderer and delivered him to the friends of the deceased to be dealt with according to the nature of the deed.

After the conclusion of the address by Alumoppees, Shickelemy arose and entered into a full account of the unhappy affair, which is very long and interesting. When the conference with the Indians was ended, a feast was prepared, to which the Governor's messengers were invited. Mr. Weiser states that there were about one hundred persons present, to whom, after they had in great silence, devoured a fat bear, the eldest of the chiefs made a speech.

The Moravian Mission was kept open till Braddock's defeat in 1755, when the alarming aspect of affairs caused the brethren to abandon it and fly to Bethlehem. What success they had among the Indians is nowhere positively stated, but it is presumed that they succeeded in converting several. As late as 1755, an individual named Grube, is spoken of as going up the river to *Quenishachshachki*—where Linden now stands—to see some baptized Indians that lived there. They also frequently made excursions to Long Island and Great Island.

Shickelemy was a chief of the Cayuga tribe, who was stationed at Shamokin to rule over the Indians. He was truly an excellent and good man, possessed of many noble qualities of mind, that would do honor to many white men laying claims to greater refinement and intelligence. He was possessed of great dignity, sobriety and prudence, and was particularly noted for his extreme kindness to the whites and missionaries. He was the most intimate and valued friend of Conrad Weiser, who entertained great respect for him. On several important occasions he attended the sittings of the Provincial Council at Philadelphia, and performed embassies between the government of Pennsylvania and the Six Nations. Conrad Weiser visited him frequently at his house in Shamokin, on business for the government, and was in turn visited by him at Tulpehocken. He had several sons, one of which was "Logan, the Mingo Chief," and another named *Taghneghdoarus*, who assumed the duties of chief, after the death of his father. He was the eldest.

Shickelemy died in 1749, and in his death the whites lost the best and truest friend they ever had among the tawny sons of the forest. Loskiel, who knew him well, thus describes his character:

"Being the first magistrate and head chief of all the Iroquois Indians living on the banks of the Susquehanna, as far as Onondaga, he thought it incumbent upon him to be very circumspect in his dealings with the white people. He mistrusted the brethren at first, but upon discovering their sincerity, became their firm and real friend. Being much engaged in political affairs, he had learned the art of concealing his sentiments; and, therefore, never contradicted those who endeavored to prejudice his mind against the missionaries, though he always suspected their motives. In the last years of his life he became less reserved, and received those brethren who came to Shamokin into his house. He assisted them in building, and defended them against the insults of the drunken Indians; being himself never addicted to drinking, because, as he expressed it, he never wished to become a fool. He had built his house upon pillars for safety, in which he always shut himself up when any drunken frolic was going on in the village. In this house Bishop Johannes Von Watteville and his company visited and preached the Gospel to him. It was then that the Lord opened his heart; he listened with great attention; and at last, with tears, respected the doctrine of a crucified Jesus, and received it in faith. During his visit in Bethlehem, a remarkable change took place in his heart which he could not conceal. He found comfort, peace, and joy, by faith in his Redeemer, and the Brethren considered him as a candidate for baptism; but hearing that he had been already baptized, by a Roman Catholic priest, in Canada, they only endeavored to impress his mind with a proper idea of his sacramental ordinance, upon which he destroyed a small idol, which he wore about his neck. After his return to Shamokin, the grace of God bestowed upon him was truly manifest, and his behavior was remarkably peaceable and contented. In this state of mind he was taken ill, was attended by Br. David Zeisberger, and in his presence fell happy asleep in the Lord, in full assurance of obtaining eternal life through the merits of Jesus Christ."

Conrad Weiser was ordered to visit Shamokin in April, 1749, on business for the government, in reference to the death of Shickelemy, and he wrote to Governor Hamilton, that he had met the eldest and youngest son of his deceased friend, at the trading house of Thomas McKee, some twenty miles down the river, who informed him that all the Indians had left Shamokin for a short time, on account of the scarcity of provisions. Here he delivered the message from the Governor to the young men, and three others of the Six Nations, one of whom was *Toganogon*, a noted Cayuga. In reference to the interview, he says:

"All what I had to do was to let the children and grand-children of our deceased friend, Shickelimy, know that the Governor of Pensilvania and his Council condoled with them for the death of their father, which I did accordingly, and gave them a small present, in order to wipe off their tears, according to the custom of the Indians; the present consisted of six Strowd Matchcoats and seven Shirts, with a string of Wampum; after this was over, I gave another string of Wampum to *Tagheneghdoarus*, Shickelimy's eldest son, and desired him to take upon him the care of a chief in the stead of his deceased father, and to be our true corespondent, untill there should be a meeting between the Governor of Pensilvania and some of the Six Nation Chiefs, and then he should be recommended by the Governor to the Six Nation Chiefs and confirmed, If he would follow the foot steps of his deceased father. He accepted thereof, and I sent a string of Wampum by Toganogon, (who was then seting out for Cayuckquo) to Onantago to let the Counsel of the Six Nation Know of Shickelimy's death and my transaction by order of the Governor. There was a necessity for my doing so."

CHAPTER VIII.

SETTLEMENT ON PENN'S CREEK—NAMES OF THE SETTLERS—FRENCH AND INDIAN WAR—MASSACRE OF THE SETTLERS—HARRIS' PARTY—BLOODY FIGHT—THE LINDEN TREE—STORY OF DUKE HOLLAND, SHOWING THE WONDERFUL SAGACITY OF AN INDIAN.

WHEN the first settlements were made at Shamokin, and on the west side of the river at Penn's Creek, these lands were embraced in the limits of Berks and Cumberland counties. Berks was organized in 1752, and took in all the region of country on the east side of the river as far northward as the limits of the Province. Cumberland was formed in 1750, and took in all the lands on the west side of the river.

The feeling of amity that had existed between the whites and Indians for a period of upwards of seventy years, was about to be broken, and a spirit of hatred and revenge began to manifest itself. The Indians became dissatisfied with the whites on account of their recent treaties, wherein they discovered that they were cheated and deceived. The evil passions of the Indians once aroused, they were capable of committing the most horrid and fiendish crimes. Once they were estranged from the English, they united with the French, and shortly afterwards followed those terrible massacres, during the French and Indian wars.

As early as 1745, an extensive settlement was made at Penn's Creek, a few miles below Shamokin, on the west side of the river. The settlers were mostly Scotch-Irish, from the Kittatinny Valley. They pitched their tents in the wilderness, on the inviting land around the stream, and commenced to open up little patches of ground. They were hardy and industrious—well calculated to endure the sufferings to be encountered in a new country, among painted savages and wild beasts. They enjoyed none of the comforts of refined life—they were the hardy pioneers of civilization.

The proud savage viewed the gradual encroachment of the whites upon his favorite hunting grounds with feelings of distrust. He had been to them a friend—had extended to them the hospitalities of his humble wigwam, and ministered to their wants. But they had cheated and deceived him in return. His proud nature could not endure such treatment—it was inconsistent with his views of justice and right. He turned away from them with feelings of scorn, deeply tinctured with the malignancy of vindictive passion.

The names of a few of the first settlers at Penn's Creek have been preserved, and are as follows: Jacob Le Roy, George Auchmudy, Abraham Sourkill, George Snabble, George Gliwell, John McCahan, Edmund Matthews, John Young, Mark Curry, William Daran, John Simmons, George Aberheart, Daniel Braugh, Gotfried Fryer, Dennis Mucklehenny, George Linn, and several others.

The settlers soon became alarmed at the dark clouds that were fast gathering, and threatening them with danger. Actual hostilities between the French and their Indian allies, had already commenced with the English.

An awful crisis was approaching—the frontier settlers were in a panic. The Indians, true to their character, when enemies, struck whenever an opportunity presented —neither sex nor age was spared—the vindictive savage knew *no* pity.

Petitions were sent in to the Provincial Government praying for protection on the frontiers. The government, seriously alarmed, made some attempt to devise a plan for protection, but it availed but little.

In 1755, the disastrous defeat of Braddock occurred on the banks of the Monongahela. This unfortunate and unexpected event, cast a pall of gloom over the minds of the settlers, and they feared the worst consequences.

True to their expectations, scarce three months had elapsed after this event, till a body of Indians from the West Branch, fell upon the settlement at Penn's Creek. The attack was made upon the 15th of October, 1755, and every person in the settlement, consisting of twenty-five, including men, women and children, with the exception of one man, who made his escape, though dangerously wounded, were either killed or carried into captivity. The scene of havoc and devastation presented in this once happy settlement, is described to have been mournful in the extreme. They barbarously killed and scalped a large number, and carried the rest into captivity. Their houses were burned, and their fields laid waste. A number of settlers near the scene of the massacre, immediately came up to bury the dead. They describe the scene as follows:

"We found but thirteen, who were men and elderly women. The children, we suppose to be carried away, prisoners. The house where we suppose they finished their murder, we found burnt up; the man of it, named Jacob King, a Swisser, lying just by it. He lay on his back, barbarously burnt, and two tomahawks sticking in his forehead; one of those marked newly W. D. We have sent them to your Honor. The terror of which, has driven away almost all the back inhabitants, except the subscribers, with a few more, who are willing to stay and defend the land; but as we are not at all able to defend it for the want of guns and ammunition, and few in numbers, so that without assistance, we must flee and leave the country to the mercy of the enemy."

Jacob King, alias Jacob Le Roy, who was so inhumanly butchered, had only lately arrived from Europe. At the time of his murder, his daughter, Anne Mary Le Roy, and some others, were made prisoners and taken to Kittanning, where she was kept a captive for about four years.

This massacre spread terror and consternation throughout the settlements; and on intelligence being received below, about the 20th of October, a party of forty-five, commanded by John Harris, set out from Harris' Ferry, (now Harrisburg,) and proceeded to the scene of the disaster, where they found and buried a number of the mangled bodies of the victims also. From this place they proceeded to Shamokin to see the Indians and prevail upon them, if possible, to remain neutral. This visit, it is alleged, they were persuaded to make by John Shickelemy and Old Belt. Their reception at the village was civil, but not cordial, and they perceived, as they thought, that their visit had disconcerted the savages. They remained there till the next morning. During the night they heard some Indians, about twelve in number, talking to this purpose: "What are the English come here for?" Says another: "To kill us I suppose; can we then send off some of our nimble young men to give our friends notice, that can soon be here?" They soon after sang the war song, and four

Indians went off, in two canoes, well armed—one canoe went down the river, and the other across.

In the morning they made a few presents to the Indians, who *promised* to remain neutral, and assist them against a large scalping party of French and Indians, that they had learned were on their way across the Alleghany mountains to attack the settlements. They were distrustful of the good faith of the Indians, after what they had heard the previous night, and were anxious to get away. Before leaving the village on their return, they were privately warned by Andrew Montour, a half breed Indian interpreter, not to take the road on the western side of the river, but continue on down the eastern side, as he believed it to be dangerous. They, however, disregarded his warning, either relying on the good faith of the Indians at Shamokin, or suspecting that *he* intended to lead them into an ambuscade, and marched along the flats on the west side of the river. The fording place across Penn's Creek was then at the place where the stream divides, one part passing south, the other and main embouchure turning nearly due east, towards the Susquehanna—this was the branch which Harris and his party were to pass. The northern shore of the creek, where they entered the water, was low; on the southern side—the head of the Isle of Queu—was a high and steep bank, near, and parallel, to which was a deep natural hollow where the savages, some thirty in number, lay concealed. Before the whites, partly on foot, and partly mounted, had well time to ascend the bank, the savages rose and fired on them. Four were killed. Harris states that himself and about fifteen of his men, immediately took to trees and returned the fire, killing four Indians, with the loss of three more men. They retreated to the river, and passed it with the loss of four or five men drowned. Harris was mounted, and in the flight was entreated by one of the footmen, a large fat man, and a doctor, to suffer him to mount behind him. With some unwillingness he consented (fortunately for himself,) and they entered the river. They had not got entirely out of rifle distance, when a shot struck the doctor in the back, and he fell wounded into the river, from whence he never rose. The horse was wounded by another shot, and failing, Harris was obliged to abandon him and swim part of the way. The remainder of the party after several days of toilsome marching through the rugged country, reached home in safety.

To mark the spot where this fight occurred, a party who came up to bury the dead, drove a wedge through the body of a Linden sapling, standing on the ground. This tree a few years ago was some eighteen or twenty inches in diameter, and still retained the marks of the wedge, about five or six feet from the ground.

The next day a party of Indians from Shamokin went down to where the engagement had taken place. They informed David Zeisberger that *they* found three white men killed, lying near together; and on the river side they found another dead man, not shot, but supposed to have been drowned trying to escape; a short distance further they discovered a suit of women's clothes, with a pair of new shoes, lying near the river, which they thought must have belonged to some one who endeavored to escape by crossing the river. They then followed the trail further into the woods, where they espied a sapling cut down, and near by a grub twisted. They were certain these marks indicated

5

something, and on carefully searching around discovered a parcel of leaves carefully raked together, upon removing which they found a fresh grave that contained an Indian who had been shot. He was well dressed: all the hairs of his head were removed, with the exception of a small tuft on the crown, which indicated him to be a French Mohawk.

They also found a glove, all bloody, lying by a tree that was much shot, which they supposed to have belonged to Thomas McKee, an Indian trader. From here they went down to George Gabriel's farm, where they saw Indian tracks in the plowed ground. His corn was burnt and destroyed, and no person about.

As the enemy was prowling around the settlements, watching an opportunity to murder and scalp, it is impossible to imagine the fear and consternation that seized the inhabitants. Their only safety was to flee and leave all to the enemy. They had in vain looked for relief from the Government. Houses that had been occupied, barns that had been filled with the fruits of a rich and plenteous harvest, and newly sowed fields, and standing corn, were all abandoned to the mercy of the savages.

A friendly Indian named Duke Holland, of the Delaware tribe, who was much esteemed by the whites, was about the settlement at the time of the massacre. The surviving whites in their rage, partly resolved to satiate their revenge by murdering him. This Indian, satisfied that his nation was incapable of committing such a foul murder in time of profound peace, told the enraged settlers that he was sure the Delawares were not in any manner concerned in it, and that it was the act of some wicked Mingoes or Iroquois, whose custom it was to involve other nations in wars with each other by clandestinely committing murders, so that they might be laid to the charge of others than themselves. But all his representations were vain; he could not convince exasperated men, whose minds were fully bent on revenge. At last, he offered that if they would give him a party to accompany him, he would go with them in quest of the murderers, and was sure he could discover them by the prints of their feet and other marks well known to him, by which he would convince them that the real perpetrators of the crime belonged to the Six Nations. His proposal was accepted; he marched at the head of a party of whites, and led them into the tracks. They soon found themselves in the most rocky parts of the mountain, where not one of those who accompanied him was able to discover a single track, nor would they believe that ever a man had trodden on this ground, as they had to jump over a number of crevices between the rocks, and in some instances to crawl over them. Now they began to believe that the Indian had led them across those rugged mountains in order to give the enemy time to escape, and threatened him with instant death the moment they should be fully convinced of the fraud. The Indian, true to his promise, would take pains to make them perceive that an enemy had passed along the places through which he was leading them; here he would show them that the moss on the rock had been trodden down by the weight of a human foot, then that it had been torn and dragged forward from its place; further, he would point out to them that pebbles or small stones on the rocks had been removed from their beds by the foot hitting against them, that dry sticks by being trodden upon were broken, and even that in a particular place, an Indian's blanket had dragged over the rocks, and removed or loosened the leaves lying there, so that they lay no more flat, as in other places; all which the Indian could perceive as he walked along, without ever stopping. At last arriving at the foot of the mountain, on soft ground, where the tracks were deep, he found that the enemy were eight in number, and from the freshness of the foot-prints, he concluded that they must be encamped at no great distance. This proved to be the exact truth; for, after gaining the eminence on the other side of the valley, the Indians were seen encamped, some having already laid down to sleep, while others were drawing off their leggings for the same purpose, and the scalps they had taken were hanged up to dry. "See!" said Duke Holland to his astonished companions, "there is the enemy! not of my nation, but Mingoes, as I truly told you. They are in our power; in less than half an hour they will all be fast asleep. We need not fire a gun, but go up and tomahawk them. We are nearly two to one and need apprehend no danger. Come on, and you will now have your full revenge!" But the whites overcome with fear, did not choose to follow the Indian's advice, and urged him to take them back by the nearest and best way, which he did, and when they arrived at home late at night, they reported the number of the Indians to have been so great, that they durst not venture to attack them.

This story is said to be strictly true by Heckewelder, the Indian historian, and is illustrative, in a nice degree, of the wonderful sagacity and cunning of the Indians.

CHAPTER IX.

ANDREW MONTOUR VISITS THE GREAT ISLAND—PROCLAMATION OF GOV. MORRIS—A REWARD FOR INDIAN SCALPS—SHAMOKIN ABANDONED AND BURNED BY THE INDIANS—REFLECTIONS.

THE consternation and excitement that prevailed throughout the country, at the time of the massacre on Penn's Creek, is better imagined than described. The most exaggerated rumors were put in circulation, many of which were devoid of all truth. But, notwithstanding, they had reasons to be alarmed, as the danger was really great.

About the latter part of October, 1755, Andrew Montour, and an Indian named Monagatootha, were sent for by the Delawares to visit them at the Great Island. They started up, accompanied by three other Indians. On arriving there they found six Delaware and four Shawanese, who informed them that overtures had been made them by the French. Large bodies of French and Indians had crossed the Alleghany mountains, for the purpose of murdering, scalping and burning. This Montour reported to the Provisional Government, and also recommended the erection of a fort at Shamokin.

It was the intention of the French to overrun this portion of the country, and erect fortifications at different points, making Shamokin their head-quarters.

In the latter part of October, 1755, a few weeks after

the big massacre, the Indians again appeared in considerable numbers around the Shamokin region; and during the following month committed several barbarous murders upon the remaining whites. No particulars, however, are preserved, and notwithstanding the most careful research, I have been unable to gather them.

During the month of November, at a Council held at Philadelphia, the old Indian Chief Scarroyady, was present, and gave some interesting information. It was to the effect that two messengers had recently come from Ohio to the Indian town at Big Island, where they found a white man who accidentally happened to be there. These Indians were very much enraged on seeing him, and insisted upon having him killed. The other Indians would not permit him to be injured, stating that *they* would not kill him nor allow *them* to do it, as they had lived on good terms with the English, and did not wish to shed blood. These messengers were sent by the French to estrange these friendly Indians if possible.

In 1756, the Governor of the Province of Pennsylvania, on account of the hostility of the Indians, was obliged to issue the following proclamation, which I copy from the 7th volume of the Colonial Records, page 88:

"A PROCLAMATION.

" *Whereas*, the Delaware tribe of Indians, and others in confederacy with them, have for some time past, without the least provocation, and contrary to their most solemn treaties, fallen upon this province, and in a most cruel, savage and perfidious manner, killed and butchered great numbers of the inhabitants, and carried others into barbarous captivity; burning and destroying their habitations, and laying waste the country. *And whereas*, notwithstanding the friendly remonstrances made to them by this Government, and the interposition and positive orders of our faithful friends and allies the Six Nations, to whom they owe obedience and subjection, requiring and commanding them to desist from any further acts of hostility against us, and to return to their allegiance, the said Indians do still continue their cruel murders and ravages, sparing neither age nor sex; I have, therefore, by and with the advice and consent of the Council, thought fit to issue this Proclamation; and do hereby declare the said Delaware Indians, and all others who, in conjunction with them, have committed hostilities against His Majesty's subjects within this Province, to be enemies, rebels, and traitors to His Most Sacred Majesty; and I do hereby require all His Majesty's subjects of this Province, and earnestly invite those of the neighboring Provinces to embrace all opportunities of pursuing, taking, killing, and destroying the said Delaware Indians, and all others confederated with them in committing hostilities, incursions, murders, or ravages, upon this Province.

" *And whereas,* many Delawares and other Indians abhorring the ungrateful, cruel and perfidious behavior of that part of the Delaware tribe and others that have been concerned in the late inhuman ravages, have removed into the settled and inhabited parts of the country, put themselves under the protection of this and the neighboring governments, and live in a peaceable manner with the King's subjects; *I do therefore declare,* that the said friendly Indians that have so separated themselves from our said enemies and all others who shall join or act with us in the prosecution of this just and necessary War, are expressly excepted out of this Declaration, and it is recommended to all officers and others to afford them protection and assistance. *And whereas,* the Commissioners appointed with me to dispose of the *sixty thousand pounds* lately granted by act of General Assembly for His Majesty's use, have, by their letters to me of the tenth inst., agreed to pay out of the same the several rewards for prisoners and scalps herein after specified; and, therefore, as a further inducement and encouragement to all His Majesty's Liege People, and to all the several tribes of Indians who continue in friendship and alliance with us, to exert and use their utmost endeavor to pursue, attack, take, and destroy our said enemy Indians, and to release, redeem, and recover such of his Majesty's subjects as have been taken and made prisoners by the same enemies; *I do* hereby declare and promise, that there shall be paid out of the said sixty thousand pounds to all and every person and persons, as well Indians as Christians not in the pay of the province, the several and respective premiums and bounties following, that is to say: For every male Indian enemy above twelve years old who shall be taken prisoner and delivered at any forts garrisoned by the troops in the pay of this Province, or at any of the County towns, to the keepers of the common jails there, the sum of one hundred and fifty Spanish dollars or pieces of eight; for the scalp of every male Indian enemy above the age of twelve years, produced as evidence of their being killed, the sum of one hundred and thirty pieces of eight; for every female Indian taken prisoner and brought in as aforesaid, and for every male Indian prisoner under the age of twelve years taken and brought in as aforesaid, one hundred and thirty pieces of eight; for the scalp of every Indian woman, produced as evidence of their being killed, the sum of fifty pieces of eight; and for every English subject that has been taken and carried from this Province into captivity that shall be recovered and brought in and delivered at the city of Philadelphia to the Governor of this Province, the sum of one hundred and fifty pieces of eight, but nothing for their scalps; and there shall be paid to every officer or soldier as are or shall be in the pay of this Province who shall redeem and deliver any English subject carried into captivity as aforesaid, or shall take, bring in and produce any enemy prisoner, or scalp as aforesaid, one half of the said several and respective premiums and bounties.

Given under my hand and the Great Seal of the Province, at Philadelphia, the fourteenth day of April, in the twenty-ninth year of His Majesty's reign, and in the year of our Lord one thousand seven hundred and fifty-six.

"ROBERT H. MORRIS.

"By His Honor's Command,

RICHARD PETERS, Secretary.

GOD SAVE THE KING."

From this document it will be perceived that the whites were encouraged to scalp the Indians, by a reward offered by the Governor. It is thought to have been very barbarous for the Indians to scalp the killed, but at the same time it is not generally known that the English were hired to do the same. Such being the fact then, are the Indians to be blamed for their conduct? Certainly not. But it will be argued, probably, that they first commenced the barbarous practice. Granting such to be the fact, was that any reason that people claiming to be enlightened, should adopt the custom of savages?

About this time the Indians abandoned the town of Shamokin, probably on account of fear of the English, who were expected there in considerable force, to erect a fort, and make preparations for the defence of the frontier. On the third of June, 1756, a scout, consisting of George Allen, Abraham Loverhill, James Crampton, John Gallaher, John Murrah, and Robert Egar, were sent up the river to reconnoitre the enemy at Shamokin. They reported that they arrived there on Saturday night, and not observing any enemy, went to the place where the town had been, but found all the houses consumed, and no trace of it left. They remained there till ten o'clock the next day, but observed no signs of Indians.

Shortly after the massacre on Penn's Creek, the Moravian Mission at Shamokin was broken up, and the settlers fled to Bethlehem. This they were compelled to do in order to save their lives, as the Indians were very rude, and probably would have murdered them if they had remained much longer.

Thus was the ancient town of Shamokin destroyed by its own inhabitants. It seemed that they were anxious to obliterate all trace of their settlement at this point, when they found that the whites were encroaching so rapidly upon their lands. Like the Russians, they were determined to leave nothing behind, that could be of any benefit to the enemy.

Shamokin having been such an important point among them from time immemorial, no doubt they left it with regret, and the dusky warrior as he turned into the forest, could not refrain from looking back at the spot he loved so well, that was to be abandoned forever. The flames of the burning wigwams lighted up the gloom of the surrounding wilderness—the little pappooses clung closer to their mothers, and looked wistfully around. This closed the first act in the drama. The curtain will rise upon a new scene.

CHAPTER X.

COL. CLAPHAM SENT TO BUILD FORT AUGUSTA—HIS INSTRUCTIONS—DIFFICULTIES AT FORT HALIFAX—HIS ARRIVAL—TROUBLES CONTINUE—MEETING OF THE OFFICERS—THE COL.'S PITHY LETTER TO GOV. MORRIS.

It being fully determined by the Provincial Government to erect a fort at Shamokin, instructions were issued to Col. William Clapham, by Gov. Morris, in June, 1756, as follows:

"Herewith you will also receive two Planns of Forts, the one a Pentagon, the other a Square with one Ravelin to Protect the Curtain where the gate is, with a ditch, covered way, and Glacis. But as it is impossible to give any explicit directions, the Particular form of a fort, without viewing and Considering the ground on which it is to stand, I must leave it to you to build it in such form as will best answer for its own Defence, the command of the river and of the Country in its neighborhood, and the Plans herewith will serve to shew the Proportion that the Different parts of the works should bear to Each other.

"As to the place upon which this fort is to be erected, that must be in a great measure left to your Judgment; but it is necessary to inform you that it must be on the East side of the Susquehanna, the Lands on the West at ye forks and between the branches not being purchased from the Indians, besides which it would be impossible to relieve and support a garrison that side in the winter time. From all the information that I have been able to Collect, the Land on ye south side of the east branch, opposite the middle of the Island, is the highest of any of the low land thereabout, and the best place for a fort, as the Guns you have will form a Rampart of a moderate highth, command the main river; but as these Informations come from persons not acquainted with the nature of such things, I am fearfull they are not much to be depended on, and your own Judgment must therefore direct you.

"When you have completed the fort you will cause the ground to be cleared about it, so to a convenient distance and openings to be made to the river, and you will Erect such buildings within the fort and place them in such a manner as you shall Judge best.

"Without the fort, at a convenient distance, under the command of the Guns, it will be necessary to build some log houses for Indians, that they may have places to Lodge in without being in the fort where numbers of them, however friendly, should not be admitted but in a formal manner, and the guard turned out, this will be esteemed a compliment by our friends, and if enemies should at any time be concealed under that name, it will give them proper notions of our vigilance and prevent them from attempting to surprise it.

"As soon as you are in possession of the Ground at Shamokin, you will secure yourself by a breastwork in the best manner you can, so that you ever may work in safety, and you will inform me of everything committed to their care."

This extract embraces the principal part of the instructions relating to this point, and may be found at length in the Archives of the State, page 668.

When Col. Clapham received these instructions, he was at Fort Halifax, at the mouth of Armstrong's Creek, thirty-two miles below Shamokin, with a body of several hundred men. He had a number of mechanics also engaged in building boats for the transportation of their provisions, and munitions of war. These boats were pushed against the current. Navigating the river at that time, and in such a manner, was very laborious as well as dangerous; for the savages were constantly on the look out to surprise them. He also manufactured carriages at this place for his cannons, but the number is not given. It is inferred, however, from letters, that he had a number of pieces.

It appears that the Colonel had some difficulty with his men here, on account of pay already due them. Not being able to pay them, on account of the scarcity of funds, some of the soldiers, and the bateau-men, became very obstreperous, and refused to perform their duty. The latter were Dutchmen, according to his account, and twenty-six in number. They were arrested, and confined for mutiny.

The march was continued under great difficulty, and in July, 1756, the Colonel arrived at Shamokin with a command of about four hundred men. Temporary breastworks were hastily thrown up for their better protection, and preparations made to build a fort without delay. The men, however, were much dissatisfied about their pay, and it was with great difficulty that they could be restrained from returning. Matters finally assumed such a serious aspect, that on the 13th of July, a council was held in the camp, to take into consideration what was best to be done. As it shows clearly the troubles encountered by the commander, and forms an important feature in the history of Fort Augusta, I copy it entire, as follows :

" Present—all the Officers of Colonel Clapham's Regiment, except Capt. Miles, who Commands the Garrison at Fort Halifax.

"The Subalterns complain, that after expectation given them by several Gentlemen, Commissioners, of receiving seven Shillings and Six Pence each Lieut., & five Shillings & Six Pence each Ensign per day, the Commissary has received Instructions to pay a Lieut. but five shillings and six pence, and an Ensign four Shillings.

" Capt. Salter affirms, that the Gentlemen Commissioners assur'd him that the Subalterns pay was Augmented from five Shillings and six pence, and four Shillings to the sums mention'd above.

" Lieut. Davies reports, that Mr. Fox assured him that the pay of a Lieut. in this Regiment woud be Established at seven Shillings &

six Pence per Day, and that Mr. Peters, the Provincial Secretary, told him the same as a thing concluded upon, but hinted at the same time that he might expect but five shillings and sixpence per Day, before he came into the Regiment.

"Lieut. Garraway says, that Mr. Hamilton told him at Dinner, at Mr. Cunninghams, that the Pay of a Captain in this Regiment was to be ten Shillings, a Liutenants seven Shillings & six pence, & an Ensigns five Shillings & Sixpence.

"Capt. Lloyd says, that Mr. Hughs, one of the Gentlemen Commissioners told him the same thing.

"The Gentlemen Officers beg leave to Appeal to his Honor, the Governor, as an Evidence that that Opinion Universally Prevailed thro'out the Regiment, and thinking themselves unjustly dealt wth by the Gentlemen Commissrs., are Unanimously Determined not to Honor their most hearty and sincere thanks for the Favours received, the grateful impressions of wch they shall never forget, and at the same time request a permission from your Honör to Resign on the Twentieth day of Augst next, desiring to be relieved accordingly.

"[Signed] Levi Trump, Patrick Davis, Daniel Clark, Chas. Garraway, Asher Clayton, Wm. Anderson, John Hambright, William Pluñkett, Sam. Jno. Atlee, Chas. Brodhead, Wm. Patterson, Joseph Scott, John Morgan, Samuel Miles, James Bryan, Pat. Allison."

From this document, which may be found on page 700 of the Pennsylvania Archives, and volume first, it will be perceived that considerable difficulty existed between the government and the officers, which threatened seriously to impair the harmony that should exist between them.

James Young, who appears to have been a paymaster in the service of the government, visited Shamokin about this time, and found great confusion and dissatisfaction existing among the officers. On the 18th of July, 1756, he wrote a long letter to Gov. Morris, detailing the troubles in the camp. Col. Clapham, he states, was much displeased, on account of there not being a sufficiency of money forwarded to pay the troops. He complained loudly, of what he termed his ill usage, and went so far as to threaten to leave the service, and join the Indians, if something was not done soon.

Young, it appears, did not pay any of the officers, on account of their claiming more than he was instructed to allow them. All of them, with the exception of three or four, had been under arrest by order of the Colonel, and released at his pleasure without trial. *He* much doubted the propriety of building a fort at this point, as there was great danger of it being deserted by the men, and given up to the enemy.

On the same day Colonel Clapham and James Burd, wrote a long letter to Governor Morris, setting forth their grievances as follows :—

"SHAMOKIN, July 18th, 1756.

"SIR; I am desir'd herewith to Transmit to your Honor the results of a Council held at the Camp at Shamokin, July the 13th, in consequence of a disappointment in the Pay of ye Subalterns, from wch it will appear to your Honor that they think Themselves ill-treated by the Gentlemen Commissioners, whose Honor they rely'd on and several of whose promises they recite in Regard to their Pay, and that they are unanimously determined to resign their Commissions on the 20th day of August next if the respective Promises and Assurances of the Gentlemen Commissioners on that Head are not fully Comply'd with before that time.

"I further beg leave to address your Honor wth a Complaint in behalf of myself, and the other Captains and Officers of this Regiment. I had the honor to receive from you, Sr., a Commission as Captain in the Regiment under my command, dated March the 29th, for which the Gentlemen Commissioners, notwithstanding it was represented to them, have been pleased to withhold my pay and Assign'd as a Reason that a man can execute but one Office at a time, and ought to devote his whole service to it, which is not only an unjust remark, but affronting to all Gentlemen who have the Honor to hold directly from his Majesty or from any of his Majesty's Officers more than one Commission at the same time, by supposing them deficient in some part of their Duty, and is virtually an invective against the Government of Great Britain itself. They have likewise been pleased to deal with Major Burd upon the same principles and have paid him only as a Captain, which must be confessed is a very concise method of reducing without the Sentence or even the Sanction of a Court Martial.

"The several Captains think themselves affronted by the Commissrs Instructions to the Commissary to pay but two Serjeants and forty-eight Private Men in each Company, notwithstanding two Corporalls and one Drummer were appointed in each Company by your Honor's express Command, this instruction appears to them also as a contempt of your Honor's Orders, and have accordingly paid these non-commissioned officers out of their own Pockets.

"I entered into this service at the Solicitation of some of the Gentlemen Commissioners, in Dependence on Promises, which they have never performed, and have acted ever since not only in two Capacities but in twenty, having besides the Duties of my Commissions as Col. & Captain been obliged to discharge those of an Engineer and Overseer at the same time, and undergone in the Service incredible Fatigues without Materials and without thanks. But as I am to be paid only as a Col. I intend while I remain in this Service only to fulfill the Duties of that Commission, which never was yet supposed to include building forts and ten thousand other Services which I have performed, so that the Gentlemen Commissioners have only to send Engineers, Pioneers and other Laborers, with the necessary Teams and Utensils, while I, as Col. preside over the Works, see that your Honor's orders are punctually executed, & only Defend the Persons engaged in the Execution of them. In pursuance of a resolution of your Honor and the Gentlemen Commissioners to allow me an Aid-De-Camp who was to be paid as a Supernumerary Capt. in the Regiment; I according appointed Capt. Lloyd as my Aid-De-Camp on April 2nd, 1756, who has ever since acted as such in the most Fatiguing and disagreeable Service on Earth, and received only Captain's Pay.

"Your Honor was pleased to appoint Lieut. Clayton Adjutant to the Regiment under my command by a Commission, bearing date the 24th day of May, 1756, but the Gentlemen Commissrs have, in Defiance of all known rules, resolved that an Officer can Discharge but one duty in a day, and have paid him only as a Lieutenant. Impowered by your Honor's orders, and in Compliance with the Exigencies of the Services, I hir'd a number of Battoe men at 2–6 per day, as will appear by the return made herewith to your Honor, and upon demanding from the Paymaster General money for the Payment of the respective Ballances due to them, was surprized to find that the Commissy had by their instructions restraing him from Paying any incidental Charges whatever, as thinking them properly Cognizable only by themselves.

"'Tis extremely Cruel, Sr, and unjust to the last degree That men who cheerfully ventured their lives in the most dangerous and Fatiguing services of their Country, who have numerous Families dependant on their labor, and who have many of them while they were engaged in that service, suffered more from the neglect of their Farms and Crops at home than the Value of their whole pay. In short, whose Affairs are ruined by the Services done their Country should some of them receive no pay at all for those services, if this is the case I plainly perceive that all Service is at an end, and foresee that whoever has the command of this Garrison will inevitably be Obliged to Abandon his Post very shortly for want of a Suply of Provisions. Your Honr will not be surprized to hear that in a government where its Servants are so well rewarded I have but one Team of Draught Horses, which, according to the Commissioners remark, can but do the Business of one Team in a day from whence you will easily Judge that the Works must proceed very slowly and the Expence in the end be proportionable.

"Permit me, Sr, in the most grateful manner to thank your Honr for the Favour conferred on me and on the Regiment under my Command which I am sensible were meant as well in Friendship to the Province as myself. I have executed the trust Reposed in me wth all Possible Fidelity and to the best of my Knowledge, but my endeavours as well as those of every other Officer in the Service have met with so ungenerous a Return so contracted a Reward that we can no longer serve with any Pleasure on such terms. And if we are not for the Future to receive from your Honr our Orders, our Supplys and our Pay beg Leave unanimously to resign on the Twentieth of August next, & will abandon the Post accordingly at that time, in which Case I would recommend it to the Gentlemen Commissioners to take great Care to prevent that universal Desertion of the men which will otherwise certainly ensue.

"Thus much I thought it necessary to say in my own Vindication, and I am besides by the rest of the Gentlemen requested to add, that they have still further cause of Camplaint from a Quarter where they little expected it, & are conscious to themselves they never deserved it, esteeming much lighter their Treatment from the other Gentlemen Commissioners in regard to their Pay than the ungenerous Reflections of one of those Gentlemen on the Conduct of an Expedition which it too plainly appears it was never his Study to Promote, and will Appeal to their Country and to your Honor for ye Justice of their Conduct in the present Step.

"'Tis wth utmost concern & Reluctance that the Gentlemen of this Regiment see themselves reduced to the necessity of this Declaration and assure your Honr that nothing but such a Continued series of Discouragements could have ever extorted it from those who hope that they have not used any Expressions inconsistent wth that high Regard they have for your Honor, and beg leave with me to Subscribe themselves,

"Your Honor's
Most obedient humble Servant,
WILL'M CLAPHAM,
JAMES BURD."

Notwithstanding these complaints, government was slow to supply the wants of the soldiers, occasioned no doubt by the scarcity of funds and provisions. The command of Colonel Clapham still remained at Shamokin, and on the 14th of August, 1756, he again writes to Governor Morris that their wants were still unsupplied, and that they only had about half a pound of powder to each man, and none for the cannon. Their stock of provisions was also low—winter was approaching, and the prospect of famine stared them in the face, unless a supply was laid in. Boats had been despatched to Harris' for flour, but they encountered so much danger in passing down to Halifax, that their safe return was almost despaired of.

In this same letter the Colonel informs the Governor, that he was obliged to put Lieutenant Plunkett under arrest for mutiny, and only awaited the arrival of the Judge Advocate, to have him tried by Court Martial.

CHAPTER XI.

BUILDING OF FORT AUGUSTA CONTINUED—REPORT OF THE GOODS ON HAND—STORY OF THE BLOODY SPRING—DESCRIPTION OF THE FORT—CAPTAIN HAMBRIGHT'S EXPEDITION UP THE WEST BRANCH—MATERIAL OF WAR ON HAND IN THE FORT IN 1758—THE FRENCH EXPEDITION—JOB CHILLOWAY.

NOTWITHSTANDING the difficulties that existed in the command of Colonel Clapham, and the threats of the officers, that they would throw up their commissions, and abandon the post by the 20th of August, if they were not paid, it nowhere appears that any of them carried this threat into execution. The commanding officer, no doubt, on more deliberate and calm reflection, came to the conclusion that they had a savage and wily enemy to contend with, and that it was absolutely necessary for their *own* preservation, that defences should speedily be erected, to guard the frontier against their incursions. In view of this, and the more patriotic feelings that triumphed over the minor considerations of personal bickerings, the work of erecting Fort Augusta steadily progressed. In September, they received some supplies from below, which tended to revive their drooping spirits. Previous to this, the men were placed upon short allowances of flour.

Peter Bard writes to Governor Morris, September 14th, 1756, and states, that "the fort is now almost finished, and a fine one it is; we want a large flag to grace it." They had labored, it appears, indefatigably, for some six weeks upon the works. The commanding officer was in a better humor, and about this time informs Benjamin Franklin, that in his opinion, this post is of the utmost consequence to the Province, and that it is defensible against all the power of musketry. From its position, however, he feared that it was more exposed to a descent on the West Branch, and recommended that it be made stronger.

It may be interesting to the people of Sunbury, to know what kind of provisions, the quantity, and the materials of war, were possessed by the garrison of Fort Augusta one hundred years ago. In view of this, I transcribe the first report of the Commissary, Peter Bard, made in September, 1756, as follows:

Provisions in Store, September ye 1st.

46 bbs. beef and pork.
9 Do. of flour.
5 Do. of peas.
1 Bullock.

Brought up September ye 1st.

3 cwt. powder.
6 Do. of Lead.
92 Pair Shoes.
4 Lanthorns.
1301 Grape shot.
46 hand granades.
58 Cannon ball.
50 blankets.
4 brass kettles.
6 falling axes.
11 frying pans.
1 Stock Lock.
A Lump of Chalk.
27 bags flour about 5000 cwt.
4 Iron Squares.
12 Carpenter's Compasses.
1 ream writing paper.
4 quires Cateridge Do.
Some match rope very ordinary.
33 head of Cattle.

The Indians watched them very closely, and it was not safe to venture far from the main body. About this time a soldier was murdered and scalped, a short distance down the river. His body was afterwards found and buried by Captain Lloyd and party.

One of the men attending the cattle outside of the fort, on Sunday, went to a very fine spring, half a mile distant, to get a drink. Whilst in the act of drinking, he was shot by Indians, and immediately scalped. A party came out and pursued them, but without success. This occurred in September, 1756.

This is supposed to be what is known at the present day as the "Bloody Spring," at the upper end of Sunbury. A tradition is handed down by the old settlers, that several men were shot here in harvest time, where they had gone to eat their dinner. The story is related that the blood of the murdered men ran into the spring and colored the water a crimson hue; and when their friends came and found them, they named it the "Bloody Spring," in commemoration of the tragical event. The name is preserved to this day, and many curious legends are related concerning it. It is on the original Grant farm, now owned by Peter Baldy, Esq. The peculiar rocks around the Spring have been disturbed in building the railroad, and much of its romantic beauty is lost.

Whether there was more than this one man murdered here, there is no account upon record. This single murder is well authenticated, however, and it is supposed that it alone gave rise to the name.

About this time William Denny was appointed Governor of the Province of Pennsylvania. Colonel Clapham wrote him a long letter, stating the condition of the garrison, and the amount of pay due them. Many of the soldiers left families that had become very destitute, and the government should do something to alleviate their wants. The Colonel stated that he had advanced all the money he could raise, besides borrowing, and now was without a single farthing in his pocket. His men frequently deserted, and no wonder. At this time he had three hundred and twenty under his command, which was an inadequate number to protect the frontier, and carry on the work on the fort at the same time. One hundred men were constantly employed in transporting provisions for the rest; and yet, owing to the difficulties they had to encounter, they never were able to get much of a supply ahead; and it was very necessary that a stock of provisions to last six months should be on hand.

A short time after this, in another letter to Governor Denny, Colonel Clapham says, in conclusion:

> "Two bushels of Blue Grass Seed are necessary wherewith to sow the Slopes of the Parapet & Glacis, and the Banks of the River—in eight or ten Days more the Ditch will be carried quite round the Parapet, the Barrier Gates finished and Erected, and the Pickets of the Glacis completed—after which, I shall do myself the Honor to attend your commands in person."

In due course of time Fort Augusta was completed, and was one of the strongest, as well as most important, of all the frontier forts built at that gloomy period of our history. The following description of it is taken from the original drawing in London, a copy of which may be found in the State Library at Harrisburg, and is undoubtedly correct in every respect:

> "Fort Augusta stands at about forty yards distance from the river on a bank twenty-four feet from the surface of the water. The side which fronts the river is a strong pallisade, the bases of the logs being sunk four feet into the earth, the tops hollowed and spiked into strong ribbond which run transversely and are morticed into several logs at twelve feet distance from each other, which are larger and higher than the rest, the joints between each pallisade with five logs well fitted on the inside and supported by the platform—the other

three sides are composed of logs laid horizontally, neatly dovetailed and trunnelled down, they are squared; some of the lower end three feet diameter, the least from two feet and a half to eighteen inches diameter, and are mostly white oak."

Doubtless the action of the water has considerably worn away the banks, from what they were at that day, for it is now less than "forty yards" from the spot where the fort stood to the bank of the river.

On the 8th of November, 1756, Colonel Clapham informs the Governor, that about fifty miles above Fort Augusta, on the West Branch, was a town containing ten Indian families, from whence parties were continually annoying them, and that it was some of these Indians that killed the man at the Bloody Spring. These Indians having once lived at Shamokin, were well acquainted with the country, and from their knowledge of all the defiles in the neighborhood, could lay in ambush, sally forth and commit depredations, and escape with impunity. They at length became so mischievous that Colonel Clapham resolved on sending a force against them for the purpose of their destruction. Captain Hambright was selected for the performance of this duty. His instructions were as follows:

"Sir: You are to march with a Party of 2 Serjts, 2 Corporals & 38 Private men, under your command, to attack, burn and destroy, an Indian Town or Towns, with their inhabitants, on the West Branch of Susquehanna, to which Monsieur Montoure will conduct you, whose advice you are directed to pursue in every Case. You are to attack the Town agreeable to the Plan and Disposition herewith given you, observing to intermix the men with Bayonets equally among the three Partys in the attack, and if any Indians are found there you are to kill, Scalp, and captivate as many as you can, and if no Indians are there you are to endeavor to act in such manner, and with such Caution, as to prevent the Discovery of your having been there by any

Party, which may arrive Shortly after you, for which Reason you are strictly forbid to burn, take away, Destroy or Meddle with any thing found at such Places, and immediately dispatch Monsieur Montour with one or two more to me with Intelligence; when ye come near the Place of action you are to detach Monsieur Montour, with as many men as he shall Judge necessary to reconnoitre the Parts, and to wait in concealment in the mean Time with your whole Party till his Return, then to form your measures accordingly; after having burnt and destroyed the Town, you are in your Retreat to post an officer and twelve men in Ambush, close by the Road side, at the most convenient Place for such Purpose which may offer, at about Twelve miles Distance from the Place of action, who are to surprise and cut off any Party who may attempt to pursue, or may happen to be engaged in Hunting thereabouts, and at the same Time secure the Retreat of your main Body.

"Tis very probable, that on these Moon Light Nights, you will find them engag'd in Dancing, in which case embrace that Opportunity, by all means, of attacking them, which you are not to attempt at a greater Distance than 20 or 25 yards, and be particularly carefull to prevent the Escape of the Women and Children, whose lives Humanity will direct you to preserve as much as possible; if it does not happen that you find them Dancing, the attack is to be made in the morning, just at a season when you have Light enough to Execute it, in which attempt your Party are to march to the several Houses, and bursting open the Doors, to rush in at once; let the Signal for the general attack be the Discharge of one Firelock, in the Centre Divisions.

"If there are no Indians at the Several Towns, you are in such case to proceed with the utmost Caution and Vigilance to the Road which leads to Fort Duquesne, there to lye in Ambush, and to intercept any Party or Partys of the Enemy on the march to or from the English Settlements, and there to remain with that Design till the want of Provisions obliges you to return.

"I wish you all imaginable Success, of which the Opinion I have of yourself, the Officers and Party under your Command, leave me no Room to doubt,

"Your Humble Servant,

"William Clapham."

Where the Indian town was located, alluded to in the

above instructions, I have been unable to ascertain; notwithstanding the most careful research, as all traces of it were undoubtedly obliterated more than three-quarters of a century ago. The probability is, however, that it might have stood at the mouth of Loyal Sock Creek.

As to the success of Captain Hambright's expedition, and whether he burned the town, and scalped the inhabitants, is no where pointed out. If he executed the orders, he undoubtedly made a report, which would give his operations in detail, but I have searched for it in vain. An accurate report of such an expedition, up this river at that early period, would certainly be possessed of deep interest; and if it ever was made and lost, it is to be very much regretted. But as it is, we have to content ourselves with nothing but conjecture concerning it.

Considerable suffering was experienced among the garrison at Fort Augusta for the want of a physician, as no one had been provided for that post for a long time.

In 1757 or 1758, Major James Burd succeeded Col. Clapham, in the command of Fort Augusta. At this time they had the fort placed in a good condition, to resist the attack of an enemy. Below I annex a copy of the report of military stores, made December 6, 1758, by Adam Henry:

"12 Pieces of Cannon in good order.
2 Swivels in good order.
4 Blunderbusses in good order.
700 Rounds of cannon balls.
123 Bags of grape shot.
383 Cartridges of powder, made for cannon.
112 Cartridges of powder, made for swivels.
12 Barrels of powder.
46 Hand granades.
29 Rounds of cut shot."

With this amount of *materiel* of war on hand, there is no doubt but the garrison would have made a formidable show of resistance.

About this time Major Burd received intelligence that the French had commenced to build a fort at a place called by the Indians, *Achtschingi Clammui*, which the whites corrupted into *Chingleclamoose*. This was on the site now occupied by the flourishing village of Clearfield. The design of the French in erecting a fortification at this point, was with the view of making it a depot, from whence they intended to start on an expedition against Fort Augusta. The expedition was fitted out, and passed down the West Branch on rafts and boats. Tradition says that it numbered about eight hundred French and Indians. Be this as it may, it is pretty well authenticated that they came to the point of the high hill, overhanging the river, and directly opposite the fort, from whence the French engineers took such observations as satisfied them, that no effective attack could be made against it without the aid of cannon, which they were unable to bring with them through the wilderness.

The French did not remain long, but the Indians continued about the hill for several days, amusing themselves by trying to shoot poisoned arrows across the river with powerful bows. The distance was too great, however, and their missiles fell short of the mark. They occasionally expressed their supreme contempt of the whites by turning up their posterior extremities in an insulting manner. A round shot was fired from the fort one day, and cutting off a large limb immediately over their heads, so frightened them that they suddenly abandoned this kind of *amusement*, gave a terrific whoop, and scampered off into the woods.

Peace having been concluded with the Delawares and Shawaneese, the Governor of Pennsylvania invited them to make a settlement at Shamokin. It was to be under the charge of Thomas McKee, the Indian trader, who writes that he had arrived with the Indians, "who had drunk much on the road; and had mostly gone on, but few staying." Conrad Weiser afterwards recommended a trading house here.

On the 20th of January, 1758, Capt. Joseph Shippen writes to Major Burd, who appears to have been absent, probably at the seat of government, that several small parties of Delaware Indians had arrived at the fort, with skins to trade at the store. Among them also came old King Neutimus, Joseph, and all their families, amounting to forty-three in the aggregate.

Job Chilloway also came here, from the Monsey country, about this time. He spoke the English language well, and gave the Captain some important information. Job was a firm friend of the English, and always proved true. He was born and bred at a place called Egg-Harbor. He had a brother Bill. He informed Capt. Shippen that the Monsey tribe, on the West Branch, were determined to continue the war against the English. He intended to return to the Monsey country in a few days, to bring away his effects, when he would live among the whites.

Job Chilloway acted a conspicuous part in the history of the Valley, and proved himself of great use on several occasions. Further mention will be made of him at the proper place.

CHAPTER XII.

THE MAGAZINE AT THE FORT—REINFORCEMENTS—SHIKELLEMY—THE LIQUOR TROUBLE—COLONEL BURD'S SPICY LETTER—SPEECH OF KING, THE INDIAN CHIEF—THE INDIANS WANT AN HONEST MAN TO KEEP STORE—EXPEDITION FROM CUMBERLAND COUNTY—THEY GO TO THE GREAT ISLAND.

TIME passed on. Nothing very remarkable occurred at Fort Augusta for several years. We have accounts of various Indian meetings being held here, however, speeches made by the chiefs, and other business transacted.

Captain Gordon, who acted in the capacity of Engineer, recommended that a substantial magazine should be erected in one of the bastions of the fort. His description of the manner in which it should be constructed is very precise, and as it is in a tolerably good state of preservation, I copy his specification as follows:

"A Magazine ought to be built in the South Bastion, 12 by 20 feet in the clear, also a Laboratory of the same dimensions in the East Bastion. The Wall of the Magazine to be 2½ Foot thick, with three Buttresses, 2 Foot thick at the bottom, levelling to 9 inches at Top, in each side. The breadth of Buttresses, 3½ Ft. The Magazine to have an arch of 2½ Brick thick, and to be under ground within 1½ Foot of the Top of the Arch. The Walls seven foot high from the Level of the Floor, and to have a Foundation 2 Foot below the Floor; great care taken to lay the Joists, and to fill up between with Ruble

Stone and Gravel, rammed; the Joists to be covered with Plank 2½ inch thick. An Air Hole 1 foot Square to be practised in the Gavel end, opposite the Door. The Passage to the Magazine to have a zig-zag, and over the Arch some Fine Plaister laid, then covered with Fine Gravel and 4 foot of Earth a Top.

"The Laboratory likewise to be arched, but with 1½ Brick, and without Buttresses.

"A Fraise ought to be compleated round the Fort, to be introduced upon the Horizontal Line, at 20 Degrees of Elevation, or as much as will be sufficient to discover it underneath from the Flanks. This Fraise to be 2½ feet in the Ground, 3½ without, not to exceed 5 inches in Thickness, the Breadth from 4 to 7; a number of these Fraises ought, before set in the Wall, to be tunnelled on a Piece of Slab or Plank, of 5 inches broad, within 6 inches of the ends, which gives an inch at the end clear of the Slab; the distance from one another, 2½. After made fast to this Slab, to be introduced in the Wall, and the Earth ramm'd well between. When the Earth is well fixed and the whole set round, or a considerable way, another Piece of 3 inches broad and 2 thick, should be nailed al along close to the wall, which will bind the whole very fast together."

This document bears date, May 6th, 1758. It is rendered more interesting at the present day, as the magazine can yet be seen. It will probably last for many years to come.

In July following, a small reinforcement arrived at the fort. The total number of available men, including officers, in the garrison, at this time, amounted to but one hundred and eighty-nine. They were pretty well supplied, however, with munitions of war, and could have made a formidable stand against superior numbers.

The commanding officer received instructions to confine all the French deserters, that had been enlisted as soldiers, and send them under guard to Lancaster jail. This was to prevent them from again joining the French, on their expedition from *Chingleclamoose.*

About this time a new flag staff, seventy feet in height,

was erected, but unfortunately their old colors were entirely worn out, and they had to wait some time for the arrival of new ones.

John Shikellemy, who, during the French and Indian war, had became estranged from the English, appears again about Shamokin in 1759 or 1760. The Governor, it seems, sent him a string of wampum, and solicited his attendance at a council to be held at the fort. He also extended to him his hand, thanked him sincerely, and greeted him as a friend. This was to gain his esteem, for Shikellemy had been a little treacherous. He attended the conference, and, after it was over, requested some provisions to last him home. They gave him a hundred weight of flour and some meat, and he started in fine spirits.

Nothing further of any importance is reported to have transpired about the fort, till July 12th, 1762, when quite an excitement was raised on a report of liquor being furnished the Indians. The Indian Agent informed Lieutenant Graydon, who had command in the absence of Colonel Burd, that he had detected his (Col. Burd's) storekeeper in selling liquor to them, and had sufficient proof to convict him. He demanded of the Lieutenant that the liquor be seized, and as the instructions from the Governor were strict, he was obliged to do it. The storekeeper, however, denied the fact. It appeared that Mr. Holland, Colonel Burd's good friend, had been posted at a "peep hole" made in the wall, in the adjacent house, from whence he could see in the Colonel's store; and the proof was that he saw some squaws in the house with the storekeeper—that one of them asked for rum, and showed a dollar, on which the door was closed, and the rum delivered to her. Lieutenant Graydon was accused of being in the store at the same time. He was very much incensed about it, and admitted having been there, but saw no liquor sold to them. He forthwith informed Colonel Burd of the accusation, who wrote from Lancaster under date of July 18th, 1762, as follows:

"I am pestered with that fellow Nathaniel Holland, Clerk to the Indian Store at Fort Augusta. He has accused Mr. Dennis McCormack, my clerk, for Issuing Provisions at that place, with having carried on a trade with the Indians, in Conseqnence of which he has seized all the Rum in Store, and he further says that this Clandestine Trade is carried on by my Particular orders. Mr. Holland has sent an Express to Philada., and Mr. McCormack has come down to me here, and in order that this letter may come to your hand soon and safe, I have sent him with it to you.

"Inclosed is Mr. McCormack's Deposition, which was taken here, as I intended to have sent him back to Augusta, if I could have forwarded my letters by a safe hand to Philadelphia, but failing of this I am under the Necessity of sending himself.

"Now Sir, as to a trade being carried on with the Indians By me, for me, by my Clerk, by the Officers, or Garrison of Fort Augusta, or in any manner, or way whatsoever, at Fort Augusta, to my knowledge, I hereby declare to be absolutely False, & to the truth of this I am ready & willing to take my oath in any words that the Commissioners, or even that Scoundrell Holland would Commit to paper, and further, I can procure if Necessary the oaths of the Officers and Garrison of Augusta to the same purpose, & of every person living on the Susquehanna from Harris's to Augusta, that I never brought a skin or any other Indian Commodity whatever to their knowledge from Augusta.

"You will observe by the Deposition that Mr. McCormack did want of an Indian Squa a thin Indian dressed winter Skin to line a pair of plush britches for himself which he was getting; if this is the ground of the Complaint it must appear to His Honr the Govr & Commissrs to be intirely malitious in Holland, & not from a well grounded zeal of serving his Country.

"It Really vexes me much to be eternally plagued in this manner by Holland, and the more so that it is an accusation of the highest breatch of trust for me to break a well known Law of that Government whose bread I daily eat.

"I must therefore beg your friendly offers in laying the state of the case clearly before the Governor if Necessary; and if this affair is mentioned to my disadvantage, that you would represent it as it really is, & you are fully at liberty to show this letter to any Person whatsoever, as I shall support it in every particular, &c."

From the tone of this letter it will readily be inferred that Colonel Burd was not in the best humor when he wrote. How the matter was finally adjusted, or whether anything further grew out of it, does not appear upon record.

At a conference with the Indians, held at Lancaster, on Monday, the 23d of August, 1762, Gov. Hamilton presiding, Thomas King, one of the chiefs and representatives of the Six Nations, rose and said:

"Now all the different tribes of us present, desire that you will call your soldiers away from Shamokin, for we have concluded a peace, and are as one brother, having one head and one heart.

"If you take away your soldiers, we desire you would keep your trading house there, and have some *honest* man in it, because our cousins follow their hunting there, and will want a trade. This is the way for us to live peaceably together.

"Brother Onas: (The name for Penn.)

"I must tell you again these soldiers *must* go away from Shamokin fort; I desire it, and let there only be traders living there; you know who are the *honest* people; we desire that only *honest* people may live there, and that you will not be too hard with us, when they may buy our skins and furs, and such things as we may have to sell. This will be the way for us to live peaceably together; but for you to keep soldiers there, is not the way to live peaceable. Your soldiers are very often unruly, and our warriors are often unruly, and when such get together they do not agree, for as you have now made peace with all our nations, there is no occasion for soldiers to live there any longer."

There is no doubt that the Indians would have been

much gratified to have had the garrison removed from Shamokin, as it was a cherished spot where they loved to dwell, and where reposed the mouldering bones of their ancestors. The proposition to place an "*honest*" man there to keep a store, is a scathing commentary upon the probity of the whites, in their dealings with these dusky children of the forest. Judging from the manner in which they dealt with them, it is doubtful whether a man could have been found that would have conducted business in accordance with this old Indian's idea of "*honesty*." It seemed that they were destined to be cheated on every occasion, and in the most shameful manner too.

The soldiers were not removed from Fort Augusta. Such a course would have proved very bad policy, for the cup of the Indian's destiny was not full, and bloody scenes were yet to be enacted, before he turned his face for the last time upon the blue hills of Shamokin.

In 1765, a number of men from Cumberland, in the neighborhood of Carlisle, went up to Shamokin, for the purpose of murdering what Indians they might find there. On the alarm being given, they hastily collected their families together and fled.

They came to Shamokin, and appeared on the opposite side of the river, next the Blue Hill. Three of them, says Lieut. Graydon, came over to the fort and reported that they were from Cumberland county, and that there was fifty of them in company. They alleged that their object was to look at the land on the river, and at the Great Island, where some of them proposed to go and settle. Some of the party returned before they got that far—others went on to the Great Island. Some of them settled where Lock Haven now stands.

7

"We cannot conjecture," continues the Lieutenant, "what these people's intentions were, but they seemed very inquisitive about Indians, which made us suspect that they had a design against those who were about us."

The names of the three men that came over to the fort were, John Woods, James McMein, and James Dickey.

About this time a number of Indian families intended settling on the Great Island, and erecting cabins. Whether they went is not definitely known, but it is supposed they did.

William Maclay seems to have been the next commander of Fort Augusta, and Col. Hunter succeeded him. The time when Col. Hunter assumed the command is not stated, but it was probably about 1770.

Crane's Arcade, Jersey Shore, Pa.

CHAPTER XIII.

THE ISLE OF QUE—THE FRENCH NAME—INDIAN RELICS—AN EXTENSIVE BURYING GROUND—THE FIRST SETTLER—THE WEISERS—AN INDIAN'S REVENGE—JOHN SNYDER—ANTHONY SELIN, THE FOUNDER OF SELINSGROVE—HIS HISTORY—UNEXPECTED ARRIVAL FROM EUROPE.

SETTLERS continued to come in slowly from 1765 up to 1770, and locate along the river, in what was called the "Shamokin region." The post at Fort Augusta was an inducement for them to venture into the wilds of the wilderness, as it served as a place of protection whither they could fly in time of danger. [For many interesting reminiscences in the early history of Selinsgrove, and the Isle of Que, I am indebted to George A. Snyder, Esq., a son of Governor Snyder, who settled there in 1785.]

The Isle of Que was a favorite place with the Indians more than a hundred years ago. The name is evidently a misspelling, being in fact *Isle à Queue*, (Tail Island) a title which was undoubtedly given by the French traders, who used in former times, before the arrival of the whites, to descend the Susquehanna from Canada, to traffic with the Indians of this neighborhood. Why this name was given, it is now impossible to ascertain. It was probably a translation of the Indian name long since forgotten.

This beautiful and fertile island consists of a sandy alluvion, resting upon a compact clay, and appears to have been formed by the wash of the Susquehanna, after the occupation of the country by the Indians, for, (when the canal was being dug,) on arriving at the clay bed, numerous hearths of stones, with charcoal remaining in the interstices, were found, near which were fragments of Indian pots made of *talc*, stone hatchets, arrow heads of flint, &c., precisely such as were found in use among the savages, on the arrival of the whites in America.

Had the inquiry been made by the first settlers, it is not improbable that some account of the inundation by which the island was formed, might have been given by the Aborigines. A thousand years, however, would not be too remote a date to assign to the event. The oaks, buttonwoods, and other trees on the isle, have long since attained the largest size to which they ordinarily reach; and the vegetable mould is of a thickness which proves that vast quantities of trees, and other plants, must have perished; consequently, many centuries must have elapsed since the isle was a barren sandbank.

At the early period of which I speak, game was plenty in the forest, and fish were taken in abundance in the river. A tradition is handed down that the place was very unhealthy at a certain season of the year, and the Indians generally left the place about the beginning of August, and retired to the hilly country, where they remained until the fall of the leaf. During the intervening period, the only human being to be seen, was occasionally a hunter, whom the game had drawn from the hills, and who always avoided sleeping in the low ground. The children were carefully kept in their mountain retreats, for the malaria was particularly fatal to them.

The general burying ground of the Indians was on the Isle of Que, near its southern extremity, and must contain hundreds, nay thousands of bodies; for the skeletons have been found over a quarter of a mile in length and breadth. In digging for the foundation of Christian Fisher's house, seven skeletons were found, and at the other end of the lane leading from said house to George Fisher's, several more were found. Others were dug up at various places between the above-mentioned points.

The country, after it came into the hands of the whites, continued to be sickly, but for how long I am unable to tell. It became healthy, however, and so continued until the year 1800, when agues became very common, and the proper treatment of bilious diseases being little understood, many cases of obstinate and lingering sickness occurred.

The first white settler on the Isle of Que, is believed to have been Christian Fisher. Christian, in his youthful days, was not what his surname would indicate. In fact he was a hard goer, a prime hand at a fight, a horse race, or a drinking bout. At length his father finding remonstrances unavailing, notified him that he must now shift for himself. At the same time he offered him the fee simple of a large tract of land on the Isle of Que—then in the heart of the wilderness—which Christian accepted.

Having tied himself for better or for worse, to the daughter of one of his neighbors, Christian set out, his whole worldly wealth consisting of a horse, a rifle, an axe, and a bed. With these he landed on the "isle, far off and alone" truly, though neither on a "blue summer ocean," nor in any other respect resembling the isle of

Tom Moore's fancy. Christian's bed was spread for the first night at the foot of a tree. Next morning he commenced a hut, in which for a year or two he found shelter, and commenced cultivating and populating the isle.

His descendants, in considerable numbers, continue to flourish in this vicinity, and his tract of land, divided into small farms, makes many of them pass for rich men.

Conrad Weiser, grandson of the celebrated Indian Agent and interpreter of that name, was an early settler here also. He was a great landholder, owning in connection with his brother Jabez and his cousin Benjamin, a tract about twelve miles long on the river, and of several miles in width from east to west. Conrad being well acquainted with several of the Indian languages, and possessing their confidence, through his honesty and fair dealing, was much esteemed by them. He died about the year 1802, leaving his family in good circumstances, as to landed property, which, had they properly taken care of, would have been, by this time, of great value.

Jabez Weiser, it appears, never resided in this part of the country, although he owned a large body of land.

Benjamin lived on the Isle of Que, and must have been fond of shade, for he suffered the elder bushes to grow up around his cabin until it was entirely concealed from the view of the passer-by. You might, perchance, on walking along the shore of the river, says Mr. Snyder in his reminiscences, have observed a narrow path leading from the water's edge into the forest. Following this through the thickly growing elders and other shrubs, the traveller would find himself suddenly brought up by Benjamin's door, for the shrubs grew so closely around the house that there was not room for a cat to run around after her tail, anywhere nearer than on the pebbly beach of the river.

Jacob Fry, of Middletown, Dauphin county, was a trader frequently associated with Conrad Weiser, senr., in his dealings with the savages. John Esh, a tall and very strong young man, was for some years in Fry's employ. After the removal of the Indians from their last foothold in the north of Pennsylvania, Esh removed to Kentucky, and settled near Knoxville, where he was murdered by an Indian. The savage was given up by his tribe to the civil authorities, tried and sentenced to death. Before his execution, he stated that he had committed the murder out of revenge, Esh having flogged him on the Susquehanna, and that he had travelled three hundred miles to effect his purpose.

John Snyder, brother to the Governor, was one of the early settlers on the Isle of Que. He was a man of great strength and resolution, but addicted to gaming. A short time before the Revolutionary War, an officer of a body of British soldiers who were stationed in Lancaster, happened to make some insulting expressions concerning the Americans, in John's presence. He not only repelled his insults, but attacked and flogged him soundly. The consequence may readily be guessed. A number of British soldiers pursued him with fixed bayonets, determined to wash out the insult to their commander in blood. John was, however, too swift for them, and effected his escape. This occurred in his nineteenth year.

He settled on the Isle of Que, on which, and the main land, he owned a large tract of land. He was considered rich, and might have been richer, but for his inordinate love of gaming. He was the original proprietor of

Selinsgrove. Soon after the town was laid out, he wagered one of the lots upon the result of a horse race at Stumpstown, but was unfortunately thrown from his horse and killed. This lot was for many years known as the "unfortunate lot."

Anthony Selin, the founder of the present town of Selinsgrove, was a Swiss, who bore a captain's commission in the American army during the Revolution. When the war was over he came to this part of the country—then called Shamokin—and being a handsome, active young man, captivated the affections of a young lady named Agnes Snyder, who was a sister of the Governor's, and married her. This happened near the time of John Snyder's unfortunate death. Simon Snyder and John Miller were appointed administrators of the estate of John Snyder, and after a few years found that the estate was encumbered with debt to such a degree that it became necessary to sell the whole of it. This was accordingly done, and Selin became the purchaser, at a price which was then considered high. John Snyder's widow had, meantime, married a man named Jacob Kendig, who lived upon the fine farm lying at the eastern end of the long bridge across Penn's Creek, about one mile above Selinsgrove.

Selin, finding that the draft of John Snyder's town would not fit the ground, caused the whole to be resurveyed and laid out anew, and named it Selinsgrove. What name John Snyder had given, or intended to give the town, does not appear.

Selin had two children, Anthony Charles and Agnes. After he had lived for some time on the farm adjoining the northern line of Selinsgrove, a young Swiss, of about seventeen years, made his appearance and saluted him with the endearing name of *father!* and indeed it proved that master Zifhareus Selin, was veritably the son of Anthony; and that his mother, lawful wife to the said Anthony, was alive, and living amid the romantic mountains of Switzerland, and sent her respectful compliments to her truant husband!

Selin's mortification and distress on this occasion was so great, as to produce a fever, which shortly resulted in his death. Fortunately for the children, Anthony and Agnes, their half brother, Zifhareus, was not of sound mind. Had he been, he would probably have remained here long enough to establish himself in the possession of his father's estate. His claim could not have been contested, for Selin had acknowledged him. Being, however, but little removed from absolute idiocy, he only claimed and received his father's "Decoration," as member of the Cincinnati—and contented with this high and important acquisition, he set out for Europe. He never afterwards returned to claim his inheritance, and in fact, was never heard from, so that it is impossible to say whether he arrived at his home, or perished at sea.

CHAPTER XIV.

FIRST HOUSE IN SELINSGROVE—JIMMY SILVERWOOD, "MASTER OF THE SEVEN ISLANDS"—STORY OF GAHL, THE PHYSICIAN—DISCOVERY OF HIS SECRET—TOMMY PRICE—HIS REMARKABLE ESCAPE FROM AN ENGLISH PRISON IN NOVA SCOTIA.

THE first house built in the town of Selinsgrove, was erected by a man named Kern, a clockmaker. At what time it was built I did not learn, but presume it was at a very early period. It stood on the street leading to the Isle of Que, and was a few years ago still in the possession of his widow, who, after his death, married a man named Rhoads. When asked why he had not built upon the main street of the town plot, Kern answered that it could be of no advantage to him, for there *never* would be a street there. This occurred immediately after the town had been laid out, and the whole ground was as yet covered with a forest of pines, and a dense underbrush.

The cluster of islands, in the Susquehanna, opposite the Isle of Que, were first settled and cultivated by old Jimmy Silverwood, an Englishman, who used pompously to entitle himself "master of the seven islands;" which title borne across the Atlantic in his letters, gave his English relations and friends an undue idea of his wealth and consequence. Could the old man have transferred his islands to England, their extent and fertility would have made their possessor a rich landholder; and even here, had he known how to take care of his property, he might have became a man of considerable fortune.

Soon after Silverwood came into possession of the islands, the country began to be filled with people, and shad became a good article in the home market, and Silverwood's islands presented several excellent localities for fisheries. Immense numbers were caught; three, four, and five thousand at one haul of the seine being not uncommon—and even at the low price of six dollars per hundred, they were a source of profit. Silverwood made money, but, alas! he did not make provision for the future; he spent, and suffered his sons to spend, as if the shad fisheries were an inexhaustible mine of wealth. Of course he died poor, and left a poor family behind him.

These islands were originally covered with a heavy growth of excellent timber, and almost entirely free from underbrush. The banks were clear, and presented no obstruction to the vision, besides their steepness, and the overhanging, in some parts, of the sod sustained by the roots of the huge trees. Cultivation has, however, worked material changes here. The trees having been cut away, the banks have become more sloping, by the crumbling of the upper portion. The cattle being kept off by the fences and the care of the farmer, seeds of divers sorts of trees have lodged and been permitted to grow, and the islands are now surrounded by an impenetrable thicket, presenting in summer an encircling wall of the liveliest verdure. But for their loneliness and seclusion, I know of no more desirable residence than these islands would furnish.

At an early period a man named Gahl, who afterwards became the first curer of agues and intermittent fevers in the Shamokin region, came and settled with his father near where Sunbury now stands. The old man purchased a farm soon after his location; and before Peter commenced practice as a physician, his mother died. The intelligence having been spread, many of the neighbors called at the house to condole with the afflicted husband, but found no living being at home. After waiting for some time, the old man came in from the fields, where he had been at work, set down for a few minutes, and then rose to return to his work, saying, "Well, neighbors, just try and amuse yourselves as well as you can till Peter comes in, and then he'll play the fiddle for you!"

When agues in that region of country became common, and the proper treatment of bilious diseases being little understood, many cases of extreme and lingering sickness occurred. The physicians generally administered Peruvian bark, but not being aware of the necessity of previously freeing the stomach from bile, the bark frequently failed of the desired effect. Peter Gahl, who was a French West Indian, commenced the practice of medicine. Although an arrant quack, he was the only person who generally succeeded in curing agues and intermittent fevers, having probably acquired his knowledge in St. Domingo. His remedy he kept a profound secret, and the other physicians of the country were too little acquainted with chemistry to be able to discover the real nature of his nostrum, through the disguise in which he had shrouded it. The remedy was contained in a gallypot, and the directions to the patient were that he should take the contents in three rather unequal portions, on three consecutive days. The first day's dose made the patient vomit, the second purged him, and the third and largest dose produced the cure.

The composition of this prescription was discovered in a singular manner. There was, about that time, living with Simon Snyder, a nephew, a rough lad of fifteen or sixteen, named George Kremer, who, on one occasion, was sent to Gahl to procure some of the famous medicine. It so happened that he had none ready, and therefore mixed a gallypot full in George's presence. George, who was naturally a remarkably shrewd boy, was attentive to the process, and asked the name of each ingredient used. Gahl, unsuspectingly told him the names, which George did not fail to remember. First in the gallypot was an ounce of bark, above this was a portion of some active cathartic—calomel and jalap—and at the top was an emetic. A little essence of cinnamon was added to disguise the nature of the ingredients. The next time that Dr. Young, Snyder's family physician, came to the house, the important secret was imparted to him. He forthwith imparted it to his brethren of the medical profession, and they were soon able to treat agues and fevers more successfully than Gahl. Being acquainted with medicine as a science, they were able to apply the remedy more judiciously than the ignorant West Indian.

Tommy Price, another old settler, lived on Water street, Selinsgrove. In his younger days he had been a soldier, and on one occasion was made prisoner by the British, and carried to Halifax, in Nova Scotia. There being a vast extent of forest intervening between Nova Scotia and the nearest American settlements, it was not deemed necessary to be particularly watchful on the land side. Of which circumstance, Tommy taking advantage, eluded the sentries and made for his home. Travelling westward, he was stopped by the waters of the Bay of Fundy, but not being discouraged by this check, he travelled round the head of the bay, and after a journey of many hundreds of miles, through a wilderness, during which he was exposed, without arms, to the mercies of savages, and wild beasts, he arrived at the settlements in New England.

After the Revolutionary War he came to Selinsgrove, where he built a small log-house, and resided during the balance of his life. Notwithstanding the decision of character indicated by Tommy's remarkable escape from Nova Scotia, he was a very idle personage—in fact an inveterate fisherman, and would sit on the bank of the creek for hours, patiently waiting for a nibble.

In due course of time, Tommy died and was buried. Some days after his death, some one on seeing the widow looking very sad, inquired of her, "Well, Rosina, what is the matter?" "Oh!" said she, whining and shaking her left foot, "Tummas is ded and I's got de agee!"

CHAPTER XV.

MURDER OF TEN INDIANS BY FREDERICK STUMP—EXCITEMENT THROUGHOUT THE PROVINCE—PROCLAMATION OF GOV. PENN—HIS ARREST AND CONFINEMENT IN CARLISLE JAIL—RESCUED BY A MOB—HIS DESCRIPTION—FINAL ESCAPE AND DEATH.

PEACE having been restored with the Indian tribes, settlers gradually came forward, pitched their tents in the wilderness, and commenced to make improvements. Nothing unusual occurred till early in the winter of 1768, when an event transpired that caused great excitement in the settlements around Shamokin, and gave the Governor great uneasiness.

It appears from the records of that early period, that a man named Frederick Stump, a German of Penn's township, in the county of Cumberland, (now Snyder,) not far from where Selinsgrove stands, and near the mouth of Middle Creek, did, in violation of the public faith, and in defiance of all law, inhumanly and wickedly kill, without any provocation, four Indian men, and two Indian women, in his own house, on Sunday, the 10th day of January, 1768. Not content with this inhuman murder, he went the next day to an Indian cabin fourteen miles up the creek, and there barbarously put to death, and burnt, an Indian woman, two girls, and a young child!

As soon as this cool, deliberate, and bloody murder became known, the most intense excitement prevailed throughout the country. The people were astounded at the magnitude and relentless barbarity of the act. The Indians, who were friendly, and had come from the Great Island, and pitched their rude wigwams on the creek, in order to be near and claim the protection of the whites, had given him no cause for thus barbarously murdering them. The whites were alarmed, too, for fear that when the sad intelligence reached the friends of these Indians, that they would rise up and commence to burn, murder and scalp all that they could find, in order to be revenged.

Stump had an accomplice in this bloody tragedy, named John Ironcutter, who acted in the capacity of a servant to him. He was a German also.

A few Indians being in the neighborhood, on repairing to the spot, found the remains of their friends, and being apprised that Stump was the murderer, forthwith proceeded to look for him. He fled to Fort Augusta, and entering a house in the occupancy of the mother and aunts of the late Mrs. Grant, claimed their protection; alleging that he was pursued by Indians. The ladies, noticing from his countenance that all was not right, at first refused to have anything to do with him, fearing that the Indians might come and murder them, too, on finding him secreted in the house. He begged so piteously, however, for protection, that they relented, and snugly stowed him away between two beds. But a few minutes elapsed before the arrival of the infuriated Indians, who had tracked him to the house. They inquired if he had been seen there, and blustered and threatened considerably, but the ladies insisted that they knew nothing about him, when they were reluctantly compelled to depart without finding him. Before leaving, however, they picked up a cat, pulled out all her hair, and tore her to pieces before the family, by way of illustrating how they would have treated Stump if they had caught him!

The only excuse Stump had to offer for the murder, was, that the Indians came to his house on Sunday evening in a state of intoxication, and were somewhat disorderly. He endeavored to persuade them to leave, but they refused to do it, and being apprehensive that they intended to do him some harm, killed them all; and in order to conceal their bodies, dragged them down to the creek, made a hole in the ice, and threw them in. Fearing that the killing of them might come to the ears of some of their friends near by, he went the next day fourteen miles up the creek, to two cabins, where he found one squaw, two girls, and a small child, whom he killed, and setting fire to the cabins, consumed their bodies!

The intelligence of this inhuman butchery coming to the ears of John Penn, Governor of the Province, accompanied by numerous depositions, so shocked him, that he felt himself in duty bound to have the murderer speedily brought to justice. The matter was laid before the Council, then in session in Philadelphia, and resolutions were passed instructing the Governor to write to the magistrates of Cumberland county, requiring them to exert themselves, and have him arrested immediately. Also, to acquaint the sheriffs of the adjoining counties of Lancaster and Berks, to be on the lookout, and arrest him, should he come into their districts.

The Council further advised the Governor to write to

General Gage and Sir William Johnson, acquainting them with the unhappy event, and request them to communicate the same as soon as possible to the Six Nations, in the most favorable manner in their power, to prevent their taking immediate revenge for this great injury committed on their people; and to assure them of the firm and sincere design of the government to give them full satisfaction at all times, for all wrongs done to them, and that they would leave nothing undone to bring the murderer to condign punishment.

On the 19th of January, 1768, Governor John Penn addressed himself in a long letter to the magistrates of Cumberland county, giving them the necessary instructions how to act. Amongst other things, he says:—

"I am persuaded Gentlemen, that the Love of Justice, a sense of Duty, and a regard for the Public Safety, will be sufficient inducements with you to exert yourselves in such a manner as to leave no measures untried which may be likely to apprehend and bring to punishment the Perpetrator of so horrid a Crime, which, in its consequences, will certainly involve us again in all the Calamities of an Indian War, and be attended with the Effusion of much innocent Blood, unless by a proper Exertion of the Powers of Government, and a due Execution of the Laws, we can satisfy our Indian Allies that the Government does not countenance those who wantonly Spill their Blood, and convince them that we think ourselves bound by the Solemn Treaties made with them. I have this matter so much at heart, that I have determined to give a Reward of Two Hundred Pounds to any Person or Persons who shall apprehend the said Frederick Stump, and bring him to justice," &c.

A similar letter was also forwarded to the magistrates of Berks and Lancaster counties, enjoining upon them the necessity of acting with promptitude, should the murderer escape into their territory.

Accompanying this letter was a public proclamation,

issued in a formal manner, bearing the broad seal of the Province, in which it was strictly commanded, "that all Judges, Justices, Sheriffs, Constables, Officers Civil and Military, and all other, his Majesty's faithful and Liege Subjects within this Province, to make diligent search and enquiry after the said Frederick Stump, and that they use all possible means to apprehend and secure him in one of the Public Gaols of this Province, to be proceeded against according to Law."

Governor Penn also sent a message by an Indian named Billy Champion, to Newaleeka, the chief of the Delawares, and other Indians, residing at the Great Island, acquainting them with the cruel murder of their friends; and assuring them that the most speedy measures would be taken, to have the ends of justice accomplished. For carrying this message, the Council allowed Billy for his services, a "blanket, a shirt, a hat, a pair of shoes, a pair of Indian stockings, a breech cloth, and four pounds two shillings and six pence, in cash."

Stump was finally arrested and lodged in the jail at Carlisle. The account of his capture is given as follows:—

"Captain William Patterson, lately in the Provincial service, now living on Juniata, about twenty miles from Frederick Stumps, hearing of the murder committed by him and his servant, on the bodies of a number of Indians, engaged nineteen men, at two shillings and six pence per diem wages, to go with him to take them. On their approach, Stump fled to the woods; but Patterson pretended to the people in the house, that he came there to get Stump to go with them and kill the Indians at the Great Island; this decoy had the desired effect. Some one went out, found and brought Stump to the house. On his coming in, Patterson arrested, bound and brought him, with his servant, John Ironcutter, without delay, to Carlisle jail, where he was lodged on Saturday evening, the 23d of March, 1768."

Thus it seemed that the ends of justice were about to

be accomplished, and the murderers receive the punishment which they so justly deserved. A difficulty, however, arose among the magnates of the law at Carlisle, about where he should be tried.

It was intended to take him to Philadelphia for trial, and a discussion arose upon this point. The account is continued as follows:

"The Court just then concluding, all the justices were in town. The Monday morning following, the sheriff was preparing to carry him to Philadelphia, agreeable to the express mandate of the chief justice's warrant; but a doubt arose amongst the justices and towns-people, as is pretended, whether the sheriff had a right to remove him, he being committed to their jail by two justices, Armstrong and Miller. But the truth was, they apprehended a design to try him at Philadelphia, though the chief justice's warrant expressly commanded that he should be brought down for examination—and thereupon the sheriff was directed to proceed in his duty.

"Wednesday, several justices again met, to consult about sending him down; while they were consulting, about forty of the country people assembled, and marched near the town, declaring they would take him out of jail, as they understood he was to be taken to Philadelphia. A gentleman advised them not to go into town, but send in two of their party, to know the sentiments of the magistrates on that head. The two messengers came into town, and received assurances that Stump should not be sent to Philadelphia, but receive his trial at Carlisle, upon which the messengers returned, and the company dispersed, and went to their respective dwellings.

"Thus matters quietly rested until Friday, when a company from Sherman's Valley, about fifteen miles from Carlisle, and Stump's neighborhood, assembled, and came near the town, about eight of whom came in by couples; the first two that entered the prison, asked the jailer for a dram, or some liquor; which he went to get for them, and when he brought it, the others entered. They directly drew a cutlass, and presented a pistol, swearing they would kill him, if he resisted, or made the least noise; the same care was taken as to the jailer's wife. Immediately came up the general company, of about sixty armed men, and surrounded the jail; the rioters within had a sledge, crowbar, and axe, with which (as some say) they broke the inner jail door; while others assert, that they had procured the keys of the dungeon from a girl in the jail. They proceeded down to the dungeon, where Stump lay handcuffed, the chain which fastened him to the floor having been taken off two days before. They then brought him up. In the meantime came the sheriff, Col. John Armstrong, Robert Miller, Esq., and Parson Steel, who were admitted within the circle of armed men round the jail, but not knowing of others being within, went on the steps of the jail, and declared they would defend it with their lives. By this time those within came with Stump to the door—the sheriff seizing him, when one of the men made a thrust with a cutlass, which passed close by his throat, and immediately the whole body surrounded the sheriff and justices, and carried them to the middle of the street, but happily did not touch a hair of their heads, and went off with Stump, greatly shouting; but first took him to a smith, whom they obliged to cut off his irons. The sheriff and justices immediately went after them, and overtook one-half of the company; but the rest, with Stump, were gone over the hills to Sherman's Valley.

"Some of them declared they would give Mr. Patterson the interest of his £200 reward, which should not be of any service to him, and great danger was apprehended to his person and property, for his upright and spirited behavior in the cause of virtue and his country."

Ironcutter was also rescued at the same time, and carried off with Stump.

This violent demonstration, on the part of the people, against the enforcement of the civil law, as may be expected, caused a tremendous excitement throughout the Province. The Governor was astounded, and scarcely knew how to act. Not daunted by the violence of the people, a party, composed of the sheriff, clergy, magistrates, and several other reputable inhabitants, speedily assembled and proceeded to Sherman's Valley, to remonstrate with those that rescued Stump, against such lawless proceedings. They represented to them the dangerous consequences of such conduct, and the bad example they were setting. They manifested some contrition, and partially promised to return him in three days. They did not do it, however.

The people of the frontier were very much alarmed at this lawless demonstration, and many of them left their homes. Captain Patterson being threatened by the rescuers of Stump, was obliged to keep a guard in his house night and day.

The reasons given by the mob for their conduct, was, that the government always manifested a greater concern at the killing of an Indian than a white man. That numbers of the whites had been barbarously murdered and no lamentations were made, nor exertions of the goverment to bring *their* murderers to justice. That their wives and children must be insulted by Indians, and a number of them receive the fatal blow, before they *dare* say it is war. In view of this they were determined *no* longer to submit.

Governor Penn ordered proceedings to be instituted against those who had thus violated the law, and forcibly rescued Stump. Testimony was speedily obtained against twenty-one of them, including the ringleaders, and warrants issued for their arrest. Whether they were arrested does not appear.

The most positive instructions were issued by the Governor for the re-arrest of Stump and Ironcutter, and a warrant from the chief justice forwarded to the authorities, to convey them to Philadelphia, accompanied by a second proclamation, offering an additional reward of two hundred pounds for Stump, and one hundred for Ironcutter. He also caused a description of their persons to be published, to assist in their apprehension.

The description of the culprits is as föllows, and is copied from the official records of the State:

> "Frederick Stump, born in Heidleburg township, Lancaster county, in Pennsylvania, of German parents. He is about 33 years of age, 5 feet 8 inches high, a stout fellow, and well proportioned; of a brown complexion, thin visaged, has small black eyes, with a downcast look, and wears short black hair; he speaks the German language well, and the English but indifferently. He had on, when rescued, a light brown cloth coat, a blue great coat, an old hat, leather breeches, blue leggins and moccasins.
>
> "John Ironcutter, born in Germany, is about 19 years of age, 5 feet 6 inches high, a thick, clumsy fellow, round shouldered, of a dark brown complexion, has a smooth, full face, grey eyes, wears short brown hair, and speaks very little English. He had on, when rescued, a blanket coat, an old felt hat, buckskin breeches, a pair of long trousers, coarse white yarn stockings, and shoes with brass buckles."

After their rescue they came back to the neighborhood in which the murder was committed. From thence Stump went to hi sfather's, in Tulpehocken. Ironcutter was carried off, and secreted by some Germans. Afterwards they escaped to Virginia, and never were arrested again. Stump, it is said by an old settler, died there only twenty-five or thirty years ago, at a very advanced age. So ends the history of Stump, the Indian killer.

CHAPTER XVI.

ORGANIZATION OF NORTHUMBERLAND COUNTY—ITS ORIGINAL BOUNDARIES—SUNBURY FOUNDED—NAMES OF THE SETTLERS ALONG THE RIVER—TROUBLES AND PRIVATIONS—THE GRANT FAMILY—DR. PLUNKETT—SKETCH OF HIS LIFE—ANECDOTES.

THE County of Northumberland was organized, March 12th, 1772, out of Lancaster, Cumberland, Berks, Northampton and Bedford. It embraced a large extent of territory. The following description of its boundaries is from the first section of the act erecting it:

"That all and singular the lands lying and being within the boundaries following, that is to say, beginning at the mouth of Mahontongo creek, on the west side of the river Susquehanna, thence up the south side of said creek, by the several courses thereof, to the head of Robert Meteer's spring; thence west by north to the top of Tussey's mountain; thence south westerly, along the summit of the mountain to Little Juniata; thence up the north-easterly side of the main branch of little Juniata, to the head thereof; thence north to the line of Berks county; thence east along the said line, to the extremity of the Province; thence east along the northern boundary, to that part thereof of the Great Swamp; thence south to the most northern part of the Swamp aforesaid; thence with a straight line to the head of the Lehigh, or Mill creek; thence down the said creek so far, that a line run west south-west will strike the forks of Mahontongo creek where Pine creek falls into the same, at the place called the Spread Eagle, on the east side of the Susquehanna, thence down the southerly side of said creek to the river aforesaid; thence down and across the river to the place of beginning."

It was directed by the Provincial authorities, that the courts be held at Fort Augusta, till a Court House, and the necessary public buildings, could be erected. A committee composed of William Maclay, Samuel Hunter, John Loudon, Joseph Wallis, and Robert Moody, were appointed to purchase a piece of land, in some convenient place in the county, subject to the approval of the Governor, on which to erect a court house and jail.

Joshua Elden, James Patten, Jesse Lukens and William Lukens, were appointed "to run, mark out and distinguish the boundary lines between Lancaster, Cumberland, Berks, Northampton, Bedford, and Northumberland counties."

At that time Northumberland embraced all of the West Branch Valley, as far as Lycoming creek. The river above that point was the boundary on the south side. The north side was in dispute. Most of the territory was a dense forest, where the red man had roamed with untrammeled freedom, from time immemorial, but the onward march of civilization was about to drive him from these favorite haunts, and compel him to seek a new home in distant wilds. He sullenly retired from the cherished scenes of his childhood, after being overcome by the superior numbers and intelligence of the race that, it seemed, were destined to dispossess him. Such seemed to be his fate. But the vindictive passions of his savage breast were aroused, and he fought for his home and hunting grounds. It was natural that he should do so—the present race of whites, claiming a greater amount of refinement and intelligence, would do the same. They would scalp, too, before they would surrender their hearths and firesides to another race, and leave all the endearing associations of home. The territory of the Indian was acquired by *purchase* and aggression, treachery and duplicity. His noble nature knew no guile—he thought the white man was *honest!* Alas! what a sad mistake.

The territory on the north side of the Otzinachson—now called the West Branch—was not included in the purchase of 1768, at Fort Stanwix, further west than Lycoming creek, which was supposed to be the Tiadaghton of the Indians. The mistake was not discovered till at the treaty of 1784, held at the same place, when the Indians informed the Pennsylvania Commissioners that what the whites called Pine creek, was the *real* Tiadaghton.

The town of Sunbury was laid out in the same year that the county was erected, 1772, by John Lukens, the Surveyor General, on the beautiful plain one mile below Fort Augusta. He erected a frame house, which was, probably, the first building put up in the town. William Maclay, of whom mention has already been made, shortly afterwards erected a stone building, which is still standing, fronting on the river.

At this time Mungo Reed resided on what was then called Shamokin island, near the confluence of the two rivers, and a few yards above the fort. Thomas Grant and Colonel Hunter, commander of the fort, lived on two farms which they had taken up close by. Robert Murdock also had a farm here. These gentlemen are considered among the first *bona fide* settlers at this point, who formed the nucleus around which the other immigrants clustered.

The Grant family were identified, to a considerable extent, with the history of the eventful period of the Revolution. Mr. Grant was a Captain in the Revolutionary War, and had command of a frontier fort. His widow was a remarkably fine woman, of great mind and resolution, and universally esteemed and beloved by all who knew her, for her many social virtues. She is well remembered, and feelingly spoken of, by many of the old people now living. When Sherman Day visited her, about 1840, he describes her as a venerable old lady, living in a fine mansion, surrounded by her children and grandchildren. Her memory extended back for a period of eighty years, yet she did not appear to be over fifty.

Robert Martin, originally from New Jersey, was the father of Mrs. Grant. He first settled at Wyoming under the Pennsylvania title, but being unable to live there in peace, abandoned his farm, and removed to Northumberland. He erected a house, and kept tavern here, previous to the purchase of 1768. His house, at that time, was the only one to be seen about Northumberland Point, or even on the other side, except in Fort Augusta. He was undoubtedly the first settler on the site of Northumberland, near eighty years ago. After the purchase of 1768, his house was thronged with numerous speculators, pioneers, surveyors, and adventurers, who came to view and settle upon the lands of the West Branch.

Colonel Hunter is distinguished in the history of that period. He had command of Fort Augusta during the time of the Revolution, when it was the great point to which all the settlers of both Branches converged, when compelled to abandon their homes in the wilderness, by the attacks of the savages. All the forts erected along the West Branch were under his supervision, and the duties that devolved upon him were great. He may be considered the watchful guardian of the frontier. Scenes of the most thrilling character were enacted at that period.

A fine brick mansion now stands on the identical spot formerly occupied by the fort. It is owned by Miss Hunter, a lineal descendant of the old Colonel. Truly, it is built on sacred ground.

In 1772, according to the best and most reliable information that I have been able to collect, there was but one house where Sunbury now stands, one at Fort Augusta, and one on the Grant farms, one on Shamokin island, one in Northumberland, and but four between that point and where Milton now stands, where there was one. Between Milton and Muncy hills there were six families, and not more than eight or ten on the river above.

Captain Lowden, and a Mr. Patterson, it appears, became owners of the land at Northumberland. They afterwards sold a part to Reuben Haynes, a brewer from the city of Philadelphia, who laid out the town of Northumberland, in 1775. This was at a very gloomy period of our history, and it made but slow progress for several years. The settlers were often compelled to abandon their homes, and fly to Fort Augusta for protection.

Ludwig Derr, a German, settled in Buffalo Valley, where Lewisburg now stands, about 1772 or 1773. A patent for a tract of land containing three hundred and twenty acres, was granted to Richard Peters, August 11th, 1772; and on the 17th of November, 1773, it was deeded to Ludwig Derr.

Colonel John Kelly, a distinguished hero of the Revolutionary period, settled in Buffalo Valley, as early as 1768, immediately after the purchase from the Indians.

He was one of the *first* pioneers in this region, and endured many hardships.

Captain John Brady, with a large family, also immigrated to the West Branch, about 1772, and located opposite where Lewisburg now stands. This family was one of the most remarkable that ever resided in the romantic vale of the Otzinachson, and their history, replete with some of the most daring and thrilling events, will occupy a large space.

The following persons were also among the early settlers:—Samuel and Joseph Wallis, William Hutchinson, Cornelius Atkinson, Moses Kirk, John and Robert Eson, Captain Gray, Robert Frait, Walter and William Clark, William Wilson, Robert Clark, James Steedman, Scotts, &c.

Captain Simpson was among the first settlers in Sunbury. He participated in the disastrous battle of Wyoming. His descendants still live there.

Paul Baldy also located here at a very early period. He erected a log-house, and it is related by some of the citizens of the present day, that he traded with the Indians through the cracks of the building, not daring to permit them to enter at the door.

Of the troubles and privations endured by those settlers, we can scarcely form a just conception. It is related that during the time of the Indian wars, when hideously painted savages skulked like demons through the forest, many of the first settlers about Sunbury, were often obliged to take their families in canoes, and moor them in the middle of the river during the night, to escape the scalping knife of the ever-vigilant foe. Contrast those times with the peace and comfort now enjoyed, gentle reader, and rejoice that you did not live at that day.

Amongst the early settlers at Sunbury, it must not be forgotten to mention the name of Dr. William Plunkett, sometimes called Colonel Plunkett, for having commanded an expedition against Wyoming, and also one against the Connecticut settlers on the West Branch. The Doctor, as he was familiarly called, was quite a character at that time, and was extensively known. He is said by some to have been an Englishman, and, by others, an Irishman.

Many anecdotes are related concerning him, one of which is, that once upon a time in England, in a public house, he was in an adjoining room, where a number of gentlemen were assembled, with several friends, talking in a loud tone of voice. One of the gentlemen in the adjoining room, observed to his companions, that he did not believe the loud-talking man could tell the time of day by the watch, and taking a valuable one from his pocket, sent it in with his servant to see. The servant informed the Doctor of his errand. Being somewhat irritated, he took the watch, and assuming a very defiant attitude, held it out and exclaimed: "Here is a watch, sent to see if *I* can tell the time of day by it; will the owner please step forward, and *I will* soon inform him?" The gentry became alarmed at his bold appearance, and the owner was *afraid* to make himself known, fearing a flogging for thus trying to insult him. "As nobody will own the watch," said the Doctor, "*I will keep it*," and quietly putting it in his pocket, went about his business!

The Doctor was compelled to leave Europe rather abruptly,* for being concerned with one James Maclean, in committing a robbery on Lord Eglintoun. He was arrested and thrown into prison, but escaped, and was

* Miner's History Wyoming, page 179–80.

smuggled on shipboard in a barrel, and brought to America.

His loyalty to the king was so great, that "neither the blandishments of ambition, the persuasions of interest, nor the terrors of proscription could shake him for a moment." Up to the day of his death he never took the oath of allegiance, which would concede the death of royalty in America. Being free-spoken and fearless, he was frequently assailed. He went armed with the loaded butt of a riding whip, prepared to defend or chastise. Previous to the Revolution, he acted for a time as a Justice of the Peace. His manner of inflicting punishment was odd, if not arbitrary and severe. As the old English whipping-post and stocks were never erected in Sunbury, the Doctor had a stout worm fence, and he sometimes placed the neck of the culprit between the rails, making them both pillory and stocks at the same time! He was for many years one of the Associate Judges of Northumberland county.

Plunkett was afterwards recognized in America by a person who had known him in England, and who kept his secret. He regretted this action, as one of his youthful crimes, and afterwards became a very useful member of society. His services as a physician were invaluable on many occasions, in the dressing of wounds.

The Doctor is said to have been acquainted with several Indian languages, and when travelling up the river one day on a lonely path, met an Indian. He addressed him in all the languages he was master of, without making him understand; when, as a last alternative, he spoke to him in English, and strange enough the Indian understood him. He inquired what tribe he belonged to, and on being informed, exclaimed, "*Very bad; very bad tribe.*" The Indian in turn asked him what nation *he* belonged to, and on being informed that it was the English, looked him in the face and said, "*Ah, berry bad tribe, berry bad indeed, more badder dan poor Indian!*"

The Doctor was an old bachelor, and lived to a great age. Some say that he became blind. He died at Sunbury in 1801 or 2.

Residence of L A. Mackey, Lock Haven, Pa.

CHAPTER XVII.

DERR'S OLD MILL STILL STANDING AT LEWISBURG—SETTLEMENT ON WARRIOR RUN—NAMES OF THE SETTLERS—MRS. DERRICKSON—FIRST COURT IN NORTHUMBERLAND COUNTY—NAMES OF THE OFFICERS—ORIGINAL TOWNSHIPS—NAMES OF THE CONSTABLES—FIRST GRAND JURY—MACLAY'S SPICY LETTER.

LUDWIG DERR, who located where Lewisburg now stands, had a trading house and did an extensive business with the Indians. He also erected a small mill on what is now known as Wilson's Run, which, it is worthy of remark, is standing at the present day in a good state of preservation. It is the only continental mill standing in the valley, the others having been burned during the "Big Runaway," or since destroyed. It is a small square building, constructed of roughly hewn logs. A large building has been erected alongside of it, which is used as a mill now, the old building being used for the reception of grain. The mill is owned by John Brown. Derr also had a sawmill here, but all trace of it is gone. Derr's mill was an important place for many years among the settlers. They often came forty miles from above to get a small grist of flour. Two or three settlers would unite, take a canoe, push down to Derr's mill, get their flour and return in three or four days to their families. They were obliged to go armed, and exercise great caution in order not to be surprised by the savages.

Meanwhile their families awaited their arrival with great suspense, and when the canoe hove in sight with its scanty supply of flour, joy and gladness rang through the humble dwelling. Then again how often were they disappointed, on receiving the sad intelligence that the husbands and fathers were killed and scalped, and the little children were obliged to go supperless and fatherless to bed.

I now come to an important point in the history of the West Branch Valley, viz: to give an account of the first white settlement on Warrior Run, where Fort Freeland was erected, and where some bloody scenes were enacted. I am pleased to be able to give a correct account, having obtained the particulars from Mrs. Mary Derrickson,* a daughter of Mr. Cornelius Vincent, one of the original settlers.

In 1772, they immigrated from Essex county, New

* On visiting this venerable old lady in July, 1856, I found her with a mind bright and unimpaired, and able to relate the thrilling scenes enacted at Fort Freeland, with remarkable accuracy. She could give the dates of the occurrences, and remembered the incidents of the battle, the names of the principal actors, and everything else of importance, in a manner that was truly astonishing. She was the sister of Bethuel Vincent, a name well remembered throughout this region of country. She was very small at the time of the taking of the fort in 1778, but being a sprightly child, everything was so strongly impressed upon her mind, that death alone can obliterate it. Her father had five sons and four daughters. The sons were named, Isaac, Daniel, Bethuel, Benjamin, and John; the daughters, Sarah, Elizabeth, Rebecca, and Mary. Of this number, but two or three survive. Mary, of whom I obtained this information, is in her 78th year, and enjoying the comforts of a hale old age, surrounded by her children and grandchildren. She is a woman of extensive and varied information, free to converse upon the topics of the day. The only disadvantage under which she labors is a slight deafness. The name of the Vincents is inseparably associated with the history of this Valley. Their descendants are very numerous. Mrs. Derrickson resides in the family of her son-in-law, Jacob Sensenbach, of Williamsport.

Jersey. Their names were: Jacob Freeland, John Vincent, Cornelius Vincent and Peter Vincent, with their families. The next year they were reinforced by Timothy Williams with a very large family, together with Samuel Gould and family. Freeland settled on Warrior Run, a few miles above its mouth. The Vincents settled one mile below the mouth, on the river. This was the first nucleus of a settlement formed in this part of the country, around which other settlers clustered, till they had quite a little community.

These hardy pioneers pitched their tents in the wilderness, and commenced to make improvements. They were men of nerve, resolution and daring, and soon became inured to the hardships and privations incident to the settlement of a new country.

In 1773, Jacob Freeland commenced to build a small mill on Warrior Run, having brought the necessary irons with him the previous year from New Jersey. The mill was completed, and proved a valuable acquisition to the settlement. The fort was built in 1775, about half a mile north-east of where the Warrior Run Church now stands. It was a Stockade fortification, not very strong, and destitute of cannon.

About this time, 1772, the Connecticut people from Wyoming, commenced to settle on the West Branch, about the Muncy flats and vicinity. As the difficulties that took place between them and the Pennsylvanians were long and serious, it is thought best to devote a chapter or two exclusively to them.

The first Court in Northumberland County was held at Fort Augusta. Thinking that the record, together with the names of those concerned as officers, jurymen, &c., would be interesting at the present day, and also show who were the first settlers, I have transcribed it from the old books of the County, in the office of the Prothonotary at Sunbury. It is as follows:

RECORD OF THE FIRST COURT.

"At a Court of private sessions of the peace held at fort Augusta for the County of Northumberland on the ninth day of April in the twelfth year of the reign of our Sovereign Lord George the Third by the Grace of God, of Great Britain, France and Ireland, King, defender of the Faith, and in the year of our Lord God one thousand seven hundred and seventy-two, before William Plunkett, Esq., and his Associate Justices assigned, &c., within the said County of Northumberland, viz:

"A Commission from his Honor the Governor, bearing date the 24th day of March anno domini one thousand seven hundred and seventy-two, appointing William Plunkett, Turbutt Francis, Samuel Hunter, James Potter, William Maclay, Caleb Graydon, Benjamin Allison, Robert Moodie, John Lowdon, Thos. Lemon, Ellis Hughes and Benjamin Weiser, Esqrs., Justices of the Court of General Quarter Sessions of the Peace and jail delivery for the said County of Northumberland was published in Court.

"On motion made, the said County of Northd., or as much of the Extent of the same as is now purchased from the Indians, is divided into the following townships, to be hereafter called and known by the names of Penn's twp.*—Augusta twp.—Turbutt twp.—Buffalo twp.—Bald Eagle twp.—Muncy twp.—and Wyoming twp., each described and bounded as follows:

"DESCRIPTION OF BUFFALO TOWNSHIP.

"Beginning at the mouth of Penn's creek at the head of the isle of Que, thence up the same to the forks, thence by a north line to the West Branch of Susquehanna, thence down the West Branch of Susquehanna to the forks, thence down Susquehanna to place of beginning.

"DESCRIPTION OF BALD EAGLE TOWNSHIP.

"Beginning at the forks of Penn's creek, thence by a north line

* The descriptions of Penn's, Augusta, and Wyoming townships, are omitted, as not being pertinent to the Valley of the West Branch.

to the West Branch of Susquehanna, thence up the same to where the County line crosses it, thence by the County line south to the head of little Juniata, thence down the same to the end of Tussey's mountain, thence along the top of the same easterly to the place of beginning.

"DESCRIPTION OF TURBUTT TOWNSHIP.

"Beginning on the east side of Susquehanna at Fort Augusta, thence up the easterly side of the N. E. Branch to the old line formerly run for a division between Berks and Northampton counties, thence by the same line North West to the top of Muncy hill, thence along the top of the same westerly to the West Branch of Susquehanna, and crossing the same to the west side and down the same to the junction of the branches, and crossing Susquehanna to the place of beginning—so as to include the forks and island.

"DESCRIPTION OF MUNCY TOWNSHIP.

"Beginning on the west side of the West Branch of Susquehanna, opposite the end of Muncy hill, thence up the West Branch to opposite the mouth of Lycoming,* thence crossing the branch, up Lycoming to the heads thereof, thence by a south-east line to the Muncy hill, thence along the top of the same to the West Branch, and crossing to beginning."

The names of the Constables appointed for these respective townships, on the same occasion, were as follows:

"Turbutt	twp.	William McMein.
Buffalo	"	Robert King.
Bald Eagle	"	Samuel Long.
Muncy	"	James Robb."

This appears to have been all the business transacted at this Court—which was of a preliminary character—at least nothing else appears upon the record.

The second Court was held at the same place in Au-

* The reader will observe that Lycoming was the line of the County on the north side of the river, and was *supposed* to be the *Tiadaghton* of the Indians.

gust following, of the same year. The record runs as follows:

"At a Court of General Sessions of the Peace, held at fort Augusta for the County of Northd., the fourth Tuesday in August, in the twelfth year of the reign of our Sovereign Lord, Geo. the Third, by the Grace of God of Great Britain, France and Ireland, King, defender of the faith, &c., Before William Plunkett, Esq., and his Associates, Justices assigned, &c., within the said County of Northd., viz:

"Upon petition to the Court, Adam Haveling, Marcus Hulings, Jr., Martin Kost, Samuel Weiser; and John Alexander, are recommended to his Honor the Governor for his license to keep public houses where they respectively dwell in this County, they giving bond, &c., agreeable to the laws of this Province in such cases made, &c."

The *first* Grand Jury in the County was empanneled at this Court. Their names are given below. I copy from the record:

"George Nagel, Esq.,* High Sheriff for the County aforesaid, returned his writ of *venire* to him directed, with the panel annexed, which being called over after proclamation, made the following persons appear, who were accordingly sworn on the grand inquest for our Sovereign Lord the King, for the body of the County.

John Brady, Foreman,	Geo. Ran,
Geo. Overmyer,	And. Heffer,
John Rhowick,	Hawkins Boon,
Leonard Peter,	George Wolf,
Gerhard Freeland,	William Cook,
John Jost,	John Kelly,
William Grey,	James Poke,
Ludwig Derr,	John Walker."

At the November Sessions of 1775, the report for the *first* road, up the river, was received as follows:

* George Nagel was Sheriff of Berks county when Northumberland was organized. He, however, served in Northumberland, till William Cook was elected in October, 1772.

"The report of Henry Antes, Cookson Long, Samuel Horn, Alexander Hamilton, Jonathan Albridge, and Samuel Harris, the six men appointed at August Sessions to view and, if they saw cause, to lay out a *Bridle Road* from the mouth of Bald Eagle creek to the town of Sunbury, was read in Court, by which it appears that they have thought *it necessary*, and have according laid out a *Bridle Road* as follows: 'Beginning at a post at the mouth of Bald Eagle Creek, thence north 81 deg.,' &c., on to a Black oak on the *West Branch* of Susquehanna opposite the town of Sunbury."

These names also go to show who were among the first settlers of the County at that early period, some eighty-four years ago. Of these men, not one is now living—they are all numbered with the dead, and the wild flower blooms on their graves.

It may be interesting to belligerent gentlemen of the present day, to state that the early Courts of Northumberland county, only fined a man *five shillings for assault and battery*. The *luxury* of fighting being so cheap then, it was very much indulged in, and sparring matches were common. Such a law would suit the *chivalry* of this period. They could *cane* one another to their hearts' content at a *very* trifling expense!

They appear to have had some trouble at Fort Augusta, in reference to their public buildings, and the want of a jail, as may be inferred from the following spicy letter, written by William Maclay, to J. Tilghman, April 2d, 1773:—

"Sir: I inclose to you a Letter from three of the Trustees for the publick Buildings of this County, respecting some measures which we have lately fallen on to rescue us from the scandal of living intirely without any Place of confinement or punishment for Villains; Captain Hunter had address enough to render abortive every attempt that was made last summer, for keeping a regular Jail, even after I had been at considerable expense in fitting up this Magazine, under which there is a small But compleat Dungeon, I am sorry to inform you That he has given our present Measures the most Obstinate Resistance in his power and impeded Us with every embarrassment in the Compass of his Invention, we know nothing of the Footing on which Captain Hunter has possession of these Buildings, and only beg that the County may be accommodated with this old Magazine, with the addition proposed to be made to it, and with the House in which I now live, to hold our courts in; I have repaired the House in which I now live, But expect to have an House ready to remove to in Sunbury, before our November Court. As the present repairs are done intirely by subscription, you will readily guess that Captain Hunter is not among the number of subscribers. As there are many pieces of old Iron, &c., which formerly belonged to the fort, not of any use at present, the Trustees propose using any of them which can be converted to any advantage, for Grates, &c., for our temporary Gaol, unless they receive contrary Directions from Philada. If Hell is justly considered as the rendivous of Rascals, we cannot entertain a doubt of Wioming being the Place. Burn'd Hands, cut Ears, &c., are considered as the certain certificates of superior merit; we have certain Accounts of their having had several meetings lately to chuse a Sovereign and settle the State, &c., for it seems they have not now any Dependance on the Government of Connecticut. The Time of the Descent on the West Branch, Fort Augusta, &c., is now fixed for May next; I have no Doubt but the Desperate Tempers of these People will hurry them into some tragical affair, which will at last rouse our Government, when it may be too late to repair the mischief done by them. At the same time I am told there are some among them, who would willingly become quiet subjects, and are afraid to own their sentiments. Patterson has the other day been offered 1200 0 0, for the same number of acres, not far from your Land. I would not have you sell. Doctor Plunkett goes down in a few days; 'tis likely I may send another long letter by him.

"And am with the greatest Esteem,

Sir.

Your most Obedient humble Servant,

WM. MACLAY."

It appears that Mr. Maclay had a particular aversion to the settlers at Wyoming, and regarded them as the most arrant knaves. This is illustrative of the feeling that existed between the two parties.

As to the particulars in reference to the difficulty with Colonel Hunter, they are nowhere preserved, or, at least, I have been unable to find them.

CHAPTER XVIII.

CONNECTICUT SETTLEMENT AT MUNCY—THE TOWNSHIPS OF JUDEA AND CHARLESTON—DIFFICULTIES—JOHN VINCENT A JUSTICE—PROCLAMATION OF GOVERNOR PENN—THE TROUBLES INCREASE—ZEBULON BUTLER APPOINTED A JUSTICE—GOVERNOR PENN INFORMS THE PEOPLE NOT TO MIND HIM.

THE Connecticut settlement at Wyoming was extended to the West Branch at a very early period. As early as 1769, says Colonel Franklin in his journal, the Susquehanna Company passed a vote to send on 540 settlers, 300 of whom were to have lands as a gratuity on the West Branch. The settlement was made on the beautiful rolling plain around where Muncy now stands, and was called the "Muncy Settlement." Two townships were surveyed here as early as 1771. One was named Charleston,* and the other Judea. The names of the actual settlers are lost.

This settlement was not at first included in the limits of Westmoreland, by the Connecticut grant, which extended only fifteen miles beyond the North Branch—not reaching within twenty miles of Muncy. In May, 1775, an act was passed by the Connecticut Council to extend the limits of the town of Westmoreland, as far westward as the line fixed upon with the Indians at the treaty of Fort Stanwix, in 1768. This, then, included the set-

* Miner's Hist. Wyoming, p. 166, 7, 8.

tlements on the West Branch, as far up as Lycoming creek.

The name of John Vincent appears as one of the actors in the Connecticut, or Wyoming, troubles on the West Branch. In 1775, he was appointed a Justice of the Peace for Litchfield county. In August of the same year, it is alleged that said Vincent, with several others, went to Wyoming, and requested a number of people to go on to the West Branch and settle, in order to extend the jurisdiction and authority of Connecticut to that place as soon as possible. In answer to his appeal, William Judd and Joseph Sluman, Esqrs., with a company of about eighty others, proceeded to the West Branch in September, and commenced to make a settlement.

A bad feeling existed between the Connecticut settlers at Wyoming, and those of Pennsylvania. The latter looked upon the former as invaders of a territory that in no wise belonged to them, and their settlements were viewed with a jealous eye. Serious difficulties ensued between the two parties, which assumed quite a belligerent attitude, and in one or two instances resulted in loss of life. It is very difficult, at this late day, to get a correct version of the troubles that ensued, as but little was written and preserved concerning them. Some account is found in the Colonial Records, and in Miner's History of Wyoming, but neither of them give the details in full. I shall endeavor to give an account of these difficulties, in accordance with what data I have been able to collect.

The feeling of jealousy assumed such a pitch, that the inhabitants of Northumberland remonstrated against the Connecticut claimants, and went so far as to send in a petition to Governor Penn, as follows:

"That your Petitioners being seated, in Consequence of regular Purchase from the Proprietaries of Pennsylvania, in the said County of Northumberland, within the known Limits, and under the Protection of the Laws of the Province of Pennsylvania, have nevertheless been under the necessity of Combatting and struggling with many Difficulties and Embarrassments of so alarming a nature as scarce to be paralleled in the History of any Civilized Country; that the Colony of Connecticut sets up a Claim to the lands seated, improved, and rendered Valuable by your Petitioners' Labour; happy might your Petitioners be, would those Claimants bring their Pretensions to some Tribunal whose decision would equally bind both Parties, but with them Violence usurps the Place of Argument, and force, of Legal Decision; that about two years ago a number of your Petitioners were in a Hostile manner ousted of their Possessions at Wyoming, and Cruelly Stripped and Plundered of their Effects; that, not content with the acquisition of Wyoming and the Parts adjacent, sundry attempts have been made to extend their Conquests. A large Body of Armed Men from Connecticut in June last attempted to disposess the Inhabitants of the West Branch of Susquehanna, and, though prevented, it was not without much Fatigue, Expence, and Great Danger of Bloodshed; these People, lawless among themselves, afford an Assylum and secure Retreat to disorderly Persons, not only of this Government, but of all the neighboring Provinces, by which accessions, and the Constant Countenance of the Colony of Connecticut, their numbers have of late greatly increased; that the avowal of their Intentions is uniformly the same, especially since the account from Connecticut that 'the Government has openly espoused their Cause, and taken them under their Protection.' Deplorable indeed must be the situation of your Petitioners, if called on to defend by Force of Arms their Infant Settlements against the Power of a whole Colony; that the Consequence must be ruin to their fortunes and families in their Present distracted Situation; as common subjects of the Province, and entitled to the protection of the Laws, your Petitioners cannot help looking up to your Honor for the aid of Government; they have hitherto maintained an unequal Contest, possessed of property themselves, they have been obliged with arms in their hands to defend it against those who had no property, subject themselves to Law, they have had to Contend with those who refused Subjection to any Law, and have not been able to reduce them to order, which is confessing a Weakness they can no longer conceal; that the whole

Posse of the County is not sufficient to enforce the Laws at Wyoming, as the Inhabitants have not hitherto been able to prevent the Continuance of the Connecticut Intruders in that Part of the Province contrary to Law, and the Repeated Proclamations of Government, they fear their utmost Efforts will not be sufficient to keep their Possessions without the Interposition and Protection of the Legislature, which, therefore, they Implore, and from the Known Clemency and Justice of the administration, consider themselves as having reason to expect."

This petition was signed by the magistrates, grand jury, and other principal inhabitants of Northumberland, and laid before the Board of Council, by the Governor, in session at Philadelphia, December 9th, 1773. After receiving due consideration, it was the opinion of the Council that it should be laid before the Assembly, accompanied by a message from the Governor, to enforce it.

On the 14th of December, the message from the Governor was laid before the Assembly, and reads as follows:

"Gentlemen:—The distresses of the Inhabitants of the County of Northumberland, expressed in their Petition, which will be delivered to you by the Secretary, appear to be of a very alarming Nature, and justly to call for the particular attention of this Government.

"The Insolent Outrages of a set of Men who have long bid defiance to the Laws of the Country, and have afforded Protection to Offenders of the most Heinous Kind, ought not, Certainly, in a Well regulated Society, to be suffered to pass with Impunity; but when these men embody themselves, sally forth with arms in their Hands, and in a Warlike Manner attempt to dispossess the peaceable Inhabitants of the County lately laid out and Established by Act of Assembly, within the known bounds of the Province, it is a procedure of so dangerous a Tendency as not only to threaten the Destruction of that Infant County, but strikes at the Peace of the whole Province.

"I think it therefore Incumbent on me, Gentlemen, to recommend this Matter to your most serious Consideration, and to request you will Fall upon such Measures as will Strengthen the Hands of Government on this Extraordinary and Alarming Occasion, repel the Violence of these lawless Intruders, and afford the Petitioners that Immediate Protection and Relief which Necessities and Situation Require.

"JOHN PENN."

A long and spirited correspondence took place between the Governor of the Colony of Connecticut, and John Penn, in reference to the pending difficulty, which may be found at length, commencing on page 118 of Volume X., of the Colonial Records. All propositions to settle the difficulty proved unavailing, and the Assembly finally instructed the Governor to issue a proclamation to the magistrates and officers of Northumberland county, to be vigilant in the discharge of their duty, and see that the intruders from Wyoming no longer impose upon the Pennsylvania settlers. The proclamation is long and quite spicy. It may be found on the 153d page of the same volume.

It appears that Zebulon Butler, of Wyoming, had issued a notice and distributed it through Northumberland county, that he was appointed a justice by the authorities of Connecticut, whereupon Governor Penn, in his proclamation, most strictly forbids the people to pay any attention whatever to him, as he has no right to act in this Province.

CHAPTER XIX.

TROUBLES CONTINUE—ARRIVAL OF AN ARMED FORCE AT WARRIOR RUN FROM WYOMING—DEPOSITION OF PETER SMITH—SETTLERS DRIVEN OFF BY COLONEL PLUNKETT—GREAT EXCITEMENT—PLUNKETT'S INVASION OF WYOMING—HIS DEFEAT AND SUDDEN RETREAT.

THE spirit of the respective parties ran high. The Connecticut people were determined to occupy the valuable lands of the West Branch, and the Pennsylvania settlers were determined that they *should not.* The former claimed the land as belonging to them, and the latter insisted that they had no right to it, and determined to resort to force for their expulsion, if they did not peaceably leave. A crisis was inevitably approaching which could not be averted. The authorities of Pennsylvania had issued instructions to the officers of Northumberland county, which could not be mistaken.

On the 22d of September, 1775, William Maclay writes from Sunbury to J. Shippen, Jr. The following extract from his letter is in reference to the Connecticut troubles:

"The Congress at the last meeting ordered the Memorials respecting the Connecticut Intrusion, to lye on their Table to the next Meeting, on the 5th of Sepr, in the mean Time their Delegates were directed to enjoin a Peaceable Behaviour on their People; the 5th of Sepr is come and past, the Injunction therefore is no longer binding, according to their mode of reasoning—we never had more rumor about them, and their Designs; Sam Wallis has just now been with me respecting the Conduct of one Vincent, who lives near Mr. Modie—this man was some time ago appointed a Connecticut Magistrate, and is now at Wioming, in order to pilot down 300 of them to the West Branch, his son was with him, and is returned, and gives out, that his Father only waited untill the Armament would be ready. Wallis says he has taken some Pains to examine into the story, and for his part veryly believes it to be true; if so, we shall soon hear of them, they have lately been at great pains to enlist their Adherents among Us into the 24th or Butler's Regiment. It is highly probable that every motion of the People at Wioming, is in Consequence of Orders from the Colony of Connecticut, if so, it is incontrovertible That they intend, perfas nefasque, to possess themselves of the Country. It seems mysterious They should be so intent upon pushing their Incroachments so far Southward into the Pennsylvania Settlement, while the Lands west of Wioming, large and quite unoccupied, are quite disregarded; perhaps a west Line from the most Southern Settlement they can effect, by Art or Force may be contemplated by them, as the Boundary of their future Empire, That is, in case they intend to leave Pennsylvania a name or Place at all among the Colonys."

It appears that his fears were justly founded that an armed body of men, from Wyoming, were about to make a descent upon the West Branch. The following letter, however, from J. Sluman and William Judd, two of the Connecticut leaders, addressed to William Plunkett, at Sunbury, on the 25th of September, from Warrior Run, would not tend to create that impression. But it was doubtless intended to deceive them:

"Sir,—This acquaints you that we arrived at this place on Saturday Evening last, with a number of other men, purposing to view the Vacant Lands in this Branch of the Susqhh River, and to make a Settlement on the Vacant Lands if we find any place or places that shall be agreeable. And as this may be a matter of much Conversation among the present Inhabitants, we are willing to acquaint you the principles on which we are come. In the first place we Intend no Hostilities, we will not Disturb, Molest or Endeavor to Dispossess any Person of his property, or any ways abuse his person by Threats or any action that shall tend Thereto. And as we are Commissioners of the peace for the Colony of Connecticut, we mean to be governed by the Laws of that Colony, and shall not Refuse the Exercise of the Law to those of the Inhabitants that are now Dwellers here on their Request, as the Colony of Connecticut Extended last May their Jurisdiction over the Land. Finally, as we are Determined to govern ourselves as abovementioned, we Expect that those who think the Tittle of this Land is not in this Colony, will give us no uneasiness or Disturbance in our proposed settlement."

Contrary to the declarations expressed in this communication, "*that we intend no hostilities*," but one or two days elapsed before intelligence reached Sunbury, that an armed force, supposed to consist of three hundred men, had, arrived at Freeland's Mill,* on Warrior Run. It was supposed to be a detachment from Colonel Butler's regiment, and made up of "Connecticut intruders," as they expressed it. They brought neither women nor children, and, immediately on their arrival, commenced intrenching themselves in a strong position.

The report of the arrival of this armed band, spread through the thinly settled county, with the rapidity of wild fire. Preparations were speedily made to resist them with force of arms, if necessary. A company of fifty men immediately left Fort Augusta, to unite with other companies, from various parts of the county, to "meet and demand the reason of this intrusion and hostile appearance."

The following deposition of Peter Smith, taken before

* Vide Pennsylvania Archives, Vol. III., page 662, 3, 4, 5.

Robert Robb, Esq., one of the Justices of the Peace for the County of Northumberland, will throw some additional light on this matter:

"Northumberland County, ss.

"Before me, one of his Majesty's Justices assigned to keep the Peace for said County, personally appeared, Peter Smith, who being sworn according to Law, Deposeth and saith, that on the evening of Monday, the twenty-fifth of September last, this Deponent went to the house of Garrot Freeland, of the Warrior's Run, and there saw a number of men from Wyoming on Guard in a School house, who pressed him much to join with them, and acquainted him that they were come to enforce the Connecticut Laws, and Settle the Vacant Land, and sundrie fair promises to him if he would join with them. This Deponent saith he was then advised to go to the house of John Vincent, on the Warrior's Run, which he did, and there saw a number of men paraded and under arms, amongst whom was one they called the Major, who informed the men that he expected they would be attacked that night or the next Morning, and exhorted them to stand together like men, that they were come to enforce the Connecticut Laws, & Settle the Vacant Lands, and that they would do it or die every man on the spot, and for the honor of their Country, that they would behave better than a party of them that had gone before some time ago, who run away or were taken prisoners, and also if this party were too small to effect their design, they would send to Connecticut, and their Government would send them Two Thousand men. He the said Major, advised the men to sleep with their arms by them, and their Pouches and Horns about their Necks, that they might be ready in a minutes notice. And further, this Deponent heard one whom he took to be a Captain, speak to Major Judd, and say that there was a fence that would be much in the way, if they were obliged to draw up their men in that place, and that he thought it would be proper to move it away, and Major Judd said he would speak to Mr. Vincent about it, so he bid the men good night, and went into the house. This Deponent followed him into the house, and desired to speak with him; Major Judd asked if he, this Deponent, and was answered he was no foe; then Major Judd read this Deponent a number of Papers, which he said was orders from Government, the contents of which this Deponent cannot recollect;

he then said if he would join with him, he would warrant him a hundred acres, as also every one that would do so and come under their Laws, which this Deponent refused, so the Major said they that are not for us, are against us, and likewise said the Major, those that will not joyn us if we get the Land, we will use them accordingly; This Deponent then said, that if he could not get Land without fighting for it he would take what he had and leav the parts entirely."

This deposition was duly signed, and sworn to, the 5th day of October, 1775.

Whatever became of this large force, or whether it was an exaggeration, is nowhere stated. It is evident that some mistake must exist, or the facts have been grossly perverted. Mr. Miner, in his history of Wyoming, when speaking about the difficulties on the West Branch, does not allude to an armed force having been despatched there.

Strange as it may seem, after having positive evidence that a large body of armed men actually came from Wyoming, Mr. Miner goes on to state, that in September the "settlement was comparatively small and unsupported, and offered an inviting prize to the cupidity of those who, at some risk, should think proper to seize it. And that in the same month, September, 1775, Colonel Plunkett, under orders from the Government, detailed a strong force from the Northumberland militia, and marched to break up the settlements at Charleston and Judea. The spirit or extent of resistance, is no where preserved, but is presumed to have been inconsiderable. One life was lost, and several persons of the Connecticut party were wounded. It has not been ascertained whether any loss was sustained by the Pennsylvania troops. After burning the buildings, and gathering together, for distribution among the victors, all the moveable property, the men taken were marched as prisoners, and confined in Sunbury jail; while the women and children were sent to Wyoming, where most of them had relations and friends.

Where was the brave Major Judd, who harangued his men so valorously a few days before at Warrior Run, and desired them to fight till they would die, before they should yield to the Northumberland militia? Where was he, with his warlike party, that the resistance offered to Colonel Plunkett should have been "inconsiderable?" He must have been there, for Colonel Franklin states in his journal that he was taken prisoner with Joseph Sluman, Esq., and sent to the Philadelphia jail!

Franklin's account of this affair was, that Plunkett had a force of about five hundred men, and that the Connecticut folks were only about eighty strong. He is evidently in error, too, for it is doubtful whether so large a force could have been raised on the West Branch at that time. I am satisfied that the accounts on both sides were very much exaggerated. But it is nevertheless true, that Plunkett did march against them and drove them off by force. Numbers were carried to Sunbury and imprisoned. Plunkett acted under the instructions of John Penn, Governor of the Province, who ordered that the laws must be obeyed, and that all expence incurred in this duty would be defrayed by the government.

Thus was the Connecticut settlement on the West Branch broken up, and never afterwards renewed, leaving the disputed territory in full possession of the Pennsylvania claimants.

On the 27th of October, 1775, the Assembly of the

Province of Pennsylvania, having had the subject of these troubles under consideration, came to the conclusion that the settlers had done their duty, and resolved,

"That the Inhabitants of the County of Northumberland, settled under the Jurisdiction of this Province, were justifiable, and did their duty in repelling the said Intruders, and preventing the further Extension of their settlements," &c.

Great excitement prevailed on both sides, and a number of boats belonging to Wyoming, and trading down the river, were seized as they passed Fort Augusta, and their cargoes confiscated. Colonel Plunkett, probably elated with his late success, commenced making preparations to march against Wyoming itself, for the purpose of driving the settlers therefrom.

On receipt of the contemplated invasion, the greatest excitement prevailed throughout the settlement at Wyoming, and an agent was sent to lay the condition of things before Congress, and solicit their friendly interposition. Preparations, however, were made to resist the expected attack, and every man capable of bearing arms, was directed to hold himself ready at a moment's notice. It was in the winter time. Between two and three hundred men enrolled themselves.

On the 20th of December, the invading army was reported to be approaching the settlement as rapidly as they could, considering the great quantities of ice in the river. The prayers of the people went up, in humble petitions, for the ice to prevent their further progress.

About this time Congress interposed, and adopted the following important resolution:

"Resolved, That it is the opinion of this Congress and it is accordingly recommended, that the contending parties immediately cease all hostilities, and avoid every appearance of force until the dispute can be legally decided. That all property taken and detained, be immediately restored to the original owners; that no interruption be given to either party, to the free passing and repassing, if behaving themselves peaceably, through the disputed territory, as well by land as by water, without molestation of either persons or property; that all persons seized and detained on account of said dispute on either side, be dismissed and permitted to go to their respective homes, and that things being put in the same situation they were before the late unhappy contest, they continue to behave themselves peaceably on their respective possessions and improvements, until a legal decision can be had on said dispute, or this Congress shall take further order thereon, and nothing herein done, shall be construed in prejudice of the claim of either party."

This important resolution did not come in time to arrest the attack of Plunkett and his army on Wyoming —he had arrived on the 23d of December, near to the settlement. The account of the battle is given as follows by Mr. Miner in his History of Wyoming:

"Col. Zebulon Butler, who commanded the Yankees, by the most strenuous exertions had mustered about three hundred men and boys, but there were not guns enough to arm the whole, and several appeared on the ground with scythes fastened upon handles projecting straight as possible; a formidable weapon in the hands of an active soldier, if they should be brought to close quarters, but otherwise useless. These weapons the men sportively called 'the end of time.' On the night of the 23d, he encamped on a flat near the union of Harvey's creek with the river. From this point he despatched Major John Garrett, his second in command, to visit Col. Plunkett with a flag, and desire to know the meaning of his extraordinary movements, and to demand his intentions in approaching Wyoming with so imposing a military array? The answer given was, that he came peaceably as an attendant on Sheriff Cook, who was authorized to arrest several persons at Wyoming, for violating the laws of Pennsylvania, and he trusted there would be no opposition to a measure so reasonable and pacific. Maj. Garrett reported that the enemy outnumbered the Yankees more than two to one. 'The conflict will be a sharp one, boys,' said he. 'I for one am ready to die, if need be, for my country.' Things wore a different aspect from what they had done formerly. Men then, were almost the only inhabitants. Now the Valley abounded with old men, women and children, brought out by the confidence inspired by three years of peace and prosperity. It was a season of gloomy apprehension.

"Col. Butler was humane as he was brave—polite as he was undaunted. Several positions existed below the Nanticoke falls where the river leaves the valley, and takes its way for four or five miles between precipitous mountains, where a stand might have been made with almost certain success. It was thought better, however justifiable as would have been such a course, to wait the attack within the valley itself. Orders were also given to this effect—not to take life unless rendered unavoidable in self-defence. Leaving Ensign Mason Fitch Alden, with eighteen men on the ground where he had bivouacked, Col. Butler retired on the morning of the 23d, and detached Capt. Stewart with twenty men across to the east side of the river, above the Nanticoke falls, with orders to lie in ambush, and prevent any boat's crew from landing on that shore.

"On the morning of the 24th, about 11 o'clock, Ensign Alden was apprised of the approach of Plunkett and his army, who came up with martial music playing. Keeping at a respectful distance, no shot was fired from either side, and Alden joining Col. Butler, reported the approach of the foe.

"Displaying his columns on the flat just abandoned by the Yankees, Col. Plunkett directed a spirited advance in pursuit of Alden, not doubting but the main forces of the Yankees were near, and the hour of battle had come. In less than thirty minutes the advancing line was arrested by the word, Halt! and Plunkett, who was in the front a little on the right, observing Col. Butler's position, was heard to exclaim, 'My God! what a breastwork!'

"Harvey's creek coming in from the north, cuts the high mountain which here approaches the river, deep to its base. A precipitous ledge of rocks, from near the summit, runs southerly to the river, presenting to the west by south a lofty natural barrier, for a mile along the ravine; and where the defence was not perfect, Col. Butler had made it so by ramparts of logs, so that it would require a powerful, as well as bold enemy, to dislodge him. Nothing could have been more perfectly military than the selection of the spot, and the whole preparations of defence. So it was regarded by his soldiers. Mr. John

Carey says in respect to the conduct of Col. Butler, in all that affair: 'I loved the man—he was an honor to the human species.' Such a declaration speaks the merits of Col. Butler in language more impressive than the most labored eulogium. To take life was not the object, but orders were given for a general discharge all along the line of the defence by platoons, so as to impress Col. Plunkett with a proper idea of the strength and spirit of its defenders. No one was hurt, but considerable confusion was seen to prevail in his ranks as Plunkett's men recoiled from the formidable breastwork. A boat was forthwith despatched by him, with a number of soldiers to the opposite shore, it being the intention of the invaders to cross over and enter the settlement by a way apparently less obstructed, for Sheriff Cook to serve his civil process. The passage of the boat and crew was watched by both parties with intense anxiety. A few minutes decided its fate. As it approached the shore, Capt. Stewart opened a fire, which wounded one man, and killed a dog that was on board, probably specially aimed at, when instantly pulling their oars with a will, the men gained the suction of the falls, through which they sped among the breakers with the rapid flight of an arrow, fortunately without further injury.

"Thus closed the battle for the day. Col. Plunkett retired and encamped on the ground occupied by Col. Butler two nights previously. Early on the ensuing morning the contest was renewed, Col. Plunkett returning to the attack, and determining to outflank the Yankees, while at the same moment he would storm the breastwork. His troops displayed; they approached the line of Yankee defence, covering themselves by trees and loose rocks which lay below, and opened a spirited fire all along the line. While he thus assailed Col. Butler in front, a detachment of his most determined and alert men was sent up the mountain on the left, by a rapid march, concealed as much as possible, to turn the right flank of the Connecticut people. But this danger having been foreseen, and guarded against, the flanking party was repelled. During this contest several lives were lost, and a number on both sides wounded, how many, no record has been kept. A son of Surveyor General Lukens fell in the engagement; a fine young man deeply lamented on all sides; but it was the fortune of war.

"A circumstance truly affecting grew out of this battle. A great portion of the male population on the upper waters of the Susquehanna, it is known, in after times sawed lumber during the winter, and descended with it in rafts to market in the spring. The most cordial good understanding had for many years subsisted between the Yankee raftsmen and the inhabitants below; the latter being remarkable for their hospitality and kindness. A person who was in the battle saw one of Plunkett's men approach with great intrepidity very near the Yankee line, who, taking shelter behind a rock to load, would step out and fire wherever he could bring his rifle to bear. Already several men had fallen—the blood was up; it had become a matter of life or death, and the aims became more close and deadly. The relator watched the opportunity, and as the head of Plunkett's brave soldier rose above the rocks, he fired, and the man fell. After the battle was decided, going to the place, the relator found a hat-band cut by a bullet; the man and the hat were gone.

"Being down the river on a raft, many years afterwards, and staying all night with a fine hospitable old gentleman, they talked of Wyoming, and the ancient troubles there. 'I lost a beloved son in the Plunkett invasion,' said the aged father, as a tear fell. 'See here,' producing a hat perforated by a ball, 'the bullet must have cut the band.' The narrator said he never before experienced the depth of the calamities of war—the scene was most painful. Of course he did not avow the deed, but most deeply deplored it, although never doubting he was doing right at the time, and under the circumstances, in defending his home from the invaders.

"Finding Col. Butler's position too strong to be carried by storm, Col. Plunkett concluded his rash enterprise by a retreat. On Christmas day he withdrew his troops, they marching as they had come up, on the west side of the river. In the mean time, a party of the Yankees followed on the east side, with a view to capture one of the boats, but Mr. Harvey, who was a prisoner on board, calling to them not to fire, for they might injure their friends, they returned and left the retreating army to pass down without further pursuit."

Thus ended the memorable Plunkett invasion of Wyoming, in December, 1775. It was certainly ill-timed, rash, and injudicious, but such was the character of the man, "when invested with a little brief authority." He returned to Fort Augusta with his army, considerably chop fallen in spirits, and a worse opinion of the "Yankee intruders" than ever.

The difficulties between the two States, Connecticut and Pennsylvania, after long, intricate, and tedious litigation, were ultimately decided in favor of the latter, in 1801; and so the trouble ended.

Residence of John A. Gamble, Jersey Shore, Pa.

CHAPTER XX.

INDIAN NAME OF MUNCY CREEK—MUNCY MANOR—NAMES OF THE SETTLERS UPON IT—MUNCY FARM—NUMBER OF ACRES IN IT—MONTOUR'S RESERVE—INDIAN NAME OF LOYAL SOCK AND LYCOMING—EEL TOWN, NEWALEGAN'S CABINS, &C.

A PIECE of land was surveyed on the flats south of Muncy Creek as early as 1768, and called the "Muncy Manor." It contained sixteen hundred and fifteen acres and allowances, and belonged to the Proprietaries of Pennsylvania. It was probably first occupied by the Connecticut settlers from Wyoming.

It is worthy of mention that on the arrival of the first white men at this point, they found a fine meadow near the mouth of Glade Run, on the south side.

The Indian name of Muncy Creek—at least the one given the oftenest in the old papers—is what may be denominated a "hard one." It was called *Occohpocheny*, and by some tribes *Loneserango*. The level land around the south side of the creek was called *Occohpocheny flats*. Pronounced, Oko-po-cheny.

Orders were given by the Proprietaries of the Muncy Manor, on the 15th day of May, 1776, to have it divided into farms or lots. The survey was made, and an excellent draft executed, which is yet in a good state of preservation. The following is the report of the surveyors, giving the size of the lots, and the settlers thereon, which accompanies the draft. It may be relied upon for correctness. It is a valuable, as well as interesting, document:

"No. 1.—Containing Three hundred acres and 139 perches and an allowance of six per cent. &c. Settled on and improved by Mordecai McKinney.

"No. 2.—Containing Two hundred and ninety-nine acres & an half and allowance, &c. Settled on & improved by Peter Smith & Paulus Sheep.

"No. 3.—Containing Three hundred acres and seventy-six perches, and allowance as afd. Settled on and improved by John Brady.

No. 4.—Containing Three hundred acres & 61 perches & allowance, &c. Settled on and improved by Caleb Knapp.

"No. 5.—Containing Three hundred & one acres & 105 perches & allowance, &c. Settled on and improved by John Scudder who is displeased with the manner in which it is laid out alledging there is not Timber sufficient on it for Fencing &c. and desires his Lott may be laid out agreeably to the red lines (which contains Two hundred & fifty-four acres & 74 perches & allowce &c.) which would greatly lesson the value of the Lott Brady possesses—The S 30 E Line runs thro' of Brady's Improvement & takes near all the Rail Timber from Brady's Lott, that is on the south side of the Glade Run, so that upon the whole we judge it most convenient, and to the general advantage of the Plantations that the black line show'd remain as the Boundary between Brady & Scudder, we have therefore laid down Scudder's complaint that it may be judged of by His Honour the Governor.

"It is by no means convenient that any of the Plantations show'd cross the Creek as the banks on the north side are high, and the Creek in time of Freshets flows so very Considerable that it is thereby render'd impassable for several days—It is settled on & improved by Jerome Vanest & John Young as described in the Draft &c.—in Young's Improvt, thirty acres & in Vanest's sixty-seven acres."

Signed,

Jo. J. Wallis,
Jno. Henderson.

To Jno. Lukens, Esqr., Surv'r General.

The large tract of land called the Muncy Farm, but now better known as "Hall's Farms," contained thirty-nine hundred acres, and originally belonged to Samuel Wallis. Fort Muncy was built on it, near where the old mansion-house stands, on Carpenter's Run. In 1802, it was sold at sheriff's sale, as the property of Samuel Wallis, by Sheriff Vanderslice. It is now divided and subdivided into numerous farms, all owned by Mrs. Hall.

Andrew Montour, the Indian interpreter and agent, who always proved friendly to the whites, and was much esteemed by them, had a grant of land, from the government, at the mouth of Loyal Sock Creek. It contained eight hundred and eighty acres, including both sides of the creek, and was given to him in consideration of his valuable services. It was surveyed the 3d of November, 1769, and called "Montour's Reserve." The name of Andrew Montour is perpetuated in the beautiful and flourishing village of Montoursville, which is located upon his "Reserve."

As early as 1769, Thomas Brown settled and made an improvement two miles up Loyal Sock. He was one of the *first* settlers in that region. The Indian name for the creek was *Stonehauge.*

A large and populous Indian town was located at the mouth of Loyal Sock Creek, on the north side. It is supposed to have been the Otstuagy, mentioned by Conrad Weiser. The land here was applied for by John Campbell.

Joseph Bonser was an early settler above Loyal Sock, on the small stream that still bears his name. At the point where the great Sheshequin path intersected the run, Rev. David Brainerd first met, and preached the Gospel, to the Indians west of Muncy hills. This was in 1746—more than one hundred years ago.

A manor, containing five hundred and seventy-nine acres, was surveyed on the east side of Lycoming Creek, the 20th of March, 1769, by William Scull, for the Proprietary, John Penn.

A man named Thompson, settled at an early day on Lycoming Creek, about five miles from the mouth, where an Indian village called Eel town stood. It was in a sharp bend of the stream. A settlement was also made at a place called Newalegan's cabins, one mile above Eel town, at an early period.

The Indian name for Lycoming Creek appears to have been *Lacomick*. It is spelled various ways in the old papers, however, but this appears to have been the most generally used. Hence it will readily be perceived how easy it was for the whites to corrupt the name into *Lycoming*.

It would have been much better to have preserved the original names of the streams, as there is always a peculiar beauty about them that is to be admired. These names, although they may appear outlandish to some, and hard of pronunciation, always had a meaning which was significant. I regret exceedingly that I am unable to give the translation of any of them. I will give a few of the names of those persons who made early improvements on the south side of the river.

In 1768, Edward Burd, settled and made a small improvement on the river, five miles above the mouth of Buffalo Creek. His claim included an Indian town, probably where New Columbia now stands.

Richard Steel made an improvement in White Deer Hole Valley, before 1769. An Indian named *Cochnehaw*, had a wigwam, for a long time, near the mouth of White Deer Hole Creek, for hunting purposes. An Indian town, and the remains of a fortification, also stood on Black Hole Bottom. At this time White Deer Creek was called White Flint Creek.

Edmund Huff, as early as 1768, settled and made an improvement on the land now embraced in the farm of General McMicken, in Nippenose Bottom.

As Lycoming Creek was the boundary of the Province on the north side of the river, and occupied by the Indians, it is thought best to devote a chapter or two to that portion, and enumerate the names of the principal original settlers who took possession of the land in violation of the laws of the State, as forming a very interesting part of the work.

CHAPTER XXI.

SETTLEMENTS WEST OF LYCOMING CREEK—NAMES OF THE SETTLERS—PROCLAMATION OF GOVERNOR PENN—NO ATTENTION PAID TO IT—THE DISPUTED TERRITORY TAKEN UP—THE HUGHES AND TONER SETTLE NEAR PINE RUN.

THAT portion of the West Branch Valley above Lycoming Creek, had frequently been visited by the Scotch-Irish rangers from Kittatinny Valley, long before any permanent settlements were made, in their excursions after the Indians; and they did not fail to notice its romantic beauty and extreme fertility. No sooner was the purchase of 1768 known, than a crowd of hardy adventurers pushed westward, to occupy the land. So great was the pressure when the land office was opened in April, it was found necessary to decide the priority of location by lottery. The purchases were also limited to three hundred acres for each individual, at £5 per 100 acres, and one penny per acre quit-rent. An allotment was also made of 104,000 acres of land to the officers of the Provincial regiments who had served during the Indian campaigns, and were desirous of settling together. About this time the dispute arose whether Lycoming was the Tiadaghton of the Indians, or Pine Creek, which was the boundary of the purchase, mentioned in the treaty. The question remained unsettled for sixteen years. During this time it was not the desire of the government that the land should be occupied for fear of insulting the Indians, and inciting them to violence.

Notwithstanding this fact, however, the temptation was too great, and settlers commenced locating upon the disputed territory, and made improvements. Joseph Haines appears to have been the first settler, at the mouth of the creek, on the west side. He located there in 1773, and made an improvement.

Captain Simon Cool settled at the mouth of Larry's Creek in 1772. This creek, it may as well be mentioned here, inherits its name from an Indian trader named Larry Burt, who was married to an Indian woman, and had a cabin, which stood a few yards above where the bridge now crosses the stream. It is nowhere stated at what time he located here, but it is presumed to have been about 1770. In 1768, John Henry made an improvement nearly opposite the mouth of Nippenose Creek.

As early as 1770, James Armstrong settled on the land at the upper end of Jersey Shore, now embraced in the farm of Mark Slonaker, Esq., where he erected a cabin and cleared a patch of ground. In 1773, James Alexander ascended Pine Creek, to where Henry Tomb now resides, and made an improvement.

In 1773, Robert King, John King, and Adam King, came and settled on the west side of Pine Creek, where they only remained about a year, when they abandoned the place under the impression that the land was not good, and located below Larry's Creek on the hills. They were much mistaken. The land above Pine Creek at that time was destitute of large timber, and covered with small bushes and underbrush, familiarly known as "barrens." Now, this beautiful plain contains some of the best farms in the State.

William McElhattan settled on the south side of the river, on the stream of water now bearing his name, at a very early period. Mention is made of him having a small mill there in 1771–2. This was in Northumberland county, it will be observed.

In 1772, an improvement was made opposite the Great Island, by Samuel Harris. On the 20th of November, 1774, he conveyed it to William Dunn. The tract embraced three hundred acres, and included the Indian village, which stood, probably, where Dunnstown now stands. Dunn also became the owner of the island, which was a famous place with the Indians. It contains three hundred acres.

The earliest settlement, of which I have any account, that was made up the river on the south side, was by a man named Clarey Campbell, from the Juniata. His cabin stood on the river, in the upper part of Lock Haven. In 1776, a trial took place between him and William Glass, who claimed his land. Charles Lukens, Deputy Surveyor of Berks county, being a witness, testified as follows: "When I went up in March, 1769, to make the Officers' Surveys, I found Clarey Campbell living on this land with his family."

John Long, a silversmith, from Juniata also, settled above and adjoining Clarey Campbell, about the same time.

Two families settled about the mouth of Young Woman's Creek, as early as 1770, or 1771, and made some improvements. One of their names was Reed.

The settlements on the north side of the river, and west of Lycoming Creek, were made in violation of the laws of the Province, on land yet unpurchased from the Indians. It seemed that the hardy adventurers of that period, knowing the danger that they would incur, could not resist the temptation of taking possession of these beautiful lands. The Indians looked upon these encroachments with alarm. They beheld their favorite hunting grounds taken and appropriated by the whites. True to the Indian character, they remonstrated, but in vain. On complaint being made, the Provincial Government became alarmed, and at a meeting of the Council, held at Philadelphia, the 18th of September, 1773, reference was made to this matter, as follows:

"The Governor informed the Board that he had received Information that several Families had lately seated themselves on Lands on the North side of the West Branch of Susquehanna, beyond the Boundaries of the last purchase made of the Indians at the Treaty of Fort Stanwix, and it being Considered that the making settlements on the Indian's Lands would create Great uneasiness among them, and if not immediately removed, and prevented for the future, might be attended with Fatal Consequences, it was the opinion of the Board that a Proclamation, commanding the Magistrates and other Peace Officers to enforce and Carry the Laws for preventing Persons settling on any of the unpurchased Lands in this Province into Execution, against all Persons who had already made any such settlements, or should hereafter Transgress the same Law; The Secretary was accordingly directed to prepare a Draught of a Proclamation for that purpose."

The Proclamation was immediately drawn up by the Secretary, and approved by the Governor, on the 20th of September, 1773. Orders were given forthwith, to have it published throughout the Province. It is given as follows, in full:

"*By the Honourable John Penn, Esquire, Governor and Commander-in-Chief of the Province of Pennsylvania, and Counties of New-Castle, Kent, and Sussex, on Delaware.*

"A PROCLAMATION.*

"WHEREAS, I have received information that several Ill disposed Persons, in Disobedience to His Majesty's express orders, and in direct Violation of the Laws, have Lately presumed to seat themselves upon Lands within the Limits of this Province, not as yet purchased of the Indians: *And Whereas*, the making such Settlements doth greatly tend to irritate the minds of the Indians, and may be productive of dangerous and Fatal consequences to the Peace and Safety of His Majesty's good Subjects: *And Whereas*, by an Act of General Assembly of this Province, passed in the ninth year of His Majesty's Reign, for preventing Persons from Settling upon Lands not purchased of the Indians, it is enacted, 'that if any Person or Persons, after the Publication of this Act, either singly or in Companies, shall presume to settle upon any Lands within the Boundaries of this Province, not purchased of the Indians, or shall make, or cause any Surveys to be made of any part thereof, or mark or cut down any Trees thereon, with design to settle or appropriate the same to his own, or the use of any other Person, or Persons whatsoever, every such person or persons so offending, being legally Convicted thereof, in any Court of Quarter Sessions of the County where such offenders shall be apprehended (in which said Court the said offences are hereby made Cognizable,) shall forfeit and pay for every such offence the sum of Five hundred Pounds, and suffer Twelve Month's Imprisonment, without Bail or Main-Prize, and shall moreover find Surety for Good Behavior during the space of twelve Months from and after the Expiration of the Term of such Imprisonment. I have therefore thought Proper, by and with the advice of the Council, to issue this my Proclamation, hereby strictly enjoyning and requiring all and every Person and Persons, already settled or Residing on any Lands beyond the Boundary Line of the Last Indian Purchase, immediately to evacuate their illegal Settlements, and to depart and remove themselves from the said Lands without Delay, on pain of being prosecuted with the

* Vide Vol. X. Col. Records, and 95th page.

utmost rigour of the Law. And I do hereby prohibit and forbid all His Majesty's Subjects of this, or any other Province or Colony, on any pretence whatsoever, to intrude upon, Settle or Possess any of the aforesaid unpurchased Lands, as they will answer the Contrary at their Peril. And I do also hereby strictly Command and require all Magistrates, Sheriffs, and other Peace officers within this Province, to enforce and Carry into strict execution the said Act of General Assembly, as well against the present offenders in the Premises, as all others who may hereafter Transgress the same.

"*Given* under my Hand, and the Great Seal of the said Province, at Philadelphia, the twentieth day of September, in the thirteenth year of the Reign of our Sovereign Lord George the Third, by the Grace of God of Great Britain, France and Ireland, King, Defender of the Faith, and so forth, and in the year of our Lord one thousand seven hundred and seventy-three.

"JOHN PENN.

"By His Honour's Command,

"JOSEPH SHIPPEN, Junior, Secretary.

"GOD SAVE THE KING."

Notwithstanding this proclamation, and the punishment that was to be inflicted upon all who violated it, it appears that not the *least* attention whatever was paid to it, and settlers quietly came in, and seated themselves upon the forbidden lands. Whether any arrests were made, does not appear, but it is presumed there were none.

In 1774, after this sharp proclamation had been issued, Thomas Ferguson settled west of Lycoming creek, on the farm now owned by James Grier. A family of Kings, named William, Joseph, and Reeder, also settled near the mouth of the creek. Edmund Huff settled one mile above the mouth, in the same year. William McMein located here in 1774. Henry Dougherty came in 1775, and made some improvements.

In the same year, 1775, Andrew Armstrong settled

at a place called the "*big spring*," below Linden, on the farm now occupied by Colonel A. Stewart.

John, James, and Thomas Hughes settled a short distance west of Linden in 1774. Bratton Caldwell, afterwards noted as a *fair play* man, settled where John Hughes now resides, the same year. John Toner also settled in this neighborhood in 1773.

CHAPTER XXII.

NAMES OF THE SETTLERS CONTINUED—THE VENERABLE MRS. HAMILTON—FAIR PLAY MEN—THEIR MANNER OF DOING BUSINESS—MODE OF EJECTMENT—THE CASE OF CLARK—A MAGNANIMOUS SAVAGE—ANECDOTE OF PETER RODEY—FIRST WEDDING.

Michael Seely settled and made some improvements as early as 1775, about half a mile below where Jersey Shore now stands, on the bank of the river. During the same year, Jacob Mattox settled on the land now occupied by the town, and made an improvement also.

George Morrison settled on the land embraced in the farm of Mrs. Ferguson, at the upper end of the town, in 1774. About the same time, Thomas Nichols settled and made an improvement on the small stream now bearing his name, and emptying into Pine Creek.

Benjamin Walker settled on the flat on the west side of the first fork of Pine Creek, near where the M. E. Church now stands, as early as 1775, and made an improvement.

Francis Clark settled on the farm now owned by John Pfouts, a short distance above Jersey Shore, in 1774. Mention will be made of him again.

Edward McMasters settled on the point of land on the west side of Pine Creek, in 1774. Robert Plunkett also made some improvements there the same year, on what is now known as the Crist and Simmons farms. McMasters, it appears, left the settlement in 1775, and immediately joined the American army at Cambridge.

Amongst other early settlers along the river, above Pine Creek, may be mentioned the following: William Campbell, Alexander Donaldson, Alexander Hamilton, John Jackson,* Adam Carson, Henry McCracken, Rev. Cornelius Kincaid, Adam Dewitt, and James Parr, afterwards Captain Parr, in the Revolution.

I have been more particular in giving the names of the settlers west of Lycoming Creek, and the time they came, than at any other point, from the fact that this was the disputed territory, and not recognized by the Provincial government. From this fact originated the *Fair Play* system, which forms such an interesting feature in the history of the Valley. These names and dates may

* Four miles above Jersey Shore, on the right of the main road leading to Lock Haven, resides the venerable Mrs. Hamilton, in the 89th year of her age. She was the daughter of Mr. Jackson, and came to this place in 1773, from Orange county, N. Y., where she has lived till the present time. She became the wife of Robert Hamilton, who is now dead.

When I visited this venerable old lady in June last, I found her with her faculties bright and unimpaired, and as free and communicative as a woman of fifty. She is an extraordinary woman, possessed of a strong mind and very retentive memory. The scenes of the "Big Runaway," and the privations endured at that period, were fresh in her mind, and she could relate them with remarkable accuracy and minuteness. All the old settlers, already alluded to, were acquaintances of hers, and she feelingly spoke of them. She is the *only* survivor, and gave me much valuable information.

Mrs. Hamilton is a woman much esteemed and respected by a large circle of acquaintances, for her many virtues and social qualities which she possesses in an eminent degree. She is living in her mature old age in comfortable circumstances, surrounded by her numerous descendants, who are amongst the most respectable citizens of this part of the Valley.

be relied upon as being strictly correct, as they were taken from the official papers. Many more names might be given, but these are deemed sufficient.

As I have already stated, this part of the Valley being in dispute, and *supposed* to belong to the Indians, the settlements were made in direct opposition to the proclamation of the Governor, and the laws of the Province, quoted in the foregoing chapter. Such being the fact, then, they were considered a class of outlaws, living beyond the pale of civilization, without any government or organization.

In view of this fact, and being impressed with the necessity of entering into some measures whereby an organization and code of laws could be effected and adopted for their better government and preservation, as an independent republic in the midst of the wilderness, the *Fair Play* system was first adopted.

The following note, from the 195th page of the second volume of Smith's Laws, gives a very clear idea of the *fair play* system:

"There existed a great number of locations of the 3d of April, 1769, for the choicest lands on the West Branch of Susquehanna, between the mouths of Lycoming and Pine Creeks, but the proprietaries from extreme caution, the result of that experience, which had also produced the very penal laws of 1768 and 1769, and the proclamation already stated, had prohibited any surveys being made beyond the Lycoming. In the meantime, in violation of all law, a set of hardy adventurers had from time to time seated themselves on this doubtful territory. They made improvements, and formed a very considerable population. It is true, so far as regarded the rights of real property, they were not under the protection of the laws of the country; and were we to adopt the visionary theories of some philosophers, who have drawn their arguments from a supposed state of nature, we might be led to believe that the state of these people would have been a state of continual warfare; and that in contests for property the weakest must give way to the strongest. To prevent the consequences, real or supposed, of this state of things, they formed a mutual compact among themselves. They annually elected a tribunal, in rotation, of three of their settlers, whom they called *fair-play-men*, who were to decide all controversies, and settle disputed boundaries. From their decision there was no appeal. There could be no resistance. The decree was enforced by the whole body, who started up in mass, at the mandate of the court, and execution and conviction was as sudden and irresistible as the judgment. Every new comer was obliged to apply to this powerful tribunal, and upon his solemn engagement to submit in all respects to the law of the land, he was permitted to take possession of some vacant spot. Their decrees, were however, just; and when their settlements were recognized by law, and fair play had ceased, their decisions were received in evidence, and confirmed by judgments of courts."

Many of the names mentioned in this, and the previous chapter, were prominent *fair play* men. They had a regular code of laws for their own government, but it has been lost. I have made the most diligent search and inquiry for it, but it never was preserved. This is to be much regretted, as it would now be looked upon as an interesting document.

It is stated in some authorities that the place of holding the *fair play* courts, was where Chatham's mill now stands, on the stream of the same name, some distance below Lock Haven. But it is pretty clearly established that they had no *regular* place of meeting, or stated periods either, for the transaction of business. The court could be convened at any place within the territory over which it exercised jurisdiction, and on short notice, to try any case that might be on hand. In other words, the sittings of the *fair play* courts were convened to suit the exigency of the case, without regard to time or place.

When any person in the territory of the *fair play* men,

refused to be governed by their decisions, and the laws they had established for their guidance, it is stated that he was immediately ejected from the district by being placed in a canoe and rowed down to Lycoming Creek, the boundary of civilization, and there sent adrift.

Many interesting cases, settled by the *fair play* men, together with anecdotes, are related. Joseph Antes, Esq., son of Colonel Antes, relates the following:—Francis Clark, who, the reader will remember, was mentioned in the previous chapter, settled on the land now owned by John Pfouts, a short distance above Jersey Shore. By some means or other he got a dog in his possession that belonged to an Indian. On learning where the dog was, the Indian complained to the *fair play* men that he had stolen it. They forthwith had him arrested and tried for the alleged theft. He was convicted, and sentenced to receive a certain number of lashes. It was decided by lot who should flog him, by placing a grain of corn for each man, together with one red grain, in a bag, and drawing them therefrom. The man that would draw the red grain was to do the whipping. It was drawn by Philip Antes, and preparations were immediately made to carry the sentence into execution. On seeing that the punishment was about to be inflicted, the Indian, who seems to have been a very magnanimous savage, became sympathetic, and made a proposition that if he would abandon the land where he had settled, the punishment should be remitted. A few minutes were allowed him for consideration, when he acted upon the suggestion, and left. He settled in Nippenose Valley, in 1795.

He conveyed the land he had taken up to Andrew Boggs, who afterwards disposed of it to Samuel Campbell, and he conveyed it to James Foster, &c.

An anecdote is related—which is illustrative of *fair play* principles—that once upon a time when Chief Justice McKean was holding Court in this district, he inquired, partly from curiosity, and partly in reference to the case before him, of a shrewd old Irishman, named Peter Rodey, if he could tell him what the provisions of the *fair play* code were. Peter's memory did not exactly serve him as to details, and he could only convey an idea of them by comparison, so, scratching his head, he answered:

"All I can say is, that since your Honor's coorts have come among us, *fair play* has entirely ceased, and law has taken its place."

This sharp rejoinder created a good deal of merriment in court, and the judge was satisfied to ask no more impertinent questions, reflecting upon the legal tribunal over which Peter had in turn presided.

The first wedding west of Lycoming Creek is said to have taken place in the winter of 1775. The parties married were Bratton Caldwell, and Miss Elcy Hughes. The wedding took place at a cabin on the farm now owned by Colonel George Crane. The party crossed the river on the ice, and had quite a jollification on the occasion.

CHAPTER XXIII.

PLEASANT PROSPECTS—CONFERENCE WITH THE INDIANS AT FORT AUGUSTA—THEY RETIRE—DERR "DREETS" THEM—BRADY UPSETS THE BARREL OF LIQUOR—COMMITTEE OF SAFETY—NAMES OF OFFICERS—PETITION TO THE CENTRAL COMMITTEE—SERIOUS DIFFICULTY WITH CAPTAIN ROBB, OF MUNCY TOWNSHIP—EXPLANATION.

THE settlements rapidly extended up the valley—houses were built—fields were cleared, and improvements made. Everything betokened peace and prosperity. Although the hardy pioneers had many privations to endure, they were contented, and labored assiduously to clear the ground and sow their fields. They looked forward with joy to the ripening of their crops, when they would be able to obtain flour and provisions of their own raising. They had brought their families to the valley, and where the pappooses of the Indians had played under the wide-spreading branches of the mighty oak, the white children now sported, and made the forest resound with the melody of their voices. The axe of the sturdy pioneer resounded on every hand, and the crash of the falling monarchs of the forest, that had withstood the storms and tempests of ages, caused the wild beasts to start from their lairs and plunge further into the gloomy depths of the wilderness. The proud Aborigine beheld the onward march of civilization—he plainly saw the tracings of mysterious characters by the hand of destiny—he turned aside and groaned in spirit that he must soon depart towards the setting sun, and bid farewell forever to the cherished scenes and happy associations of his youth. It was a hard lot, but such was the decree of fate.

The valley filled up very rapidly with settlers from one end to the other. All was hope, and excitement. Contrasting their pleasures and enjoyments, with the hard lot fate had in store for them, how appropriate are the following beautiful lines from Gray:

> "Fair laughs the morn, and soft the zephyr blows,
> While proudly riding o'er the azure realm
> In gallant trim the gilded vessel goes,
> Youth on the prow, and pleasure at the helm;
> Regardless of the sweeping whirlwind's sway,
> That, hushed in grim repose, expects his evening prey."

But the settlers on the West Branch Valley were not to remain long in this happy state of mind. The war of the Revolution had now commenced, and the clangor of arms resounded in the east. Soldiers were wanted to fight the battles of liberty and freedom. The whole country was in a state of confusion, which extended to this region, and materially affected the settlements. As the colonies were weak, and had a powerful foe to contend with, almost superhuman exertions were made to repel the invaders. It was also feared that they would tamper with the Indians, and once more incite them to deeds of violence and bloodshed. This was a fearful anticipation, but hope, the anchor of the soul, could not roll back the cloud that hung suspended over the frontiers. Their anticipations were too true.

At this time the Seneca and Monsey tribes were in

considerable force, and Pine and Lycoming Creeks were almost navigable to the State line for canoes. Fort Augusta at that time was garrisoned by about fifty men, under Col. Hunter. They were called "*a fearless few.*"

Captain John Brady, at this time, suggested to his friends at Fort Augusta, the propriety of making a treaty with the Seneca and Monsey tribes, knowing them to be at variance with the Delawares. By doing so, it was thought that their friendship and assistance might be secured against the Delawares, should *they* commence any inroads upon the settlements. His proposition was approved of, and petitions were sent to the Council praying that Commissioners might be appointed, and Fort Augusta designated as the place of holding the conference. The request was granted, and Commissioners were appointed. Notice was given to the two tribes, by Brady and two others, selected for the purpose.

They met the chiefs and laid before them the proposition. They appeared to be delighted, and listened to the proposal with pleasure. After smoking the pipe of peace, and promising to attend at Fort Augusta on the appointed day, they led them out of the camp, shook hands with them cordially, and parted in seeming friendship.

Brady, who was very shrewd, feared to trust the friendship so warmly expressed, and took a different route in returning with his company, to guard against being waylaid and surprised.

On the day appointed for holding the treaty, the Indians appeared with their wives and children. The warriors numbered about one hundred, and were dressed in their war costume. Care had been taken to make the fort look as fierce as possible, and every man was at his post.

In former treaties, the Indians had received large presents, and were expecting them here; but finding the fort too poor to give anything of value, (and an Indian never trusts,) all efforts to form a treaty with them proved abortive. They left the fort, however, apparently in good humor, and well satisfied with their treatment, and taking to their canoes, proceeded homeward. The remainder of the day was chiefly spent by the officers and people of the fort in devising means of protection against anticipated attacks of the Indians. Late in the day, Brady thought of Derr's trading house, and foreboding evil from that point, mounted a small mare he had at the fort, and crossing the North Branch, rode with all possible speed. On his arrival, he saw the canoes of the Indians on the bank of the river near Derr's. When near enough to observe, he saw the squaws exerting themselves to the utmost, at their paddles, to work the canoes over to his side of the river; and that when they landed they made for thickets of sumach, which grew in abundance on his* land to the height of a man's head, and very thick upon the ground. He was not slow in conjecturing the cause. He rode on to where the squaws were landing, and saw that they were conveying rifles, tomahawks and knives, into the sumach thickets, and hiding them. He immediately jumped into a canoe and crossed to Derr's trading house, where he found the Indians brutally drunk. He saw a barrel of rum standing on end before Derr's door, the head out. He instantly overset it, and spilled the rum, saying to Derr, "My God, Frederick, what have you done?" Derr replied: *"Dey dells me you gif um no dreet town on*

* The reader will remember this was where Brady first settled when he came to the Valley.

de fort, so dinks as I gif um one here, als he go home in bease!"

One of the Indians, who saw the rum spilled, but was unable to prevent it, told Brady he would one day rue the spilling of that barrel. Being well acquainted with the Indian character, he knew death was the penalty of his offence, and was constantly on his guard.

Next day the Indians started off. They did not soon attack the settlements, but carried arms for their allies, the English, in other parts.

As the Revolution had become general, the most active preparations were made to devise means of defence. Companies of volunteers were raised, and every laudable effort used to induce the patriots of that period to march to the defence of their country. A central Committee of Safety was established at Philadelphia; and Committees in the various counties were organized and under the control of the Central Committee. The subordinate Committees were in correspondence with the Central one, and kept it posted up in every movement in their respective districts.

A Committee of Safety for Northumberland county was appointed. They held regular meetings, and kept a record of their proceedings in a large book, kept for the purpose. This book was given to Joseph G. Wallace, of Lewisburg, (deceased,) many years ago, by his uncle, Captain Gray, a Revolutionary hero. It contained the names of the principal men of the County, the business transacted at their meetings, &c., which was very interesting. This book, it is to be regretted, has been carried off and probably lost. The family should spare no efforts to recover it, and preserve it as a precious relic of the olden time.

Sherman Day examined the book some fifteen years ago, when he was collecting materials for his "Historical Collections of Pennsylvania," and made a few extracts from it. He was compelled to be as brief as possible, as the limits of his work would not permit of lengthy extracts. To him, then, are we indebted for *all* that has been taken from that interesting, as well as official document.

From it I learn that on the 8th of February, 1776, the following gentlemen, being previously nominated by the respective townships to serve in the Committee for the space of six months, met at the house of Richard Malone, at the mouth of Chilisquaque Creek: For Augusta township, John Weitzel, Esq., Alexander Hunter, Esq., Thomond Ball; Mahoning township, William Cook, Esq., Benjamin Alison, Esq., Mr. Thomas Hewet; Turbut township, Captain John Hambright, Wm. McKnight, William Shaw; Muncy township, Robert Robb, Esq., William Watson, John Buckalow; Bald Eagle township, Mr. Wm. Dunn, Thos. Hughes, Alexander Hamilton; Buffalo township, Mr. Walter Clark, Wm. Irwin, Joseph Green; White Deer township, Walter Clarke, Matthew Brown, Marcus Hulings.

Captain John Hambright was elected chairman, and Thomond Ball, clerk. The field officers of the battalion of the lower division of the county, were Samuel Hunter, Esq., Colonel; Wm. Cook, Lieutenant Colonel; Casper Weitzel, first Major; Mr. John Lee, second Major. Those of the upper battalion appear to have been Wm. Plunkett, Colonel; James Murray, Lieutenant Colonel; Mr. John Brady, first Major; Mr. Cookson Long, second Major.

Each Captain was ordered to return at least forty privates. Each battalion consisted of six companies. The Captains of the lower battalion were Nicolas Miller, Chas. Gillespie, Hugh White, Wm. Scull, James McMahon, Wm. Clarke, and afterwards, Captain John Simpson; and of the upper, or Colonel Plunkett's battalion, Henry Antes, Esq., Samuel Wallis, John Robb, Wm. Murray, Wm. McElhatten, Simon Cool, David Berry.

Many of the proceedings consisted of forms possessing no special interest. Reference was frequently made to their difficulties with Wyoming.

On the 13th of March, 1776, in their despatch to the Committee of Safety at Philadelphia, they made certain complaints of grievances, suffered in their infant settlement, on account of so many recruiting officers sent among them. On the 27th of the same month, they sent in the following petition:

"We are now, gentlemen, to inform you of what we think a grievance to this young and thinly inhabited county, viz: A constant succession of recruiting officers from different counties in this Province. Our zeal for the cause of American Liberty has hitherto prevented our taking any steps to hinder the raising of men for its service; but finding the evil increasing so fast upon us as almost to threaten the depopulation of the county, we cannot help appealing to the wisdom and justice of your committee to know whether the quota of men that may be demanded from this county under their own officers is not as much as can reasonably be expected from it. Whether—at a time when we are uncertain of peace with the Indians, (well knowing that our enemies are tampering with them) and a claim is set up to the greatest part of the Province by a neighboring colony, who have their hostile abettors at our very breasts, as well as their emissaries among us—is it prudent to drain an infant frontier county of its strength of men? and whether the safety of the interior parts of the province would not be better secured by adding strength to the frontier? Whether our honourable assembly by disposing of commissions to gentlemen in different counties to raise companies, which are to form the number of battalions thought necessary for the defence of this province, did not intend that the respective Captains should raise their Companies where they were appointed, and not distress one County by taking from it all the men necessary for the business of agriculture, as well as the defence of the same. From our knowledge of the state of this County, we make free to give our opinion of what would be most for its advantage, as well as that of the province—between which we hope there never will be a difference—and first are to inform you of the poverty of the people, many of whom came bare and naked here, being plundered by a banditti who called themselves Yankees; and those who brought some property with them, from the necessary delay of cultivating a wilderness before they could have any produce to live upon, together with the necessity of still continuing the closest application to labor and industry for their support, renders it morally improbable that a well disciplined militia can be established here, as the distance which some men are obliged to go to muster is the loss of two days to them; which not being paid for, they will not, nor indeed can they, so often attend as is necessary to complete them even in the manual exercise. We would recommend that two or more companies be raised, and put in pay for the use of the province, to be ready to march when and where the service may require them, and when not wanted for the service of the public at any particular place, to be stationed in this county, in order to be near and defend our frontiers should they be attacked by our enemies of any denomination; the good effect of which we imagine would be considerable—as, though they may be too few to repel, they may stop the progress of an enemy until the militia could be raised to assist them. Should this proposal appear eligible, please to inform us thereof, and we will recommend such gentlemen for officers as we think will be most suitable for the service, and agreeable to the people. We are, gentlemen, with due respect, &c.

Signed for and in behalf of the Committee."

JOHN HAMBRIGHT, Chairman.

It is believed that the Committee partially acceded to the requests of the petitioners, as companies were afterwards stationed in the Valley.

The Committee changed once in six months, when

only a part of the former members seem to have been re-elected. They often met at Laughlan McCartney's, a member of Mahoning township.

On the 10th of September, 1776, the Committee learned that Levy & Ballion had a quantity of salt on hand, which they refused to sell for cash—as it seems they had been ordered by a former resolution of the Committee—whereupon they ordered Mr. William Sayers to take possession of it, and sell it at the rate of fifteen shillings per bushel, and not above half a bushel to each family, and return the money to the Committee.

This Committee also attended to receiving from the Philadelphia Committee, their share of arms and ammunition, iron, and salt, for this County, and distributed it very carefully among the soldiers and people.

Captain Robert Robb, of Muncy township, formerly one of the Committee, seems to have given them a deal of trouble. He was charged with having in his possession, "a paper supposed to be from Lord Howe, concerning conditions of peace," of which said Robb said, "this is the very thing I would be at;" and said further, that "Mr. Frankling (Dr. Franklin,) was a rogue, he well knew, and that he had led the government into two or three scrapes already known to him; also, it was thought Frankling had a pension from home; likewise it was thought the Convention was bribed." Also, that said Robb says, "that Lord Howe used the members of Congress politely that was sent to treat with him, but that they used him ill."

It appears that the Committee ordered, that Robb should "either take his gun and march with the militia of the County into actual service, to prove his attachment to the American cause, or else be confined until released by further authority."

Colonel James Murray was appointed to arrest and confine him; who, having full confidence in Robb's patriotism, and "out of lenity to said Robb's family, saw fit to appoint the mansion house of said Robb as a prison for him, on a promise of his good behavior for the future."

Robb, however, seems to have practised good behavior—*as he understood it;* for when one Peter Smith had intruded himself several times into the company of Robb and another gentleman, who were "drinking a half pint together," Robb knocked him down, and bruised him severely—and thereupon further "said, that the Committee were a set of rascals—some of them were robbers, some were horse thieves, and some of them were murderers—and further saith not."

This so incensed the Committee, that they ordered Colonel Murray to take him to Philadelphia; Murray resigned, however, and two other men were appointed to perform the unpleasant duty.*

Here, Mr. Day ceased with his extracts from the record, and it is not known how the difficulty was settled, or whether he was taken to Philadelphia. It is to be regretted exceedingly, that the book was suffered to be carried off, as it would unquestionably have thrown much light upon that interesting period of our history.

From the records of the same Committee, it appears that a great scarcity of grain prevailed in 1777. In

* There appears to be some mistake with this affair, and since writing the above, I have learned that Robb *was* a patriotic citizen; that the difficulty grew out of the Committee wishing to force him into some measures in reference to the local dispute with Wyoming. He was taken a prisoner to Lancaster, where, after the matter was explained to the authorities, he was *honorably* acquitted and returned. I am happy to make this correction, in justice to his descendants, who are very respectable and patriotic citizens of the same township.

February of the same year, they ordered, "that no stiller in Bald Eagle township shall buy any more grain, or still any more than he has by him, during the season."

It appears that they were somewhat inclined to morality, too, and exercised their authority to stop "a certain Henry Sterret, of the same township, from profaning the Sabbath, in an unchristian and scandalous manner, causing his servants to maul rails, &c., on that day, and beating and abusing them if they offered to disobey such his unlawful demands."

Sterret, probably, resided on Long Island, opposite Jersey Shore, at this time, when the Committee were compelled to have a change effected in his morals.

No doubt, they had their hands full to attend to the affairs of the County at that time, and the history of their proceedings would be full of interest to the people of the present day.

CHAPTER XXIV.

YOUNG SAM BRADY AT BOSTON—HIS FATHER WOUNDED AT THE BATTLE OF BRANDYWINE—DISCUSSION ON INDEPENDENCE AT NORTHUMBERLAND—DR. PLUNKETT—NAMES AND LOCALITIES OF THE FORTS IN THE VALLEY—COLONEL ANTES—ANECDOTES OF JOB CHILLOWAY—HIS WIFE BETSEY—MURDERS.

ALTHOUGH the settlements on the West Branch were comparatively weak, the call for men, for the Revolution, was nobly responded to, and volunteers flocked to the American standard. Captain John Lowden raised a company of volunteer riflemen, seventy in number, all unmarried, and marched to Boston. Young Sam Brady,* son of John Brady, was one of the number. It was the intention of the Captain that he should be an officer, but his father objected, saying, "let him first learn the duties of a soldier, and then he will know how to act as an officer."

Whilst the riflemen lay in the vicinity of Boston, many skirmishes took place. On one occasion, Lowden was ordered to take some able-bodied men, and wade to an island, and drive off some cattle belonging to the enemy. Brady was considered too young for the service, and was left behind; but to the astonishment of

* For full particulars of the daring exploits of young Brady in the West, the reader is referred to the articles of Kishkeminetas in the 9th and 10th volumes of Hazard's Register.

the Captain, he followed, and was the second man on the island. In 1776, he was appointed a 1st Lieutenant in Captain Doyle's company from Lancaster county. He was with the army in all the principal engagements, till after the battle of Monmouth, when he was promoted to a Captaincy, and ordered to the West under General Broadhead.

During the same year, his father was appointed a Captain in the 12th Pennsylvania regiment, and was badly wounded at the battle of Brandywine, after which he returned home.

At this time, the question of Independence, or no Independence, became so warm at Northumberland, that it was decided to have a discussion on the subject. A scaffold was erected, near where the market house now stands, and the discussion took place. Colonels Cooke and Hunter took the stand on the side of Liberty and Independence, and Dr. Plunkett and Charles Cooke took the side of loyalty. Considerable warmth was manifested on both sides.

In 1778, Cooke received orders to join General Washington with his regiment, which was composed in part of three companies, raised in Northumberland county, commanded by Captains Gray, Buyors, and Brady.

In 1779, Colonel Cooke asked leave to resign his Commission, on account of ill health, occasioned by a pulmonary disease. He was appointed Commissary, however, for the army of the north, which office he held during the war. He died in 1804.

Charles Cooke and Dr. Plunkett, on account of their loyal sentiments, were ordered by the government to leave the country in ten days. Not being prepared to leave on such short notice, they kept themselves secreted for a long time. Colonel Cooke accompanied his brother Charles to New York, to sail for Europe. There they exchanged watches as a token of remembrance of each other. Charles was afterwards sent as an ambassador from England to France.

As the struggle for Liberty increased, and the infant Colonies were straining every nerve, a new danger, of a very alarming character, began to exhibit itself on the northern and western frontiers. The British had tampered with the Indians, and induced them to take up the hatchet against the whites. A stipulated price was also paid for scalps, as an inducement for them to kill and destroy. The West Branch Valley was an exposed and defenceless frontier, at the mercy of the infuriated savages. Great consternation prevailed among the inhabitants, and the government was petitioned for assistance.

It was found necessary to construct forts at different points, where small bodies of men were stationed, to guard the settlements. On an alarm of Indians being given, the settlers fled to these stations, for refuge and protection. Colonel Hunter commanded at Fort Augusta.

Freeland's Fort, it will be remembered, was built on Warrior Run, in 1773. A small stockade was erected one mile above Milton, and called Fort Schwartz. This was probably in 1777–8. Boon's Fort stood at the mouth of Muddy Run. It was commanded by Captain Boon. Fort Menninger was at the mouth of Warrior Run. Fort Rice was on Chillisquaque Creek, near where Washingtonville now stands; it became the frontier Fort, and held out until the close of the war.

John Brady, who had removed from opposite Lewisburg, and settled on the Muncy manor, erected a small fortification for the protection of his own family, and that of his neighbors, on the south side of Muncy Creek, near where the town now stands. It was called Fort Brady, and has often been confounded with Muncy Fort. The latter, as I have already observed, was erected on the Muncy farm, some miles above the town, near the old mansion of Mrs. E. Hall. It was often called Fort Wallis, after Samuel Wallis, who took up the land, now embraced in Halls' farms. It was quite an important place.

A small enclosure was erected near the mouth of Lycoming Creek, where Jaysburg stands, and called Fort Huff, after a settler of that name.

Lieutenant Colonel Henry Antes,* a famous character in the history of the Valley, erected a fort on the high ground, near where the mill now stands, at the mouth of Nippenose Creek, a short distance above Jersey Shore, in the summer of 1776. It was a very important place during the terrible times previous to the *big runaway*, and was a picketed enclosure, defended by a regular garrison of militia. He also built a mill on the site occupied by the present one. It is related that when they were building it, they made their flour by grinding the wheat in an old iron coffee mill, and removed the bran with a hair sieve. One man was kept grinding nearly all the time. The old coffee mill was preserved in the family for many years.

* Colonel Antes was born in 1736, near Philadelphia. He was distinguished during the war for his services at this point. He had a large number of children. Jos. Antes, Esq., is the youngest now surviving. He died, July 13th, 1820, aged 83 years and nine months. His descendants are quite numerous.

Horn's Fort was built on the south side of the river, a short distance below the mouth of Chatham's Run, on what is now known as Crispin's Run. In 1777, Elizabeth Carson was outside of the fort; an Indian, lying in ambush, fired upon her—the bullet passed through the folds of her dress, making fourteen holes, and left her uninjured!

Reed's Fort was erected on the site now occupied by J. Grafius' house in Lock Haven. It was a place of some importance at first, being the most advanced on the frontier. It was commanded by Colonel Long, familiarly known among the old settlers as "Cookey" Long.

Adam Carson had a small fortification, midway between Reed's and Harris' Forts, on the same side of the river, but it was almost immediately abandoned on the commencement of the troubles, on account of water.

These were the fortifications of the West Branch Valley. It is true, that they scarcely merited the name, with the exception of one or two, and were destitute of cannon, but they served admirable purposes at that time. The settlers were obliged to abandon their rude cabins, their little fields of grain, and seek refuge within these enclosures from the scalping knife of the savage. The women and children remained in the forts, whilst the men, in armed companies, would venture to their fields and houses, and cut their crops. Those who refused to seek the forts, generally paid for their rashness with their lives.

These, indeed, were terrible times, and the quiet occupants of this beautiful and fertile Valley, at the present day, cannot form the most remote conception of the privations and sufferings that were then endured. It was unsafe to venture any distance from the forts, unarmed and alone. The wily Indian lurked in ambush—quietly he watched his approaching and unconscious victim, till within range—then the sharp crack of his rifle awoke the echoes of the forest—his victim fell pierced through the heart—a savage yell followed, and the scalp was rudely torn from his head, and borne off in triumph.

In the year 1777, a company of men under Colonel Kelly, were stationed for three months on the Great Island, to guard the advanced settlements. Nothing remarkable, however, occurred at that time. Moses Van Campen, afterwards a distinguished Indian killer and adventurer, was among them. This was his first service.

Previous to this year, in 1776, the Indians at the Great Island, removed their squaws and children, and all their effects. They also cut down their corn and destroyed everything they could. During the next year, they had abandoned the entire Valley, and retired back in the wilderness, where they were making preparations to fall upon the settlements.

Job Chilloway, a friendly Indian, who frequently visited Fort Antes, informed the whites that the Indians would shortly make a descent upon the Valley. Job frequently gave valuable informatioh, and always proved to be what he pretended—*a friend to the settlers.* At this time he was compelled to leave his hunting cabins in Nippenose and Sugar valleys, and remain about Fort Antes, for fear of the Indians, for they would have murdered him also. Job had a handsome young squaw named Betsey, for a wife, but she was treacherous to the whites, and would give all the information she could to the Indians. This was a source of much vexation to her husband, and at length he was compelled to inform them to keep her as much in ignorance as possible, as she could not be trusted. She was continually roving about, and would frequently make journeys to Philadelphia alone, and return loaded with trinkets and finery. She finally abandoned her husband, and joined the Indians. Some say, she never returned, and others that he got her again.

Job Chilloway is described as being "a tall, muscular man, with his ears cut so as to hang pendant, like a pair of ear-rings." He lived much in the Juniata Valley. In his old age he was much addicted to strong drink. He is said to have been found dead in his cabin, about the close of the last century. He went with Colonel Potter's regiment to Delaware—rendered essential service, and was in the company commanded by Lieutenant Daniel McHenry, at the battle of Red Bank.

Shaney John, one of his compatriots, is often alluded to by the old people. He was a friendly Indian also. After the Revolution he frequently visited Robert Hamilton, above Pine Creek. He is said to have been very pious, and what was peculiar about him, always removed his shirt before saying his prayers, on retiring.

Mr. Joseph Antes relates an anecdote about Job, that he heard from his father. One day he was walking about the fort, and discovered a sentinel—one of the outposts probably—asleep, leaning against a tree. Quietly slipping up behind him, he reached around the tree and grappled him like a bear. The man could not see who it was, and was terribly frightened, and struggled hard to get away. On seeing it was Job, he begged him not to inform Colonel Antes, as the punishment for such an offence would be severe. Job promised that he would not. He also censured the man for being so careless, and informed him that he might have been killed and scalped. "Yes," replied the sentinel, "I might have been caught by an Indian, and killed and scalped before I had known anything about it."

"It was an Indian that caught you," replied Job, "but you may thank God he was your friend!"

This circumstance so amused Job, that he would frequently burst out into the most violent fits of laughter during the day, which attracted the attention of Colonel Antes. He inquired what amused him, but no persuasion or offer of reward would induce him to tell. At length he informed the Colonel that a curious circumstance had occurred with one of his men, but he had pledged his word not to tell. He informed him, however, that he could detect it in the countenance of the man when they were paraded. They were scrutinized sharply, and this man at last confessed to his commander. He did not punish him, but gave him some wholesome advice not to be caught so again.

CHAPTER XXV.

DECLARATION OF INDEPENDENCE ON PINE CREEK—SINGULAR COINCIDENCE—BLOODY TRAGEDY OPPOSITE ANTES' FORT—DE-WITT'S ESCAPE—BROWN'S HOUSE BURNED ON LOYAL SOCK—CRUEL MURDER OF BENJAMIN—COOKEY LONG'S ADVENTURE, PILLAGE AND MURDER—THE INDIAN AT REED'S FORT—AN INGRATE WRETCH.

EARLY in the summer of 1776, the leading *fair play* men, and settlers, along the river above and below Pine Creek, had received intelligence from Philadelphia, that Congress had it in contemplation to declare the colonies independent, absolving them from all allegiance to Great Britain. This was good news to the little settlement up the West Branch, that was considered out of the jurisdiction of all civil law, and they set about making preparations to endorse the movement, and ratify it in a formal manner. Accordingly, on the 4th day of July, 1776, they assembled on the plains above Pine Creek in considerable numbers. A good supply of "old rye" was laid in as a *sine qua non* on this momentous occasion. The subject of independence was proposed, and freely discussed in several patriotic speeches; and, as their patriotism warmed up, it was finally decided to ratify the proposition under discussion in Congress, by a formal declaration of independence. A set of resolutions were drawn up and passed, absolving *themselves* from all allegiance to Great Britain, and henceforth declaring themselves *free and independent!* What was remarkable about *this declaration* was, that it took place about the same time that the Declaration was signed in Philadelphia! It was indeed a remarkable coincidence that two such important events should take place about the same time, hundreds of miles apart, without any communication. When the old bell proclaimed, in thunder tones to the citizens of Philadelphia, that the colonies were declared independent, the shout of liberty went up from the banks of Pine Creek, and resounded along the base of Bald Eagle mountain.

The following names of settlers that participated in this glorious festival, have been collected:

Thomas, Francis, and John Clark; Alexander Donaldson, William Campbell, Alexander Hamilton, John Jackson, Adam Carson, Henry McCracken, Adam Dewitt, Robert Love, Hugh Nichol, and many others from below the creek not now remembered.

One fine Sunday morning in June, 1777, Zephaniah Miller, Abel Cady, James Armstrong, and Isaac Bouser, left Antes' Fort with two women, and crossed the river to milk the cows that remained on the opposite side, on what is now known as Pfouts' farm. The settlers all around here had fled to the fort for safety.

When they landed, all the cows were found but the one with the bell, which they heard back in the bushes. The idea never occurred to them that Indians were about. They were there, however, and managed to keep this cow back about thirty rods from the river, so that they would be obliged to come for her. Cady, Armstrong, and Miller, started after her. As soon as they went back there, they were fired upon and severely wounded. Miller was scalped immediately. Cady was also scalped and left weltering in his blood. Armstrong was severely wounded in the back of his head, but ran a short distance.

As soon as the firing commenced, the women ran with Bouser and secreted themselves in a rye field close by. The garrison in the fort were alarmed, and rushed forth immediately, regardless of the orders of Colonel Antes, who feared it might be a decoy to draw them away from the fort, when it would be assailed from the other side. They paid no attention to his orders, however, and seizing upon the canoes, crossed the river immediately to the relief of their comrades. They went and found Miller and Cady where they fell. Cady was not dead. They carried him to the river bank, where his wife met him. On seeing her he reached out his hand and immediately expired. He had recently returned from the army, and was one of the original settlers along the river. Armstrong was taken over to the fort, where he lingered in great agony till Monday night, when he expired.

A party immediately pursued the Indians, and coming on them at a place called the "Race Ground," they stood and fired—then broke and fled—pursued by the whites. They ran across what is now the upper part of the town of Jersey Shore, and escaped into the swamp, a short distance above where Lawshe's Tannery now stands. The whites fired upon them several times, and probably did some execution, as marks of blood were visible where they had apparently dragged away their killed or wounded.

In the winter of the same year, three men left Horn's Fort, and proceeded across the river to the Muncy town flats, above Lockport. They were fired upon by a lurking party of Indians, and one man killed near Sugar

Run. The other two fled, and were pursued across the ice. One of them, named Dewitt, in the hurry of the flight, ran into an air hole. He caught hold of the edge of the ice, however, and managed to keep his head above water. The Indians were afraid to venture too near. They commenced firing at his head, but watching the flash of the gun, he dodged under water like a duck, and eluded the ball. Several shots were fired at him, when, thinking he was dead, they left. Dewitt, in an exhausted state, succeeded in crawling from the water on the ice, and escaped to the fort.

The other man having crossed to the south side of the river, was pursued by a single Indian, who gained on him rapidly. He had a gun which was supposed to be worthless, but as the Indian neared him, he turned and pointed it at him, thinking to intimidate him, but did'nt pull the trigger. This he repeated several times, when the savage thinking it was unloaded, would point his tomahawk at him in derision, and exclaim, "*pooh, pooh.*" The pursuit continued, and the Indian came up close, feeling certain of his victim. As a last resort, he instinctively raised his gun, as it were, and pulled the trigger, when, to his astonishment, it went off and shot the Indian dead. He escaped to the fort in safety.

A party turned out and pursued the Indians as far as Youngwoman's Creek. They noticed that they had carried and dragged the body of the dead Indian all the way with them, from the marks in the snow.

The next attack made by the Indians in the autumn of 1777, was on Loyal Sock Creek, on the families of Brown and Benjamin.* Daniel Brown, it will be remem-

* The Benjamin family lived back of Williamsport; the Indians came and attacked them. Three brothers, and a small sister, were carried into

bered by the reader, settled at a very early period at this place. He had two daughters, married to two brothers, named Benjamin. On the alarm of the approaching Indians being given, the Benjamins, with their wives and children, took refuge at the house of Mr. Brown, and made preparations to defend themselves. The enemy came, and assaulted the house. A brisk resistance was maintained for some time, during which an Indian was killed by a shot from Benjamin's rifle. Finding they could not dislodge them, they set the house on fire. The flames spread rapidly, and a horrid death stared them in the face. What was to be done? Remain inside and be burned, or come forth to be despatched by the tomahawks of the savage? Either alternative was a fearful one.

The Benjamins at length determined to come forth and trust themselves to the mercies of the Indians. Brown refused, and remaining in the burning building, with his wife and daughter, was consumed with them, preferring rather to meet death in this way, than fall into the hands of the enemy and be tortured in a horrible manner.

When the Benjamins, with their families, came forth, one of them was carrying his youngest child in his arms. The savages received them at the door. A big Indian brandished his tomahawk aloft, and with a fiendish yell

captivity. Their names were William, Nathan, and Ezekiel. The name of the sister is not now remembered. The boys returned in a few years, but the sister remained. She grew up among them and married a chief, and had several children. Years after peace was made, William went after her, and brought her to Williamsport, where she remained some time, but in a very unhappy state of mind. Mr. Calvert, of Jersey Shore, remembers seeing her, and states that she was very wild, and shunned all society. It was difficult to get a view of her face. On account of her unhappiness, she was permitted to return to her Indian comrades.

that made the forest resound, buried the glittering steel in his brain. As he fell forward, his wife, with a shriek, caught the little child in her arms. His scalp was immediately torn from his head, and exultingly shook in her face. The remainder of the survivors were carried into captivity. This bloody massacre occurred on what is now known as the Buckley Farm, on Loyal Sock.

A man named Cook, with his wife, were taken by the same party, and carried into captivity.

The report of these murders spread terror throughout the settlements along the river. Most of the families fled to the different forts for protection, leaving their houses, fields and cattle, to the mercy of the savages.

About the close of the year, the Indians killed a man named Saltzman, on the Sinnemahoning. About the same time, another named Daniel Jones, who owned what the settlers called "the little mill," on a stream this side of Farrandsville, was murdered also, with another man. His wife escaped to the fort. These settlers had been warned to leave, but refused to do it, alleging there was no danger. Their lives paid for their incredulity.

At this time Colonel Cooksey Long gathered a company of about twenty men, and went up to Young-woman's Creek, to look for Indians. They suddenly espied a number of warriors on the opposite side, marching along in file, painted and dressed in war costume. The whites being undiscovered concealed themselves. The men were very anxious to select each his man, and fire upon them, but the *brave* Colonel refused. There was not more than twenty or thirty Indians, and the whites could undoubtedly have done good execution.

The Colonel remained in his concealed position till

they had passed by, when he returned to the fort, and reported that a large body of savages were approaching. It was probably one of the scalping parties.

Notwithstanding the utmost vigilance, a man was killed on the 23d of December, 1777, near the mouth of Pine Creek; and about the 1st of January, '78, one was killed two miles above the Great Island. Their names are not now remembered.

Petitions having been sent in to the Council, praying for some plan to be devised for the defence of the inhabitants of the Valley, instructions were at length forwarded to Colonel Hunter, ordering out the fifth class of the militia of the County. On the 14th of January, 1778, Colonel Hunter writes to President Wharton, and informs him what orders he had given. Colonel Antes also came down to Fort Augusta to consult what was best to be done, as parties of Indians were constantly seen prowling around. Three companies of Colonel Long's battalion were ordered to hold themselves in readiness at a moment's warning, subject to the order of Colonel Antes.

The party of Indians that murdered the man about the 1st of January, above the Great Island, were eleven in number. They were pursued by Antes' command, and as a light snow had fallen, were tracked easily. The whites came up with them, and succeeded in killing two. The rest fled, and could not be overtaken, although they followed them for a long distance.

Arms were very scarce. Colonel Hunter informs President Wharton, on the 28th of March, 1778, that he had endeavored to purchase "some good guns," but could get none. Two rifles and sixty ordinary muskets were all the public arms in the County at that time.

It is supposed, however, that nearly all the settlers had private arms of their own. All the guns worth repairing were being put in order, and, says Colonel Hunter, "I have promised the gunsmiths their pay for so doing."

It appears that the fifth class of militia, as they were called, were only to serve two months. As soon as their term expired, the sixth class were ordered to relieve them. The people complained that if no troops were stationed above Muncy, they would be obliged to abandon their settlements, and go down the river.

On the 5th of May, Colonel Hunter writes, that he could get no provisions to buy for them. All that could be obtained was some beef and pork, that had been purchased, by Colonel Hugh White, for the Continental stores. Of flour there was a small quantity.

About this time Colonel John Kelly's battalion was ordered to Penn's Valley, to perform duty for two months, where Jacob Stanford, his wife and daughter, were inhumanly killed and scalped, and his son, a lad of ten years, carried into captivity.

Some time in the year 1778, an Indian suddenly appeared on the bank of the river where Lockport now stands—having come down the deep ravine at that place—and made signs to the garrison at Reed's Fort to come with a canoe, and take him over. They feared, however, that he might be a decoy, and refused to venture for him. He insisted, however, and to show his good intentions, waded out into the river as far as he could. One of the women, supposed to be Mrs. Reed, seeing that none of the men would venture, jumped into a canoe, crossed over alone and brought him with safety. He proved to be a friendly Indian, and had travelled a long way to warn the settlers that a powerful band was preparing to make a descent upon the Valley, for the purpose of exterminating the settlements.

Being much exhausted, and feeling perfectly safe, after delivering his message, he went and laid down to seek some repose, and was soon buried in a profound slumber.

A number of men about the fort were shooting at a mark, amongst whom was one named Dewitt, who was slightly intoxicated. Loading his rifle, he observed to some of them that he would make the bullet he was putting in, kill an Indian. Little attention was paid to the remark at the time. He made good his word, however; and instead of shooting at the mark, fired at the sleeping Indian, and *shot him dead!* A baser act of ingratitude cannot well be conceived. The murder was unprovoked and cowardly, and rendered doubly worse, from the fact that the Indian had travelled many miles to inform them of their danger!

The garrison were so exasperated at this inhuman and ungrateful act, that they threatened to lynch him on the spot; when, becoming alarmed, he fled, and was suffered to escape. He never was heard of more, and probably fell, as he richly deserved, by the tomahawk of the enemy.

A party of Indians having penetrated into Buffalo Valley, and secured a large amount of plunder, were hotly pursued by Lieutenant Moses Van Campen, with a party of men. They came so close upon them that they were obliged to abandon their ill-gotten booty, at a large spring near the residence of Mr. George Brown, back of Jersey Shore. It is stated that several valuable articles, such as silver tankards, &c., were recovered at this place.

Residence of D. K. Jackman, Lock Haven, Pa.

CHAPTER XXVI.

MURDER OF WINTERS' PARTY—SETTLERS CARRIED INTO CAPTIVITY—CAPTURE OF ANDREW ARMSTRONG AND HIS SON—ESCAPE OF HIS WIFE—A HARD CASE FOR HER TO DECIDE—THE SURPRISE AT PINE CREEK—ESCAPE OF JOHN HAMILTON—THE COVENHOVEN FAMILY—CAPTAIN BERRY'S EXPEDITION—SURPRISE AT LOYAL SOCK—DEATH OF JAMES COVENHOVEN—ESCAPE OF ROBERT.

In the summer of 1778, William Winters, who was an early settler, came up from Berks county with several men to cut hay, in a field a short distance above where Williamsport now stands; with a view of bringing up his stock that fall. There were some ten or eleven men in the company. Six of them were in the field, near the river, mowing, when a party of Indians suddenly appeared, and shot and scalped them all in a few moments. The others were at the cabin, which stood near where the public road now passes; Winters was preparing dinner, when the sharp reports of the rifles, and the exultant yells of the savages were heard. Being satisfied that their comrades were killed, they immediately fled, and secreted themselves in the woods till night. The Indians not suspecting that any others were near, passed on. In the night, Winters and his men ventured forth and went to the meadow, where they collected the bodies of the murdered men in a pile, and instead of burying them, covered them carefully with a large quantity of freshly mown hay. Then proceeding as quickly as possible to the river, they raised their canoes that had been sunk to conceal them, and sorrowfully commenced their return.

The following spring he returned with a body of armed men, and strange to relate, found the bodies of the six men undisturbed, just as he had placed them, and in a remarkably good state of preservation. Very little, if any, change having taken place.

Their bodies were taken, and carefully buried in what is now the old Lycoming graveyard. Probably they were the first interred there.

An Indian war had now commenced, and was raging along the Valley. All improvements were at an end, and most of the settlers' houses burned, whilst the terrified inhabitants were fleeing from the country.

In May, the sixth and seventh classes of Colonel Long's battalion were ordered to be embodied by Colonel Hunter, and scout along the frontier, until the sixth and seventh classes of Colonel Murray's and Hosterman's battalions should arrive at the Great Island, to cover the frontier there.

Colonel Hunter writes to Mr. Wharton, President of the Council, under date of May 14th, 1778, as follows, concerning these detachments:

"These last Classes would have marched before this time only for want of Provisions, as for meat there is very little to be had in this County, and that very dear; Bacon sells at 4*s* 6*d* ℔ pound, and flower at three pounds ten shillings ℔ Hundred wt. I have ordered some People that lives nigh the Great Island to preserve Shad and Barrel them up for the use of the Militia that will be stationed there this summer.

Col. William Cook will undertake to provide Provisions for the Militia of this County, in case he was supplied with Cash at this present time, as he would go to some other County to purchase some meat, for I am certain it will be Very much wanted, in case the Savages Commence a war with the frontiers, all must turn out to prevent if possible, such a Crual Enemy from makeing inroads into our part of the Country. We are scarce of Guns, not more than one half of the Militia is provided with Arms, and a number of them Very Ordinary; Our Powder is Exceeding Bad, and not fit for Rifles in any shape. And as for Flints we can get none to Buy; all this I think proper to acquaint the Council with, &c."

On the 16th of May, near the mouth of Bald Eagle Creek, three men who were at work putting in a small field of corn, were attacked by a party of Indians, killed and scalped. Two days following this, near Pine Creek, a man, woman, and child, were taken prisoners, probably by the same party, and carried off.

On the 20th of the same month, two men, and seven women and children, were taken from one house, near Lycoming Creek. They were all carried away as prisoners.

About the same time, three families, consisting of sixteen in number, were killed and carried away from Loyal Sock. A party that went up from Wallis' only found two dead bodies, from which they supposed the remainder were taken prisoners. Their houses were all reduced to ashes.

It is to be very much regretted that the names of all those mentioned above, who were killed or carried into captivity, were not preserved.

About this time, Andrew Armstrong, who settled at the "big spring," below where Linden now stands, was visited by a party of Indians. They came very suddenly. On the alarm being given, Mrs. Armstrong, who was *enciente*, slipped under the bed. The Indians entered the house, and seizing Armstrong, his little son, and a woman named Nancy Bunday, made preparations to carry them away. Armstrong told his wife to lay still, which she did, and escaped. They were in a great hurry, on account of a small body of men being stationed a short distance below, and did not take time to fire the building. They turned up the creek with their prisoners. Mrs. Armstrong crawled from her hiding place, and looking out of the window, beheld her husband and little son disappear in the forest with them. Years rolled away, and no tidings were had from Andrew Armstrong. No doubt they had cruelly murdered him. The little son was also given up for lost, and the mother had ceased to mourn, and became resigned to her hard lot.

Many years after peace had been restored, and the settlers had returned to their homes, an aged Indian, with a young man by his side, bearing unmistakable signs of having white blood in his veins, knocked at the cottage door of the widow Armstrong, one pleasant autumn afternoon. He alleged that this was her son that had been carried off years ago, when a mere child. But he was grown to manhood, and partook so much of the character and disposition of an Indian, that she could not recognize him as her long lost son. The scenes of that sorrowful day were brought fresh to her mind, and her heart yearned for the little flaxen haired boy. Could this noble youth, of athletic form, and piercing eye, be he? Could he be so changed? Thus she reasoned. She could not feel positive that he was her son—neither was she *certain* that he was not. If she was to own him, and he was *not* hers, she never could extend to him the affections of a mother; and if she turned him away, and he *was* her son, oh! what remorse of conscience would she feel. A terrible conflict was going on in her mind. She never could bring herself, however, to believe that he was in *reality* her boy. Doubts still remained in her mind. He remained about the settlement for some time, but had all the manners and habits of an Indian, and never seemed to readily embrace the usages of civilized life. He finally left the neighborhood, on finding that she would not recognize him as her son, and returned to his tawny comrades of the forest. He never came again.

It was evident that white blood coursed in his veins, but he was in every other respect an Indian. Many of the old settlers believed that he was, *in reality*, the lost boy.

About this time, in the same year, four men, named Robert Fleming, Robert Donaldson, James McMichael, and John Hamilton, started from Fort Antes, to go to Horn's Fort, in a canoe. Nothing occurred till they came opposite the mouth of Pine Creek, when they were suddenly fired upon by a party of Indians, who lay concealed in a sink hole on the south side of the river, and all were killed but Hamilton. He immediately sprang out of the canoe into the water, and keeping it between him and the Indians, by holding on with one hand, managed with the other to work his way across the river. Several shots were fired at him without effect. He managed to dodge his head behind the canoe. As soon as he reached the shore, he sprang out and ran through the "barrens," till he came opposite to Fort Antes, where he cried for assistance, and was speedily brought over. Nearly all the clothing was stripped from his body in his rapid flight through the bushes.

The same day that this melancholy affair took place, a party of men were driving some cattle down from above the Great Island. Crossing the plains near where Liberty now stands, they were fired upon by a party of Indians. The whites immediately returned the fire, when an Indian was observed to fall, and was carried off. A man, named Samuel Fleming, was shot through the shoulder. The Indians fled very precipitately, and abandoned a large amount of plunder, principally consisting of blankets, which fell into the hands of the whites.

Andrew Fleming settled on Pine Creek, in the vicinity of where Matthew McKinney's house now stands. On Christmas-day, 1778, he took down his rifle, and observed to his wife, that he would go and kill a deer. He started up the ravine, and had not been gone long, before the report of a gun was heard. The day wore away and he did not return. His wife became alarmed at his protracted absence, and feared that evil might have befallen him. Proceeding up the ravine to look for him, she suddenly perceived three savages skulking in the bushes, and her worst suspicions were at once aroused. Returning hastily, she gave the alarm, and a number of neighbors collected, and proceeded to search for her husband. They had gone but a short distance, when they came to his dead body. Three balls had passed through him,—one having entered his eye. The scalp was removed. It was supposed that the guns had been fired simultaneously, making but one report.

About the commencement of the Revolution, the father of Robert Covenhoven, immigrated from New Jersey, and settled on Loyal Sock Creek. He had three sons, named respectively, James, Thomas, and Robert. The latter became distinguished as a guide, a spy, and

Indian killer; and was in several battles of the Revolution. Shortly after coming to this Valley, the old man lost all his effects by a sudden freshet in the creek.

Late in the year 1777, Robert returned to the West Branch, from the Continental army, his term of enlistment having expired. His extensive knowledge of the country, the character, habits, and disposition of the Indians, acquired whilst serving with surveying parties, was of great service, and he was disposed to make good use of it for the benefit of the settlement.

An old man named Wychoff, who appears to have been an uncle to the Covenhovens, also settled about Loyal Sock. He was a Tanner by trade, and soon erected a rude tannery, and commenced making leather for the settlement. One day, in the summer of 1778, the Covenhoven boys were mowing in a meadow, and the old man Wychoff, was at work in his tannery. A dog suddenly commenced barking, and exhibited great symptoms of alarm; he would run towards the woods, snuff the air, and return. The boys were satisfied that Indians were lurking near. They took their rifles and warned the old man to leave; this he at first refused to do, alleging that there was no danger. They finally induced him to go with them; they had not proceeded far, till one of them hissed the dog, when he bounded into the bushes, and seized an Indian by the leg, where he was lying concealed. He rose immediately, and shot the faithful animal. The whites, who were in all, six in number, immediately jumped to trees—the Indians did the same, and the firing commenced. Wychoff, who was very much hump-backed, got behind a tree that was too small to hide all of his person. Fortunately for him, another small tree stood between him and the Indians, and as they fired at him, their bullets struck this tree, and made the bark fly around Robert Covenhoven who was near. He yelled at the old man to stand up straight, or he would be hit. As he was loading his rifle, his ramrod was shot in two, but luckily he had a wiper, with which he rammed down the bullet. Just at this moment, he observed an Indian stealthily creeping round to get a fair shot at old Wychoff; watching him closely, till he attempted to crawl over a log, he fired, and shot him through the body. He sprang in the air, gave a tremendous yell, and fell. His comrades rushed up and bore him off, when the whites made away as rapidly as possible. He appeared to be the chief, or commander of the party, and no doubt it was lucky for the whites that he was shot.

The danger became so great, and such a panic seized the inhabitants, that nearly all of them about Muncy fled to Brady's Fort. Those above that, up to Lycoming creek, took refuge at Wallis'. All above Lycoming and Pine creeks, were at Antes' and Horn's Forts. The inhabitants of Penn's Valley, gathered to Potter's Fort. Those below the Muncy Hills, to Chilisquaque, were assembled at Freeland's and Boon's Forts, and Sunbury. Those in White Deer, and Buffalo Valleys, fled to the river, and forted themselves at various points. This took place in the summer of 1778.* Colonel Hunter, in a letter to John Hambright, says, that it was very distressing to see the poor settlers flying and leaving their homes. The immigrants from New Jersey, who had come up that spring and winter, set off again as rapidly as they could travel to their old homes.

Colonel Hepburn, afterwards Judge Hepburn, was sta-

* See page 570 of Penna. Archives for 1777–8.

tioned for a while at Muncy Fort, and commanded it. Colonel Hosterman, Captain Reynolds, Captain Berry, and others, were sent up soon after, to assist in protecting the frontier.

A number of horses had strayed away, and were supposed to have gone to Loyal Sock. Captain Berry was ordered to take a company of twelve men, and look after them. Robert Covenhoven, his two brothers, James and Thomas, and his uncle, William Wychoff, were in the expedition. They proceeded to Loyal Sock, where, it appears, they separated. Peter Shoefelt, William Wychoff, and a man named Thompson, went above the creek, towards Williamsport, to Thompson's house, for the purpose of saving some of his property.

The remainder of the party continued up the creek. They proceeded cautiously through the narrows, but saw no signs of Indians. Not finding the horses, it was concluded to return. Covenhoven was suspicious that Indians were about, and advised Captain Berry not to return by the path they had come, as he feared an ambuscade. Berry thought there was no danger, and paid but little attention to him, who still *insisted* on taking another route over the mountain. Berry at length accused him of cowardice, and being needlessly alarmed. This irritated him very much, but he insisted no more, and going to his brothers, communicated to them his fears that they would be attacked by the enemy and probably all killed. He requested them to keep a sharp lookout, and if the flash of a gun was seen, to jump to trees immediately.

They travelled on without any molestation, till they came to the narrows, and true to Covenhoven's expectation, were suddenly fired upon by a party of savages in ambush. Most of the party, including the reckless

Capt. Berry, were shot down. James was shot through the shoulder, and disabled. He cried to Robert that he was wounded, and could do nothing, who immediately told him to run across the creek, and he would try and cover his retreat. He succeeded in getting to the opposite side, when a ball struck him on the back part of the head, and he fell back on the edge of the creek dead. Robert ran for life, and jumped into an old tree top, where he loaded his rifle. He had not been there many minutes, till a big savage came and stood on a log within a few feet of where he lay, looking all around and up the hill. He watched his eye, and was prepared to shoot the moment he was discovered, and then run for his life. Had the Indian but cast his eye down at his feet, he would have beheld Covenhoven. He soon ran back over the creek, where they were scalping the killed. The shrieks of the wounded, and the yells of the savages, were terrible. Covenhoven soon crawled out of the tree top, and worked his way carefully up the mountain. An open spot of ground was before him, which he dare not cross, for fear of being seen and pursued. Coming to where an old tree had been blown out of root, he lay down in the hole and remained there till dark, when he started across the hills and reached Wallis' Fort in safety, and reported to the garrison the melancholy fate of the expedition.

His brother Thomas, with several others, was taken prisoner and carried into captivity. He returned after the war.

CHAPTER XXVII.

MURDER OF SHOEFELT AND THOMPSON—COLONEL HOSTERMAN'S PARTY—CRUEL MASSACRE WHERE WILLIAMSPORT NOW STANDS—PETER SMITH AND HIS DAUGHTER—ONE BRAVE MAN—ARRIVAL OF COLONEL HEPBURN—HORRIBLE APPEARANCE OF THE DEAD—KING'S WIFE—ORDERS TO LEAVE THE COUNTRY—THE BIG RUNAWAY—COLONEL HUNTER'S APPEAL.

WHEN Wychoff, Thompson, and Shoefelt came to Thompson's house, it is said they hitched their horses—for *they* appeared to have been riding—and went in and commenced cooking their dinner. The Indians having been quietly observing the movements of the two parties, sent a party to capture them. When they came in sight, the horses snorted and gave the alarm. Seizing their rifles, they attempted to run for the woods, but the Indians were too quick, and firing a volley, killed Thompson and Shoefelt, and shot Wychoff through the shoulder, wounding him severely. He was taken prisoner, and returned after a captivity of two years.

A story is related in connection with this tragical affair, but with how much truth I cannot say, that when Wychoff was taken prisoner, he was quite bald headed; but when he returned from captivity, he had a fine head of hair.

On the same day that this sad disaster befell Captain

Berry, Colonel Hosterman,* with Captain Reynolds, and a party of thirteen men, set out from Muncy Farm, to go to Antes' Fort and the Great Island, with ammunition for those places. When they came to Loyal Sock, they heard considerable firing and yelling up the creek. They supposed it to be nearly a mile distant, and proceeded as rapidly as possible in that direction. When they came to the place where they supposed the firing to have been, no Indians were discovered. They had probably seen them and made off. A noise was heard by them, however, as of some one striking on a hollow tree with a club, some distance ahead. A stroke appeared to be given for each man in the party. They then returned, and continued on to the residence of Thompson. When they arrived, the barn was on fire, but the house remained untouched. Thompson's powder horn was found near the house, with a bullet hole through it, and several moccasin and shoe tracks were observed. Nothing could be seen or heard of Thompson, Shoefelt, or Wychoff; the three men that were known to have gone there. Before they came to the house, however, they heard the death yells, and one that they took to be for a prisoner, given by Indians in the woods, which now impressed them with the idea, that the three men were killed or taken prisoners.

On the same day, the 10th of June, 1778, Peter Smith,† his wife and six children; William King's wife and two children; Michael Smith, Michael Campbell,

* See Penna. Archives for 1777–8, page 589.

† Colonel Hosterman, in his letter giving an account of this affair, states that the party in the wagon were travelling *to* Lycoming. This is evidently an error, as the settlers had mostly fled at this time, and they were probably flying also, and trying to reach fort Muncy.

David Chambers, —— Snodgrass, and —— Hammond; being seven men, two women, and eight children in all, started from Lycoming Creek to go to Muncy fort in a four horse wagon. They had got but a short distance, when they were met by a messenger and informed that considerable firing had been heard about Loyal Sock that day, and it was not considered safe for them to proceed. Peter Smith informed the messenger that he would not be stopped by the firing, and would continue on. He returned and reported Smith's intentions, whereupon a party pushed on to meet them. This party is supposed to have been Colonel Hosterman's. It was near night, however, and they did not reach them.

When the men with the wagon, and the women and children, reached the spot of ground now said to be occupied by Hall's foundry, in Williamsport, they were fired upon by a body of Indians, supposed to have been about twenty in number. At the first fire Snodgrass fell dead. The Indians only discharged two guns, when they made a rush, tomahawk in hand, for the wagon. They were not observed till the fire had been given, when the remaining white men immediately jumped to trees, and commenced fighting for their lives and their women and little children. The Indians closed in and endeavored to surround them, when all the men, with the exception of Campbell, *ran*, and abandoned the defenceless women and children to the horrible fate that awaited them! A little boy escaped, and running to Lycoming, informed some men there of what had happened. The men that escaped, state that they looked back, and saw the savages tomahawking the women and children; and Campbell was closely engaged with an Indian fighting nobly.

Peter Smith ran into a rye field close by, and on looking back perceived something following him; supposing it to be an Indian, he ran as fast as possible, but on climbing the fence discovered that it was his little daughter, who, with arms stretched towards him, was following as fast as she could, and imploring him to wait and save her! It is scarcely necessary to add that the *flying* father's heart was deeply touched, and waiting a moment, snatched the child up in his arms and fled for life! He escaped to fort Muncy. What became of the other men is not stated.

When the boy gave the alarm at Lycoming, they misunderstood him, and thinking it was a canoe that had been attacked in the river near where they lived, ran there at once. It was now dark, the massacre having occurred about sundown, when Colonel Hepburn, with a party that had started out, on the alarm being given by the fugitives flying from Loyal Sock, came to the spot. They found the body of Snodgrass and another, but it was too dark to do anything, and they pushed on to Lycoming Creek, where they remained till morning. The next day, being the 11th of June, they returned to the scene of the massacre, and there beheld a revolting and horrible sight. Peter Smith's wife was found shot through the body, stabbed, scalped, and a knife by her side. William King's wife was tomahawked and scalped, but still survived, and was sitting up when they came. Her husband came to her, when she leaned on him, and almost immediately expired. She appeared to be sensible, but could not speak a word, and presented a sickening sight, her face being covered with clotted blood.

A little girl was found killed and scalped, and a boy the same. Campbell was found killed, stabbed, and scalped—he had also been shot in the back, and a knife was sticking in his body. Everything around him indicated that he had maintained a fearful struggle with superior numbers, and sold his life as dearly as possible. An Indian gun was found near him broken to pieces. His gun was gone. What became of the remainder of the children is not stated, but they were probably carried into captivity. The Indians took but a few things out of the wagon, which they left standing. They probably took the horses.

A party under Captain Shaffer, it is stated, went to Thompson's house and searched for him. At length they found him and Shoefelt outside of a field among some pine grubs. Thompson had been shot through the side—Shoefelt was shot through the shoulder—they were both scalped, and lay but a short distance apart. They appeared to have been so near Thompson when he was shot, that his jacket was burned.

This was indeed a bloody day—the savages glutted themselves with murder and plunder, and returned in triumph. A gloomy pall seemed suspended over the infant settlement, and weeping and wailing was heard on every hand. Children were murdered before their parents' eyes; husbands were compelled to witness the horrid deaths of their wives—and in turn children were compelled to gaze upon the mangled bodies of their parents. Neither age, sex, nor condition was spared. The wails of helpless infants; the imploring cries of defenceless women, failed to awaken a chord of pity in the adamantine bosom of the tawny savage—he laughed their pitiful appeals to scorn, and with a fiendish grin of pleasure, plied the knife, and tore the reeking scalp from their heads.

How many of the present inhabitants of the beautiful

and flourishing town of Williamsport, are aware that on the 10th day of June, 1778, such a fearful and bloody tragedy was enacted upon the site of that town, and the cry of helpless innocence mingled with the whoop of the savage, awoke the echoes of the forest, and ascended to the azure-realms of heaven?

On the intelligence of these murders reaching Colonel Hunter, at fort Augusta, he became alarmed for the safety of those that remained above fort Muncy, and sent word to Colonel Hepburn to order them to abandon the country, and retire below. He was obliged to do this, as there was not a sufficiency of troops to guard the whole frontier, and Congress had taken no action to supply him with men and supplies. Colonel Hepburn had some trouble to get a messenger to carry the order up to Colonel Antes, so panic-stricken were the people on account of the ravages of the Indians. At length Robert Covenhoven, and a young millwright in the employ of Andrew Culbertson, volunteered their services, and started on the dangerous mission. They crossed the river and ascended Bald Eagle mountain, and kept along the summit, till they came to the gap opposite Antes' fort. They cautiously descended at the head of Nippenose Bottom, and proceeded to the fort. It was in the evening, and as they neared the fort, the report of a rifle rang upon their ears. A girl had gone outside to milk a cow, and an Indian being in ambush, fired upon her. The ball, fortunately, passed through her clothes, and she escaped unharmed. The word was passed on up to Horn's fort, and preparations made for the flight. Great excitement prevailed. Canoes were collected, rafts hastily constructed, and every available craft that would float, pressed into service; and the goods, and also the wives and children of the settlers, placed on board. The men armed with their trusty rifles, marched down on each side of the river to guard the convoy. It was indeed a sudden, as well as melancholy, flight. They were leaving their homes, their cattle, and their crops, to the mercy of the enemy, and fleeing for their lives. Nothing occurred worthy of note, during the passage to Sunbury, as the Indians did not venture to attack the armed force that marched on shore. It is said that whenever any of their crafts would ground on a bar, the women would jump out, and putting their shoulders against it, launch it into deep water.

The settlements above Muncy Fort were all abandoned, and the Indians had full possession of the country once more. Companies came up as soon as possible to secure and drive away their cattle. They found the Indians burning and destroying. When they came to Robert King's improvement—where Robert King, Junr., now lives—they found the remains of his house and barn yet smoking. Passing on to Antes' Fort, they found the mill, containing a quantity of wheat, and the surrounding buildings, reduced to ashes. As the smouldering embers were not yet extinct, the air for some distance around, was tainted with the odor of roasted wheat. They gathered up what cattle they could as soon as possible, and drove them off from this scene of desolation.

Fort Muncy, Freeland's Fort, and all the intermediate points, were abandoned about the same time. Thus was the Valley of the West Branch evacuated. This flight was called by the people of that period, the "*Big Runaway*," a name which it bears to this day.

Shortly after the *Big Runaway*, the attention of the

savages was attracted to the memorable descent upon Wyoming, which took place the 3d of July, 1778. But few remained on the West Branch, nearly all having gone to participate in that bloody massacre.

Petitions were immediately drawn up and signed, and letters written, importuning the government to send troops to Northumberland county, to protect the settlers whilst they returned to cut their harvests. The harvest was ripe—the settlers had fled, and dare not return without an armed force. What else could they do?

On the 12th of July, Colonel Hunter drew up and forwarded the following pathetic *appeal* to the Executive Council, which will be read with interest:

"*To His Excellency The President and The Honble The Executive Council of the Commonwealth of Pennsylvania.*

"The Calamities so long dreaded, and of which ye have been more than once informed must fall upon this County if not assisted by Continental Troop or the Militia of the neighboring Counties, now appear with all the Horrors attendant on an Indian war; at this date the Towns of Sunbury and Northumberland on the Frontiers where a few Virtuous Inhabitants and fugitives seem determined to stand, Tho' doubtful whether To-morrow's sun will rise on them, freemen, Captives or in eternity. Yet relying on that being who never forsakes the virtuous, and the timely assistance of the Government, which they have with Zeal and vigor endeavoured to support, they say they will remain so long as they can without incurring the censure of suicide. The Carnage at Wioming, the devastations and murders upon the West branch of Susquehanna, On Bald Eagle Creek, and in short throughout the whole County to within a few miles of these Towns (the recital of which must be shocking) I suppose must have before now have reached your ears, if not you may figure yourselves men, women, and children, Butchered and scalped, many of them after being promised quarters, and some scalped alive, of which we have miserable Instances amongst us, People in crowds driven from their farms and habitations, many of whom have not money to purchase one day's provisions for their families, which must and has already obliged many of them to Plunder and lay waste the farms as they pass along. These Calamities must if not speedily remedied by a reinforcement of men from below inevitably ruin the frontier, and incumber the interior Counties with such numbers of indigent fugitives unable to support themselves as will like locusts devour all before them. If we are assisted to stand and save our crops, we will have enough for ourselves and to spare, you need be under no apprehension of any troops you send here suffering for want of provisions if they come in time, before the few who yet remain are obliged to give way, with men it will be necessary to send arms and ammunition as we are ill provided with them. Gentlemen, ye must all know that this County cannot be strong in men after the number it has furnished to serve the united states. Their applications to us for men were always complyed with to the utmost of our abilities and with the greatest alacrity; should our supplications now be rejected I think the survivors of us, (if any) may safely say that Virtue is not rewarded, I have only to add that A few Hundreds of men well armed and immediately sent to our relief would prevent much bloodshed, confusion and devastation through many Counties of this State, as the appearance of being supported would call back many of our fugitives to save their Harvest for their subsistence, rather than suffer the inconveniences which reason tells me they do down the Country and their with their families return must ease the people below of a heavy and unprofitable Burthen. These opinions I submit to your serious Consideration.

"Signed.

"SAMUEL HUNTER.

"Sunbury, 12th July, 1778."

CHAPTER XXVIII.

ARRIVAL OF COLONEL BROADHEAD—SETTLERS RETURN AND CUT THEIR HARVEST—WALLIS' LETTER—MELANCHOLY DEATH OF YOUNG BRADY—GRIEF OF HIS MOTHER—DEATH OF THE CHIEF BALD EAGLE—REINFORCEMENTS—MORE MURDERS—ESCAPE OF MRS. M'NIGHT AND CHILD—CRUEL SCALPING OF MRS. DURHAM—HER RECOVERY.

Colonel Broadhead having been ordered to the assistance of the settlement at Wyoming, and on his arrival at Sunbury, finding it was *too* late to be of any service there, marched his command up to Fort Muncy, and took possession of the deserted country. The appearance of an armed force, and the assurance of protection, induced most of the settlers to return and cut their grain. The Colonel was very active in scouring the country, and stationing men at various points, for the protection of the harvesters. He despatched a Captain, and twenty-five men, to take post at General Potter's fort, in Penn's Valley, and protect the reapers there. This left him one hundred and twenty at Muncy.

On the evening of the 23d of July, an Indian was discovered by one of the sentinels approaching the fort, in a skulking manner. He fired on him at the distance one hundred and fifty yards, when he made off.

Samuel Wallis, (who appears to have returned also,)

writes to Colonel Matlack, on the 24th of July, from Fort Muncy, and finds a great deal of fault with Colonel Hunter; who, he alleges, on hearing of the massacre at Wyoming, became alarmed and ordered all the troops off the West Branch. This move created so much alarm, that a great number of the people of Sunbury fled, and when he (Wallis) reached that place with his family, he found that Colonel Hunter had removed *his* family and effects, and was ready at a moment to fly himself; and had it not been for Colonel Broadhead, he is of the opinion, not ten families would now have been found in the county. He was exceedingly anxious to have some regular troops sent up, as he had no dependence in the militia. Concerning them, he says:

"Such confusion has already happened by trusting to the Militia here, that I can & do declare for myself, that I will not stay a single moment longer than I can help after being assured that we are to be protected by them only. We were amused some time ago by a resolve of Congress for raising 100 six months men in this County, & Col. Hunter was pleased to assure the Counsil that the men would be readyly raised, when he at the same time knew, & was pleased to declare, in private conversation, that it was Impossible to raise 100 men amongst People so much confused and alarmed. This kind of Conduct from Col. Hunter, as well as a number of our other leading men, has brought us to the pass you now find us, & unless some speedy Interposition in our behalf, I do again with great Confidence assure you that we shall be no Longer a People in this County, & when the matter will end God only knows."

Such was the independent, yet mournful tone of Wallis' letter, which no doubt gave a pretty correct account of the state of affairs.

General Potter returned to Penn's Valley, on the 25th of July, having been absent on duty, and immediately writes that the people are pretty generally returned and cutting their harvest. The loss sustained to the county, by the *Biy Runaway*, he sets down at £40,000.

The appeals of the people to Congress, were not all in vain, and that body at length ordered Colonel Hartley to the West Branch, with his regiment. He arrived in August, and immediately took measures for strengthening the fort on Muncy Farm. A body of militia were ordered out in the county, amounting to three hundred men. The people seemed much encouraged, and returned in greater numbers.

Nothing unusual occurred till the 8th of August, when a party of Indians fell upon a number of reapers, a short distance below Williamsport, and cruelly murdered young Brady. The circumstance is about as follows:

A Corporal and four men, belonging to Colonel Hartley's regiment, and three militiamen, were ordered about two miles above Loyal Sock, on the 8th of August, 1778, to protect fourteen reapers and cradlers, who went to assist Peter Smith, the unfortunate man that had his wife and four children murdered about a month previous, to cut his crop. Smith's farm was on Turkey Run, not far from Williamsport, on the opposite side of the river.

James Brady, son of Captain John, the younger brother of Captain Sam. Brady of the Rangers, was with the party. According to custom in those days, when no commissioned officer was present, the company generally selected a leader, whom they styled "Captain," and obeyed him as such. Young James Brady was selected Captain of this little band of about twenty men.

On arriving at the field they placed two sentinels at the opposite ends, the sides having clear land around. The day being Friday, they cut the greater part of the grain, and intended to complete it the next morning. Four of the reapers improperly left that night, and returned to the fort. A strict watch was kept all night, but nothing unusual occurred. In the morning they all went to work; the cradlers, four in number, by themselves, near the house; the reapers in another part of the field. The reapers, except young Brady, placed their guns round a tree. He thought this was wrong, and placed his some distance from the rest. The morning proved to be very foggy, and about an hour after sunrise, the sentinels and reapers were surprised by a number of Indians, under cover of the fog, quietly approaching them. The sentinels fired and ran towards the reapers, when they all ran, with the exception of young Brady. He made towards his rifle, pursued by three Indians, and when within a few yards of it was fired upon by a *white man* with a pistol, (probably a tory,) but falling over a sheaf of grain, the shot missed him. He rose again, and when almost within reach of the rifle, was wounded by a shot from an Indian. Here another sentinel fired his gun, but was immediately, with a militiaman, shot down. Brady succeeded in getting his rifle, however, and shot the first Indian dead. He caught up another gun, and brought down a second savage, when they closed around him in numbers, but being a stout active man, he struggled with them for some time. At length one of them struck a tomahawk into his head, when he fell, and was wounded with a spear* in the hands of another. He was so stunned with the blow of the tomahawk, that he re-

* Penna. Archives for 1777–8, page 689; and page 307, ix. vol. Hazard's Register.

mained powerless, but strange as it may seem, retained his senses. They ruthlessly tore the scalp from his head as he lay in apparent death, and it was a glorious trophy for them, for he had long and remarkably red hair.

The cradlers, who it appears were in a low spot, in a distant part of the field, on hearing the alarm, ascended an eminence and partly beheld this unhappy affair. The Indians, as soon as they accomplished their bloody work, left instantly, probably fearing an attack from the whites.

The Corporal and three men, with the cradlers, proposed to make a stand, but the others thought it imprudent, and they all immediately left. The cradlers being acquainted with the country, took the nearest way to Wallis'; the Corporal and his three men pushed right down the road. At Loyal Sock they were fired upon by a party of Indians, probably the same that killed Brady. They returned the fire, when the Indians fled, and they retook three horses from them, and brought them to the fort in safety.

After Brady was scalped, he related that a little Indian was called and made to strike the tomahawk into his head, in four separate places. He was probably taking lessons in the art of butchery.

After coming to himself, he attempted, between walking and creeping, to reach the cabin, where an old man named Jerome Vaness, had been employed to cook for them. On hearing the report of the guns, he had hid himself, but when he saw Brady return, he came to him. James begged the old man to fly to the fort, saying, "the Indians will soon be back and will kill you." The worthy man positively refused to leave him alone, but stayed and endeavored to dress his frightful wounds. Brady requested to be assisted down to the river, where he drank large quantities of water, when he still insisted on the old man leaving him and trying to save himself, but he would not do it. He then directed his faithful old friend to load the gun that was in the cabin, which was done, and put into his hands, when he laid down and appeared to sleep.

As soon as the sad intelligence reached the fort, Captain Walker mustered a party of men and proceeded to the spot. When they came to the river bank, Brady heard the noise, and supposing it was Indians, jumped to his feet and cocked his gun. But it was friends. They made a bier and placed him on it, and brought him away. He requested to be taken to Sunbury to his mother. His request was granted, and a party started with him, amongst whom was Robert Covenhoven. He became very feverish by the way, and drank large quantities of water, and became partly delirious. It was late at night when they arrived at Sunbury, and did not intend to arouse his mother, but it seemed she had a presentiment of something that was to happen, and being awake to alarms, met them at the river and assisted to convey her wounded son to the house. He presented a frightful spectacle, and the meeting of mother and son is described to have been heart-rending. Her heart was wrung with the keenest anguish, and her lamentations were terrible to be heard.

The young Captain lived five days. The first four he was delirious, on the fifth his reason returned, and he described the whole scene he had passed through very vividly, and with great minuteness. He said the Indians were of the Seneca tribe, and amongst them were two chiefs; one of whom was a very large man, and from the description was supposed to be Cornplanter; the other he personally knew to be the celebrated chief Bald Eagle, who had his nest near where Milesburg now stands.

On the evening of the fifth day, the young Captain died, deeply regretted by all who knew him, for he was a noble and promising young man. Vengeance, "not loud, but deep," was breathed against the Bald Eagle, but he laughed it to scorn, till the fatal day at Brady's Bend on the Alleghany.*

Small parties of Indians were continually skulking about, and it was very unsafe to venture from the forts. Having gained so much plunder recently, it seemed that they had become bolder, and committed greater depredations with impunity.

On the 20th of August, Colonel Hunter writes, that in accordance with the resolution of Congress, and the instructions of the Council, he had succeeded in raising a company of volunteers to serve six months, and had appointed the officers. The Company was now doing duty, and numbered about sixty men. The expense of raising the company was considerable. Each man that furnished himself with a good rifle and accoutrements, was to have eighty dollars; this was the basis upon which it was raised.

* Several years after the death of James Brady, a large party of Senecas, under the command of Cornplanter, were marching along the Alleghany river on their way to Bald Eagle's nest. Captain Sam. Brady recognized the Bald Eagle that day, and fired at him. When the battle was over he searched for his body and found it. The ball had pierced his heart, and the blood of the young Captain at Loyal Sock was fatally avenged by the hands of his brother on the banks of the Alleghany.—*Hazard's Register*, page 237, vol. ix.

The militia who had served their turn, complained loudly about their pay. Most of them were very poor on account of losing all their property, particularly those about Loyal Sock.

At this time, one hundred men belonging to Colonel Hartley's regiment; two hundred and twenty of Lancaster County militia; one hundred and seventy of Berks County; and one hundred of the Northumberland militia, and between sixty and seventy of Captain James Murray's company of six months' men, was the number of men enrolled in the Valley—amounting to upwards of seven hundred. This was a pretty effective force, and it was stationed to the best advantage, throughout the County, by Colonel Hartley.

On the first of September, Colonel Hartley informed the Executive Council, that he considered it highly important to have a small body of horse ordered to the County. He also wrote to the Board of War, requesting them to be sent.

From his letter, we learn that Captain Walker had succeeded in making the necessary repairs at Fort Muncy, and had a four pounder mounted on the walls. He had also succeeded in inducing some of the people to put in their fall crops.

Three German militia men, without arms or permission, went out from the fort, on the last day of August, to dig potatoes. Although they were in sight of the garrison, they were immediately attacked by the savages, who were lying in ambush. The Indians discharged all their guns at once. One militia man was killed and scalped, and another was seized and had a hard struggle with a stout Indian, for a few minutes, when the garrison came to his relief.

Some days before this affair—the 23d—a man named Cottner, was killed near the fort, and on the same day, Captain Martel was wounded. From these circumstances it can be inferred how exceedingly dangerous it was to venture out of the fort in those days. A large number of the descendants of Cottner still live about Muncy.

When the settlers at Fort Freeland returned after the *Big Runaway*, Jacob Freeland picketed in half an acre of ground around the fort, into which the people all collected with their families.

Some time in the autumn of 1778, Mrs. McNight, and Mrs. Durham, with small children in their arms, and mounted on horseback—with a number of men on foot —started from Freeland's Fort, to go to Northumberland. They met with no interruption till they had got one mile below the mouth of Warrior Run, when they were unexpectedly fired upon by a party of Indians. Mrs. McNight's horse suddenly wheeled and galloped back. She came very near losing her child, but caught it by the foot, and held it firmly, dangling by her side, till the frightened horse brought her to the fort. Mrs. Durham's infant was shot in her arms, when she fell from the horse. She was immediately scalped and left for dead.

Two young men, sons of Mrs. McNight, ran, on the alarm being given, and tried to secrete themselves under the bank of the river. Their place of concealment, however, was discovered by the Indians, and they were taken and carried into captivity.

Two men, named Peter and Elias Williams, were the first to find Mrs. Durham. On coming up to where she lay, they were greatly surprised to see her rise up and call for a drink of water! She had received no other injury, save the loss of her scalp. They took her to Sunbury, where her wounded head was dressed by Dr. Plunkett. It was a long time before it healed up completely. She finally recovered, and lived till within a few years. Many of the settlers about Warrior Run remember her well.

CHAPTER XXIX.

COLONEL HARTLEY'S EXPEDITION—DEPARTURE FROM MUNCY—FOLLOW THE SHESHEQUIN PATH—BAD TRAVELLING—SIGNS OF INDIANS—A SKIRMISH—TOWNS DESTROYED—LARGE BODY OF TORIES—MARCH FROM WYALUSING—A SEVERE BATTLE—KILLED AND WOUNDED, &c.

IN September, 1778, Colonel Hartley planned an expedition to Tioga and the North Branch, to destroy some Indian towns, and break up some of their principal places of rendezvous. The following is his report of the expedition, which will be found to be very interesting:

ADDRESS OF COLONEL HARTLEY TO CONGRESS, 1778.

"With a Frontier from Wioming to Allegany, we were sensible the few regular Troops we had could not defend the necessary posts. We thought (if it were practicable,) it would be best to draw the Principal part of our Force together, as the Inhabitants would be in no great danger during our absence. I made a stroke at some of the nearest Indian towns, especially as we learnt a handsome detachment had been sent into the Enemy's Country by the way of Cherry Valley. We were in hopes we should drive the Savages to a greater distance.

"With Volunteers and others we reckoned on 400 Rank & File for the expedition, besides 17 Horse, which I mounted from my own Regt., under the command of Mr. Carbery.

"Our Rendezvous was Fort Muncy, on the West Branch, intending to penitrate, by the Sheshecunnunk Path,* to Tioga, at the Junc-

* Sheshequin Path, struck up Bouser's run below Williamsport, and came out on the head waters of Lycoming.

tion of the Cayuga, with the main North-East Branch of Susquehannah, from thence to act as circumstances might require.

"The Troops met at Muncy the 18 Septr., when we came to count and array our Force for the Expedition, they amounted only to about 200 Rank & File. We thought the number small, but as we presumed the Enemy had no notice of our Designs, we hoped at least to make a good Diversion if no more, whilst the Inhabitants were saving their grain on the Frontier.

"On the morning of the 21st, at four o'clock, we marched from Muncy, with the Force I have mentioned, we carried two Boxes of spare ammunition and Twelve days Provisions.

"In our Rout we met with great Rains & prodigious Swamps, Mountains, Defiles & Rocks impeded our march, we had to open and clear the way as we passed.

"We waded or swam the River Lycoming upwards of 20 Times. I will not trouble your honourable Body with a tedious Detail, but I cannot help observing that, I immagine, the Difficulties in Crossing the Alps, or passing up Kennipeck, could not have been greater than those our men experienced for the Time. I have the pleasure to say they surmounted them with great Resolution and Fortitude.

"In lonely woods and groves we found the Haunts and Lurking Places of the savage Murderers who had desolated our Frontier. We saw the Huts where they had dressed and dried the scalps of the helpless women & Children who had fell in their hands.

"On the morning of the 26th our Advance Party of 19 met with an equal Number of Indians on the Path, approaching each other, our People had the first Fire, a very important Indian Chief was killed and scalped, the rest fled.

"A few Miles further we discovered where upwards of 70 Warriors had lay the night before, on their March towards our Frontiers, the Panick communicated, they fled with their Brethren.

"No Time was lost, we advanced towards Sheshecunnunck, in the Neighborhood of which place we took 15 Prisoners from them, we learnt that a Man had deserted from Capt. Spalding's Company at Wioming, after the Troops had marched from thence, & had given the enemy Notice of our intended Expedition against them.

"We moved with the greatest Dispatch towards Tioga, advancing our Horse, and some Foot in Front, who did their duty very well; a number of the Enemy fled before us with Precipitation, it was near dark when we came to that town, our Troops were much fatigued; it was impossible to procced further that Night.

"We took another Prisoner, upon the whole Information, we were clear the Savages had Intelligence of us some days—That the Indians had been towards the German Flats—had taken 8 scalps & brought of 70 oxen intended for the garrison of Fort Stanwix—That on their Return they were to have attacked Wioming and the settlements on the West Branch again—That Colo. Morgan or no other Person had attempted to penetrate into the Enemy's Country, as we had been given to understand, and that the Collected force at Chemung would be upwards of 500, & that they were building a fort there.

"We also were told that young Butler had been at Tioga a few Hours before we came—that he had 300 Men with him, the most of them Tories, dressed in green—that they were returned towards Chemung, 12 Miles off, & that they determined to give us Battle in some of the Defiles near it.

"It was soon resolved we should proceed no further, but if possible, make our way good to Wioming. We burnt Tioga, Queen Hester's Palace or Town, & all the settlements on this side; several Canoes were taken and some Plunder, Part of which was destroyed.

"Mr. Carbery with the Horse only, was close on Butler, he was in Possession of the Town of Shawnee, 3 Miles up the Cayuga Branch, but as we did not advance, he returned.

"The Consternation of the Enemy was great, we pushed our good Fortune as far as we dare, nay, it is probable the good countenance we put on saved us from destruction, as we were advanced so far into the Enemy's Country & no return but what we could make with the sword. We came to Sheshecunnunk that night.

"Had we had 500 Regular Troops, and 150 Light Troops, with one or two Pieces of artillery, we probably might have destroyed Chemung, which is now the recepticle of all villainous Indians & Tories from the different Tribes and States. From this they make their Excursions against the Frontiers of N. York and Pennsylvania, Jersey & Wioming, & commit those horrid Murders and Devastations we have heard of. Niagra and Chemung are the assilums of those Tories who cannot get to New York.

"On the Morning of the 28th, we crossed the River and Marched owards Wyalusing, where we arrived that night at eleven o'Clock; our men much worn down—our Whiskey and Flour was gone.

"On the Morning of the 29th we were obliged to stay 'till eleven o'Clock to kill and cooke Beef. This necessary stop gave the Enemy Leasure to approach.

"Seventy of our Men, from real or pretended Lameness, went into the Canoes, others rode on the empty Pack Horses, we had not more than 120 Rank & File to fall in the Line of March.

"Lt. Sweeny, a valuable officer, had the Rear Guard, consisting of 30 Men, besides five active Runners under Mr. Camplen. The advanced guard was to consist of an officer & 15. There were a few Flankers, but from the Difficulty of the ground & Fatigue, they were seldom of use.

"The rest of our Little army was formed into three Divisions, those of my Regmt composed the first, Capt Spalding's the 2d, Capt Murrow's the 3d. The Light Horse was equally divided between front and rear. The Pack Horses and the Cattle we had collected, were to follow the advance guard

"In this order we moved from Wyalusing at twelve o'clock, a slight attack was made on our Front from a Hill, half an Hour afterwards a warmer one was made on the same quarter, after ordering the 2d and 3d Divisions to out Flank the Enemy, we soon drove them, but this, as I expected, was only amusement, we lost as Little time as possible with them.

"At two o'clock a very heavy attack was made on our Rear, which obliged the most of the Rear guard to give way, whilst several Indians appeared on our Left Flank. By the weight of the Firing we were soon convinced we had to oppose a Large Body.

"Capt Stoddard commanded in Front, I was in the Centre; I observed some high ground which overlooked the Enemy, orders were immediately given for the first & 3d Division to take Possession of it, whilst Capt Spalding was dispatched to support the Rear Guard. We gained the Heights almost unnoticed by the Barbarians, Capt Stoddert sent a small Party towards the Enemy's Rear; at this critical moment Capts Boone & Brady, & Lt King, with a few Brave Fellows, landed from the Canoes, joined Mr. Sweeny, and renewed the action there. The War Whoop was given by our People below and communicated round, we advanced on the Enemy on all sides, with great shouting & Noise, the Indians after a brave resistance of some minutes, conceived themselves nearly surrounded, fled with the utmost Haste, by the only passes that remained, & left ten dead on the ground.

"Our Troops wished to do their duty, but they were much overcome with Fatigue, otherwise (as the Indians immagined themselves surrounded), we should drove the Enemy into the River.

"From every account these were a select body of warriors, sent after us, consisting of near 200 Men. Their Confidence and Impetuosity probably gave the victory to us.

"After they had drove our Rear some Distance their Chief was heard to say, in the Indian Language, that which is interpreted thus: *my Brave Warriors we drive them*, be bold and strong, the day is ours, upon this they advanced very quick without sufficiently regarding their Rear.

"We had no alternative but Conquest or Death, they would have murdered us all had they succeeded, but the great God of Battles protected us in the day of Danger.

"We had 4 killed and 10 wounded. The Enemy must have had at least treble the number killed & wounded.

"They received such a Beating as prevented them from giving us any further trouble during our March to Wioming, which is more than 50 Miles from the place of action.

"The officers of my Regiment behaved well to a Man. All the party will acknowledge the greatest merit and Bravery of Capt Stoddert, I cannot say enough in his favor, he deserves the Esteem of his Country.

"Mr. Carbery with his Horse, was very active, and rendered important services, 'till his Horses were fatigued.

"Nearly all the other officers acquitted themselves with Reputation

"Capt Spalding exerted himself as much as possible.

"Capt Murrow, from his knowledge of Indian affairs, and their Mode of fighting, was serviceable. His Men were Marksmen and were useful.

"The men of my Regt were armed with Muskets & Bayonets, they were no great marksmen, and were awkward at wood Fighting. The Bullet, and three Swan shot in each Piece, made up, in some measure, for the want of skill.

"Tho' we were happy enough to succeed in this Action, yet I am convinced that a number of Lighter Troops, under good officers, are necessary for this Service. On the 3d the Savages killed and scalped 3 men, who had imprudently left the garrison at Wioming to go in search of Potatoes.

"From our observations, we imagine that the same party who had fought us, after taking Care of their *Dead & Wounded*, had come on towards Wyoming, and are now in that Neighborhood.

"I left half of my detachment there with five of my own officers, should they attempt to invest the place when their number is increased, I make no doubt but they will be disappointed.

"Our Garrisons have plenty of Beef & Salt, Tho' Flour is scarce at Wioming.

"I arrived here with the remainder of the detachment on the 5th, we have performed a Circuit of near 300 miles in about two weeks. We brought off near 50 Head of Cattle, 28 Canoes, besides many other articles.

"I would respectfully propose that the Congress would be pleased to send a Connecticut Regiment to Garrison Wyoming as soon as possible, it is but 120 miles from Fish Kills. I have done all I can for the good of the whole. I have given all the support in my Power to that Post, but if Troops are not immediately sent, these Settlements will be destroyed in Detail. In a week or less a Regiment could march from Fish Kills to Wyoming.

"My little Regiment, with two Classes of Lancaster and Berks County Militia, will be scarcely sufficient to preserve the Posts from Nescopake Falls to Muncy, and from thence to the Head of Penn's Valley.

"I am with the greatest Respect,
Your most obedt,
Humble Servt,
THOS. HARTLEY, COL."

"Sunbury, Octr. 8th, 1778."

An unanimous vote of thanks was passed by the Executive Council, for Colonel Hartley's "brave and prudent conduct in covering the North Western frontiers," &c. See Col. Rec., Vol. XI., p. 640. And, for this report, see Archives for 1778–9, p. 5.

CHAPTER XXX.

COLONEL HARTLEY LEAVES THE VALLEY—DEATH OF CAPTAIN BRADY—NEGLECTED STATE OF HIS GRAVE—SAMUEL BRADY'S VOW—CAPTAIN WALKER'S LETTER—M'CLAY'S PROPOSITION TO HUNT THE INDIANS WITH DOGS—BATTLE NEAR MUNCY—A TRADITION—WARRIOR SPRING—NATURAL HOTEL—FORT MUNCY EVACUATED AGAIN—TERRIBLE SCENES OF MURDER AND DEVASTATION FOLLOW.

On the 7th of October, 1778, two serjeants belonging to Colonel Hartley's regiment, stationed at Muncy, were surprised by the Indians a short distance from the fort, and one of them killed and scalped. The other was supposed to have been taken prisoner and carried off, as he could not be found.

As Colonel Hartley had left a portion of his regiment at Wyoming, the West Branch was again destitute of the requisite number of troops to guard the settlers, and it was necessary that a fresh supply should be sent. The volunteer company raised for six months' service, and commanded by Captain Murrows, had refused to do their duty, till the sum of eighty dollars per man, promised them by the government, was paid.

In view of this state of affairs, and the urgent necessity for fresh troops to be sent to protect the Valley from the daily inroads of the savages, a number of prominent citizens were induced to request Colonel Hartley to send

George Tombs' Buildings, Jersey Shore, Pa.

Colonel Antes, Captain Chambers, and Mr. Maffit, as Commissioners to the Executive Council, to lay their grievances before that body, and solicit timely assistance.

During the month of November, the savages were very bad. They burnt and destroyed much on the North Branch, and on the 9th, a body, consisting of seventy warriors, came to the forks of Chilisquaque, and took several prisoners.

About the close of the year 1778, Colonel Hartley left the West Branch for another field of duty. His departure from the command of the troops was very much regretted by Colonel Hunter, and others, as he had done more for the country during his stay, than any other person. Colonel Hunter complained that his lot, as commander of the militia, was a hard one; and that the militia of this County were harder to govern than any others, and never could be brought under the same degree of discipline as regulars.

He also informed President Reed, at the same time, that agreeably to the resolution of Congress, and the instructions of Council, to raise a Company of volunteers to serve six months, he had appointed the following officers: James Murrows, Captain; Robert Arthur, 1st Lieutenant; Samuel Fulton, 2d Lieutenant; William Reed, 3d Lieutenant; and Andrew Donaldson, Ensign. Their term of service was about to expire, and Captain Murrows had gone to the Board of War, with the muster roll, to receive their pay. Some of the men had paid as high as thirty pounds for a good rifle, hence the government should be prompt in paying them.

Captain John Brady, it will be remembered, commanded the fort which bore his name, near Muncy Creek. It was merely a local affair, and garrisoned by the inhabitants for their own protection.

In April, 1779, it became necessary to go up the river some distance, to procure supplies for the fort, and Captain Brady, taking with him a wagon, team, and guard, went and procured what could be had. As he was returning in the afternoon, riding a fine mare, and near where the road forked, being some distance behind the team, in conversation with Peter Smith, he suggested the propriety of taking a different route from the one the wagon had gone, as it was shorter. They travelled together, till they came to a small stream of water, where the other road came in. Brady observed,* "this would be a good place for the Indians to secrete themselves." Smith said, "Yes." That instant three rifles cracked, and Brady fell dead! The mare ran past Smith, who threw himself upon her, and was carried to the fort in a few seconds. The garrison hearing the report of the rifles, ran out, and on seeing Smith coming at full speed, anxiously inquired for Captain Brady. His wife was amongst the foremost, and feared the worst. Smith replied, "*in heaven or hell, or on his road to Tioga!*" Meaning he was either killed or taken prisoner by the Indians.

The men immediately ran to the spot, to which the wagon guard had also been attracted by the firing, and found the brave Captain lying in the road, his scalp taken off, and his rifle gone. The Indians were in such haste, that they had not taken either his watch or shot pouch.

This was a hard stroke on Mrs. Brady, bowed down as she was in mourning for the death of her beloved son James, the previous year. Now, her husband and pro-

* See the article by Kiskeminetas, Vol. IX. Hazard's Register, p. 307.

tector was cruelly murdered by the same relentless hand. Truly, her lot was hard.

The Peter Smith in company with him, was the same whose wife and children were killed near Lycoming, and on whose farm his son James was so barbarously murdered, when assisting to cut his harvest. It seemed that bad luck attended this unfortunate man wherever he went.*

The place where Captain John Brady was killed, was little more than a quarter of a mile from the fort, by the old path, and near where the main road, from Muncy to Williamsport, now crosses Wolf Run. He was taken and buried in the graveyard on Muncy Farm. For many years, all trace of the hero's grave was lost, and his son, General Hugh Brady, frequently sought for it in vain. One of his daughters, the wife of Major Backus, was providentially made acquainted with the spot, during a visit a few years ago, where her grandfather was interred. An old Revolutionary soldier, named Henry Lebo, who was well acquainted with the Captain, and served in his company, had known and marked the spot, and on his death-bed, described it, and requested to be buried by his side. His request was granted; and there lie side by side, the Captain and his brave compatriot.

The grave, I am sorry to say, is shamefully neglected, and can only be found by the marks of the latter. The people of Lycoming county, cannot show a better appreciation of true patriotism, than by erecting an *humble* slab, at least, in perpetuation of the memory of the gallant Brady. Let the sacred spot where his ashes repose, be marked in this way, with a tablet on which to inscribe the many virtues of the noble dead.

* After the war, Smith is said to have settled in the Genessee Country and become a wealthy man. Good luck returned.

The death of Brady took place on the 11th of April, 1779. His son Samuel was at Pittsburg when the sad intelligence reached him. He also mourned the death of his brother James, but this news served to fill his cup of sorrow, and, in the first phrensy of grief, he is said to have raised his hand on high, and swore: "*Aided by Him who formed yonder Sun and Heavens, I will revenge the murder of my father; nor while I live will I ever be at peace with the Indians of any tribe!*" This fearful vow was uttered in the first moments of anguished feeling, but it was never effaced from his memory. He became a devoted man-killer, reckless of all sympathy, and destitute of all humanity towards the Indian race. The vow was fearfully fulfilled, and many a dusky warrior bit the dust. His daring adventures on the Alleghany would fill a volume. They may be found at length, in the numbers by Kiskeminetas, in the ninth and tenth volumes of Hazard's Register.

On the 17th of April, Captain Andrew Walker, who commanded Fort Muncy, writes to the Executive Council, giving them an account of the repairs done to the fort, and the sufferings endured by the garrison. His letter is quite interesting. I quote the greater part of it, *verbatim*, as follows:

"On the 2d of Augt, wee ware ordred by Colonel Hartley to build this Fort; wee Immeadiately begon and Finnish'd by the 18th of Sepr, with these Exceptions—There was but one row of Abbeties round it, wee had built Neither Barrack's Store or Magazine.

"On the 20th of Sepr, the Garrason, which Consifted of 1 Capt, 2 Subs, 4 Sergts, & 60 Rank and File, ware drawn out (Except 1 Subn & 18) on an Expedition under the Command of Col. Hartley—on the 9th of Sepr wee Again marched into it; bad weather comeing on we began our Barraks Magazine, Storehouse, &c; when this was Finesh'd, wee ware Comfortably Prepared Again the winter; but in the Spring I found the Works much Impeared; I then set the Garreson to Repair the Works, and raised them Eighteen Inches; Then wee put two rowes more of Abberties round the works—this is Just now Finesh'd; it is to be Observ'd that in the Course of this time, one third of our men ware Constantly Imployed as Guards to the Inhabitants, and, I may Aferm, in Harvest the one halfe ware Imployed the same way, nor can anny man in the County say he ever asked a guard (when he had a Just Occation) and was denied. Dureing this time the Troops ware not supplied even with Ration Whiskey, allmoste Neaked for want of Blankets and Cloathes, and yet I have the Satisfaction to infoarm you they done their Duty Cheerfully. I from time to time did promise them some Compensation for their Troble and Industrey. The works are now finished, and, in my oppinion, Taneble again anny nomber our Savage Enemy can bring again it; as to my own part, I begg lave to observe That I neither clame Meret or Reward for what I have done—it's anough that I have done my Duty. Yet, Sir, as I have Promised these men a Compensation for there Industry, I begg you will Please to lay before the Hon'ble Councel, the Inclosed Plan, which will Inable them to Judge wheather the Troops deserve a Reward for their labour or not.

"The sole cost this fort is to the States is, to building two Roomes for the Officers. Makeing the gate & two Sentry Boxes.

"(Signed)

ANDW. WALKER,
Capt. Com'g Fort Muncy."

Captain Walker certainly deserved much credit for his services at this post, and although he claims neither "Meret or Reward," was eminently entitled to something. Whether government gave him a vote of thanks, even, does not appear.

On the 26th of the same month, a party of Indians, supposed to be thirty or forty in number, suddenly appeared in the vicinity of Fort Freeland, and succeeded in killing and capturing seven men belonging to that place. Among those taken prisoners was James McNight, Esq.,* one of the Assemblymen for the county of Nor-

* See Pennsylvania Archives for 1778–9, page 346.

thumberland, and *probably* the husband of Mrs. McNight, who made such a narrow escape from the Indians, sometime before.

The same day a party of thirteen men went in search of their horses, about five miles from Fort Muncy. They were fired upon, probably by the same party of Indians, and all killed or taken prisoners, except one man, who made his escape. Captain Walker, on hearing the firing, immediately turned out with a company of thirty-four men, and proceeded to the spot, where he found the bodies of four men lying dead, and their scalps taken.

It appeared that great preparations were making by the various tribes to unite, and make a sudden descent upon the valley in overwhelming numbers, and exterminate the infant settlements at one fell swoop. They seemed to be resolved upon their destruction, and the people were justly alarmed, for in all probability, if strong measures were not taken to guard against it, the tragedies of Wyoming would be re-enacted in the beautiful vale of the Otzinachson.

The great danger, and the urgent necessity of speedy action, induced William Maclay to submit a proposition to Council for employing dogs to hunt the savages. The following extract is taken from his letter, bearing date the 27th of April, 1779:

"I have sustained some Ridicule for a Scheme which I have long recommended, Viz., that of hunting tho Scalping parties of Indians with Horsemen & Dogs. The iminent Services which Dogs have rendered to our People in some late instances, seems to open People's Eyes to a Method of this kind. We know that Dogs will follow them, that they will discover them and even seize them, when hunted on by their Masters.

"History informs us That it was in this Manner That the Indians were extirpated out of whole Country's in South America. It may be objected That we have not Proper Dogs. It is true that every new thing must be learned; But we have, even now, Dogs that will follow them, and the arrantest Cur will both follow and fight in Company. I cannot help being of opinion that a Single Troop of Light Horse, attended by Dogs, (and who might occasionally carry a footman behind them, that the pursuit might not be interrupted by Morasses or Mountains,) under honest and active officers, would destroy more Indians than five thousand Men stationed in forts along the Frontiers; I am not altogether singular in this opinion, could not such a Thing be tryed?"

This letter was written from Sunbury. It nowhere appears how his views were received by the Executive Council; but it is certain that the scheme was never adopted and "tryed."

About this period a battle was fought near the summit of the Muncy Hills, on the War Path leading from Muncy to Shamokin, between a party of Indians and whites that accidentally met there. It is said the whites behaved gallantly, and gained a complete victory. They were under the command of William Patterson, grandfather of the late J. Potter Patterson, of Muncy. The numbers engaged on each side, and the losses sustained, it is to be regretted, have not been preserved. Tomahawks, and other relics of the contest, have often been found on the spot.

A tradition is handed down to this day, that at a very early period, a party of Indians massacred a white man on this spot, by burning him at the stake. They stuck his body full of pitch pine splinters, and danced around him in fiendish glee, awaking the echoes of those dismal mountain solitudes with their demoniac yells. A little superstition is also blended with the tradition, to the effect that no herbage has ever been known to grow in the circle where the terrible deed was consummated.

The Indians that met the whites on this lonely path, had lain the previous night, at the Warrior Spring, near Fort Brady. It was a great place of resort, and rose in the bank of the river near where Port Penn now stands, and is the largest head of spring water known in the Muncy Valley at the present day. The quality of the water has no superior, both for its low degree of temperature, and crystalline appearance.

At this spring, old Egohowen, a Muncy Chief, and his compatriots, exhibited their hospitalities to Newaleeka, of the Great Island, and his other allies and friends. It was one of Nature's Hotels, at the head of Muncy Ripples. The Elm tree that overhung the shore was both hitching-post and manger, whilst the *voyageur* was regaled at the gravelly bar.

The ravages of the Indians had become so great on both branches of the Susquehanna, that it was resolved to march a large army into their country, and destroy their villages and cornfields. It was thought that by so doing, their arrangements would be so disconcerted that they could no longer carry on their system of warfare with advantage, and would be compelled to abandon their designs. The command of the expedition was given to General Sullivan, and it proved pretty successful. He marched up the North Branch in June.

General Sullivan required all the available troops that could be spared for him in this Valley. In view of this, the garrison was withdrawn from Fort Muncy, being the second time it was evacuated during the Revolutionary war; and the settlements above Freeland's Fort were again left in a defenceless and unprotected condition.

But few settlers remained, however, to trust themselves to the roving bands of savages.

The troops were scarcely withdrawn from this post till the enemy appeared in considerable numbers, and commenced to burn, murder, and destroy everything before them. On the third of the month, (June, 1779,) they killed two men, and took three prisoners, at Lycoming Creek. Their names are not given. Following up their work of destruction, they burned the widow Smith's mills, and killed one man, on the 8th. These mills are said to have stood where the White Deer Mills now stand. The irons were discovered a few years ago in a slough near the river.

On the 17th they penetrated near Fort Brady, where they killed two men, and took three prisoners; burned Starrets' flouring mill, and *all* the principal houses in Muncy township. This mill stood where the Muncy mills now stand, near the centre of the valley. Desolation and blood marked their course. Many families were carried into captivity, amongst which was the family of Joseph Webster, who lived on Muncy Farm. Four of his children were attacked. The eldest, a son, was killed, and the others, two daughters, and a son, were carried into captivity. Some of the descendants reside near Muncy at the present time.

Pushing on their ravages with impunity, they appeared near Fort Freeland on the 21st, and surprised several men at work in a cornfield. A son of Jacob Freeland, and Isaac Vincent, were killed; and Michael Freeland and Benjamin Vincent taken prisoners.

It is related of young Freeland, that on the alarm being given, he ran towards a stone quarry, but was pursued and speared in the thigh. He fell near the edge of the quarry, when the Indian pounced upon him, but suddenly rising with him on his shoulders, pitched him over the precipice, and would have escaped, but another Indian came running up, and killed him.

Great alarm existed among the few remaining settlers, and they scarcely knew what to do. Savages lurked behind every bush, and no man was safe when absent from the Fort. It was also rumored that an extensive body of British and Indians were making preparations to descend upon the Valley, whilst Sullivan was marching up the North Branch, and penetrate to Fort Augusta, kill and burn everything before them, and take possession of that stronghold.

A recital of the bloody scenes that followed must be reserved for another chapter.

CHAPTER XXXI.

COVENHOVEN, AS A SPY—DISCOVERS THE ENEMY—RETURNS AND GIVES THE ALARM—THE FLIGHT—THEY APPROACH AND BURN FORT MUNCY—FORT FREELAND INVESTED—THE BATTLE AND SURRENDER—CAPTAIN BOON'S SPARTAN BAND—LIST OF THE KILLED—THE WOMEN AND CHILDREN—DEATH OF JOHN MONTOUR—HIS BURIAL AT PAINTED POST.

As the rumor of the approaching body of British and Indians increased, it was determined to send an active man, well acquainted with all the paths and defiles, as a spy, to see what intelligence he could glean of their movements. Robert Covenhoven, who was then acting as a guide and scout for the garrison, being an expert woodsman, was selected for the dangerous task. He started alone, preferring no company, as he thought he could better elude observation, than if accompanied by several men, who might not obey his instructions. Purposely avoiding all the Indian paths, he shaped his course through the wilderness, towards the head waters of Lycoming Creek, and travelling all night, soon arrived in the vicinity of the enemy's camp. Secreting himself in a secure position, he lay, during the day, and heard several hundred shots, from which he judged that they were cleaning their guns. Being satisfied that a large body was about to advance, he started back over the rugged mountains, hungry and fatigued, and made as rapid progress as the nature of his path would admit. Striking an Indian path near Loyal Sock, it *forcibly* occurred to him that he might meet Indians if he continued in it, and stepping out behind a tree to rest himself, had been there but a few minutes, till two Indians rapidly passed him, humming a tune as they went. Had he continued on without stopping, they would have met him.

When he arrived at the settlements, he gave the alarm, and the terrified women and children were hastily put in boats, and sent down to Fort Augusta, under his charge. Fort Meninger, at the mouth of Warrior Run, was abandoned, and intelligence sent up to Freeland's Fort, to make preparations to leave as soon as possible. Thinking, probably, that he was magnifying the danger, they were slow to move. The garrison at Boon's Fort, at the mouth of Muddy Run, also remained behind.

In the meantime the enemy, consisting of about three hundred British and Indians; the former under the command of Captain McDonald, and the latter under Hiokoto, a veteran brave of the Seneca tribe, were rapidly advancing. They burned fort Muncy on their way down, and laid the country waste.

They approached Fort Freeland, and appeared there early on the morning of the 29th of June, 1779. The inhabitants were not aware of their being so near, and fancied themselves secure. Delusive fancy!

About daylight, on the morning of that memorable day, an aged man, named James Watt, left the fort to look for his sheep, and had proceeded but a short distance in the direction of the creek, when an Indian, named John Montour, who was lying in ambush, suddenly sprang upon him, and attempted to drag him off, but Watt resisted and cried loudly for assistance. The Indian then felled him with his tomahawk, and attempted to scalp him, when he was wounded in the back by a rifle ball fired from the fort, which compelled him to fly. Two young men were also out at the same time, but immediately ran in. One of them stopped in the gate to look back, when a ball struck him in the forehead. The other pulled him in and closed the gate. Thus the attack commenced.

The fort only contained twenty-one effective men, and a large number of women and children. The names of a few are given as follows: Captain John Lytle, John Vincent, Cornelius Vincent, Daniel Vincent, Bethuel Vincent, George Pack, Elias Williams, Henry Gilfillen, &c.

As soon as the attack began, Mary Kirk and Phœbe Vincent, commenced to run bullets, and continued as long as they had a dish or spoon that would melt. Heroic women!

The savages set up a terrible yell, and advanced to the attack, under cover of trees, bushes, &c. Those in the fort also maintained a stout resistance, and fired vigorously upon the enemy, but with little effect. After continuing the assault for some minutes, and finding that little impression could be made upon the works, Captain McDonald hoisted a white flag, and proposed terms of capitulation. Captain John Lytle, accompanied by John Vincent, went out and held a conference with McDonald, who proposed the following terms:

1. That Lytle should give up the fort, without further resistance.

2. That for so doing, McDonald would take no prison-

ers but the able-bodied and efficient men, and all the women, children, and old men, would be permitted to leave the place, without danger or molestation.

In the event of refusing these terms, McDonald stated that he should renew the attack, and if his party were victorious—as he doubted not they would be—it would be out of his power to prevent a general massacre of all who were found in the fort, not excepting the women and children.

Thirty minutes being allowed Captain Lytle to decide on the expediency of accepting the proposed terms, he immediately returned to the fort for consultation with his friends. The fortification was poorly constructed, being nothing more than three logs laid one upon another, and it covered more space than there were men to man it. The garrison, therefore, believing there was no possible chance for success, if a battle ensued, resolved to surrender the fort, as soon as the thirty minutes expired.

These thirty minutes were not, however, spent in idleness by the females in the fort. Every woman put on as much clothing as she could possibly wear, taking care also, to load her pockets with every little thing of value that she could lay hands on. William Kirk, a young man of feminine appearance, was dressed in female costume, by his mother, and escaped with the women. This is the *only* case of this kind that *actually* took place, although several have been published.

It was about nine o'clock in the morning when the articles of capitulation were signed, and the prisoners marched forth. McDonald was true to his word, and no massacre took place.

As soon as the Indians took possession of the fort,

the squaws began to display their inherent mischievous disposition. They took all the feather beds they could find, ripped them open, emptied the feathers in a heap, set them in a blaze, and danced around them with tremendous yells of satisfaction. They then packed the ticks full of clothes and goods, destroying everything that was too unwieldy for removal, preparatory to their retreat. One of the squaws, in passing a white girl, snatched a handkerchief from her neck, and refused to give it up. McDonald very generously gave the poor girl his own, in lieu of it, and appeared to be much exasperated against the thievish disposition of the savages, which he found impossible to control.

The Indians having rifled the fort of all that was valuable, and having gathered together all the provisions they could find, proceeded to the creek below the mill—the squaws riding away on the side-saddles they had stolen, in mockery of the white females—where they kindled their fires, cooked their meats, and made preparations for a sumptuous repast. Their enjoyment, however, was of short duration.

News of the attack having spread around the neighborhood, and the firing being distinctly heard at Boon's Fort, caused Captain Hawkins Boon to set himself vigorously to work to collect a party and proceed to the assistance of the garrison. In a short time he collected together thirty-three as daring patriots as ever fired a gun, out of the Chilisquaque settlement, and marched to the scene of action.

About 11 o'clock, whilst the Indians were enjoying their meal, this Spartan band reached the opposite side of the creek, within seventy-five or eighty yards of the enemy, without being discovered. Each man was cautioned to take sure aim, and when all were ready, at a given signal they fired, and at least thirty of the savages fell dead without a moment's warning. As soon as they could reload, they crossed the bridge, and made directly for the fort, but when they had run about half way across the meadow, they discovered it to be on fire. As this was evidence that the fort had been abandoned, Boon ordered a retreat to the woods, where he felt confident that he could better cope with the savages in their own peculiar way. The Indians seeing the white men so few in number, endeavored to cut off this retreat by throwing themselves before the bridge, but they were unsuccessful. One of Boon's men, named Dougherty, made a short cut for the creek, and while endeavoring to cross it, got entangled in some vines. While in this situation, an Indian called to him to surrender, but he answered with an oath that he would not, and taking his hunting-knife, with a few vigorous blows, cut his way out, and reached his companions in safety, who gave him a hearty cheer.

A brisk fire was now kept up across the creek, until two o'clock in the afternoon, the whites fighting against the odds of *nine* to one! They stood their ground nobly, until *seventeen* of their number, including the brave Captain Boon, were slain, when the survivors gave up the fight, and each man made the best escape he could. All of these brave fellows were closely hunted by the savages, and several of them made very narrow escapes. A man named Doyle, darted in among a bunch of hazel-bushes close by where he had been fighting, and remained in safety until night, although Indians passed several times within a few feet of him.

During the fight, William Hood and Major McMahon,

crossed the creek to where the women were collected together, spoke a few words with them, and retreated with safety.

Samuel Brady, brother to Captain John, who was killed at Wolf Run, and the uncle of the celebrated Samuel Brady of the Rangers, was at Fort Freeland the day of its capture. He was determined not to be carried off as a prisoner, and watching an opportunity, suddenly dashed into the hazel-bushes and ran for life. He escaped through the bushes and came upon a plain, hotly pursued by several Indians. He was determined, as he was afterwards heard to say, to "*make his eternal escape!*"

After running a considerable distance, he looked back and found himself pursued by two Indians, one a large dangerous looking fellow, the other of small stature. He renewed his speed, and was getting along pretty well, when his foot slipped into a hole, and he fell down. The large Indian was foremost, but Brady had fallen with a loaded rifle in his hand, with which he shot at the savage, who gave a wild yell and fell dead. The other, fearing that there might be more rifles about, gave up the pursuit and returned. Brady yelled after him at the top of his voice—"*You murdering thief—you didn't know it was Brady!*"

The only one of the band taken was Henry Gilpin, who was caught the next day in a dilapidated fort—probably Fort Muncy—while in the act of milking a cow to obtain some nourishment, which he had not tasted for twenty-four hours. He was tomahawked on the spot.

The survivors of this Spartan band took an active part in the skirmishes which took place during the remainder of the war. Many of their descendants still reside in Chilisquaque, and no doubt inherit the same patriotism and love of liberty, that distinguished their heroic ancestors.

The following is a list of the names of those killed in the fort:—James Watt, John McClintock, William McClung, James Miles, Henry Gilfillen. The names of *all* the killed in Captain Boon's company are not now remembered. The following is a part of them:—Capt. Boon, Capt. Samuel Dougherty, Natte Smith, John Jones, Edward Costikan, Ezra Green, Samuel Neel, Matthew McClintock, Hugh McGill, Edward Woods.

Fifty-two women and children, and four old men, were permitted to depart for Sunbury, by Captain McDonald. Great consternation prevailed throughout the country after this battle, and the road leading to Fort Augusta was filled with the terrified and unprotected women and children. John Vincent was one of the old men allowed to remain—his wife was a cripple, and unable to walk. He carried her to the lower end of the meadow, and laid her down, where they remained till morning, without any covering; during the night it rained on them. He caught a horse that came to them, and making a bridle out of hickory bark, succeeded in getting her to Sunbury.

The enemy burned and destroyed all the houses, barns and stacks of hay, leaving behind them one dread scene of devastation and ruin, which remained untouched for several years, as a memento of their cruelty.

The first night after the surrender, the prisoners were confined in an ash-house near Muncy. One of them had attempted to escape during the day, and was placed on the second floor of the building, when John Montour came in and pointed his gun at him, as if about to shoot. He was followed by old Catreen—his sister—who exclaimed to him, "Ah! you debil, you tschot me." Frightened until his knees knocked together, he replied, "No, I never shot anybody." "You lie, you debil; I got my wrist cut by you," and she waved her tomahawk as if about to hurl it at his head. "I've a good mind to scalp you," she continued, after looking at him until she thought him sufficiently frightened not to attempt running away again. It is said that such was the fright he received at this time, that for years he could not divest himself of the idea that the rustling of the leaves as he passed through the woods, was the noise of the tread of the Indian in pursuit.

John Montour suffered much from the wound he received when attempting to scalp old Mr. Watt, and finally had to be carried on horseback. The second or third day he is said to have died. A post was erected near his grave, and painted red, and the place to this day is known by the name of the "Painted Post." Montour was a distinguished warrior, and his death was much regretted by the Indians.

CHAPTER XXXII.

DANIEL VINCENT'S RETURN FROM CAPTIVITY—MEETING BETWEEN HIM AND HIS WIFE—CAPTAIN LYTLE'S WIFE RETURNS TO WARRIOR RUN—IS DECEIVED, AND MARRIES ANOTHER MAN—THE CAPTAIN RETURNS—ARRIVAL OF TROOPS—CAPTAIN ROBINSON—HIS LETTER—MORE MURDERS—SCALPING OF CATHARINE STORM—ESCAPE OF HER COMRADE—KILLING OF TATE, &C.

THE enemy seemed contented after capturing Freeland's Fort, and did not continue their ravages any further down the river. It is not known why they retreated so precipitately, as the expedition was obviously planned for the purpose of trying to capture Fort Augusta; and had they advanced rapidly against it, after the fall of Freeland's Fort, there is but little doubt that they would, with their superior numbers, have given it a hard brush.

Of the Vincents, Bethuel, Cornelius, and Daniel, were taken prisoners. Benjamin, a lad of only eleven years, was taken at the first attack on the 21st of July. He remained in captivity for five years, when he returned.

The captives were taken to Tioga river, thence into the Genessee country, and from there to Niagara, and Lower Canada. The country through which they passed was one vast wilderness, and they did not see a white man's dwelling, after they left Lycoming Creek, until they arrived at Fort Niagara. A little beef without salt, roasted on the end of a stick, was their chief article of food. They were treated as well as they had reason to expect, and much better than many others in similar situations.

Daniel Vincent had been recently married, and after the capture, his wife, full of sorrow and grief, worked her way back to New Jersey, to her father's house. Three years rolled away, and no tidings came from her captive husband, but she still *hoped* to see him again. One evening in winter time, a sleighing party were about leaving a house in New Jersey to go on a short excursion. The young wife had been induced to go with them, for the first time. As they were on the eve of starting, a neighbor, in company with a roughly dressed man, with a heavy beard, rode up. He inquired for Mrs. Vincent, and informed her that here was a man that could tell her something about her husband. The stranger stepped forward and shook her warmly by the hand, and entered into conversation with her. She made many anxious inquiries respecting him, when, finding that she did not recognize him, on account of his changed appearance, he could restrain his pent up feelings no longer, and calling her by name, exclaimed, "*Do you not know your husband; I am he?*" With a shriek of joy, she bounded into his arms, and wept tears of gladness.

Cornelius, the father of Daniel, returned about the same time from captivity. He was heavily ironed, for a period of eighteen months. When he died, the marks of the British fetters were still plainly visible on his ankles.

Previous to the return of the captives, some of their

wifes ventured back to their desolated homes. Amongst these—it is said by a writer on the 88th page of the tenth volume of Hazard's Register—came the wife of Captain Lytle, and her children, in company with a single man of good reputation, who was a cropper. After some time, this man became attached to Mrs. Lytle, and in consequence, made proposals of marriage, which were rejected with a declaration of her determination never to accept the addresses of any man, while in her breast she could cherish the fond hopes of the return of her husband from captivity. To effect his purpose, certain letters were circulated, stating that Captain L. was certainly dead at the time; and after giving her time to mourn the death of her husband, still alive, the young man resumed his addresses, which were then accepted, and they were finally married. But time at length released Captain L. from captivity, and with fond anticipation, hastened his return to the caresses of his wife and little children, from whom he had been so long separated. But what were his feelings when he first heard of the marriage of his wife to another man? It is said that he refused to see her, until an understanding was effected by some well-disposed persons, who investigated the matter, and discovered that the letters were basely forged for the purpose of deceiving her. On being satisfied of this fact, Captain Lytle became reconciled to his wife, and her deceiver was compelled to fly, in order to escape the rigor of the law. Captain Lytle and family resided in the Warrior Run settlement for a number of years. He has been dead for half a century.

The distress of the inhabitants was great, and on the 30th of July, Colonel Hunter writes, that Northumberland town was the frontier the previous night. The entire Valley of the West Branch was abandoned.

Preparations were speedily made to follow the enemy, for the purpose of trying to recover some of the cattle, as they had driven all away they could find. On the 3d of August, Colonel Matthew Smith arrived at Sunbury, with sixty Paxton boys, and several more companies were expected from neighboring counties. These detachments came without special orders from the Executive Council. By the 5th, they numbered five hundred strong, and marched immediately for Muncy, under command of Colonel Smith, determined to seek the enemy. But they had retired far in the wilderness, beyond the reach of all pursuit.

General Sullivan having commenced his march into their country, attracted their attention, and they were compelled to fly before him, and abandon their towns. He destroyed everything in the shape of Indian wigwams, cornfields, &c., which so disconcerted them, that but few predatory bands appeared on the West Branch for a year or two. The blow given them by Sullivan, was such a severe one, that they never finally recovered from it.

In the fall of 1779, Henry McHenry,* with a party of ten men, came to Loyal Sock from Fort Rice, to thresh some grain. Sentinels were carefully posted. McHenry was one, and took up his position in a thick clump of bushes. He soon observed an Indian creeping along on his hands and feet, to get a shot at the men in the barn. Watching an opportunity, he fired and shot him through the small of the back, when he sprang off a short distance and fell. His comrades were observed to carry him off. They did not return.

During the year 1780, we have but few accounts of

* See Archives for 1781-3, p. 70.

Indian depredations. The inhabitants, encouraged by the prospect of protection, and the absence of the enemy, again returned slowly to their deserted homes, and commenced improving.

On the 14th of July of this year, however, one man and three children were murdered by Indians, near the mouth of Buffalo Creek; and on the following day, Captain McMahon was taken prisoner, by an Indian and tory, six miles from Northumberland, on the West Branch, but he escaped by killing the tory when the Indian had gone to his company, that lay near at hand. This tory was Captain Caldwell, a noted villain.

Early in the spring of 1781, Captain Robinson came to the county, and commenced raising a company. General Potter also returned about the same time, and on the 12th, he writes to President Reed, that Robinson had succeeded in enlisting forty men, but many of them were so destitute of clothing, that they were unfit for duty. Not a blanket was found among them!

In the month of March, a small band of savages penetrated into Chilisquaque or Buffalo Valley, and attacked an old man, his son and daughter. The boy was shot dead, and scalped, and the girl made a prisoner. The old man had a stick in his hand, with which he stoutly defended himself against one of the Indians, who had a tomahawk, and made him drop his weapon. Colonel Kelly, and a few of his neighbors, being in a house at a short distance, heard the alarm, and came running to his assistance. They obliged the Indians to fly so suddenly that they left the young girl, and all their blankets, and the brave old gentleman with his stick, behind them. They outran Colonel Kelly and his party, and got off safe. The name of the old man is not given in General

Potter's letter,* and I have been unable to ascertain it. On the 8th of the same month, a party came to the house of a man named Darmes, about five miles from Sunbury, on the Sabbath-day. Immediately on entering, they shot Darmes, and plundered the house of every thing valuable. There were four women there, and a number of children; and what is strange, they took all the plunder, leaving them behind. They were pursued early the next day, but effected their escape.

Colonel Joseph Solomon, living about five miles from Northumberland, on the main road leading to Danville, was surprised by the same party of Indians and made prisoner. His wife escaped to the woods, where, that night, she brought forth her first born! A hired girl escaped by running up stairs, and shutting down a trap door.

They travelled with Solomon four days, when they met another party of Indians, and turned him over to them. One of them was called Shenap, and said, "Solly, you shan't be hurt." They soon fell in with a large body of savages, who had another prisoner, named Williamson. They were to run the gauntlet. Williamson refused, and was beaten to death. Solomon started very rapidly, and plunged through fearfully, receiving but a few trifling bruises, when Shenap came up, and shaking him by the hand, laughingly said, "Solly, you run like debil—you run like hoss."

He was exchanged in a short time, and returned to his home in safety. He lived and died on Fishing Creek, and left a very respectable family.

On the 15th of June, 1781, Captain Thomas Robinson wrote to President Reed, as follows:

* He was the father of A. H. McHenry, Esq., of Jersey Shore.

"I take this opportunity of adressing your Excellency and Council in order to Inform you of the Present state of my Company. I have used every exertion in Recruiting that my Cercumstances would admit of. I Have Engaged 52 men During the war the want of necessary Clothing and money puts it out of my Pour to Render that service to this Distressed part of the Country I Could otherwise do most of them are naked they have not a sufficiency to Cover themselves. Blankits they have none. I Hope Council by this time will be able to afford me sufficient Clothing and what money is due them to the first of June this will not only be Doing Proper Justice to the Company but will enable me to fill my Company very soon. Lieut. Grove has Raised 17 men for seven months. Mr. Saml. McGredey has Raised 20 men for the same time and has been extreamely active with them. I have with the advice of Gen. Potter nominated him as a Lieut. to command that Detachment I hope this will meet with your Excellences approbation. I Have Raisd 14 men for 7 months and as we have mostly Been Devided in small Detachments it was Impossible for Mr. Vancamp & myself to Do the necessary duty. I have therefore with the advice of Col. Hunter and the approbation of Genl. Potter nominated Mr. Sam'l Quinn as an Ensn he has been Doing the Duty of an officer since the first of May this I Hope will also be acceptable to you if the number of our men would admit, it would be more agreeable to me to Confer the Rank of Lt on him. The Country being without a Pay master I suppose severals will be applying for that office whose abilities will not allow them to do that Duty, if your Excellency should think proper to confer that office in addition to the other on the Bearer Mr. Quinn I know he can Execute it without preventing him from doing Duty as an officer or at least to the appointment of Paying my men and the Present Temporary troops in the County I think allowing him some Pay for the Extra Duty will be Cheaper to the County than appointing one merely for that Purpose—another thing I Beg Leave to Inform your Excellency and Earnestly beg your attention thereto is the appointment of a surgeon there is not one in the County not within forty miles that I know. Some Incouragement given for that Purpose a Surgeant might be had. I know of none that would be willing to Com here but Michael Jenneys or Doctor Smith of Lancaster County.

"One thing more I Beg your attention to is the Establishing the Posts in this County. I have for sometime had in Contemplation to

Rebuild Fort Muncy, this Gen. Potter is extremely fond of and looks upon it as the most advantages Post in the County for many Reasons; should this meet with your approbation, I Request your Instructions therein by the Bearer in this and aney other thing necessary for me to know.

("Signed)

"THOMAS ROBINSON, CAPT.

P. RANGERS."

Captain Johnson came to Sunbury, on the 18th of July, with twenty-six militiamen, to serve the balance of their time in the County. Fourteen of them were destitute of guns, and no ammunition could be furnished them, even if arms could be secured. Colonel Hunter wrote respecting them, that they had "no stores of any kind, not even provisions."

A few miles above Northumberland, on what was known as Judge McPherson's farm, resided a man named John Tate; probably in 1780 or 1781. A large field of flax grew near the house. It was harvest time, and a number of men were engaged in the field, some distance from the house. The path ran by this field of flax, where a party of Indians came out and laid to watch for the men returning from dinner. Owing to some cause or other, they went to the field another way, and they missed their victims. Waiting for some time, they at length rose and went to the house, where they found a young woman named Catharine Storm, and another, engaged in spinning flax. Miss Storm was knocked over, with a tomahawk, and scalped; the other girl secreted herself behind the door and escaped. They then went to the field, and killed Tate.

Catharine Storm was not killed by the blow of the tomahawk, only stunned. She finally recovered, and lived for many years. No hair grew on her head where the scalp was removed.

A law having been passed for the furnishing of supplies, and the levying of tax from each County, it was found to require more tax from Northumberland than could be raised from the sale of all the property in the County. William Clark and William Antes, the Commissioners, immediately wrote to President Reed of the Council, as follows:

"Believe us, sir, it is with the utmost pain, and yet greatest truth, that we are obliged to declare our utter inability to Comply with the Demands of that Law. We now know that all the inhabitants in this County are not Equal in number to those of some Townships.in the interior Countys. Those who have property sufficient to support themselves are removed and gone. Shall then the Quota of the County be Levyed on the miserable few that remain. Their whole personal property, if removed to a place where hard Cash could be had for it, and sold, would not pay the tax. The old returns will not do, as a Rule to lay a Tax on Asentees. The improvements are grown up, burnt or destroyed, the personal property removed and now paying tax in the lower Countys. As to the men for the Supply of the Federal Army, (if those already inlisted are excepted) they are not to be here without taking the heads of Familys, and those we well know, cannot be had, as no money whatever would induce them to abandon their Familys in our Situation. We Sincerely wish to render a Ready Obedience to all Laws of the State, But in our Circumstances, it intirely puts it out of our power. We beg you, Sir, to Consider this as the Language of Genuine Truth, Extorted from us by Distressing Necessity," &c.

This letter shows in plain language, the miserable condition of the settlers in this beautiful Valley, three quarters of a century ago. It shows the promptings of honest hearts, clothed in the language of "genuine truth."

CHAPTER XXXIII.

INTERESTING ACCOUNT OF THE CAPTIVITY AND ESCAPE OF CAPTAIN JAMES THOMPSON—HIS SUFFERINGS IN THE CANOE—CAPTURE OF MARY YOUNG AT THE SAME TIME—HER RETURN—THE MARE AND THE COLT—A SINGULAR CIRCUMSTANCE—THE KLINESMITH FAMILY—CAPTURE OF THE TWO SISTERS—ONE OF THEM KILLS AN INDIAN, AND BOTH ESCAPE.

Captain James Thompson was an early settler in Buffalo Valley, and during a predatory incursion of savages, was taken, and carried into captivity. Several incorrect publications of his sufferings have been made, but the following is believed to be correct, as it was taken down from his own lips, in 1832, by James F. Linn, Esq., of Lewisburg, and entered in his journal.

Some time previous to his capture, he had removed his wife and children to Penn's Creek, for greater security against the Indians. In March, 1781, he was going from Lewisburg (then Derr's town,) to his farm, preparatory to moving down the country. On the road between the farms of John Linn and Colonel John Kelly, he was suddenly surprised by four Indians, and compelled to go along with them. When they came to the hollow, half a mile from Kelly's house, they discovered a fresh track in the soft clay. One of the Indians exclaimed, "*Squaw.*" Two of them immediately set off on a run, and two remained to guard him, one behind and one before. They soon heard a female scream, when the one behind struck him on the back with his gun and cried, " *Waugh*," (run.) They started off on a run, and on coming to the top of the hill, saw the other two with a woman, when they pushed off immediately for an Indian town on Towanda Creek.

They crossed the White Deer, and other mountains, north of Buffalo Valley, and came to the river near the mouth of Lycoming Creek, which they crossed in canoes. During the night they tied his arms behind him, and fastened the cord to grubs in the ground.

One night while encamped on Lycoming Creek, not being tied very securely, he succeeded in releasing his arms. Two of the Indians lay on one side of the fire with the girl,* and two on the other side with him. He first endeavored to get one of their tomahawks, but he discovered that they were all lying on their arms. He then got a stone, which they had used for crushing corn, and raised on his knees, preparatory to giving one of them a mortal stroke on the temple, and securing a tomahawk. But on account of his head being wrapped in a blanket, he struck too high to effect his object. The Indian gave a yell, which awoke the other. He now attempted to run, but the cord, with which he was tied, and stretched between the two grubs, intercepted him, and as he stepped back to get around it, one of the savages caught him by the collar of his coat, and in the struggle, tore it to the bottom. He drew his tomahawk to strike him on the head, but desisted, and spoke to the one he had wounded in his own language, and then drew it again, desisted, and spoke to the wounded Indian, and

* The name of the young woman was Mary Young, the daughter of Matthew Young, who lived on a farm adjoining Captain Thompson's.

then drew it the third time. He expected to receive it this time, and was resolved to try and catch it and wrest it from his hand. But they finally concluded not to kill him, reserving him for a more formal execution. They then tied a hollow gourd containing shot, to his waist, telling him this was his *death warrant.*

He could have easily escaped himself, but his object was to kill the Indians, and thereby rescue the young woman also, but he failed in the attempt.

After this they tied him so tight that he lost all feeling in his hands and arms. They continued on towards their place of destination. One day they shot a wild turkey, and taking out the entrails, rolled them round a stick without any cleaning, roasted them in the fire, and gave them to the prisoners to eat. Before this they had only a few grains of corn per day, and this change of diet, said Mr. Thompson, was quite a delicacy!

When they got to Towanda the Indians became less careful, thinking he would not attempt to run away again. In the evening they made him gather wood for their night fires. On one occasion when gathering wood, he managed to go further away for each load, till he got as far as he thought it was prudent to try, and watching an opportunity when they were not observing him, darted off into the woods as fast as he could run, with *twenty-two* grains of corn in his pocket, for provision, to travel a journey of many miles through the wilderness.

He said he could have made his escape on several occasions before, but he could not think of leaving Mary Young a prisoner with them. She frequently told him to escape, and not try to rescue her, as it would only defeat both. She was resigned to her fate.

He took a different route at first from that toward home,

to deceive the Indians in pursuit. In running, he stepped on a rotten stick, which broke, and made a noise; at the same time he heard two trees rubbing together with the wind, which he took to be the Indians in pursuit. Being terribly frightened, he ran into a pond, and hid himself in the brush, with nothing out but his head, where he lay till he was satisfied they were not coming that way. He then proceeded on his journey, keeping along the mountains, lest he might meet Indians in the valleys. One night he ran almost into an Indian encampment before seeing it. He went a little higher up the hill, where he could plainly see the Indians pass between him and the fire. At another time he came very near an encampment, when an Indian gave a yell. He supposed he was discovered, but squatted down immediately and remained quiet in the bushes; in a short time one of the Indians commenced chopping wood, when he knew they had not seen him, and carefully passed around them.

He struck the West Branch a few rods above where they had crossed it going out, and found one of the canoes on the bank, the river having fallen. Being so weak, he was unable to push it in, but getting two round sticks under it for rollers, with the aid of a hand-spike, succeeded in launching it. On getting in, he discovered the other canoe sunk, when he went to work and bailed it out, and lashing the two together, started with two paddles on his voyage. He rowed to the middle of the river, so that if the Indians should pursue him and shoot, they would not be so likely to hit him. One of his paddles accidentally dropped out and floated off, which he regretted very much, but, on getting into an eddy, it came floating up to his canoe, and was recovered.

When his craft got opposite to where Watsontown

now stands, he was discovered, and relieved by some friends. He was so weak that he lay in the canoe, and waved his hand to them on shore, which attracted their attention. When taken out, he was so weak that he could not relate his adventures, for several days, having to be nourished with sweet milk till he gained strength sufficient to talk. After getting able to walk, he went to his family, and removed to Chester county, where they remained till the close of the war.

The Indians took Mary Young to their towns, and set her to hoeing corn. An old negro, who was also a prisoner, told her to dig up the beans that were planted with the corn, and they would think her too dumb to learn agriculture, and sell her to the English. She took his advice, and was eventually sold to an English Captain, with whom she remained several years, when she was liberated and returned home. Having been so much exposed during her captivity, her constitution was so shattered that she survived her return but a short time. On their way out, she was obliged to wade through deep creeks, and, as the weather was very cold, her clothes were often frozen into a solid mass of ice.

She informed Captain Thompson that two of the Indians pursued him part of two days, but returned without success. They regretted his escape very much, as they intended to torture him. The wounded Indian left them soon after his escape, and she never heard of him afterwards, but supposed he died, as he was badly injured.

Captain Thompson informed Mr. Linn at the same time, that he went with his step-father,—who drove a team,—to Fort Cumberland the time of General Braddock's disastrous campaign. He was then a lad of only ten years of age.

At that time he saw a woman, a cousin to James Cornelius, who resided in Buffalo township, that had been taken a prisoner by the Indians during the French war. When they had taken her a great distance from home she managed to effect her escape, and made her way through the woods alone. The first day she came up with a mare and colt, and getting on her rode all day. When night came she turned her out to pasture, laid herself down by a log for the night, and never expected to see her again. When she awoke in the morning, the mare and colt stood by her side! She rode her all that day, and turned her out to graze whilst she slept, but the next morning the faithful animal was there, as usual, to receive her rider. She rode her each day till she arrived at the fort. By some, this peculiar circumstance would be termed an interposition of Divine Providence, to preserve the life of the woman. It is also stated that when she came to the fort the mare would allow no other person to approach, and when she was turned out to graze that night, made her escape, and was never heard of again.

In 1832, Captain Thompson went to reside with his son-in-law, Boyd Smith, in Jersey Shore, where he died in 1837, aged 93 years, and was buried in the graveyard now embraced in the limits of that borough. He was a fine old gentleman, and is distinctly remembered by a large number of people.

Early in the spring of 1782, Captain Robinson was ordered to Fort Muncy with his company, for the purpose of rebuilding and repairing that fortification. His head-quarters were at this station, and he rendered valuable services to the country, by the vigilant watch he kept on the Indians. Scouts were constantly kept out, and whenever a body of wandering savages appeared, they were pursued immediately, and obliged to fly.

In October of this year, a small body of savages came to the house of John Martin, in the Chilisquaque settlement, near the residence of Colonel James Murray, and barbarously murdered him and his wife. They also took from the house two young women, and a little girl, seven years of age, and carried them off.

On the 24th of the same month, two men named Lee and Caruthers, were sent out as spies from Fort Rice. They were waylaid, and fired upon. Lee was killed, and Caruthers taken prisoner.

About this time there lived near where the town of New Berlin now stands, a family named Klinesmith. A small party of Indians coming upon their dwelling, whilst the males of the family were busy in the harvest field of a neighbor, plundered the house, and carried away two of Klinesmith's daughters, one sixteen, the other fourteen years old. The party retreated to a spring north of New Berlin—now called the Still-House Spring—where they halted, and, not satisfied with the trifling mischief they had done, left their prisoners and booty in the care of the oldest man of the party, whilst the main body proceeded to the harvest field, in the hope of getting some scalps to carry home as trophies of their success.

The old man lighted his pipe, and sat down at the foot of a tree, keeping an eye upon his prisoners. After some time the rain began to fall, when Betsey, the eldest girl, intimated to the sentinel that she meant to cut down some branches from the trees, and cover a small bag of flour which the Indians had brought from her father's house. The Indian, little suspecting her real intention, assented, and permitted her to take one of the axes or tomahawks. She pretended to be very busily occupied with her task, but contrived to get behind the old man, and buried the axe in his head!

By this time the scalping party, finding the harvesters too numerous and well armed for their purposes, were on their return, and had already approached near enough to hear the groan or cry of the old Indian as he fell. The girls fled—the savages pursued, and fired. The younger girl, just as she was in the act of springing over a fallen tree, was pierced with a bullet, which entered below the shoulder blade, and came out at the breast. She fell, and immediately rolled herself under the log, which at that point was raised a little from the ground. The savages sprang over the log, in chase of her sister, without observing that any one lay under it.

Betsey being a strong and active lass, gave them a hard run, so that the harvesters, alarmed by the firing, came to the rescue in time to save her, and change the pursuers into fugitives. They found the little girl under the fallen tree, much terrified and weakened by loss of blood, but fortunately not dangerously wounded, the ball having passed through her body without touching any vital organ. She recovered, and afterwards married a man named Campbell. Becoming a widow, she married again. Her last husband's name was Chambers. Betsey also married, and, with her husband, removed to one of the Western States.

Residence of A. H. M'Henry, Jersey Shore, Pa.

CHAPTER XXXIV.

MURDER OF SERGEANT LEE AND JOHN WALKER—CAPTIVITY OF MRS. LEE AND TWO CHILDREN—HER CRUEL DEATH—PURSUIT OF THE SAVAGES—BURIAL OF THE DEAD—AN INCIDENT AT LEE'S FUNERAL—RECOVERY OF YOUNG LEE—VAN CAMPEN—SEVERE BATTLE ON BALD EAGLE—DEFEAT AND CAPTIVITY—NARROW ESCAPE, &c.

About the close of the Revolutionary war, Sergeant Lee and family resided in Dry Valley, a few miles above Northumberland, on a farm, since in the occupancy of a man named Irely. The Indians hated Lee, alleging that he had cheated them in a trade, and they had long thirsted for an opportunity to be revenged.

Towards the close of a fine summer day, probably in 1781, a party of savages entered the Valley, and proceeded in the direction of his house. Not far distant from where he resided, they passed an elderly man and woman sleeping in the woods, but so intent were they on surprising Lee, that they did not molest them, for fear of raising an alarm.

Lee's family, with one or two other persons, were quietly taking their tea, without any suspicion of the fate which awaited them; when the Indians suddenly burst in upon them. A young woman named Katy Stoner, escaped up stairs, and concealed herself behind the chimney, where she remained undiscovered. Lee was instantly tomahawked and scalped, and an old man named John Walker, shared the same fate. A Mrs. Boatman and daughter were also killed. Mrs. Lee, with her small child, and a larger one, named Thomas, were led away captives. The savages took the Great Path leading up that side of the Valley, crossed the White Deer mountains, came to the river, and crossed over.

One of Lee's sons, named Robert, happening to be absent at the time, escaped the fate of his parents. He was returning, however, and came in sight of the house just as the Indians were leaving it, but they did not observe him. Knowing that they were there with evil intentions, he immediately turned and fled to Northumberland, where he gave the alarm. A party of about twenty men* were hastily collected by Colonel Hunter at Fort Augusta, and started in pursuit. On arriving at Lee's house, they beheld the sufferers writhing in agony. Lee was not dead, and Mrs. Boatman's daughter also survived. Litters were hastily constructed, and they were sent to Fort Augusta, where Lee soon expired in great agony. Miss Boatman finally recovered, and lived for many years afterwards.

Colonel Hunter, and his party, without delaying to bury the dead, pushed after the savages as rapidly as possible, with a view of overtaking them. They came in sight of them above Lycoming Creek.

In crossing the mountains, Mrs. Lee was accidentally bitten by a rattlesnake on the ankle, and her leg became so much swollen, and pained her so severely, that she travelled with great difficulty. Finding

* Henry McHenry, the father of A. H. McHenry, of Jersey Shore, was in this expedition, and gave an account of it to his son.

themselves pursued, they urged her along as fast as possible, but she failed rapidly. When near the mouth of Pine Run, some four miles below Jersey Shore, she gave out, and seated herself on the ground. The whites were rapidly approaching, and the Indians were afraid she would fall into their hands. One of them stealthily slipped up behind her, and placing the muzzle of his rifle close to her head, fired. The whole upper portion of her head was blown off! One of them then snatched up her little child by the heels, and hastily dashed it against a tree, when they fled with renewed speed, and crossing the river at Smith's fording, ran up through Nippenose Bottom.

When Colonel Hunter and his men came up to where the body of Mrs. Lee laid, it was yet warm, *and the brains were smoking!* The sight was a horrible one to look upon. The child was but little injured, and was found moaning piteously, and staring wildly around.

Crossing over the river as rapidly as possible, they pursued the Indians up through the Bottom, and were so close on them, that when they came to Antes' Gap, they separated and ran up both sides of the mountain, into the swamp. Colonel Hunter considered it imprudent to follow them into the interminable thickets of the swamp, for fear of an ambuscade; and being much exhausted, they reluctantly gave up the chase, and slowly returned. Passing down, they buried the body of Mrs. Lee, and cared for her child. When they came to Lee's house, they halted, and buried the dead there. A hole was dug alongside of Walker, and his body rolled into it.

When Lee was buried at Fort Augusta, a little circumstance occurred worthy of being related. Two soldiers, having a spite at each other, were selected to bear one end of the coffin. On the way to the grave they got to quarreling, and commenced kicking at each other under the coffin. John Hunter, the Adjutant, perceiving their conduct, seized a rattan and gave them a sound threshing. This was a curious performance to take place at a funeral, and over the coffin!

Young Thomas Lee, who was taken prisoner and carried into captivity, was not recovered for many years afterwards. The son who gave the alarm on the fatal day of the murder, made arrangements with certain Indians to bring his brother to Tioga Point, where he was delivered to his friends. Such was his love of Indian life, however, having been raised amongst them, and being very reluctant to return, they were obliged to tie him, and place him on board a canoe. When near Wilkesbarre, they untied him, but as soon as the canoe touched the shore, he was out, and off like a deer. It was several hours before they succeeded in taking him again. On arriving at Northumberland, he evinced all the sullenness of a captive. Indian boys and girls, near his own age, were made to play about him for several days, before he showed any disposition to join with them. At last he began to inquire the names of things, and by degrees became civilized, and obtained a good education.

Nearly all the old people, yet living on the West Branch, are familiar with the names of Moses and Jacobus Van Campen. They were remarkable adventurers, as well as noted Indian killers, and distinguished themselves in many a well fought battle. Their services were very valuable in the protection of the frontiers.

In 1838, Major Moses Van Campen was living in the

town of Dansville, N. Y., when he applied to the government for a pension. His petition to Congress is a very interesting document. The following extract relates to the Valley of the West Branch:

"In February, 1781, I was promoted to a Lieutenancy, and entered upon the active duty of an officer by heading scouts; and as Capt. Robinson was no woodsman nor marksman, he preferred that I should encounter the danger and head the scouts. We kept up a constant chain of scouts around the frontier settlements, from the North to the West Branch of the Susquehanna by the way of the head waters of Little Fishing creek, Chilisquaque, Muncy, &c. In the spring of 1781 we built a fort on the widow McClure's plantation, called McClure's fort, where our provisions were stored. In the summer of 1781, a man was taken prisoner in Buffalo Valley, but made his escape. He came in and reported there were about 300 Indians on Sinnemahoning, hunting and laying in a store of provisions, and would make a descent on the frontiers; that they would divide into small parties, and attack the whole chain of the frontier at the same time, on the same day. Col. Hunter selected a company of five to reconnoitre, viz.: Capt. Campbell, Peter and Michael Groves, Lieut. Cramer and myself. The party was called the Grove party. We carried with us three weeks' provisions, and proceeded up the West Branch with much caution and care. We reached the Sinnemahoning, but made no discovery but old tracks. We marched up the Sinnemahoning so far that we were satisfied it was a false report. We returned; and a little below the Sinnemahoning, near night, we discovered a smoke. We were confident it was a party of Indians, which we must have passed by, or they got there some other way. We discovered there was a large party—how many we could not tell—but prepared for the attack.

"As soon as it was dark we new-primed our rifles, sharpened our flints, examined our tomahawk handles; and all being ready, we waited with great impatience till they all lay down. The time came, and with the utmost silence we advanced, trailed our rifles in one hand, and the tomahawk in the other. The night was warm: we found some of them rolled in their blankets a rod or two from their fires. Having got amongst them, we first handled our tomahawks. They rose like a dark cloud. We now fired our shots, and raised the war-yell. They took to flight in the utmost confusion, but few taking time to pick up their rifles. We remained masters of the ground and all their plunder, and took several scalps. It was a party of 25 or 30, which had been as low down as Penn's creek, and had killed and scalped two or three families. We found several scalps of different ages which they had taken, and a large quantity of domestic cloth, which was carried to Northumberland and given to the distressed who had escaped the tomahawk and knife. In Dec. 1781, our Company was ordered to Lancaster. We descended the river in boats to Middletown, where our orders were countermanded, and we were ordered to Reading, where we were joined by a part of the third and fifth Pennsylvania regiments, and a Company of the Congress regiment. We took charge of the Hessians taken prisoners with Gen. Burgoyne. In the latter part of March, at the opening of the Campaign in 1782, we were ordered by Congress to our respective stations. I marched Robinson's Company to Northumberland, where Mr. Thomas Chambers joined us, who had been recently commissioned as an ensign of our Company. We halted at Northumberland two or three days for our men to wash and rest. From thence Ensign Chambers and myself were ordered to Muncy, Samuel Wallis' plantation, there to make a stand and re-build Fort Muncy, which had been destroyed by the enemy. We reached that station and built a small block house for the storage of our provisions. About the 10th or 11th of April, Capt. Robinson came on with Esquire Culbertson, James Dougherty, William McGrady, and a Mr. Barkley. I was ordered to select 20 or 25 men, with these gentlemen, and proceed up the West Branch to the Big Island, and thence up the Bald Eagle creek, to the place where a Mr. Culbertson had been killed. On the 15th of April, at night, we reached the place and encamped. On the morning of the 16th we were attacked by 85 Indians. It was a hard fought battle. Esquire Culbertson and two others made their escape. I think we had nine killed, and the rest of us were made prisoners. We were stripped of all our clothing excepting our pantaloons. When they took off my shirt they discovered my commission. Our commissions were written on parchment, and carried in a silk case hung with a ribbon on our bosom. Several got hold of it; and one fellow cut the ribbon with his knife, and succeeded in obtaining it. They took us a little distance from the battle ground, and made the prisoners sit down in a small ring; the Indians forming another around us in close order, each with his rifle and tomahawk in his hand. They brought up five

Indians we had killed and laid them within the circle. Each one reflected for himself—our time would probably be short; and respecting myself, looking back upon the year 1780, at the party I had killed, if I was discovered to be the person, my case would be a hard one. Their prophet, or chief warrior, made a speech. As I was informed afterwards by a British Lieutenant, who belonged to the party, he was consulting the Great Spirit what to do with the prisoners—whether to kill us on the spot, or spare our lives. He came to the conclusion that there had been blood enough shed; and as to the men they had lost, it was the fate of war, and we must be taken and adopted into the families of those whom we had killed. We were then divided amongst them, according to the number of fires. Packs were prepared for us, and they returned across the river, at Big Island, in bark canoes. They then made their way across hills, and came to Pine creek, above the first forks, which they followed up to the third fork, and took the most northerly branch to the head of it—and thence to the waters of the Genesee river."

Van Campen and his fellow-prisoners were marched through the Indian villages. Some were adopted, to make up the loss of those killed in the action. Van Campen passed through all their villages undiscovered; neither was it known he had been a prisoner before, and only effected his escape by killing the party, until he had been delivered up to the British, at Fort Niagara. As soon as his name was made known, it became public among the Indians. They immediately demanded him of the British officer, and offered a number of prisoners in exchange. The commander on the station sent forthwith an officer to examine him. He stated the facts to the officer concerning his killing the party of savages. The officer replied, that his case was desperate. Van Campen observed, that he considered himself a prisoner of war to the British; that he thought they possessed more honor than to deliver him up to the Indians to be burnt at the stake; and in case they did, they might depend upon a retaliation in the life of one of their officers. The officer withdrew, but shortly returned, and informed him, that there remained no alternative for him to save his life, but to abandon the rebel cause, and join the British standard. A further inducement was offered, that he should hold the same rank in the British service that he now possessed. The answer of Van Campen was worthy the hero, and testified that the heart of the patriot never quailed under the most trying circumstances: "*No, sir, no—my life belongs to my country; give me the stake, the tomahawk, or the scalping-knife, before I will dishonor the character of an American officer!*"

In the month of March, 1783, Van Campen was exchanged by the British, and returned home. He was immediately ordered to take up arms again, which he did, and joined his company the same month at Northumberland. About that time Captain Robinson received orders to march with his company to Wyoming. Van Campen and Ensign Chambers accompanied them, and remained there till November of the same year, when the army was discharged, and they retired, poor and penniless, to the shades of private life.

CHAPTER XXXV.

ULRICH AND THE FRIENDLY SAVAGES—THE STOCK FAMILY—MURDER OF MRS. STOCK—HER HEROIC DEFENCE—PURSUIT OF THE INDIANS—THE SURPRISE AND SLAUGHTER BY THE WHITES—LIEUTENANT COOKE'S SUFFERINGS—CAPTAINS BOYD AND ROSS—THE LATTER BURNED AT THE STAKE, NEAR SINNEMAHONING—BOYD'S LIFE IS SAVED BY A SQUAW—HULING'S JUMP, THE GREATEST ON RECORD.

An old settler near Selinsgrove, informed Mr. Snyder, some fifteen or twenty years ago, that when his father, Mr. Ulrich, came to the country, several Indians still remained in the neighborhood. They came frequently to their house, and were always treated with great kindness. They had a particular liking for bread and butter, which was never refused them. In return, they brought game, maple sugar, and Indian baskets. By this kindness shown them, Ulrich's family acquired the affectionate attachment of these swarthy children of the forest; a feeling which was of infinite service to them, and in all probability, was the shield between them and the tomahawk.

On one occasion, when two Indians came to the house of Mr. Ulrich, his son George, a small lad, was much amused at the manner in which one had *beautified* himself. He had painted a bright red circular patch about his mouth, leaving the remainder of his face plain. He observed the lad laughing at him, when he said: "Well, little George, what are you laughing for? You are admiring my handsome mouth, I suppose?" This was spoken in German, which these Indians had learned from their intercourse with the whites in that settlement.

These Indians, on one occasion, requested Mr. Ulrich to leave, as a large party of hostile Indians were expected to attack the settlements. "You are our friend," said they, "and we are desirous of saving you—so you had better go to your friends in Tulpehocken." He informed them, that he could not leave his crops to be destroyed, and would rather take the risk of staying where he was. "I will send my children to Tulpehocken," said he, "and trust to your friendship." They warned him to be on his guard, however, and promised to do what they could to save him from their red brethren. They counselled him to keep as much as possible within doors, and promised to drive his cattle homewards, if they found them straying too far in the woods. They could not warrant his safety, however, for the red man, when out on a scalping party, is not easily restrained. The war parties came and ravaged the country, but during the continuance of hostilities, Ulrich remained undisturbed.

One of the most remarkable murders which occurred at that time—about 1781—was that of the Stock family, who resided about two miles west of Selinsgrove. Stock was particularly disliked by the Indians, on account of his harsh and inhospitable conduct towards them.

On the day of the murder, Stock and three of his sons, were occupied in clearing a field in a deep narrow valley, about a mile from the house; when a scalping party of about thirty Indians was drawn by the sound of the axes to the edge of the hill, overlooking the field where they were at work. Seeing that there were four stout men, armed, and on their guard, they passed on without molesting them, and proceeded to the house. In a field near the dwelling, they found another son, ploughing, whom one of the party shot and scalped, while the remainder entered the house, where they found none but Stock's wife and her daughter-in-law, recently married. The mother, a strong and courageous woman, escaped from the house, and defended herself with a canoe pole, as she retreated towards the field where her husband was. She was, however, killed by a tomahawk, thrown by one of her pursuers, and scalped. The house was hastily plundered, and the young woman carried off. It appeared by the footprints, that her strength failed from terror, in a newly ploughed field through which they were leading her, when two Indians took her between them, and supported her until they got into the woods, about one hundred yards from the house, where they killed and scalped her.

When Stock returned home, he found his house plundered, his son lying on his face in the field, dead—the young woman in the woods, inhumanly butchered, and his wife, with a deep wound in her forehead, lying on her back, with the canoe pole by her side. What a sight for the husband and father!

The neighborhood was quickly alarmed, and three experienced Indian fighters, named Grove, Pence, and Stroh, set out in pursuit of the enemy. The speed with which the Indians travelled, and the care required to keep on their trail, and avoid an ambuscade, prevented the white men from overtaking them, until they had got into the State of New York, somewhere on the head waters of the North Branch, where they found the party, encamped for the night, on the side of a hill covered with fern. Here the Indians fancied themselves safe. The distance they had travelled in safety, warranted them in believing that they had not been pursued, and they therefore kept no watch. Grove, leaving his gun at the foot of the hill, crept up through the ferns, and observed that all their rifles were piled around a tree, and that all but three or four were asleep. One of them, a large and powerful man, was narrating in high good humor, and with much impressive gesticulation, the attack on Stock's family, and described the manner in which Mrs. Stock defended herself. Grove lay quiet until the auditors fell asleep, and the orator, throwing his blanket over his head, slept also. He then returned to his comrades, Stroh and Pence, informed them of what he had seen, and concerted the plan of attack, which was put in execution, as soon as they thought the orator and his hearers fast asleep. They ascended the hill, when Grove plied his tomahawk, while Stroh and Pence took possession of the rifles, and fired among the sleepers. One of the first to awake was the orator, whom Grove despatched with a single blow, as he threw his blanket from his head, and arose. How many they killed I do not know, but they brought home a number of scalps. The Indians thinking they were attacked by a large party, fled in all directions, and abandoned everything. A white boy, about fifteen years of age, whom they had carried off, was rescued and brought back.

The survivors having fled, they selected of the best of the rifles, as many as they could conveniently carry, destroyed the remainder, and made their way to the Susquehanna, where they constructed a raft of logs and embarked. The river was so low, that their descent was both tedious and slow, and their raft unfortunately striking a rock at Nanticoke Falls, went to pieces, and they lost all of their rifles and plunder. From this place they returned home on foot in safety.

In 1781, the people of Northumberland were much alarmed on the report of a body of Indians having been seen in the neighborhood. They were informed of their approach by a man named Frank Grey, who was riding to town, but perceiving a couple of Indians jump a fence, turned and rode swiftly in another direction, and gave the alarm to a party of men working in a field, a short distance up the North Branch. They immediately furnished Pompey, an old negro belonging to Captain Cook, with a gun, and started him to give the alarm in another direction. Going along the river, he perceived two Indians standing under the bank, leaning on their rifles, and pointing in the direction of Fort Augusta. Pompey ran back very much frightened, when David Steedman jumped into a canoe, crossed over, and went down and informed the people in the fort. The following day, John Hamilton was shot, whilst at work, in a field, a short distance from town.

About the same time, Lieutenant John Cook of Northumberland, a full cousin of Colonel Cook, belonged to the company of Captain Boyd. The Captain started with a company of about forty men on an expedition to the Juniata to look for Indians. They were suddenly surprised by a large body in ambush, and fired upon. A smart engagement took place, but the whites were overcome by superior numbers, and after losing several men, were compelled to fly. Cook received several wounds, and was taken prisoner. Four Indians took him in charge, and started off, he knew not where. On the third night of his captivity they began to amuse themselves by burning his legs with firebrands, and as he was much exhausted from loss of blood from his wounds, was scarcely able to move. After travelling through the wilderness for about twenty days, fed on the entrails of wild animals, they brought him to Niagara. He was brought out one day to run the gauntlet, but being unable to run, as his legs were so badly burned, the savages at length took mercy on him, and let him off. He was then confined in prison till he was finally exchanged and returned. He is said to have had an exceedingly sharp pair of legs from the knees down, probably occasioned by the burning.

Previous to this, Cook captured an Indian near Northumberland, and brought him to town a prisoner. The scuffle between them was animated and severe, but he succeeded in getting the Indian's gun, tomahawk, and knife away from him, and finally overpowered him. The Indian remained at Northumberland for many years, and became quite civilized. Cook died in March, 1822, aged seventy-six years.

Several accounts of Captain Boyd's captivity have been published, but are said to be incorrect. The following account was furnished me by Mr. Jacob Cook, of Muncy, and is claimed to be correct:

After the defeat of Captain Boyd's party, he tried to make his escape by running, but was pursued and received three severe gashes in his head with a tomahawk, when he was taken. The Indians immediately struck across the country, and came to the West Branch, near the mouth of the Sinnemahoning Creek. They also had another prisoner, named Ross, who was wounded very badly. Being unable to travel further, they determined to massacre him in a very cruel and inhuman manner. He was fastened to a stake, and his body stuck full of pitch pine splinters, when fire was applied, and they danced round him, making the woods resound with their hideous yells. His tortures were terrible, but at length death put an end to his sufferings.

During this time Captain Boyd, faint from the loss of blood, was tied to a small white oak sapling, and compelled to be a silent spectator of the diabolical scene. His turn was to come next, and he summoned up courage, and quietly resigned himself to his fate. Whilst these incarnate fiends of Pandemonium were making preparations to torture him to death by inches, he sang a very pretty Free Mason song, with a plaintive air, which attracted their attention, and they listened to it very closely, till he was through. At this critical moment an elderly squaw came up, and claimed him as her son. The Indians did not interfere. She immediately dressed his wounds, and attended to him carefully during their journey to Canada. She accompanied him to Quebec, where he was placed in the hospital, and attended by an English surgeon, and rapidly recovered. He was then turned out into the street without money or friends. As he passed along, a large sign, with the letters, "Masonic Inn," painted on it, attracted his attention, and observing the landlord standing in the door, gave him the sign of the Order, which was recognized. He was kindly taken in, and cared for till he was exchanged. The wounds on his head occasioned him to keep up a continual winking.

The old squaw who was the means of preserving his life, belonged to the Oneida tribe. Boyd remembered her as his *best* friend, and often sent her presents of money. On one occasion he made a journey personally to visit her. Boyd died in Northumberland.

A story is related,* that about the time of the Indian troubles, a man named Marcus Huling, living in the town of Northumberland, was on the west side of the river, when he was suddenly chased by a number of Indians. He ran as swiftly as he could towards the precipice at Blue Hill, but they gained so rapidly upon him, that he expected to be taken there. They also fancied him secure in their grasp. Being drove to the edge of the frightful precipice, with the savages yelling in his rear, he determined to make the dreadful leap, preferring to die in this manner, rather than fall beneath the tomahawk of the Indian. Seizing a large branch of a tree in his hands, he jumped over, and landed some *ninety* feet below, on a shelf of the rock, unhurt! From this point he jumped *forty* feet further, and escaped with only the dislocation of his shoulder. The savages were obliged to run round for a mile, when he escaped. This jump, if true, is certainly the greatest one on record. It is supposed the branch broke his fall, and saved his life. Huling, on being asked about it, replied, that he "jumped for a great wager—he jumped for his life!"

* By Jacob Cook, Esq., of Muncy.

Residence of J. J. Sanderson, Jersey Shore, Pa.

CHAPTER XXXVI.

CAPTURE OF ROBERT LYON—CARRIED TO CANADA—UNEXPECTEDLY MEETS HIS BROTHER—HIS FAITHFUL DOG FOLLOWS HIM AND RETURNS—ARREST OF A TORY—HIS DEATH—GROVE'S ENCOUNTER WITH INDIANS ON SINNEMAHONING—A BLOODY DEED—DIES IN NIPPENOSE VALLEY—ADVENTURE IN THE GENESEE COUNTRY—PETER PENCE.

SOMEWHERE about the close of the Revolutionary war, Robert Lyon* was despatched from Fort Augusta to Wyoming, with a canoe loaded with supplies for a company of men stationed at that point. In the afternoon of the first day he landed his canoe at the mouth of Fishing Creek, and leaving his dog and gun in it, hastened to the house of Mr. Cooper, who had two very interesting daughters, one of whom he had taken quite a fancy to. He had scarcely seated himself in Mr. Cooper's house, and entered into conversation with his intended, till he observed her sister leave the house. At this moment an inward monitor seemed to warn him of approaching danger, and but a few minutes elapsed till three hideously painted savages rushed in at the door. The only weapon within reach that he could lay his hands on, was a dull case knife, lying on the table.

* I am indebted for this information respecting Mr. Lyon, to Jacob Cooke, Esq., of Muncy, as well as several other interesting reminiscences.

This he seized and endeavored to defend himself. The three Indians attacked him, and a dreadful struggle ensued. He managed to floor two of them, when the third one sprang upon his back, and endeavored to pinion his arms. The old case knife was used vigorously, and he tried, with all his strength, to thrust it into their bodies, but it was too blunt. If he had been in possession of a good knife, there is but little doubt he would have despatched all three. In the midst of the struggle, four more Indians came to the door, and one of them cried out in English, "Give up, Lyon, you sha'nt be hurt." Seeing the number increasing, he yielded, and suffered himself to be bound and led away.

The first night he was bound hand and foot, and placed between two Indians, in a thicket of underbrush, about seven miles from where he was captured. The notorious Shenap commanded this marauding band; he could talk English sufficiently plain to be easily understood, and informed his prisoner that his life would be spared, but he would be compelled to run the gauntlet, when they got to the end of their journey.

After many days of toilsome traveling, through swamps, and over hills, Lyon became much exhausted, and his wrists and ankles became very sore and much swollen, from the effects of the cords used in tying him at night. At length they arrived at the Niagara river, about three miles above where the town stood. He was placed in a canoe, and conveyed down to the village to run the gauntlet. A long row of warriors, squaws, and young ones, were drawn up ready for the amusement, armed with clubs, stones, and all manner of weapons. Shenap pointed to the door of the Council House, and informed him if he reached it, he was safe, and encouraged him to run rapidly. Lyon was well aware of his situation, and knew that if he attempted to run round them, his life would be the forfeit. He plunged in between the two ranks, knocking and kicking them about at such a furious rate, that he only received two or three light strokes, and arriving at the goal, was safe.

After the race was over, he was taken and placed in prison, where he remained about two weeks, without seeing the face of any person, save his keeper, when he was visited by a very gentlemanly officer, clothed in the uniform of the British army, who asked him many questions concerning himself, his brothers, sisters, &c. Lyon informed him that he was an Irishman by birth, and when a small lad had come to America with his brother Benjamin, but what had become of him he was unable to say. At this juncture the officer abruptly turned away and left, without saying another word. When the keeper came, he inquired if he had been visited by an officer, and on being answered in the affirmative, said, "You will fare well; *that officer is your own brother!*" He was thunderstruck, as it were, and could scarcely believe that such was his good fortune as to fall into the hands of his long lost brother so unexpectedly. He had not seen him since he was seven years of age, and had almost entirely forgotten him. In three days' time he was released from prison, and set at liberty.

Whilst he was confined, the jailor informed him that a large yellow dog had come to the door of the prison, and remained there manifesting much uneasiness. From the description, he knew him to be his own faithful animal, that he had not seen since he left him with his rifle in the canoe at Fishing Creek, and was satisfied that he had followed him through the wilderness to this place.

He desired the keeper to take charge of him, which he promised, but he disappeared suddenly that night.

The people of Northumberland and vicinity, had not learned the fate of Lyon, and wondered what had become of him. One day, his dog came to the house of Mr. McKee, in Buffalo Valley, apparently much distressed and half starved. He acted very strangely, and seemed as if he wanted to tell them something. The faithful animal was returning from the door of his master's prison in Canada, to inform them of his captivity, *but he was not gifted with the power of speech*, and had to manifest his errand by signs! They offered him food, but he refused to eat. Mr. McKee knew the dog, and judging there was something wrong, mounted his horse and rode to Northumberland to make inquiry, where he learned that Lyon was supposed to be a captive.

When Lyon returned home, his noble dog was lying behind the house, but he scented him when forty yards distant, and running to meet him, placed his paws on his shoulders, and licked his face with gladness!

The fact of Lyon having disappeared so mysteriously from the house of Cooper, together with other evidences, convinced the people that he was a tory, and endeavoring to further the interest of the enemy. A party of men from Northumberland, proceeded to his house and arrested him as a traitor, and placed him in a boat to convey him to Sunbury jail. On their passage down, a rifle belonging to a man named Doyle, was accidentally lost overboard. Doyle in his fury, accused Cooper of throwing it in, which he denied, and an altercation taking place, he seized a hatchet, and buried it in Cooper's skull. The unfortunate man lived about twenty days, when he expired in prison.

Lyon afterwards married a young lady of another family, and resided in Northumberland county till his death, which took place in 1822. He left two sons; one named Robert, still survives, and lives on the main road leading to Milton, about five miles above Northumberland.

In 1781 or 1782, a party of Indians suddenly made a descent upon Buffalo Valley, and succeeded in killing and scalping one or two. To avenge this outrage, Captain Peter Grove, Lieutenant Cramer, William Campbell, and Michael Grove, followed them, resolved not to return without at least some scalps, even if they had to pursue them to their towns. In the afternoon of the third or fourth day after they had left Northumberland, they came in sight of the Indians. At this time they were between the Great Island and Youngwomanstown, and ascertained them to be forty or fifty in number.

As the Indians did not consider themselves sufficiently safe to kindle their fires that evening, our heroes delayed their attack on that account, and patiently awaited a more favorable moment. They stealthily pursued them all the next day, resolved to attack them the first favorable opportunity, notwithstanding their numbers. This was afforded them that evening, when the Indians encamped on the bank of Sinnemahoning Creek, about twelve miles from its mouth, and fancying themselves secure, kindled their fires for the first time.

The desires of the pursuers were now accomplished, and silently creeping up, they observed the number of Indians, the position of their arms, and the manner in which they had retired to rest. They now patiently waited till they were all wrapped in sleep before commencing the attack. One old Indian annoyed them very much. He was troubled with a severe cough, and frequently rose up and looked carefully around, seeming from his peculiar actions, to anticipate danger. At length the old man fell asleep, when they commenced creeping up, intending to use their tomahawks first. One of them unexpectedly crawled over an Indian, who had laid himself down some distance from the rest, and the old man also rose up at this moment. Finding themselves discovered, they rushed on them. Michael Grove with a powerful stroke of his hatchet, clove the skull of the old Indian in twain, and dexterously striking it into the back of another, was unable to withdraw it, when the Indian drew him over the bank into the creek, where, however, he succeeded in killing and scalping him. They plied their tomahawks to the best advantage, and then used their rifles. Several Indians were killed, when they fled to the opposite side of the creek, and finding that the attacking party was small, commenced a brisk fire, and being between them and the light, had the advantage, which prevented them from returning to scalp the killed. They bore off two scalps, however, and commenced their retreat immediately. To avoid pursuit, they waded down the creek to its mouth, and taking the hills, continued to where Lock Haven now stands, when they passed up over "Proctor's Farm,"* to the summit of the Bald Eagle Ridge, and continuing along it for several miles, reached their homes in safety.

Grove was a celebrated Indian killer, and many a sa-

* The traveller along the river, when near the Great Island, will observe a large bare spot of land covered with stones, on the north side of Bald Eagle Mountain. This is called "Proctor's Farm," and takes its name from a land speculator, who first owned it.

vage was made by him to pay the death penalty. He was an inveterate hater of the race, and never let an opportunity slip to give one of them a passport to the spirit-land. He was one of the first settlers in Buffalo Valley, about two and-a-half miles east of Mifflinburg. If all his daring deeds, hair-breadth escapes, and remarkable adventures had been preserved, they would fill a volume. But they are obscured by the dark curtain of eternity.

Visiting a daughter who resided in Nippenose Valley, at an advanced age, he was suddenly taken ill, and shortly afterwards expired. He was attended in his last moments by Dr. A. Davidson, of Jersey Shore, to whom he related the bloody affair on Sinnemahoning, and gave a vivid account of his killing the old Indian. This was the only act of his life that worked upon his mind, and he seemed to manifest some contrition of spirit for the unceremonious manner in which he had launched the spirit of the old man into eternity. His death took place about 1827.

Another adventure of this Indian-hunter is preserved, which I will here relate:

On one of his hunting excursions he wandered into the Genesee county, where he lost himself, and was under the necessity of entering an Indian village for information. During his conference with them, he remarked that the attention of the Indians appeared to be directed very particularly to his hunting-pouch and horn. These articles he had taken from a renowned warrior, whom he had slain some years before; and he now conjectured that he was of this tribe, and they knew who they had among them, and would certainly have blood for blood, if an opportunity offered. Grove kept his countenance and his counsel, and, having received his directions, set out. He walked very quietly and unconcernedly away, but so soon as out of sight, put forth his speed and strength—in which he had never found his superior—and fairly outran his vindictive foes. This he considered the most imminent danger to which he had ever been exposed.

There was another remarkable hunter and Indian-killer in this valley, named Peter Pence, of whom many wonderful stories are related. He is described by those who remember him, as being a savage-looking customer, and always went armed with his rifle, tomahawk and knife, years after peace was made.

The accounts of his adventures with the Indians being in such a vague and unsatisfactory form, I have concluded to omit them altogether, rather than detail them incorrectly. I much regret this, since I made some effort to get a correct sketch of them. It is said that an account of his life was published some thirty years ago, and is remembered by some, but the most careful research has failed to develop it.

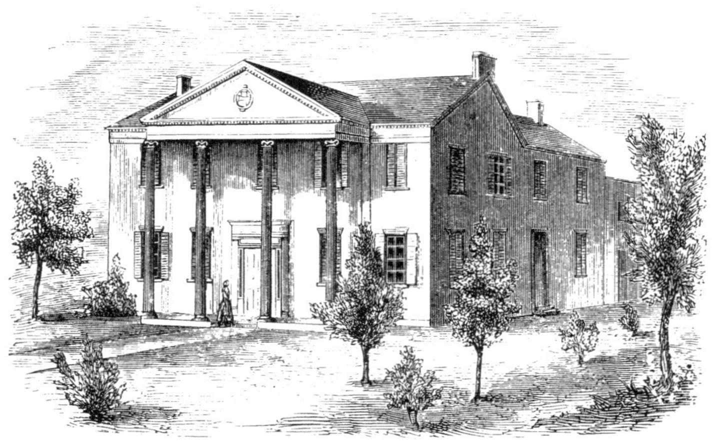

Residence of M. Slonaker, Jersey Shore, Pa.

CHAPTER XXXVII.

THE TREATY OF 1784—THE REAL TIADAGHTON MADE KNOWN—HUGHES, DOUGHERTY, TONER, AND SWEENY'S DIFFICULTY ABOUT LAND—SETTLERS OF '85—DR. DAVIDSON—COLONEL HUGH WHITE—COPY OF HIS COMMISSION—SKETCH OF THE MONTOUR FAMILY—THEIR GRANTS OF LAND.

I NOW come to the close of the Revolutionary war, and the treaty of Fort Stanwix. The troubles and difficulties incident upon the bloody Indian wars, are about to cease, and peace—happy peace—usurp her reign once more. The struggle for freedom is over—the battle has been won, and the flag of American Liberty is unfurled to the breeze in this Western World.

The last treaty at Fort Stanwix, with the Indians, took place in October, 1784.* One important feature of this treaty, was the settlement of the difficulty that had existed for some sixteen years between the whites, in relation to the boundary line embraced by *Tiadaghton.* It will be remembered that some contended that Lycoming Creek was the line, and others that it was Pine Creek.

At this treaty the Pennsylvania Commissioners were specially instructed to inquire of the Indians, which stream was *really* the Tiadaghton, and also the Indian

* See Smith's Laws, Vol. II., page 123. Fort Stanwix was located on the site now occupied by the town of Rome, in the State of New York.

name of Burnett's Hills, left blank in the deed of 1768. The Indians informed them *Tiadaghton* was what the whites called Pine Creek, being the largest stream emptying into the West Branch. As to *Burnett's Hills*, they called them the *Long Mountains*, and knew them by no other name.

At this treaty a purchase was made of the residue of the Indian lands within the limits of Pennsylvania, and the deed signed by the chiefs of the Six Nations, is dated October 23, 1784. The boundaries are thus described:

"Beginning on the south side of the river Ohio, where the western boundary of the State of Pennsylvania crosses the said river, near Shingo's old town, at the mouth of Beaver Creek, and thence by a due north line to the end of the forty-second and beginning of the forty-third degrees of north latitude, thence by a due east line separating the forty-second and forty-third degrees of north latitude, to the east side of the east branch of the river Susquehanna, thence by the bounds of the late purchase made at Fort Stanwix, the fifth day of November, *Anno Domini*, one thousand seven hundred and sixty-eight, as follows: Down the said east branch of Susquehanna, on the east side thereof, till it came opposite to the mouth of a creek called by the Indians, *Awandac*, and across the river, and up the said creek on the south side thereof, all along the range of hills called *Burnett's Hills* by the English, and by the Indians ———, on the north side of them, to the head of a creek which runs into the west branch of *Susquehanna*, which creek is by the Indians called *Tiadaghton*, but by the Pennsylvanians, *Pine Creek*, and down the said creek on the south side thereof to the said west branch of Susquehanna, then crossing the said river, and running up the same on the south side thereof to the fork of the same river, which lies nearest to a place on the river Ohio, called *Kittanning* aforesaid, and then down the said river Ohio, by the several courses thereof to where the western bounds of the said State of Pennsylvania crosses the same river, at the place of beginning."

At a treaty held at Fort McIntosh, with the Wyandott

and Delaware Indians, by the same Commissioners, January, 1785, a deed was executed by those nations, for the same lands, in the same words, with the same boundaries, dated January 21st, 1785. Both of these deeds, with the treaties, or conferences, are printed at large in the appendix to the Journal of the Assembly for February, 1785.

Thus, in a period of about one hundred and two years, was the whole right of the Indians to the soil of Pennsylvania extinguished. The Legislature, at the time of this last treaty, being apprehensive that the directions given to the Commissioners to ascertain the precise boundaries of the purchase of 1768, might produce some inconveniences, passed an act as follows:

> "That the said directors did not give, nor ought not to be construed to give to the said commissioners, any authority to ascertain, definitely, the boundary lines aforesaid, and that the lines of the purchase so made, as aforesaid, in the year one thousand seven hundred and sixty-eight, striking the line of the west branch of Susquehanna, at the mouth of *Lycomick* or *Lycoming* creek, shall be the boundaries of the same purchase, to all legal intents and purposes, until the general assembly shall otherwise regulate and declare the same."

This last accession of lands was called by the whites the "New Purchase," and when the land office opened in 1785, settlers rapidly flocked to the West Branch above Lycoming Creek, to take up the choice lands in that region. Nearly all the original settlers, or *squatters*, on this disputed territory, previous to the "Big Runaway," now returned and claimed their lands.

The dispute about this territory being settled, some trouble was likely to arise with the original settlers. In view of this, the Legislature passed the following act, which may be found in Smith's Laws, Vol. II., page 195:

"And whereas divers persons, who have heretofore occupied and cultivated small tracts of lands, without the bounds of the purchase made as aforesaid in the year 1768, and within the purchase made or now to be made, have, *by their resolute stand and sufferings during the late war*, merited, that those settlers should have the pre-emption of their respective plantations, it is enacted, that all and every person, or persons, and *their legal representatives*, who has, or have heretofore settled, on the north side of the West Branch of Susquehanna, between *Lycomick* or *Lycoming* Creek on the east, and Tyadaghton, or Pine Creek, on the west, as well as other lands within the said residuary purchase from the Indians, of the territory within this State, (excepting always the lands hereinbefore excepted,) shall be allowed a right of pre-emption to their respective possessions, at the price aforesaid."

No person was to be entitled to the benefit of this pre-emption act, unless he had made an actual settlement before 1780, and no claim was to be admitted for more than 300 acres of land, &c., and the consideration thereof tendered to the Receiver General of the Land Office, on or before the 1st of November, 1785.

Several cases of litigation took place between some of these settlers, that were decided under the pre-emption clause. The first was John Hughes, against Henry Dougherty, tried in 1791. The plaintiff claimed under a warrant of May 2d, 1785, for the premises, and a survey made thereon the 10th of Jan., 1786. On the 20th of June, 1785, the defendant entered a *caveat* against the claims of the plaintiff, and on the 5th of October following, took out a warrant for the land in dispute, on which he was then settled. Both claimed the pre-emption of 1784. The facts given in evidence are as follows:

"In 1773, one James Hughes, a brother of the plaintiff, settled on the land in question, and made some small improvements. In the next year he enlarged his improvement, and cut logs to build a house. In the winter following, he went to his father's, in Donegal, in Lancaster Co., and died there. His elder brother, Thomas, was at that time settled on the Indian land, and one of the fair play men, who assembled together and made a resolution, (which they agreed to enforce as the law of the place,) that 'if any person was absent from his settlement for six weeks, he should forfeit his right.'"

In the spring of 1775, Dougherty came to the settlement, and was advised by the *fair play* men to settle on the premises which Hughes had left. This he did, and built a cabin. The plaintiff soon after came, claiming it in right of his brother, and, aided by Thomas Hughes, took possession of the cabin. But Dougherty collecting his friends, a fight ensued, in which Hughes was beaten off, and he remained in possession. He continued to improve; built a house and stable, and cleared about ten acres. In 1778 he was driven off by the enemy, and went into the army. At the close of the war, both parties returned and claimed the land. After hearing the argument, the jury decided in favor of Dougherty.

The next case was between John Toner and Morgan Sweeny. Toner went upon the Indian land in 1773, and made a settlement; but he exchanged it for another, on which he continued, with a view to make a settlement for his family, till the war broke out, and there was a call for soldiers. He inclined to list, but was afraid of losing his land, and his friends attempted to dissuade him. However, they promised to preserve his settlement for him, and he enlisted.

In 1775, Sweeny went up, and there was some contract in writing, by way of lease, between him and Toner, and by virtue of that he entered into possession of the premises. The terms of the lease were, that he should make certain improvements on the place for the benefit of Toner. This lease was deposited in the hands of a third person, and Sweeny's wife, by a trick, got hold of it, and she and her husband determined to destroy it, and so make the place their own. They continued there till driven off by the Indians. During all this time, Toner was absent from the settlement, but in the service of his country. The suit was decided in favor of Toner.

The Valley rapidly filled up with settlers—improvements were made, barns and houses erected, and in a short time peace and plenty abounded.

Amongst some of the settlers, after the war, I will mention the names of Stewart, Davidson, and White.

Samuel Stewart came with his father, and settled on the river, in Nippenose Bottom. He became quite a leading man in after years, and was one of the first sheriffs of Lycoming county. He fought a duel, with pistols, opposite the town of Lewisburg, with John Binns, a printer of Northumberland. Neither one was injured. Mr. Stewart lived till an advanced age, and only died a few years ago.

Dr. James Davidson settled a short distance below the mouth of Pine Creek in 1785. He was a surgeon in the army during the Revolutionary period, and was present at a number of battles. A case of surgical instruments used by him at the battle of Eutaw Springs, is now in the possession of his son, Dr. A. Davidson, of Jersey Shore. They are carefully preserved as a valuable relic of that dark and gloomy period. Dr. Davidson was a useful man in his time, and filled several important offices. He was one of the first Associate Judges of Lycoming County, and afterwards a member of the State Legislature. For many years he enjoyed an extensive practice of medicine, and was beloved and respected for his many acts of benevolence and humanity.

His death occurred in 1825, at the age of 73, when his mantle descended upon his son, who has been a successful practitioner forty years, and yet enjoys the confidence and respect of the community.

Colonel Hugh White,* who held a commission in the army of the Revolution, settled, about this time, some five miles above Jersey Shore. He acted for some time

* A correct copy of Colonel White's commission, as Captain, is herewith appended, to show the manner and style of commissioning meritorious individuals at that day. The *original* document is now in the possession of his son, Henry White, of Williamsport:

"*Pennsylvania ss.*

IN ASSEMBLY.

April 19th, 1776.

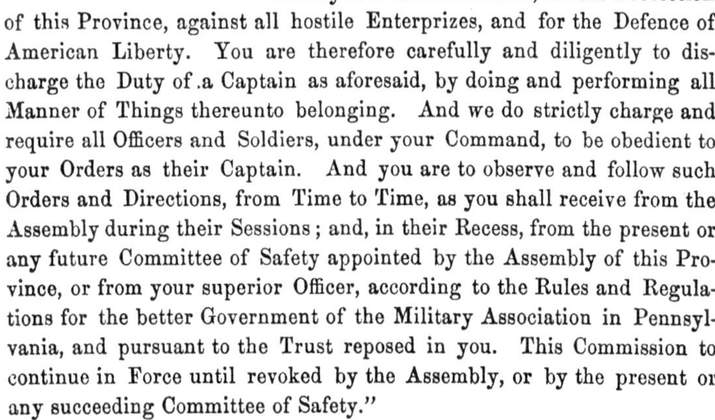

To Hugh White, Esq.

WE reposing especial Trust and confidence in your Patriotism, Valour, Conduct and Fidelity, DO, by those Presents, constitute and appoint you to be Captain of a Company of Foot in the 1st Battalion of Associators in the County of Northumberland, for the Protection of this Province, against all hostile Enterprizes, and for the Defence of American Liberty. You are therefore carefully and diligently to discharge the Duty of .a Captain as aforesaid, by doing and performing all Manner of Things thereunto belonging. And we do strictly charge and require all Officers and Soldiers, under your Command, to be obedient to your Orders as their Captain. And you are to observe and follow such Orders and Directions, from Time to Time, as you shall receive from the Assembly during their Sessions; and, in their Recess, from the present or any future Committee of Safety appointed by the Assembly of this Province, or from your superior Officer, according to the Rules and Regulations for the better Government of the Military Association in Pennsylvania, and pursuant to the Trust reposed in you. This Commission to continue in Force until revoked by the Assembly, or by the present or any succeeding Committee of Safety."

Signed by Order of the Assembly,

JOHN MORTON, *Speaker.*

He proved himself a faithful, as well as valuable Officer, and subsequently rose to the rank of Colonel.

in the capacity of a Commissary, and mention is frequently made of him in the Colonial Records. He was an active, as well as useful man, in his time, and was untiring in his efforts to provide supplies for the starving army of Washington. He is described, by those who remember him, as being an exceedingly polite and gentlemanly man. He died in 1822, at the age of 85—from injuries received by being thrown from a horse—leaving behind him ten sons and two daughters, who are amongst the most respectable and leading citizens of the Valley.

Colonel John Chatham took up land in 1785, and settled at the mouth of Chatham's run, where Judge Crawford now resides.

I might mention many others, and give interesting biographical sketches of their lives, but the limits of this work will not permit of it, and I must forego that pleasant duty, and hasten on to more general topics of history.

THE MONTOUR FAMILY.

Of the Montour family I have failed to glean much of the history, as they flourished at such an early period, that no record appears to have been kept of them. John and Roland Montour were two roving braves of the Seneca tribe. They also had a sister named Catrina, who was a remarkable woman, and unrelenting, like her brother John, in her hatred to the whites.

Roland Montour married a French woman, by whom he had three sons, Andrew, Henry, and Robert. If they had any more children, mention is not made of them. They lived at Shamokin when that place was first visited by the English. The two brothers are described to have been men of fine proportions—noble specimens of the Indian race—and inveterate haters of the English.

Roland appears to have died at quite an early period, and his widow, who always went by the name of Madame Montour, shortly afterwards married another Indian, named Carondowana, alias Robert Hunter, but soon afterwards lost him in a war against the Catawbas. Madame Montour was a remarkable woman, and contrary to the disposition of her husband, very friendly to the English. When Count Zinzendorf visited Shamokin, he crossed the river and went to the town of Ostonwackin, where she resided, and was very kindly received and entertained by her for several days.

John Montour was frequently engaged in predatory incursions against the settlers on the West Branch, and was at the taking of Fort Freeland, where he received a wound that proved mortal. He is said to have been buried at the "Painted Post." Catrina was also there. She had a village on the banks of Seneca Lake.

Whatever became of Madame Montour, is not stated; but it is *probable* that she lived and died at Shamokin, from the fact that her sons became the fast friends of the English. Her sons were what was called, "French half-breeds." They became the friends of the whites on their first arrival, and always remained steadfast through the trying wars that ensued. Having acquired the English language, they soon became interpreters, and were employed by the government in that capacity. After a long and tried apprenticeship, they were found to be genuine friends, and never were known to betray the interests of their employers. For their fidelity and satisfactory performance of duty, they were much esteemed,

20

and as a recompense for their services, the Colonial Government made them large grants of land. Andrew had a tract at the mouth of Loyal Sock, and the village there now bears his name. Henry had a tract in Chilisquaque,* and the other, I believe, had a grant westward, near the Ohio river.

The name of these two Seneca warriors is perpetuated in the iron mountain, called, "Montour's Ridge," that runs from Northumberland to Danville.

* See Judge Huston's Land Titles of Pa., p. 319.

CHAPTER XXXVIII.

EARLY SETTLERS IN NORTHUMBERLAND—DR. JOSEPH PRIESTLY —SKETCH OF HIS LIFE—THOMAS COOPER SETTLES THERE ALSO —HIS HISTORY—IMPRISONED UNDER THE SEDITION LAW—APPOINTED JUDGE—REMOVED BY GOVERNOR SNYDER—AMUSING ANECDOTE OF JACK GLOVER AND THE JUDGE.

NORTHUMBERLAND, which had been partially abandoned, was re-occupied by the returning inhabitants, in 1785. It soon became the stopping place of several distinguished exiled foreigners, who came and resided here, amongst whom may be mentioned Mrs. Dash, Mr. Russell, Dr. Priestly, and Dr. Cooper.

Mrs. Dash was a very enterprising woman. She was the wife of an English banker, who failed in business; and whilst he was settling up his affairs, she came out to America, in 1794, with her three daughters, and purchased a farm of about one hundred acres of land, near Northumberland. She immediately had some twenty acres cleared, and sown in wheat—had a comfortable stone cottage erected, where she welcomed her husband on his arrival. Verily, she was a wife worth having.

Mr. Russell was an Englishman, who resided here, and purchased, in connection with a number of land speculators, large tracts of land in the north-eastern counties of this State.

Dr. Joseph Priestly, the distinguished philosopher and

theologian, spent the latter years of his life in Northumberland. His sons preceded him to America, and coming to the Susquehanna, made a large purchase of land, with a view of making it the asylum of English Dissenters, and other distinguished European exiles. Many Englishmen, friends of Dr. Priestly, removed here about the same time, amongst whom was Dr. Cooper.

Dr. Joseph Priestly was born at Fieldham, in England, in March, 1733. His father was a clothier of the Calvinistic persuasion, in which he was also himself brought up. After he had attained a respectable degree of classical acquirement, he was finally placed at the Dissenters' academy at Daventry, with a view to the ministry. He spent three years at this school, where he became acquainted with the writings of Dr. Hartley, and was gradually led into a partiality for the Arian hypothesis. He became minister of Needham Market, in Suffolk, but falling under the suspicion of Arianism, he left there and took charge of a congregation at Nantwich, to which he joined a school. In 1761, he was appointed tutor in the languages at Warrington academy. Here he published his essay on government, and several other useful works on education and history. His History of Electricity, published in 1767, procured him an admission into the Royal Society; he had previously obtained the title of doctor of laws from the University of Edinburgh. In the same year he took charge of a church at Leeds, where his opinions became decidedly Socinian. Here his attention was first drawn to the properties of fixed air, and he also composed his work on Vision, Light, and Colors. In 1773, he went to live with the Marquis of Landsdown, as librarian or literary companion. He travelled over Europe with this nobleman, and also occupied himself with scientific pursuits. In 1773, he furnished a paper in the Philosophical Transactions, on the different kinds of air, which obtained for him a gold medal. This was followed by three volumes, the publication of which forms an era in the history of aeriform fluids. He published several metaphysical works, and an edition of Hartley's Observations on Man, to which he annexed a dissertation savoring strongly of Materialism. This doctrine he still more forcibly supported in his Disquisitions on Matter and Spirit, 1777. These works resulted in a dissolution of the connection between himself and his patron, and he took charge of a dissenting congregation at Birmingham. At length, when several of his friends at Birmingham were celebrating the destruction of the Bastile, a mob assembled and set fire to the dissenting meeting-houses, and several dissenters' houses; among which was that of Dr. Priestly, although he was not present at the celebration. He lost his valuable library and apparatus, and although he obtained a legal compensation, it fell far short of his loss. On quitting Birmingham, he succeeded his friend, Dr. Price, as lecturer in the dissenting college at Hackney, where he remained some time in the cultivation of scientific pursuits, until he was goaded by party enmity to seek an asylum in the United States. He arrived at Northumberland, and fixed his residence there, in 1794. Here he dedicated himself for ten years to his accustomed pursuits, until his death on the 6th of February, 1804, in his 71st year.

Dr. Priestly was an ardent controversialist, chiefly in consequence of extreme simplicity and openness of character; but no man felt less animosity towards his opponents, and many, who entertained the strongest antipathy to his opinions, were converted into friends by his urbanity in personal intercourse. As a man of science, he stands high in the walk of invention and discovery: he discovered the existence of oxygen gas, and other aeriform fluids. As a theologian, he followed his own convictions wherever they led him, and passed through all changes, from Calvinism to a Unitarian or Socinian system, in some measure his own; but to the last, remained a zealous opposer of infidelity. In his family, he ever maintained the worship of God. His works amount to about seventy volumes, or tracts; and embrace essays on history, politics, divinity, (practical and controversial,) metaphysics and natural philosophy. His life, edited by his son, was published in 1806. The memoirs are written by the Doctor himself, down to the year 1795, and are embraced in two volumes.

The descendants of Dr. Priestly still reside at Northumberland. J. W. Priestly, Esq., Cashier of the Northumberland Bank, is one of his grandsons.

Thomas Cooper,* another distinguished Englishman, who came and settled in Northumberland, was born in London, October 22, 1759. Having been educated at Oxford, he became a proficient in Chemistry, and acquired a knowledge of the Law and Medicine, and brought these acquisitions to America, where he joined his friend Dr. Priestly, having been driven from England by the part which he took in reference to French politics, in becoming the agent of an English democratic club to a revolutionary club in France, and writing a pamphlet in reply to an attack on him by Burke, which was threatened with prosecution. In the United States, he became a Jeffersonian politician, and attacking Adams in a newspaper

* See Encyclopædia of American Literature, Vol. II., Page 331.

communication, which he published in the Pennsylvania *Reading Weekly Advertiser* of October 26, 1799, was tried for a libel under the sedition law in 1800, and sentenced to six months' imprisonment, and a fine of four hundred dollars.

The Democratic party coming into power, Governor McKean appointed Cooper, in 1806, President Judge of the Common Pleas District, embracing Northumberland county. He filled the office with energy, but was removed from it in 1811 by Governor Snyder, at the request of the Legislature, on representations chiefly of an overbearing temper. He afterwards became Professor of Chemistry in Dickinson College at Carlisle, and subsequently in 1816, held a Professorship of Mineralogy and Chemistry in the University of Pennsylvania, and shortly after, in 1819, became at first, Professor of Chemistry, then, in 1820, President of the South Carolina College. He also discharged the duties of Professor of Chemistry and Political Economy. Retiring from this post on account of age in 1834, he was employed by the Legislature of South Carolina in revising the Statutes of the State. He died May 11, 1840, at the ripe old age of eighty-one.

Judge Cooper was a man of letters, and the author of several valuable works. But being so petulant, he was much disliked by those who had business with him. When he was Judge at Northumberland, he used to fine a man one dollar for the most trifling offence, and the attorneys disliked him very much. The following anecdote concerning him is related:

Jack Glover was a singular genius that used to attend the courts at Sunbury, whither business sometimes took him, and whither he more frequently took business.

Jack was apparently possessed with an uncontrollable propensity to make a noise. When he had been expelled by the constable from the court-house for his loud talking, he would go to the *huckster's* shop, purchase a bag of chesnuts—perhaps a bushel—shoulder it and march to the court-house, followed by all the idle boys of Sunbury. When arrived there he would cut a hole in the bottom of the bag and run round the house; then came the scramble, the uproar and the battle; out came the constable, and then came the chase, until Jack was run down, brought before Judge Cooper, fined, and imprisoned for twenty-four hours.

On one of these occasions, Jack having served out his time, came into the court-house in the morning very much intoxicated, and as usual made himself rather too conspicuous for his own good.

"Bring that man before the Court," cried the Judge. Jack was brought up, when Cooper peered at him through his eye-glass, and exclaimed:

"Ah, Jack; is that you—drunk again! The Court fines you one dollar, and sentences you to be imprisoned for twenty-four hours!"

"P-l-e-a-s-e your Honor," replied Jack, "it is hard to be punished twice for the same offence!"

"Ah, Jack; but you are drunk to-day again," retorted the Judge.

"P-l-e-a-s-e your Honor," said Jack, "I hav'nt been sober yet."

The Judge was posed, and after studying a moment, said:

"Well, well, Jack; get about your business, and try to keep quiet *if* you can."

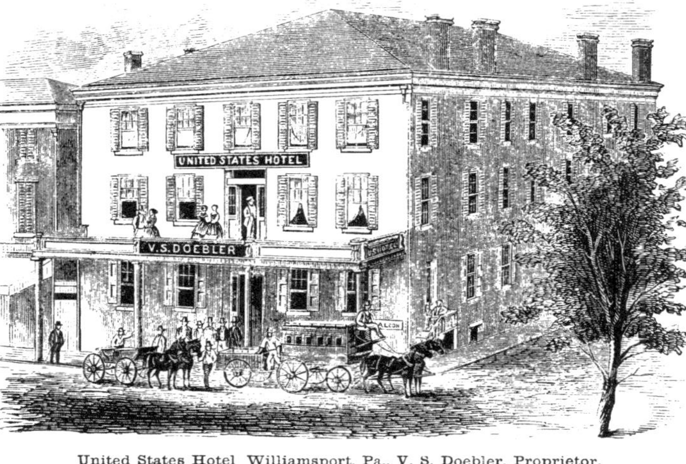

United States Hotel, Williamsport, Pa., V. S. Doebler, Proprietor.

CHAPTER XXXIX.

HISTORY OF GOVERNOR SNYDER—MRS. CARSON—SKETCH OF HER LIFE—BOLD SCHEME TO ABDUCT THE GOVERNOR'S YOUNGEST SON—HER IMPRISONMENT AND DEATH—JOE DISBURY, THE WONDERFUL THIEF—HIS TRICK ON THE FARMER—FINALLY SENTENCED TO TWENTY-ONE YEARS IMPRISONMENT—SERVES OUT HIS TIME AND RETURNS.

SIMON SNYDER was born at Lancaster, November, 1759. His father was a respectable mechanic, who immigrated to Pennsylvania from Germany, about the year 1768. The maiden name of his mother was Knippenberg, born near Oppenheim, Germany. On the 24th of April, 1774, his father died at Lancaster. In 1776 he left Lancaster, and resided at York upwards of eight years, where he learned the tanning and currying business. As a proof of his early integrity, it may be mentioned that he served four years to learn this business, without being bound by written contract. At this place he learned at a night school, kept by John Jones, a member of the Society of Friends, during eight winter months, arithmetic; and made some progress in the mathematics. Often at the midnight hour, after a hard day's work, he was found engaged in the pursuit of knowledge; and his Sundays were almost always devoted to study.

In July, 1784, he removed to the county of Northumberland, and settled in the town of Selinsgrove, where he shortly afterwards opened a store, and became the owner of a mill. He soon became useful as a scrivener, and as the friend of the poor and distressed; and so generally was he respected for his modesty and unassuming worth, that he was unanimously elected by the freeholders of a large district of country, a justice of the peace. In this capacity he continued to officiate for twelve years, under two commissions. The first was granted under the constitution of 1776, and the second under the constitution of 1790. So universally were his decisions respected, that there never was an appeal from any judgment of his to the Court of Common Pleas, and but one writ of *certiorari* was served on him during all that time.

Though the inhabitants consisted of that description of persons, amongst whom quarrels and disputes are very frequent, yet so great was his personal influence, and so strenuous his efforts to reconcile contending parties, that he generally prevailed; and so great was his influence, that during the whole period of his administration, of the many actions for assault and battery brought before him, he made return to the court of but two recognizances. These are evidences of an extraordinary degree and extent of public confidence in the judgment and general good character of Mr. Snyder, which his whole life proved to have been well deserved.

In 1789, he was elected a member of the convention which framed the constitution of this State. Though but a novice in politics, his votes point him out as the supporter of those principles best calculated to promote the happiness of the free people of this country.

In 1797, he was elected a member of the Legislature, and in 1802 became speaker of the House of Representatives. As speaker, he presided with much dignity, with a full knowledge of his duties, and a most accurate recollection and prompt application of the rules of the House.

With him originated the arbitration principle, first incorporated with other wholesome provisions for the adjustment of controversies brought before justices of the peace, in a law commonly called the $100 act. After a few years' experience, this salutary principle was engrafted upon our judiciary system. By this truly patriarchal mode of deciding controversies, more cases are decided than by ordinary mode of trial by jury.

He continued to preside in the chair till 1805. During that session he was taken up as a candidate for Governor, and ran against Thomas McKean, who was re-elected by five thousand majority.

In 1806, Mr. Snyder was again re-elected to the House of Representatives, and again chosen speaker, and was re-elected to both stations in 1807.

In 1808, he was again taken up as a candidate for Governor, and after an arduous contest, was elected by a majority of 28,000. In 1811, he was re-elected; and also in 1814. His conduct during the war of 1812, was patriotic, and worthy of a Governor of Pennsylvania.

In the session of 1813–14, a very large majority of both houses passed the bill to charter *forty banks!* The candidate for Governor was at that time nominated by the members of the Legislature. Having assembled in caucus for that purpose, it was remarked after the meeting had been organized, that the bill to charter forty banks was then before the Governor, and that it would be prudent to make no nomination till it was seen whether he would sanction it.

Within three days Governor Snyder returned the

bill, with his objections, and it did not pass that session. His independence was the theme of universal praise, and he was that year re-elected by a majority of near 30,000.

Having served the constitutional period of nine years, he retired to his former place of residence in Selinsgrove, where, at the next general election, he was elected a Senator of the State of Pennsylvania, and served one session.

The last half year of his life was evidently very unhappy. His long residence at the seat of government, during which he had not the leisure necessary for managing his extensive estate, and the liberal assistance afforded by him to his relatives and friends, had greatly embarrassed his affairs; and the death of his son Frederick taking place at this time of anxiety, broke his spirit and prepared his system for the disease which finally carried him off. He died in November, 1819.

During the time Simon Snyder was Governor, a bold scheme was concocted by a woman to abduct his youngest son, and retain him as a hostage, till a pardon was granted which she sought. The account of this affair forms an interesting feature in the life of the Governor; and in order to elucidate the case more clearly, it is necessary to give a sketch of the woman also.

Mrs. Ann Smith, *alias* Carson, was in many respects a remarkable woman, and during her life made considerable noise in the world. She was first married to a sea captain named Carson, and during his last voyage, which lasted something over two years, she pretended to believe that he was dead, and married a man named Smith, who had been a lieutenant in the army. Shortly after the marriage Carson returned, and of course took possession of his house and wife, and gave Smith notice to quit. The latter, however, manifested a disposition to keep possession of the woman. The parents and friends of Mrs. Carson endeavored to accommodate matters, and had at length succeeded, as they imagined, in prevailing upon her to renounce Smith. The latter, however, coming into the house of Carson one day, when Mrs. Carson's parents and one or two other friends were present, was ordered by Carson to leave the house. The order being disregarded, Carson advanced towards him and repeated the command, when Smith turned to Mrs. C. and said, "Shall I go, Ann?" "No: stay," was her reply; upon which he drew a pistol and shot Carson dead! For this offence he was tried and executed.

Pending the sentence of death, Mrs. Carson wrote to Mrs. Snyder, praying her to interfere in behalf of Smith, and be instrumental, if possible, in procuring from her husband a remission of the sentence. She likewise got up a petition to the Governor for the same purpose, tolerably well filled with respectable names. The application, however, signally failed.

Being disappointed in her efforts to procure a pardon in the usual manner, she had recourse to a bold, as well as quite romantic, scheme. The plot was discovered, however, and the Governor speedily apprised of it. It was as follows:

Governor Snyder was at Selinsgrove, where he usually spent the summer months, when letters arrived from Philadelphia, notifying him that Mrs. Carson, in conjunction with two or three associates, was on her way to Selinsgrove for the purpose of seizing his youngest son, and detaining him as a hostage for the life of Smith. This scheme so pleased her that she could not keep it a secret, but boasted of it till it reached the ears of the civil authorities.

On receipt of the intelligence, the Governor immediately set out for Harrisburg, leaving his three sons, Henry, George and Frederick, to guard the house. On his arrival there, his friends put themselves on the watch, and after two or three days, Mrs. Carson and two men arrived, and were recognized. They were permitted to proceed as far as Hunter's Falls, ten miles above the Capitol, where they stopped for the night at the public house of Mr. Armstrong. One of them opening his trunk in the bar-room, displayed three pistols to the bystanders. Armstrong remarked, "You are well armed." "Yes," replied the man, "if I had one of these pistols in my hand, and Governor Snyder in the other, the question of Smith's pardon would soon be settled."

They then proceeded to make many inquiries about the age of the Governor's youngest son, whether he was going to school, and divers other particulars. Soon after the party had retired to rest, a constable and posse arrived from Harrisburg, and arrested the whole three. On searching their trunks, a good stock of gimblets, saws, screw-drivers, and other house-breaking tools, were found.

It was now ascertained that the male conspirators had been but recently liberated from the penitentiary. The conspiracy to capture the young man having been clearly proved, the two men were soon safe within the walls of the penitentiary again. Mrs. Carson was convicted and sentenced to one of the city prisons of Philadelphia, where she had not long remained till she contrived a plan for her escape, which probably would have proved successful, but for her uncontrollable propensity to talk. She boasted in the presence of her keeper, that she possessed the means of effecting her escape at any time she thought proper. The keeper rightly judging that his empire was rather less pleasant than a state of freedom, grew suspicious and inquisitorial; and it was not long before he found the impression of his prison key upon a piece of soap which she had sent out with her clothes to the washerwoman. She was accordingly very carefully looked to, and served her time regularly.

Some years after these occurrences, she was convicted of passing counterfeit bank notes on an extensive scale, and sentenced to the penitentiary, where she died.

There was a notorious character named Joe Disbury, who flourished about Selinsgrove and Sunbury, near the close of the last century, concerning whom many interesting stories are related. He was possessed of prodigious strength, and had few superiors in running and skating, and in thieving and lying, was considered a match for the prince of darkness!

So bold was he, that he has been known to enter the kitchen of a house when the family were in bed, kindle a fire, cook a meal, and eat it at his leisure before decamping. On one or two occasions he was interrupted in this agreeable occupation, but such was his reliance on swiftness and stratagem that he cared little for that.

As Joe could tell *tremendous* tales about the Indian wars in which *he* had performed numberless incredible feats of heroism, he was a welcome guest of a long winter's evening, at the fireside of those who did not know him well. But he seldom suffered them to remain long in ignorance of his character and propensities—that is, if they had anything worth stealing in the house.

One day, when the river was tolerably high, Joe called on one of the lovers of the marvelous, and told him how the Indians, once upon a time, when hard pressed by their white pursuers, had buried a quantity of money, plate, watches, &c., on a certain island nearly opposite the house of his eager hearer; and that he thought he could find the exact place where the treasure was deposited. It was, therefore, agreed that the farmer should take Joe to the island in his canoe, and that they should "share the labor and the spoil." To the island they went, and dug divers holes without success, though Joe cheered his companion with assurances that the treasure must be at last discovered. Having worked until they were hungry, Joe proposed to return in the canoe to the house for refreshments, while his companion waited for his return. He went to the house, procured a loaf of bread, a piece of cold meat, and a bottle of whiskey, and stepping into the canoe, left the credulous farmer digging on the island, and set off on a voyage of discovery down the river, "and in those parts was never heard of more."

Joe became at length so notorious for his crimes, that the whole country was on the *qui vive;* he was finally taken and imprisoned in Sunbury jail, from which, however, he quickly escaped, and was honored by having a reward offered for his apprehension by the sheriff. He fled to the Isle of Que, and took refuge in a dense thicket of laurel that then grew on the isle, where he fancied himself secure.

He might have remained undiscovered and escaped, but for his inordinate love of perpetrating jokes, which proved his ruin at last. Lying on the watch near the main road cut through the thicket, Joe heard the tread of a horse, and slyly peeping from his covert, espied the sheriff's wife, on horseback, approaching him. Stepping into the road before her, he pulled off his hat, made a very polite bow, and again disappeared in the thicket.

The lady pushed on to Selinsgrove, giving the alarm as she went, and Joe was, after much chasing, ferreted out and captured by George Kremer. Fancying himself secure in that hiding place, he for a moment forgot his caution, and Kremer, having been led by Joe's evil genius to the spot, almost at the same moment, was enabled to seize him.

He was remanded to jail—had his trial on three separate indictments, and was convicted on each. The Judge on summing up, sentenced him to seven years, imprisonment on each oount. " That, may it please your honor," said Joe, with great coolness, "*makes just twenty-one years!*"

He served out the long term of his imprisonment, and again appeared in the neighborhood of his former exploits, an aged man, but as merry as a cricket. His long confinement had not served to eradicate his inordinate thievish propensities, and he would steal whenever he had an opportunity. What became of him is not known by the writer.

CHAPTER XL.

JOHN HANNAH—HIS WHIMS AND ODDITIES—GETS INTO TROUBLE WITH JUDGE COOPER—HAD OCCASION TO CHANGE HIS OPINION—PUMPKIN FLOOD—INDIAN TRADITION THAT A BIG FLOOD OCCURRED EVERY FOURTEEN YEARS—FACTS IN THE CASE—WHISKEY RIOT IN NORTHUMBERLAND—THE POWERFUL NEGRO.

An Irishman, named John Hannah, settled in Northumberland many years ago, and established himself as a dealer in flour, horse-feed, and various other necessaries for man and beast. He was prudent, attentive to business, and economical, and of course grew rich apace. Being a confirmed bachelor, however, he was addicted to peculiar whims and fancies. One of his notions was to entertain a great dislike to Free Masons in general, and to speak all manner of ill of them in the broadest and most sweeping terms; though there were many Masons among his most esteemed friends and customers. His *chief* whim was to wear the dress, and stoutly profess the principles, of the Quakers, though he could not brook an affront, and was one of the most belligerent gentlemen in the State. Possessed of great physical strength, and a willing disposition to use it, there were but few found willing to risk a second encounter with him.

When Judge Rush left the bench in Northumberland county, and Cooper succeeded him, John expressed great pleasure at the change. As he had his Irish prejudices and prepossessions hanging thickly about him, he did not like the informal and unostentatious manner in which justice was administered in America. He would have liked to see the bench crowned with wigs, and surrounded by an array of armed police, as he had been used to seeing it in the "ould coontry."

It being announced that Cooper was appointed, and that he would on the next Monday take his seat, John drew his hands from his capacious pockets, rubbed them, chuckled, and said exultingly, "Now, be the power iv the Vargin Mary, ye'll see bisiness done in the right style. The Americans are not fit for judges; they dinna how to presarve orther, but now ye'll see what a quiet Coort an ould coontry Judge will kape."

On Monday morning, John put his hands into his huge pockets—whence he had extracted them for the purpose of eating his breakfast—and straightway walked over to Sunbury, full of the grandest ideas of his new dispenser of justice. He walked into the Court House without thinking for a moment that his honor would take offence at his covered head. The Judge, however, quickly noticed him, and called, "Constable, Constable, there is a man with his hat on—bring him before the Court." John was forthwith marched up. The purblind Judge took aim with his glass, and recognizing an old acquaintance, repented somewhat of his projected severity of tone, and said peremptorily, though not angrily, "John 'Annah, pull 'hoff your 'at."

John declined the proposal, saying something about the "'at" being his own, whereupon the Judge's wrath was provoked, and he cried aloud—

"John 'Annah, the Court fines you one dollar, and sentences you to twenty-four hours imprisonment. Take him to jail, Constable!"

John Hannah's exalted opinion of European Judges ceased to exist from that day; and at the expiration of his sentence, he returned home a wiser, if not a better, man.

In 1786 a great flood occurred in the Susquehanna, which endangered the towns of Sunbury and Northumberland to a considerable extent. It is stated that a heavy rain commenced to fall on the 5th of October of that year, and on the following day grew more violent. The river rose rapidly, and that night forced itself over the banks, carrying everything before it. Many houses were soon surrounded by the rushing flood, and the inmates were unable to escape therefrom. A man and his wife, near Fishing Creek, on the North Branch, were drowned, together with a son; the daughter, a girl about seventeen years of age, becoming terrified at the rising waters, took three young children and fled to the hills, and escaped the fate of her unhappy parents, and brother, who remained.

The waters rose with the greatest rapidity all Friday, making, in the fore part of the day, nearly twelve inches perpendicular, in the space of an hour; the rain continued, but not with the same violence. The condition of the town of Sunbury was truly alarming; its situation on an island occasioned by a gut from the main branch, emptying into Shamokin Creek below the town, rendered an escape impossible.

In the lower part of the town the water was up to the first story of many of the houses, so that the inhabitants were obliged to land with their canoes on their stairs, or at the upper window. A few acres in the middle of the town, on which were three or four houses, being situated higher than the rest, showed above the water. The Register and Recorder was obliged to abandon his house, and it was feared the records of the county would be lost.

The town of Northumberland suffered considerable loss, an unfinished ferry-house, erected on the point at the confluence of the two streams, was carried off. The sufferings of the farmers on the creeks and along the river, was great, their fences, barns, &c., being swept off.

A tradition existed among the Indians, that a great flood occurred in the Susquehanna at regular intervals of fourteen years, swelling the waters six or seven feet above the average height of the freshets of the intermediate time. Subsequent experience seemed to verify this, and prove that the Indian tradition was founded on correct observation. The first regular flood on record, among the whites, occurred in 1744; the second in 1758; the third in 1772; the fourth, known as "*the great pumpkin fresh*," happened in 1786; and the fifth took place in the spring of 1800, after a heavy rain, which continued three days and three nights, and carried off a tolerably deep snow; and the sixth occurred in August, 1814, occasioning much damage along the course of the stream. According to the rule, another should have followed in 1828, but the freshets of that year were nowise remarkable—leaving the inference that the Indian rule of a flood every fourteen years, had failed and run out. Whether this failure has been caused by the clearing of the country, the extension of agriculture, and the alteration in our climate; or whether these causes have merely extended the period; or, finally, whether the regular recurrence of the great floods was not altogether fortuitous,

I shall leave for the investigations and decisions of those inclined to construct theories and philosophize. There is no doubt but the old Indian tradition was well founded, and the fact of those floods occurring at the stated periods, would go to confirm it. Perhaps the great flood of 1817 ought to be considered the first deviation from the rule, which has occurred at irregular periods down to the flood of 1847, well remembered by the people of the Valley. If the rule holds good, the next great flood will be about 1859.

Each of these floods is stated to have swelled the river to an average height of at least six feet above ordinary high water mark.

Some years after the conclusion of the Revolutionary war, Captain McDonald, the officer that commanded the British and Indians at the taking of Fort Freeland, having occasion to visit Washington, ventured to travel from Canada, down Lycoming Creek, and pass the site of the old fort where he achieved such a victory. Coming to Northumberland, he concluded to tarry there for the night, and had his horse put up for that purpose. Towards night it leaked out that the stranger was the famous Captain McDonald, and groups of men were observed putting their heads together, and talking in a serious manner. Becoming alarmed at these demonstrations, and fearing that they were concocting a plan to give him a coating of tar, the *brave* Briton quietly hired a man to row him down the river in a canoe, and left immediately, as the saying is, "on suspicion." Whether the citizens seriously meditated anything, is not positively known, but he felt guilty, and did not like their actions. His horse remained unclaimed in the possession of the landlord for near a year, when he was sold for his keeping.

In 1794 quite a difficulty took place at Northumberland, familiarly known as the "Whiskey Insurrection." The participants hoisted a Liberty Pole, which stood at the south-east corner of Second and Market streets. The Arsenal, or place where the public arms were stored, stood close by, and was under the charge of Robert Irwin. The pole was driven full of nails from the ground, ten feet upwards, so that it could not be cut down.

The insurrectionists took possession of the Arsenal, and distributed arms to the people, who resisted the law. Matters became serious, and it was feared that a bloody scene would ensue. A guard was placed round the pole day and night. Those friendly to the government could not stand the outrage any longer, and were determined to give battle, and protect the house and property of Captain John Brady, Jun., who was the district Marshal. The swords of the officers that had been sheathed since the war, were drawn from their scabbards, to protect the laws and the government. As the trouble increased, a collision was considered inevitable, if something was not done; many of the more peaceably disposed persons, together with the ladies, interfered to prevent shedding of blood. Matters remained unsettled, however, for several days, till the arrival of an armed Company of ninety-nine men and officers, from Lancaster, under the command of Captain Robert Cooke.

The pole was still guarded, and the Marshal's proclamation to clear the streets unheeded. The mob being well armed, seemed determined to maintain the position it had taken. Cooke ordered them to disperse, which not being obeyed, he commanded his company to charge them at the point of the bayonet. The order was executed, and the bayonets were already at their breasts, when they broke and fled in all directions. An axe was called for to cut the pole down. Barney Hoobley's wife came running with one, when she was met by Jacob Welker's wife, who resisted her, and a desperate fisticuff ensued between these two women about the axe. The battle was a hard contested one, but Mrs. Hoobley, who was the least of the two, succeeded, and the pole was cut down. These ladies were sisters, and much respected by the people.

Several of the ringleaders in this insurrection, were arrested and conveyed to Philadelphia, to stand their trial for resisting the laws of the United States. They were tried, convicted, and sentenced to pay a fine of one hundred pounds each, and undergo an imprisonment of six months.

The following persons were convicted and sentenced: Robert Irwin, Daniel Montgomery, John Frick, William Bonham, James Mackey, Sen., and S. McKee.

When they were marched into the presence of General Washington, the old hero was so affected that he shed tears. He pardoned them all at the end of twenty days, and they returned home, deeply impressed with the goodness and magnanimity of that great man.

In the spring of 1793, Captain John Cooke, son of Colonel Cooke, raised a company of one hundred and twenty men, in Northumberland county, and marched under General Wayne to the Miami, and participated in that bloody campaign. He returned in the autumn of 1794, with but *twenty* of his brave volunteers! He escorted General Wayne into Philadelphia, and was introduced to Washington by him. He died in 1824, aged fifty-nine years.

The Duke of Rochefoucauld Liancourt, a distinguished French traveller and exile, visited Dr. Priestly at Northumberland in 1795, and tarried several days. He afterwards published an account of his travels in America, and spoke of Northumberland as follows:

> "The average price of lands about the town is $20 to $24 per acre, near the river. Further up the river from $4 to $6. Town lots selling at $48 to $50. Houses chiefly built of logs—two only of stone, and one of brick, 'large and convenient,' lately sold at $5,200, and rented for $80—the highest rent in town. The inhabitants mostly foreigners—Irish, Dutch, and English; and Germans about Sunbury. People here were much in favor of the Whiskey insurrection. The island of 250 acres is now the property of an aged man, who lives on it in a small log-house. He bought it some seven years since for $1,600, and lately refused $3,300."

More than half a century ago, there resided in Northumberland, a gentleman named Jenkins, who owned a slave called '*Sias*, (Josiah.) He *is said* to have been a negro of Herculean strength, and almost incredible agility, over whom his master could exercise but little control. Some of the most wonderful anecdotes, and feats of strength, are related about black 'Sias, still fresh in the memories of the oldest citizens.

He occasionally officiated as a waterman, and when grog got the headway, or the whim seized him, he would, with a single jerk, snap off the stem of an oar-blade where it worked on the pivot! These stems are made of a pine log about ten inches in diameter, and from twenty-five to thirty feet in length.

On one occasion, being pursued by the constable and posse, he escaped by leaping across a deep mill-race, a distance of about thirty feet! He was subsequently seized, convicted and imprisoned. During the winter—

for his conviction took place late in the year—he escaped from prison in the evening, secured a pair of skates, went to Harrisburg and got a fiddle he had left there, and returned to Northumberland before morning!

On another occasion, *it is said*, that he skated to Harrisburg, stole a loaf of bread, which a woman on the river bank had just taken from the oven, put it under his coat, and returned to Northumberland before it had grown cold!! The distance was about fifty-five miles.

CHAPTER XLI.

SKETCH OF THE LIFE OF COLONEL JOHN KELLY—DISTINGUISHES HIMSELF IN THE REVOLUTIONARY WAR—RETURNS TO BUFFALO VALLEY—BURIES THE DEAD AT FREELAND'S FORT—ANECDOTES —HIS OPINION OF EVANGELIZING THE INDIANS—DEATH AND BURIAL, MONUMENT, &C.—HISTORY OF COLONEL HARTLEY, THE SCHOLAR, SOLDIER AND STATESMAN.

JOHN KELLY was a native of Lancaster county. He was born in February, 1747. After the purchase from the Indians, by the Proprietaries of Pennsylvania, in 1768, he left Lancaster county and settled in Buffalo Valley. Here he endured the hardships common to all settlers in new countries. He was well calculated for a new settlement, however, being about six feet two inches in height, well proportioned, vigorous and muscular, with a body inured to labor, insensible of fatigue, and fearless of danger.

He was a Major in the Revolutionary war, and distinguished himself in the brilliant actions at Trenton and Princeton.

In the course of one of their retreats, the commander-in-chief, Colonel Potter, sent an order to Major Kelly, to have a certain bridge cut down to prevent the advance of the British, who were then in sight. The Major sent for an axe, but represented that the enterprise would be very hazardous. Still the British advance must be stopped, and the order was not withdrawn. He said he could not order another to do what some would say *he* was afraid to do himself—he would cut down the bridge. Before all the logs on which the bridge lay were cut off, he was completely within the range of the British fire, and several balls struck the log on which he stood. The last log broke down sooner than he expected, and he fell with it into the swollen stream. The American soldiers moved on, not believing it possible for him to make his escape. He, however, by great exertions, reached the shore, through the high water and the floating timber, and followed the troops. Encumbered as he must have been with his wet and frozen clothes, he made a prisoner on the road of a British scout, an armed soldier, and took him into camp. History mentions that our retreating army was saved by the destruction of that bridge; but the manner in which it was done, or the name of the person who did it, is not mentioned. It was but one of a series of heroic acts, which occurred nearly every day; and our brave soldiers were more familiar with the use of the sword than the pen.

After his discharge, Major Kelly returned to his farm and his family, and during the three succeeding years the Indians were very troublesome to the settlements on the West Branch. He became Colonel of the Regiment, and it was his duty to guard the Valley against the incursions of the savages. When the "Big Runaway" occurred, Colonel Kelly was one of the first to return. For at least two harvests, reapers took their rifles to the fields, and some of the company watched whilst others wrought.

At one time Colonel Kelly had the principal command

of scouting parties in the Valley, and very often was out in person. Many nights he has laid on the branches of fallen trees to keep himself out of the mud, without a fire—because it would have indicated his position to the enemy. He became well skilled in Indian warfare, and was a terror to their marauding bands.

One circumstance in his life deserves particular notice. So greatly was he feared by the savages, that they were resolved on his destruction, and being too cowardly to attack him openly, sought his life by stealth. One night he had reason to believe that they were prowling around. Rising early the next morning, and looking through the crevices of his log-house, he ascertained that two of them, at least, were lying with their arms in such a position as to shoot him when he opened the door. Being of a quick turn of mind, he determined to thwart their design, and fixed his own rifle, and took a position so that he could open the door with a string, and watch them at the same time. The moment he pulled the door open, two balls came into the house, and the Indians rose to advance. He immediately fired and wounded one, when they both retreated. After waiting to satisfy himself that no others remained, he followed them by the blood—but they escaped.

After the capture of Freeland's Fort, Colonel Kelly, with a company of men, went up to bury the dead. On the way, along a narrow path, a deer started up. The man immediately behind him was a great "*fist bully*," but on hearing the noise, instinctively seized Kelly's coat-tail, and held on. On learning that the noise was not occasioned by Indians, he exclaimed: "*Lord God, John, what a soldier you are!*"

The Colonel was a fearless man, and not to be intimidated by trifles. A neighbor once tried his bravery by painting himself like an Indian, and hiding behind a log to await his return from a scout up Spruce Run. When Kelly came opposite the log, he raised his head, but was almost immediately detected, and Kelly's gun was leveled upon him, and he would have received the contents, had he not made himself known speedily.

For many years, Colonel Kelly held the office of a magistrate. In the administration of justice, he exhibited the same anxiety to do right, and disregard of self, which had characterized him in the military service of his country. He would at any time forgive his own fees, and, if the parties were poor, pay the constable's cost, to procure a compromise.

He was a member of the Presbyterian Church, and a devout Christian, but to show the strong force of habit in men, I will relate an anecdote concerning him.

About forty years ago, a mission was set on foot in the Northumberland Presbytery, to evangelize the savages. Colonel Kelly was called on to make a contribution. He said he would not give a cent to send preachers to the Indians, *but he would give any sum required, to buy ropes to hang them!*

He died the 18th of February, 1832, universally honored and respected, at the good old age of 88, and was interred in the Old English burying-ground in Lewisburg. On the 8th of April, 1835, amid a grand military display, a plain monument was erected to his memory, and an appropriate oration delivered by James Merrill, Esq.

Early in the spring of 1856, the monument, together with his remains, was removed to the cemetery, west of the town. It is said that a few large bones were all the visible memorials of the once powerful Indian fighter—the brave compatriot of Washington in the glories that followed the darkest night of our country's history.

Colonel Kelly left several sons, who reside on the old farm, and vicinity, about seven miles from Lewisburg. They are highly respectable and intelligent men, and in every respect worthy of their illustrious father. His name is also perpetuated by one of the most fertile and productive townships on the banks of the Otzinachson.

Colonel Thomas Hartley, whose name frequently occurs in the history of this Valley, and who was stationed for a while at Fort Augusta, was born in Berks county, in 1748. He received the rudiments of a classical education in the town of Reading, and went to York, at the age of eighteen, where he commenced the study of law, under Samuel Johnson. He pursued his studies with great diligence for three years, when he was admitted to the bar, and commenced the practice of his profession in 1769.

Young Hartley was early a distinguished and warm friend of his country, and signalized himself both in the cabinet and field. In 1774, he was elected by the citizens of York, a member of the Provincial meeting of Deputies, held at Philadelphia, in July of the same year. The subsequent year he became a member of the Provincial Convention, held in the same city.

The clangor of arms now began to resound in the east. Hartley espoused the cause of Liberty, and soon distinguished himself as a soldier. The Committee of Safety recommended a number of persons to Congress, for Field Officers of the sixth battalion ordered to be raised. Congress, on the 10th of January, 1776, elected William Irwin, as Colonel; Thomas Hartley, as Lieutenant-

Colonel; and James Dunlap, as Major. Hartley was soon afterwards promoted to the full degree of Colonel.

After three years' service, he wrote to Congress, asking permission to resign his commission. His resignation was accepted. In 1778, he was elected a member of the Legislature from York county. In 1783, he was elected a member of the Council of Censors. In 1787, he was a member of the State Convention, which adopted the Constitution of the United States.

In 1788, he was elected a member of Congress, and he continued a member of that august body for about twelve years.

In 1800, Governor McKean commissioned him a Major General of the fifth Division of the Pennsylvania Militia. Soon after receiving this appointment, he died at York, on the 21st of December, 1800, in his fifty-third year.

The name of this distinguished scholar, soldier and statesman, is perpetuated in the enterprising town of Hartleton, in Snyder county.

CHAPTER XLII.

THE BRADY FAMILY—GENERAL HUGH BRADY—HIS LIFE AND PUBLIC SERVICES—DESCRIPTION OF THEIR TRIALS IN BUFFALO VALLEY—THE YOUNG LAD AT BRANDYWINE—HUGH'S DESCRIPTION OF HIS BROTHERS—DEATH OF THE MOTHER AT THE EARLY AGE OF 48—AN ANCESTRY TO BE PROUD OF.

PERHAPS there was no family on the West Branch, more identified with its history, and deserving of a more extended notice, than the Brady family. It furnished some of the most remarkable men of that period—men whose deeds of heroism and daring, would fill a volume, and should be emblazoned on the broad page of History. The descendants of this illustrious family, now living throughout the Valley, are numerous, and respectable members of society.

Many writers, in speaking of the Bradys, have ran into errors, on account of several of the same name, and confounded them in such a manner as to render it exceedingly annoying to their descendants. I flatter myself, that I will be able in these pages to give a correct sketch, as I obtain the facts from the papers of General Hugh Brady, who died at Detroit, in 1851. Concerning himself, and the family, the General says:

"I was born on the 29th day of July, 1768, at the Standing-Stone, in Huntingdon county, Pa., and was the fifth son of John and

Mary Brady. They had six sons and four daughters. My brothers all lived to be men, in every sense of the term, and at a period when the qualities of men were put to the most severe and enduring tests. While I was yet a child, my father moved on to the West Branch, and pitched his tent about eight miles above Northumberland. At this time, titles to wild lands could be obtained by erecting a log house, and girdling a few trees, by way of improvement, or cultivation. In this way, my father, John Brady, took up a vast quantity of land; and, had he not fallen in the war of 1776, would have been one of the greatest land-holders in the State. But, owing to the dishonesty and mismanagement of those connected with him, his family received but little benefit from his exertions. Soon after the commencement of the war of 1776, he was appointed a Captain in the 12th Pennsylvania Regiment; and in a few weeks having recruited his Company, joined the army and remained with it till after the battle of Brandywine.

At this time the Indians had become very troublesome in the settlements on the Susquehanna—so much so, that application was made for regular troops to protect the frontier. Gen. Washington not being in a condition to spare any troops at that moment, ordered home Capt. John Brady, Capt. Boone, and Lieuts. John and Samuel Dougherty, to use their influence in inducing the people to sustain themselves until he could afford them other relief. And nobly did they execute his design. All that brave and experienced men could do, was done by them, even to sacrificing their lives in the defence of their country; for, in less than two years from that date, Capts. Boone and Brady, and Lieut. Samuel Dougherty, had fallen by the hands of the savages. Ten months before the death of Capt. John Brady, his son James had fallen, (an account of which has already been given.) Another son, Samuel, was then an officer in the U. S. Army. John was then at home, in charge of the family, and in his sixteenth year.

After the fall of Capt. Brady, my mother removed, with her family, to her father's place in Cumberland County, where she arrived in May, 1779, and where she remained till October of that year. She then removed to Buffalo Valley, and settled on one of our own farms. We found the tenant had left our portion of the hay and grain, which was a most fortunate circumstance. The winter following—1779 and '80—was a very severe one, and the depth of snow interdicted all traveling. Neighbors were few, and the settlement scattered—so that the winter was solitary and dreary to a most painful degree. But, whilst the depth of the snow kept us confined at home, it had also the effect to protect us from the inroads of the savages. But, with the opening of the spring the savages returned, and killed some people near our residence. This induced Mrs. Brady to take shelter, with some ten or twelve families, about three miles from our home. Pickets were placed around the houses, and the old men, women, and children remained within during the day; while all who could work and carry arms, returned to their farms, for the purpose of raising something to subsist upon. Many a day have I walked by the side of my brother John, while he was plowing, and carried my rifle in one hand, and a forked stick in the other, to clear the plowshare!

Sometimes my mother would go with us to prepare our dinner. This was contrary to our wishes; but she said that, while she shared the dangers that surrounded us, she was more contented than when left at the fort. Thus we continued till the end of the war, when peace—happy peace—again invited the people to return to their homes.

In 1783, our mother was taken from us. In '84 my brother John married, and soon after, my eldest sister followed his example. 'All the children younger than myself, lived with them. I went to the western country with my brother Capt. Samuel Brady. He had been recently disbanded, and had married a Miss Swearingen, in Washington County, Pa. He took me to his house at that place, and I made it my home until 1792, when I was appointed an Ensign in Gen. Wayne's army. Previous to this my brother had moved into Ohio County, Va., and settled a short distance above Charlestown. At that day the Indians were continually committing depredations along the frontier.

I joined with several parties in pursuit of Indians, but only met them once in action. In 1792 I was placed in a rifle company commanded by Capt. John Crawford."

The General participated in the campaign that followed under Wayne, and he gives an interesting description of it, but as it is not in the province of this work, I am obliged to omit it. At the conclusion of the war, he returned and visited the widow of his brother, Captain Samuel, in Virginia, who had died some time previous

Having been absent for ten years, he had a desire to see his brothers and sisters, and having resigned his commission in 1795, started for home. Remaining some time in Kentucky and Virginia, he finally arrived at Sunbury in 1797. He thus continues:

"I reached home about the 21st of July. I went first to Capt. William Gray's, my brother-in-law. My sister, Mrs. Gray, came to the door, and, as I enquired for Mr. Gray, she put on rather an important look, and replied—'I presume you will find him at the store'—and turned into the parlor. I was about turning on my heel, when I heard steps in the entry, and, turning round, I saw my sister Hannah. She immediately raised her hands, and exclaimed—'My brother Hugh!' and flew into my arms. This was not a little surprising, as when she saw me last, she could not have been more than eight years old. She knew me by my resemblance to my twin sister Jane. I found my connections all living happily, and moving at the head of society. I passed a happy three or four months with them, when I became weary of an idle life, and began to look for my *promised fortune*."

He remained with them till the winter of 1798–9, when he was appointed a Captain in Adams' army, and in less than two years was disbanded. He then went with his brother William to make an improvement near Pittsburg. In 1805 he married, and resided there till 1810, when he returned with his family to Northumberland, and remained till the war of 1812, when he again entered the army, and distinguished himself in the brilliant actions at Lundy's Lane and Bridgewater, where he was severely wounded. He subsequently rose to the rank of Brevet Major General in the United States Army, and his name stands indelibly recorded in the annals of his country's fame. He died in 1851. A beautiful and pathetic poem, on his death, was written by Rev. George Duffield, a few verses of which I give as follows:

"A woe is on the Nation's soul,
And soldier-hearts are sad and sore,
As through the land the tidings roll—
Our gallant BRADY is no more!

* * * * *

"But fife, nor drum, no more shall wake
The Warrior from his dreamless sleep;
Life's battle fought—the victory won—
His feet now press Fame's highest steep."

"Then kindly wrap the Nation's flag
Around the Hero's honored clay—
Fit shroud for soldier such as he,
Who knew no joy save in its ray!"

"And manly eyes may weep to-day,
As sinks the Patriot to his rest;
The Nation held no truer heart
Than that which beat in BRADY'S *breast!*"

Speaking of his brother James, who, the reader will remember, was killed below Williamsport, he says:

"James Brady was a remarkable man. Nature had done much for him. His person was fine. He lacked but a quarter of an inch of six feet, and his mind was as well finished as his person. I have ever placed him by the side of Jonathan, son of Saul, for beauty of person, and nobleness of soul, and, like him, he fell by the hands of the Philistines."

He makes allusion to his brother John as follows:

"My brother John, in his fifteenth year, was in the battle of Brandywine, and was wounded. On the retreat, he would have been captured, had not his Colonel (Cooke) taken him up behind him.

John had gone to the army with my father, in order to take home the horses ridden out, and was directed by my father to return. But John heard from Ensign Boyd, that a battle was expected to be fought soon. He, therefore, remained to see the fun; and when my father took command of his company, on the morning of the battle, he found John in the ranks, with a big rifle by his side. My father was wounded in the battle; Ensign Boyd was killed; and John received a wound during the retreat.

As one good turn deserves another, two of my brothers many years after, married two of the Colonel's daughters."

He thus describes his brother Captain Sam., the great warrior and Indian-killer:

"Never was a man more devoted to his country, and few—very few—have rendered more important services, if we consider the nature of the service, and the part performed by him personally. He was 5 feet 11¾ inches in height, with a perfect form. He was rather light—his weight exceeding, at no time, one hundred and sixty-eight pounds. As I have said before, there were six brothers, viz: Samuel, James, John, William P., Hugh and Robert. There was but half an inch difference in our heights. John was six feet and an inch, and I was the shortest of them all. Is it not remarkable that I, who was considered the most feeble of all, should outlive all my brothers, after having been exposed to more dangers and vicissitudes than any, except Samuel? Is it not a proof that there is, from the beginning, 'a day appointed for man to die?' It is said—'the race is not to the swift, or the battle to the strong; but safety is of the Lord.' That has ever been my belief."

Captain Sam. Brady was a remarkable man, and in many a bloody skirmish. He was in the surprise at Paoli, and made a narrow escape. As he jumped a fence, the skirt of his great coat, was pinioned to the rail by a bayonet in the hands of a British soldier, who made a thrust at him. He afterwards was appointed to a Captaincy, and given the command of a Company called the Rangers. He was under General Wayne, and rendered efficient service in protecting the frontiers. He continued to command them to the time of his death, which occurred on Christmas day, 1795, in the 39th year of his age. He left a widow and two sons.

Mary Brady, the mother of this illustrious family,

weighed down with grief and care, died in 1783, at the early age of forty-eight, and was buried in the old English Burying Ground in Lewisburg. Her son John, the heroic lad, who remained and fought with his father at Brandywine, died at the same age, in 1809, and was laid by the side of his beloved mother.

In the spring of 1856, their remains were taken up and deposited in the Cemetery, where they will probably remain till the Archangel's trump shall awaken them to glory and to life again.

The numerous descendants of this heroic family in the enchanting vale of the Otzinachson, have just reasons to feel proud that they sprung from such a noble ancestry; and he who can stand up at this day and say that the patriotic blood of Mary and John Brady courses through his veins, should scorn to tarnish that immortal name by a base action.

Within a year or two, a township in Lycoming County has been formed out of Washington, and named BRADY, in commemoration of the revered name.

CHAPTER XLIII.

GEORGE KREMER—SKETCH OF HIS LIFE—SENT TO THE LEGISLATURE—BECOMES A MEMBER OF CONGRESS—JACKSON, CLAY AND ADAMS—THE CELEBRATED LETTER—CHARGE OF CORRUPTION—TREMENDOUS EXCITEMENT—KREMER BECOMES A LION—FINALLY DECLINES AND SINKS INTO OBSCURITY—HIS CHARACTER.

George Kremer, well remembered by the older residents of the Valley, became quite distinguished in the political world, and attracted considerable attention. A biography of his life and public services may prove interesting at this period. For the material facts, I am indebted to George A. Snyder, Esq., who is competent to detail them correctly.

George Kremer was the nephew of Governor Snyder, and came to reside with him when a mere lad. He was very ill-formed, but not the least ashamed of his ugliness, and rather inclined to feel proud of his distinction in this respect. He grew up to be stout, and soon became able to fight his own battles, in an age and a district where broils were of daily occurrence. This region, then called by the general name of Shamokin, was in those days the frontier, and looked upon by the dwellers on the sea-board, as we look upon Iowa and Kansas at the present time. It served as a place of refuge for all runaway and desperate characters from the south-eastern counties. The sheriff and constable seldom ventured into the wilds on this side of the river, which acquired the significant title of *Rascal's* creek!

George was remarkable for shrewdness, no less than for courage and bodily strength, and he became in a short time, a person of great influence among the hardy inhabitants of the new country. In addition to his other good qualities, he was strictly honest, and his word was his bond. Whatever he did, he did it with all his might. With such qualifications and endowments, it is no matter of wonder that he became a leading man so soon as he embarked in politics.

After serving several terms as a member of our State Legislature, he was elected to Congress, and here acquired the distinction which he enjoyed.

In 1825, it having been ascertained that neither of the candidates for the Presidency had received the constitutional majority of votes, the matter was referred to Congress. Mr. Adams, General Jackson, Mr. Clay, and Mr. Crawford, were the candidates, and as the choice of Congress lay between the two first, there was, of course, considerable intriguing on the part of the two latter and their friends. The friends of Jackson finding that Mr. Clay and his friends were decidedly hostile to their candidate, and, indeed, made no secret of their aversion to him, resolved, after in vain trying the arts of persuasion, to resort to intimidation. They caused a letter to be written and published in the *Columbian Observer*, of Philadelphia, which stated that a corrupt bargain had been made between Messrs. Adams and Clay, in pursuance of which the latter was to transfer his vote, and the vote of his friends to Mr. Adams, who was to make him Secretary of State as his reward.

On the day after the appearance of the letter, Mr. Clay, then Speaker of the House of Representatives, moved that a committee be appointed to inquire into the truth of this charge. Mr. Kremer seconded the motion, stating that he was ready with the proofs, and willing to meet the inquiry. The motion was opposed by Mr. McDuffie, and some others—friends to Jackson—on the ground that there was not sufficient reason to consume the time of the House in investigating a frivolous newspaper charge—a charge which no one acquainted with the parties concerned, would believe. Mr. Clay had even insisted on his right to clear his character from the stain thus publicly attempted to be fixed on it, and Mr. Kremer eagerly seconded him, exulting in the anticipated certain confounding of the Clay and Adams party.

Not one, however, of those who had put him upon writing the letters, supported him, or manifested any anxiety for the proposed inquiry. The committee was appointed. On the evening of the same day, Kremer discovered that his friends could furnish him with no evidence to support his charge, and that he must get out of the scrape as well as he could. On the succeeding day the committee notified him they were ready to proceed, in answer to which he wrote a long letter to the chairman declining to appear, alleging that as he had made no formal charges, the committee could have no jurisdiction—that his charge was made for the public, &c. This special pleading was so nearly identified with the argument of Mr. McDuffie on the preceding day—in the motion for inquiry—as to lead some to suspect that he (Mr. McDuffie) was its author; but the character of Mr. McDuffie forbids us to harbor any such suspicion. It was probably the production of Mr. Ingham, who, as afterwards appeared, was Kremer's chief prompter in this business. It was natural for him to adopt Mr. McDuffie's arguments, being the best, and indeed only mode of getting clear of the difficulty.

One might have supposed that this disgraceful retreat would have convinced the whole public of the falsehood of Kremer's charge; but political faith covers mountains, and the charge was eagerly entertained and reiterated by the disappointed partisans of Jackson. Kremer himself, as appears from the testimony of Mr. Crowninshield, doubted, at the last, and had a letter of apology ready for Mr. Clay, which Mr. Ingham found means to suppress.

Such was the eagerness with which the Pennsylvanians received the corruption story, and such the cloud of incense with which Kremer was fumigated, that it is no wonder that his brain was effected, and he really believed himself the saviour of his country's liberty! His vanity became excessive, and as Cicero of old continually rung the changes in his latter orations, on the names of Lentulus, Cethugus, and Catiline, so Kremer made corruption, and his famous letter, the eternal burden of his song. He fancied that he smelled corruption in every breeze that blew along Pennsylvania Avenue, and had Mrs. Adams invited him to tea, he would have fancied he discovered corruption in her card.

On his return home he visited Philadelphia, Harrisburg, and other places, where he was feasted and flattered by the Jacksonians, until he believed himself to be, what they pretended to think him, one of the most remarkable men of the age.

Finding that the corruption story was unsparingly used against him by the Jacksonians, notwithstanding the way in which they had backed out of the charge; and that even General Jackson had condescended to lend the authority of his name to this shameless calumny, Mr. Clay took the trouble to collect the letters, certificates, and affidavits of almost every one who could have any knowledge of the matter in agitation, and published them in a pamphlet. These testimonials, coming from upwards of fifty persons of *all* parties, formed a most triumphant refutation of the corruption story. But it was all in vain for Messrs. Adams and Clay; the popular mind had been roused to phrensy, and was utterly inaccessible to all reason. Jackson was elected in 1828 by a decided majority, and Kremer, having answered the purpose of the party, was forgotten at once. Too honest to take a part in the intrigues of his fellow-partisans at Washington, he could not make himself of any further use to them, and was pushed aside to make room for those who knew how to make the best use, for selfish purposes, of his services.

For some years after he was left out of Congress, he continued to make speeches at public meetings, the burden of which was corruption, and—"*My letter to the Columbian Observer!*" His action, in speaking, was vehement and ungraceful—his voice loud, and his accentuation false and ranting, such as schoolboys are apt to acquire under the tuition of an injudicious teacher. His honesty and zeal no one doubted, but designing demagogues contrived, by dexterous management, to keep him back, as he was too straightforward for them, and if admitted to their counsels, would mar the harmony of their best laid plans, by denouncing their selfishness and unfair dealing. There was neither selfishness nor meanness about him; and had he condescended to cringe to the party leaders in 1828–9, when his name was in the mouth of every one; or had he intimated that his influence might possibly be turned against Jackson, there is no doubt but that he could have obtained the highest reward in the form of political preferment. Indeed it was matter of wonder and remark, among his unsophisticated constituents, that he remained without office. They little thought that their favorite was altogether thrust aside by the throng of hungry office-hunters, who assailed the President with their importunate cries for the spoils of victory. He was not blind to the intrigues and foul play going on at the seat of government, for on his way home once, he met an acquaintance whom he mistook for one of his own political cast, and to whom he said:

"Adams and Clay were *corrupt*, but their corruption was child's play to what is going on at Washington now!"

CHAPTER XLIV.

ROBERT COVENHOVEN—HIS AGE AND DEATH—PETER A. CARTHAUS—HOW HE GOT HIS WIFE IN WILMINGTON—HIS IMPROVEMENTS—THE DINNER PARTY AT JUDGE POTTER'S, IN BELLEFONTE—PETER AND THE DEVIL—MISSIONARY SENT TO SINNEMAHONING—ATTEMPTS TO PREACH—THE FINALE.

Robert Covenhoven, of whom mention has already been made in several places, was born of Low Dutch parents, in Monmouth County, New Jersey. The name has since been corrupted to Crownover, and by it his descendants are known at the present day.

In his youth, Robert was much employed with surveying parties on the North and West Branches, in the capacity of hunter and axeman. By this means he acquired his great familiarity with all the paths and defiles of the wilderness, which rendered him so valuable afterwards as a scout and guide. It is needless to add, that the graduate of such a school was fearless and intrepid—skilled in all the wiles of Indian warfare, and possessed of an iron constitution.

At the commencement of the Revolution, he joined the standard of General Washington, and participated in the brilliant actions at Trenton and Princeton. In the meantime the family had left the arid sands of New Jersey, and sought a home on the West Branch. His father joined the army, and Robert was permitted to return and protect his mother. Most of his adventures have been given already in their proper place. He was one of those men who were always put forward when danger was to be encountered, but always forgotten when honors and emoluments were to be distributed. Nevertheless, he cheerfully sought the post of danger, and never shrunk from duty. Few men in those perilous days passed through more deadly encounters, or had more hairbreadth escapes.

He was very useful to General Sullivan as a spy and a guide, in his celebrated expedition up the North Branch in 1779, to the Indian country. It is said that he was in the unfortunate company commanded by Lieutenant Boyd, and was one among the few that escaped the dreadful massacre.

When the din of battle ceased, and peace was restored to the land, Covenhoven came and settled permanently on the West Branch. His old farm is four miles below Jersey Shore, on the right of the road, and is owned at the present time by William McGinness, Esq. He resided there till declining age admonished him to relinquish the pursuits of the agriculturist, and seek a more quiet and sedate life. For a part of the time he resided with his son-in-law, Colonel George Crane, near Jersey Shore; and the other part in the family of Mr. Pfouts, another son-in-law, near Northumberland, where he died in October, 1846, at the ripe old age of 90 years, 10 months, and 22 days. His remains were deposited in the grave yard at Northumberland.

PETER A. CARTHAUS.

Who has not heard of the "*Carthouse*," as it is familiarly termed by the up-river folks? The title is derived from a remarkable old Dutchman, whose name is given above. A short sketch of his life may not prove uninteresting.

When Peter A. Carthaus landed in the United States, he was a widower of some forty-five years of age, with a number of little children. In Wilmington, Del., he saw a very pretty lady of some eighteen or nineteen summers, and was immediately smitten with her charms, and grew very matrimonial in his ideas. He applied to the lady's father, who, of course, thought some little upon the subject of the disparity of years, and the number of pre-existing issue. But Peter was very rich, and his dollars were broad enough to hide all his imperfections—age, children, stinginess, ugliness, boorishness, &c., with which he was endowed. The prudent father did not, however, neglect the main chance—he insisted on a marriage settlement of $20,000. Peter made faces—he was a capital hand at driving a bargain, and so was the father. After considerable parleying, Peter, sorely straitened between his love of money, and his desire for matrimony, consented to a settlement of $15,000. He got his wife, but never forgave either her or her father, for getting, what he termed, so good a bargain out of him!

He carried his new wife, escorted by his numerous small children, triumphantly home to his paradise in the wilds of Clearfield County, where the Wilmington beauty was each night lulled to rest by those forest nightingales, the wolves! How time passed with her, history saith not, but we may readily divine the feelings of a city belle, espoused to a bear and serenaded by wolves!

Shortly after his arrival in this country, he purchased a large tract of land in Clearfield County, which was found to be well supplied with iron ore, coal, timber, &c. Being possessed of plenty of capital, he resolved to become richer by means of the aforesaid ore. Accordingly he laid out many thousands of his dollars in erecting a furnace, a forge, a large grist mill, a convenient wharf, and several large houses, all of stone. Being built in an unsettled country, they cost an immense sum of money. Peter manufactured iron, but behold! there was no way to get it to market—he made ready his mill, but alas! people grew no grain in the woods, and of course his toll-dish was not often filled. His works were very complete, but soon fell into disuse, and rapidly went to decay. They yet stand in a dilapidated condition, a monument of his folly—and the place is universally known by the name of the "*Carthouse*."

Many amusing anecdotes are related of Peter, a few of which I will give, to illustrate more fully his character.

About a year after his marriage, the father of his pretty wife, accompanied by ten or twelve brothers, sisters, cousins, uncles, aunts, &c., paid a visit to the happy couple, to witness their connubial happiness, eat venison, and listen to the music of the Clearfield nightingales. No sooner were they safely landed in Carthaus' paradise, than Judge Potter, one of the most hospitable and friendly of men, paid his respects to the new-comers, and invited them to dine with him at his residence in Bellefonte. They went, of course, and partook of the Judge's meat and drink, in company with twenty or thirty of the most respectable persons of the vicinity. When the cloth was removed, and after the wine had begun to loosen the tongues and warm the hearts of the company, some one, meaning to compliment the fair Mrs. Carthaus, remarked to Peter, that he believed the Wilmington ladies were very handsome.

"Yes," growled Peter, "dey ish very pretty, *but dey sell dem d——h high?*"

Peter once went to the house of Governor Snyder, in Harrisburg, with the model of a boat which he had constructed. It had a water wheel at the head, connected with which was a lever, to the ends of which were attached poles, whereby the boat was to be shoved against the stream. It is unnecessary to attempt a more minute description of the contrivance—suffice it to say, that it was constructed upon the *very* philosophical principle that the force of the current would turn the wheel, which would set the lever and poles in motion, and propel the boat against the stream. Something like mounting a chair to look over the top of one's own head!

Once upon a time he had occasion to go to Bellefonte, where a newly-established wagon maker had just finished a large wagon, the outside whereof was painted sky-blue, and the inside a beautiful pink; and Peter was in raptures with the glorious sight. To his eager inquiries, and offers of purchase, he was answered that this jewel upon four wheels had been made to order, and was not to be had. "Make me a new one den directly, as pretty as dis," said Peter. The promise was given, and in due time performed, though to the impatient Peter the time seemed long enough to build fifty wagons. The wagon, in all its splendor, was sent home, and its first errand was into the woods for a load of charcoal. There being no road, the vehicle had to wind its devious course among the forest trees, between two of which it got inextricably jammed with its dusty cargo, on the way homeward. Peter backed his horses and swore—he and his man next applied their shoulders to the wheels, and swore again; but neither backing the horses, nor pushing with the shoulders, sufficed, when he wished the devil might come and burn his wagon, and unhitching his horses went home to supper. The next morning, with a reinforcement of horses and men, and a sufficient reserve of curses, Peter returned for the wagon. But alas! the charcoal had not been rightly looked to—a spark lurked in the huge mass—the night wind fanned the flame, and on his arrival he found nothing but a heap of ashes. His first impression was, that the devil had taken him at his word, and he yelled with mingled terror and wrath, till the woods resounded to the echo!

Whilst up in this region, I may as well relate another amusing circumstance, which is said to have been a fact. It relates to a settlement on the Sinnemahoning Creek at quite an early day, when morals and religion were little known and practised there. Some humane persons having heard of the heathenish condition of the people, straightway made arrangements to send a missionary amongst them, for the purpose of enlightening them. In due course of time he came, and made arrangements to convert the heathen. The account of the mission is described as follows:

"ALL IS VANITY, SAITH THE PREACHER."

There is a place called Sinnemahone,
Of which but little good is known:
For sinning, ill must be its fame,
Since *Sin* begins its very name.
So well indeed its fame is known,
That people think they should begin
To drop the useless word *Mahone*,
And call the country simply, *Sin!*

But to my tale—Some years agone
The Presbytery—having heard
Of the sad state of Sin—resolved
To send some one to preach the word,
And Mr. Thompson was bid see then
To the conversion of the heathen.
I shall not linger long to tell
Of all that on the way befell;
How he was lost among the bushes,
And floundered through the reeds and rushes;
Or how, when hungry, down he sat
To corn-cobs fried in 'possum fat!
How his black coat's unusual hue,
Caused a grim hunter to pursue
And cock his gun to blow him through,
Believing, as I've heard him swear,
Our missionary was a bear.
"'Tis true," he said, "I never counted
On seeing such thing as a bear
Upon a good stout pony mounted;
But yet I can with safety swear
That such a very wondrous sight,
We might expect by day or night,
Rather than, in our hills, to note
A parson with a rale black coat!"

The news soon spread around the land,
That Parson Thompson, on next Sunday,
Would in the school-house take his stand,
And preach to them at least for one day.

The Sunday came, and with it came
All of the ragged population;
Men, women, children, dogs to hear
The tidings of salvation.

The women came in linsey-woolsey,
And tall wool hats increased their stature;
The men in shirts and leather leggins;
The brats and dogs in dress of nature!

The men who seldom stop at trifles,
Brought tomahawks and knives and rifles.

Service began—the parson wondered
To hear the singing that they made—
Some Yankee Doodle—some Old Hundred.
The hounds, astonished, howled and thund'red
Until the forest shook with dread.
The singing o'er—the prayer was said,
But scarcely had the text been read,
When, panting with fatigue and fear,
Rushed past the door a hunted deer;
Prayer, hymn and text, were all forgot,—
And for the sermon mattered not,—
Forth dashed the dogs—not one was mute—
Men, women, children, followed suit.
The men prepared the deer to slaughter,—
The girls to head it to the water.
None staid but lame old Billy French,
Who sat unwilling on his bench,
Not for the sake of hymn or prayer,
Did Billy keep his station there;
But, as he said, with rueful phiz—
"*For a darned spell of roomatiz!*"

The Parson groaned with inward pain,
And lifting up his hands amain,
Cried, dolefully, "*'tis all in vain!*"
Up starting nimbly from his bench,
"*'Tis not in vain,*" cried old Billy French,
"When my good hound old Never-fail,
Once gets his nose upon the trail,
There's not a spike buck anywhere,
Can get away from him, *I'll swear!*"

CHAPTER XLV.

ESTHER M'DOWELL FOUND BEFORE THE CABIN DOOR OF MARTIN REESE—A ROBBED AND INJURED FEMALE—GREAT EXCITEMENT PREVAILED—SHE TURNS OUT TO BE AN IMPOSTER—A HUMBUGGED COMMUNITY—HISTORY OF THE WALKER TRAGEDY ON PINE CREEK—STATISTICS OF LYCOMING COUNTY.

ABOUT the year 1803, a remarkable circumstance transpired at the upper end of the borough of Jersey Shore,* well remembered by all the old people living at that time. Pine trees, in considerable numbers, were then standing on the spot which I now speak of. An old Dutchman, named Martin Reese, had built a cabin near where the public road crosses the canal, on the farm now owned by Mark Slonaker, Esq., and made some improvements. Rising very early one frosty morning in October, he was surprised on going to his door, to find a beautiful female in a state of nudity, with her hands tied behind her back, and a gag in her mouth, standing in front of the cabin, against a tree. He relieved her from this uncomfortable position as soon as possible, and tendered her the hospitalities of his humble cabin. She appeared to be completely chilled through with the cold, and could scarcely speak for

* Sherman Day, in his Historical Collections of Pennsylvania, falls into a great error in stating that this circumstance occurred near Williamsport. Such is not the fact; it occurred as stated above, at Jersey Shore.

some time. On recovering sufficient strength, she related that she had been travelling on horseback from her father's house in Montreal, to visit an uncle that resided in Kentucky, in charge of a young man named Benjamin Connett, who was sent expressly to attend her. But having a large amount of gold in her possession, an evil spirit prompted him to rob her; and in a lonely spot near Pine Creek, he presented a pistol to her breast, compelled her to dismount and deliver up what money she possessed; when he immediately stripped her, tied her, and left her in this shameful and denuded condition, to starve with hunger or be devoured by wild beasts. She had remained in that condition nearly all night, when, after the most desperate struggles, she had released herself and made her way to his cabin. After being refreshed, she willingly went with the family to the spot, and pointed out the place where she had been tied, and the path she had beaten round the tree trying to free herself.

There was something artless in her appearance; and her modest demeanor and delicate frame, left no doubt in the minds of those who saw her, that her statements were true, and that she had been foully dealt with. She appeared to be overwhelmed with distress at the thought of her situation among strangers. She gave her name as Esther McDowell.

Rev. Mr. Grier, father of Judge Grier of the Supreme Court, resided close by, and took her into his family and kindly provided for her wants. A great deal of sympathy was excited in her behalf, and the neighbors vied with each other in making her presents of clothing. Several gentlemen, now living, presented her with valuable silk dresses, and other articles, which she accepted, and kindly thanked them for their liberality.

Meanwhile the news spread throughout the country, and the public indignation was highly excited against the villain Connett. Handbills, offering a reward for his apprehension, were put in circulation, and the chivalry of the West Branch started in all directions to look for the scoundrel. He had twenty-four hours' start, however, and being well mounted, eluded all observation and effected his escape.

The artless girl remained in the neighborhood, caressed and entertained by the sympathising people, who could not do enough to alleviate her wants. Her manners were so simple, her actions so lady-like and refined, and her description of the thief so minute, that no doubt was left of her being badly treated. Letters in the meantime were despatched to her father at Montreal, but weeks elapsed and no answer came. Still the public confidence in her was unshaken.

The intelligence having spread far and near, strangers in great numbers flocked to see her, and loaded her with presents. They were always fascinated with her beauty, her simple and captivating charms. Being at the hotel kept by Duffies, at Larry's Creek, a gentleman named Hutchinson, from Milton, called to see her. She eyed him closely, and seemed to keep shy of him, which attracted his attention, and he thought he detected something familiar in her countenance. He requested to have some private conversation with her, which she positively refused, when he exclaimed, calling her by name,—"*I believe you are the identical young man that once worked for me in Milton as a journeyman tailor!*" This was a poser, and she became greatly excited, which aroused a suspicion among the people that she *might* be an impostor. And such it ultimately turned out to be.

The pretty Esther McDowell had deceived and humbugged them in a shameful manner, and *never* was robbed as she represented.

A bundle of men's clothing had also been found near the spot where she was found, secreted in a hollow log, which went to confirm the suspicion. At length she confessed that such was the fact—that she had been playing the impostor, being of a romantic turn of mind, and had actually passed herself off as a young man, and worked as a journeyman tailor.

It was now remembered that a young man answering her description, had crossed the White Deer Mountains into Nippenose Valley, and staid over night with the family of a farmer. The evening of that day she (he) came to the house of Joseph Antes, Esq., where Major McMicken now resides, and he ferried her over the river, when she doffed her male attire and placed herself in the position in which she was found.

Whatever became of her is not distinctly known, though it is asserted that she left the country soon afterwards, and went to the West under another name, where she shortly afterwards married and became a highly repectable woman.

The case of Esther McDowell afforded much amusement for many years among the people, and when the subject is broached to the old people at the present day, their mirthfulness is at once excited, and they recount the circumstance of being so nicely humbugged with considerable gusto.

About the year 1790, a circumstance occurred on Pine Creek, a few miles above Jersey Shore, known as the "Walker Tragedy," which was a bloody, as well as an aggravated case, on both sides. Three brothers, named Benjamin, Joseph, and Henry Walker, lived on a farm not far from the mouth of the creek. Their father, John Walker, was barbarously killed and scalped near Turtle Creek, the same time the Lee family was murdered.

About the time I speak of, two Indians—one a mere youth, and the other a middle-aged man, tall and well proportioned—came into the neighborhood. They remained for some time. Being at a public house, called Stephenson's Tavern, near the mouth of the creek, on a certain occasion, where a number of people were congregated, amongst whom was the Walkers, they became intoxicated and performed many antics. The old Indian threw himself down before the Walkers, and went through several performances, exhibiting the most horrid grimaces and contortions of the face, remarking to them:—"*This is the way your father acted when I killed and scalped him!*"

The brothers were aroused at this savage and tantalizing demonstration. The murderer of their beloved father stood before them, and in mockery and derision, exhibited his death struggles. Their blood boiled with indignation, and they swore vengeance upon the savage fiend, and would have rushed upon him at the time and put an end to his existence, but were restrained by the crowd. That evening they persuaded a man named Samuel Doyle, to accompany them a short distance up the creek, where they planned the destruction of these Indians. Coming upon the encampment, they made known their intentions. The young Indian, who was a noble youth, remonstrated, cried, and begged for his life, stating that he was not concerned in the murder of the old man, but his pleadings were all in vain, and he was immediately tomahawked. They then attacked the old man, and a fearful struggle ensued with knives and tomahawks. He fought desperately for his life, and severely wounded two of the Walkers, and probably would have killed them, had they not succeeded in shooting him through the head. Their bodies were then taken and sunk in the creek not far from where Phelps' Mills now stand.

The people wondered at the sudden disappearance of the Indians from the neighborhood, and suspicion pointed to the Walkers, but the people considered that they got what they deserved, and it was soon forgotten. In course of time a freshet came, and washed their bodies ashore on a gravel bar near where Mr. H. Bailey now resides. Complaint was made to the Walkers, and, it is said, they went and buried them.

The murder now became the subject of much conversation through the neighborhood; some alleged that they were justifiable, under the circumstances, in committing the deed; and others that it was in time of peace, and a violation of the civil law. Thus matters rested for some time, till at length it came to the ears of the authorities, and proceedings were at once instituted against the murderers. So flagrant a violation of law, and the treaty now existing between the whites and Indians, could not be permitted to go unpunished. The sheriff was ordered to arrest them, and confine them in Sunbury jail for trial. They had good friends, however, and were advised of his coming in time to escape from the country. A reward was offered for their apprehension, but they never were taken.

Doyle was not so fortunate—he was taken and incarcerated in jail, charged with participating in the bloody tragedy. His trial came on—great excitement prevailed throughout the country, and hundreds were present, determined to rescue him in case of his conviction; alleging that he had been *forced* into it, and that it was *right* to kill the savages, under the circumstances. He was acquitted, however, and returned in triumph to his home. The Walkers were seldom heard of, not daring to venture back into the country.

When the intelligence of the murder of these Indians reached their friends west of the Alleghanies, they were highly incensed, and true to the vindictive character of the savage, resolved on revenge. Preparations were immediately made to invade the settlement; and it is said that a large body of warriors were on their way, when the Chief, Cornplanter, on learning that the authorities sought the murderers for punishment, considered it best to recall them, and despatching one of his swift footed young men, ordered them to return. They were bound to obey him, and reluctantly gave up the expedition.

The County of Lycoming was taken from Northumberland, by the Act of the 13th of April, 1795. It is a large County, embracing an area of about 1500 square miles, and is one of the most important in Northern Pennsylvania. According to the census of 1850, the population was 26,257. It has probably increased at the rate of six per cent. since that time. It also contained 113,264 acres of improved land; and 90,997 unimproved. The cash value of the farms was estimated at $4,110,234; and the value of farming implements, machinery, &c., at $164,611. At that time the County contained 4,066 horses; 14,230 sheep; 4,940 milch cows. Total value of *all* live stock, $429,332. Bushels of wheat raised, 285,925; rye, 95,274; Indian corn, 262,456. The County also contained 4 Baptist, 1 Episcopal, 1 Friends, 1 German Reformed, 8 Lutheran, 15 Methodist, 8 Presbyterian, 2 Roman Catholic, 2 Union, and 1 Minor Sect, Churches; the aggregate value of which was $63,000, with accommodations for 15,815 hearers.

This estimate was for the year ending the 1st of June, 1850, when the last census was taken. There has been a considerable increase since that time.

CHAPTER XLVI.

ARRIVAL OF THE TOMB FAMILY ON PINE CREEK—THE WOMEN AND THE PANTHER—A GREAT HUNTER—TAMING THE BLUE DUN—CATCHING A LIVE ELK—HUNTING EXPEDITIONS—ABUNDANCE OF FISH—IMMENSE QUANTITIES OF SNAKES—AN ADVENTURE WITH A BEAR—NARROW ESCAPE.

AMONGST some of the earliest settlers on Pine Creek, after peace was declared, was the Tomb family. Philip Tomb, one of the descendants, known as a great hunter and adventurer, recently published a work entitled, "Pioneer Life: or, Thirty Years a Hunter," which contains some remarkable statements. I shall quote liberally from it in reference to the Pine Creek region. Speaking about the arrival of the family, Mr. Tomb says:

"In 1791, my father purchased some land seventy miles up the West Branch, in the wilderness. He hired men and paid them in advance to build a house. They did not fulfil their contract, but having raised and enclosed it, left it without chimney, door, window, or floor, while the bushes, ten feet high, were left standing in the middle of the house. On the first of November my father started for his residence, and loaded a keel boat with provisions sufficient for one year, irons for a mill, and a supply of clothing. He was six days going fifty miles. He then arrived at the mouth of Pine Creek, six miles from his destination, but could proceed no farther with his boat, on account of low water. He then hired ten canoes, and started with such articles as he most needed. He arrived at his house the 20th of November. It was very cold—the men had been dragging the boats, and the women were nearly frozen. When within two miles of the house, two of the men who assisted in building it, asked the privilege of going ahead to make a fire. When we arrived in sight we saw a large fire, which revived our spirits greatly, for the snow was falling rapidly, the wind blew cold, and we were chilled through. A hole had been left for a chimney, and a fire built on that side of the house, and when we arrived the men were cutting out the brush. My father asked why things had been left in this state. They replied that they could not induce the other men to proceed any farther with the job. Father was inclined to be angry, when my mother interposed, and said if we could get through the first night it would do. We soon became warm, had our supper, went to sleep and passed the night very comfortably. The next morning all hands went to work and made a floor and chimney, and plastered the house, which was accomplished in two days. On the 25th my father commenced his mill. He had to hew and split out all the timbers to be used for building. He had also a race to dig and a dam to build, and he had it all finished by the first of March.

At that time game, such as bears, elk, deer and wild turkeys were very plenty in that section of the country. I had two brothers old enough to hunt, but they had no gun except an old musket which my father had used while training. In the morning we would frequently find the deer feeding within twenty rods of the house. Sometimes we would see a drove of elk, fifteen or twenty in number, crossing the creek. At other times we saw bears traveling back and forward. But we had no hunters among the six men, and no gun but the old musket, and that was out of order. On the 5th of December two of our nearest neighbors—who lived twelve miles distant—came to see us, bringing two guns and two dogs, but no ammunition. There was no powder or lead in that part of the country, except what my father had, and he supplied them what they needed. They then hunted about two days for my father to procure him a supply of wild meat. They killed four deer, and two fat bears."

Speaking about the inconveniences of obtaining flour, before his father's mill was in running order, he says:

"The nearest grist mill was thirty miles distant, and no road or other means of getting to it—nor had we any grain except a little which we raised in the same manner as the Indians. Every family had what was called a 'family block' or mortar, into which they pounded their corn into meal and samp."

Wild animals were numerous and dangerous at that time, judging from the following adventures, which he relates:

"A woman belonging to a family, living half a mile above the first fork, was washing at the creek, accompanied by four or five small children, when one of them looking up exclaimed, 'What a handsome big red dog is coming!' The animal stopped within fifty feet of the children, and stood looking at them. Another boy cried, 'It isn't a dog; it is a panther!' At that moment a cat came out of the house, and attempting to run up a tree, was caught by the panther and devoured. The family hurried into the house, closed the door and escaped. Shortly afterwards a man came along with a dog and gun, and shot the panther. It measured four and a half feet in length."

"Two miles from that place, on the main creek, lived a family consisting of a man and three females. The house stood on the flat lying between the river and the rocky bluff, which rose to the height of fifty feet. In the month of January the man was absent teaching school, and no one was left at home but the women. One of the women, on going to the creek one morning for a pail of water, heard a scream like the voice of a woman in distress. She hastened back and told the others. They all went to the door to ascertain the cause, when they saw an animal moving towards them, which they at first took for a dog. When it approached near enough, they saw, to their horror, that it was a panther. They retreated into the house and closed the doors. Three geese which belonged to the family, were on the ice of the creek—the panther captured one and carried it off. After he had been gone some time they went out together and procured wood and water enough to last till the next day. The next morning at the same hour the panther returned, uttering the same terrific cries, and carried away another goose. On the third morning he came and took the last one. He had become acquainted with the vicinity, and the terrified women knew not what to do. Their nearest neighbor was two miles distant. In order to prevent the animal from entering by the chimney, they covered it with boards, and kept up a fire all night. He returned the next morning, when they let out their dog. The panther closed in with him, drove him against the door, and after a short struggle killed and carried him off. The following morning a man named Rice Hamlin, happened to come to the house—he found the women almost frightened to death. On looking for the panther he discovered and shot him. He weighed two hundred pounds."

He describes an elk hunt as follows, which will be read with interest:

"In August, 1795, my father, Jacob Tomb, Jerry Morrison, and myself, started on an elk hunt. Taking provisions with us we pushed up to Round Island, but found no elk there. Morrison proposed to go to Stony Lick, near the second fork of the creek. All hands consented. When we arrived near the place, tracks were discovered. We followed them some distance, and found that one of them had been attacked and killed by a panther, and completely disemboweled. We skinned and salted the elk in the skin and placed it between two logs, and resumed our route. Early the next morning we heard the roar of an elk, and on proceeding to look for him found a large one, which we killed and salted. It weighed five hundred pounds. The horns were upwards of six feet in length, and had eleven branches, six on one, and five on the other.

"When they finished salting the meat, Morrison proposed to go over to Mud Lick himself and look for elk, leaving me and my father to watch Stony Lick. We went and concealed ourselves behind a log—my father commenced mending his moccasins, and directed me to watch. A small stream ran below me, containing some large trout. It occurred to me if I could build a dam across the stream I could take some trout. Slipping down, I threw an old log across, made a dam, and in a few minutes had threw out thirty large trout. My father on finding me asked if that was watching the lick, I told him I wanted some trout for supper. While I was stringing my fish I heard a stone rattle about a hundred yards below, and on looking up, beheld a panther gazing at me! I sprang up the bank and informed my father what I had seen. Telling me to keep quiet, and make the dog lie down, he stationed himself behind a root having a hole in it, through which he pointed his gun and awaited the panther's approach. When it came within three rods of us, it paused, with its fore feet on the bank, and its mouth open, displaying a formidable array of glistening teeth. My father fired, and it fell dead. It was a very large one."

The following description of taming a vicious horse, and capturing an elk alive, is very interesting:

"In 1799, my father being at Irving Stephenson's tavern at the mouth of Pine Creek, found a large collection of men there. A horse called the Blue Dun, was kept there. It was a very large and powerful horse, and it was with difficulty three men could take it from the stable. My father witnessed the operation and laughed, saying he could take it from the stable without any assistance. The others disputed this stoutly, saying the horse would kill him if he attempted it—upon which he offered to bet twenty dollars that he could do it. The bet was taken and the money staked, when he went in to the horse, struck him a few times on the flank, completely subdued him, brought him forth, and rode him round to the surprise of the crowd, and took him back, and won his money.

"The whole party began to drink pretty freely and talk about elk hunting. Stephenson asked my father if he could take an elk alive. He replied that he could, when Stephenson offered to bet him on it. My father asked him what he was willing to bet. He said he would bet 250 pounds. It was accepted. Stephenson pledged a house, lot and tanyard worth the amount, and my father gave seven hundred and fifty dollars' worth of lumber, and two satisfactory sureties as security for the performance of the contract. The elk was to be between fourteen and sixteen hands high, caught alive, and brought home by the first of March, allowing some six months to take it in. Articles of agreement were duly drawn. It was then considered impossible to take an elk alive.

"The first of January, 1800, he prepared for his hunt, and started, taking two of his boys and a man named Maddock, with a horse, four dogs, and ropes sufficient to hold an elk. They ascended the ice eight miles to Morrison's, and desired him to go along, but he declined, alleging that an elk was a very powerful and dangerous animal, and its capture alive attended with a good deal of peril. The party continued on. The weather was very cold, and snow began to fall. On the second or third day an elk was found and the pursuit commenced. He ran for many miles back and forth across the creek. The plan to take him was to throw a rope over his horns when he got on a rock to fight the dogs. He was finally hunted so severely that he took refuge on a large rock in the evening. A fire was built near the rock and kept up all night. The next morning, after considerable manœuvering, a noose was finally thrown over his horns, and the rope made fast to a tree. The dogs were set on behind to drive him off the rock, and when he came to the edge a sudden pull was given which jerked him off. He plunged and fought tremendously, but they succeeded in getting another rope on him, and fastening it some distance ahead managed to drive him down the hill, by untying and fastening alternately. This was a slow as well as difficult process, as he was constantly becoming entangled in his struggles. The ropes were unloosed, and two men to each end and a dog let loose to keep him going. When he went too fast, we could check him by snubbing the rope round a tree. He started and walked very gently till he reached the creek, which was covered with ice. We fastened one rope across the creek, keeping the other in our hands, and drove him upon the ice when he slipped and fell. We all went to the other side and dragged him across. As soon as he gained a footing he sprang up and walked towards us. We then fastened the ropes in opposite directions to give him no play, and as it was four o'clock in the afternoon, determined to let him remain here until we could bring a horse from Morrison's to take him home. The horse being brought the next day, we cut a road through the underbrush about one mile to the big creek. We now secured him close up to a tree, and placed a large rope about forty feet long over his horns, down near to his head, and then tied a smaller rope to the upper part of each horn. We then attached the horse to the large rope behind, and one of the hands started the horse. When he first started he plunged about considerably, and became entangled in the rope. At the end of three hours we reached the creek, a distance of one mile. Here we met with no further obstruction, as the ice was slightly covered with snow, and he found a good footing. We proceeded without much more trouble to Morrison's, and placed our captive in a stable. A heavy rain now came on and broke up the ice in the river—our horse ran off and was drowned, and we took the elk down on a float. Stephenson was informed of the capture, when he cheerfully gave up the stakes.

"This was the first grown elk caught alive on the waters of the Susquehanna. It was sixteen hands high, and had horns five and a-half feet long, with eleven branches."

Philip Tomb, who was along in this expedition, afterwards became a very successful elk hunter, and took several alive.

Fish were very plenty in those times, in the creek, as we would naturally conclude from the following account by Mr. Tomb, of taking them in a fish basket:

> "We were so abundantly supplied with fish from this source that we used them to feed our hogs, and found them very useful for that purpose. A slight rise coming in the creek, the eels began to run very fast, and the other fish came in so rapidly as to dam up the water, and let the eels go over the sides of the basket. Finding that we were losing many eels in this way, my brother brought the canoe and placed it under the basket and raked the eels in as they came. In about ten hours the creek had rose so high as to overflow the basket and put an end to our operations. We had then carried out about *twelve wagon loads of suckers*, three barrels of eels, and two barrels of salmon and rock fish, besides throwing a great quantity out of the basket to keep it from overflowing."

This may be considered a pretty large fish story, nevertheless Mr. Tomb relates it as a fact in his work. Fish were very numerous in those days before the river was obstructed by dams, booms, &c.

Rattlesnakes were very numerous also, in those days. He speaks of them thus:

> "In 1794, Mr. Jas. King and Mr. Manning went on an exploring expedition up the creek. They found the rattlesnakes so numerous, that they were obliged to anchor their canoe in the creek and remain in it over night. About the third day they arrived at the larger rock on the west side of the creek, and found as many as thirty snakes lying on it sunning themselves. They pushed their canoe to the other shore, and when passing the smaller rock, they discovered on the top, a pile of rattlesnakes as large as an out-door bake oven!"

This is undoubtedly a pretty tough snake story, although they were very numerous, and were a great annoyance to the settlers for many years.

King and Manning proceeded as far up as the Big Meadows, that had evidently been an Indian cornfield. They found a plum orchard there, supposed to contain about twenty acres, bearing plenty of fruit.

He states that there were six rattlesnake dens on Pine Creek. Some distance up the creek was a large rock, about forty feet long by fifteen wide, called Rattlesnake Rock. On this the snakes would often lie in piles.

Being engaged lumbering some twenty miles up the creek, Mr. Tomb once had an adventure with a bear, which he describes as follows:

"A large bear was passing near where I was at work. I threw stones at him, but he paid no attention to them and kept on his course. I was thinking of retreating, when I thought I would throw one more; and picking up a large stone, threw it and hit him on the forehead. He raised up, uttered a savage growl, and rushed towards me. I ran to the logs, caught up my axe and sprang upon a pair of timber wheels. Before springing on the wheels, I looked round and he was close at my heels. I raised my axe, intending to plunge it into his brain; but in the excitement missed my aim, and the handle struck his feet, which caused him to give another cry of pain. I was now on the wheels, and taking off my hat shook it at him, causing him to step back a little. I saw death staring me in the face. In a short time he moved off. I never was so badly frightened in my life."

His work is filled with marvelous stories about hunting and trapping, and much more might be selected, but the foregoing must suffice. He mentions having discovered a remarkable cave near Tumbling Run, with square rooms, stone benches, &c., bearing unmistakable signs of having been cut by hand. Considerable inquiry has recently been made concerning it, but no person in that neighborhood seems to have any knowledge of its existence.

CHAPTER XLVII.

SKETCH OF SUNBURY AND NORTHUMBERLAND—BLUE HILL—JOHN MASON—THE LEANING HOUSE—HIS GRAVE—CHURCHVILLE—SODOM—ORIGIN OF THE NAME—LIST OF THE SHERIFFS OF NORTHUMBERLAND COUNTY—STATISTICS—THE COFFIN FIGHT—A LEGISLATOR OF THE OLDEN TIME—ANECDOTES.

SUNBURY is one of the oldest towns in Northern Pennsylvania. Fort Augusta having been erected here one hundred years ago, rendered it in early times, and during the Revolution, a place of great importance, from its central position at the confluence of the North and West Branches of the Susquehanna. It was the grand depot for troops and supplies for all this region—was the point from which the emigrants radiated. Being located, too, on a beautiful rolling plain, with excellent facilities for water communication, and contiguous to the immense coal fields, Sunbury at one time seemed destined to become a great central emporium of trade. All such anticipations, in course of time, were dispelled, and for a long time the wheels of Progress seemed stayed, and the town remained *in statu quo*.

Within a few years, Sunbury has been roused from its Rip Van Winkle sleep of half a century, and has taken a fresh start in improvement. Being the converging point of several important railroads, a new impetus has been given to business, fresh energy seems infused into the citizens, and it bids fair to be an important place ere many years. It is the starting point of the Sunbury and Erie Railroad, which runs through the entire length of the West Branch Valley. The Susquehanna Railroad also terminates here, and a railroad to Mount Carmel and Shamokin, is in operation. Immense quantities of coal are shipped here. It also possesses fine advantages for water power, and I know of no place in the State better adapted, from its location, means of communication, and natural facilities, for the erection of saw mills, manufactories of cotton, iron, &c.

As the majority of buildings were erected years ago, and the people not having kept pace with the improvements of the age, of course the style is somewhat quaint, and antiquated in appearance. The buildings are substantial and comfortable. The Court House, and other public buildings, are of brick. The latter stands in the centre of a square or diamond. The town contains some fourteen stores, and a number of good hotels. Supreme Court, of the Eastern District, sits here. According to the census of 1850, it contained a population of 1218. It has increased much since that time.

An old gentleman resides here named John Colsher, Esq., in the 96th year of his age, with memory bright and unimpaired. He is a remarkable man—can write a plain legible hand, tell a good joke, and walk around the streets as comfortably as many men of younger years. He has never worn glasses in his life, and can see to read well—he can hold his arm outstretched for several minutes, without the slightest tremor.

A fine bridge is thrown across the North Branch at this point, and a few yards below it, a fine structure has recently been erected by the Sunbury and Erie Railroad

Company. A large dam was placed in the river here, by the State, for the benefit of the canal.

The site of Fort Augusta is occupied by a fine brick mansion, one mile above the town, owned by Miss Hunter. Every vestige of the fort is gone, with the exception of the magazine, which can be seen in the yard, resembling a cave. It is used for various purposes.

Many relics of the olden time are plowed up every year on this farm, consisting of hatchets, gun barrels, cannon balls, camp kettles, &c. But the most interesting of all, is a little article called a "*Crow's foot.*" This was a piece of iron made with three prongs, very sharp, and barbed at the points, and so constructed, that when thrown on the ground one of them would point upwards. Great quantities were made and strewn around the fort for the Indians to step on. They would go through a moccasin, and penetrate the foot for an inch. They were quite an ingenious contrivance, and capable of inflicting great pain. Bushels of them are plowed up at the present time.

Shamokin Creek empties into the river at Sunbury, and fourteen miles up the Creek is located the town of Shamokin, which is growing rapidly, being in the coal region. Sunbury should have been called Shamokin, as it stands where the *original* town of that name was situated.

Passing over the river we come to Northumberland, located in the forks of the two branches. It is a very old town also, and has not improved much for many years, although it has had immense advantages.

Northumberland was incorporated as a borough in 1828. It contains four churches—Old and New School Presbyterian, German Reformed and Methodist. The Bank of Northumberland, a very old and popular institution, is located here. According to the census of 1850, it contained 1041 inhabitants. The citizens are intelligent and refined, and probably more newspapers are taken here than in any other town of similar size in the State. Extensive wharves for shipping coal have recently been erected here by Messrs. Cochran, Peale & Co. They are deeply interested in the coal trade, and send large quantities to Elmira. I believe they were the first to send coal to the Empire State over this road.

The first iron foundry in the Shamokin region, was established here in 1827–8. An ingenious workman from New York, named David Rogers, came to the place, bringing with him a quantity of patent scale-beams, of which he was the inventor, or owned the right for this portion of the State. Mr. Shannon assisted him in erecting a small foundry for the purpose, specially, of casting the necessary irons. As he succeeded very well, it was his intention, in conjunction with Mr. Shannon, to enlarge the business, and make other and larger castings. Owing to cruel and wicked tricks played on him, Rogers became deranged and left his plans, and the business was discontinued, Mr. Shannon not being acquainted with the business.

The locality is inviting to the recluse. The country expands behind the town in a semi-circular form, rising in gentle swells towards Montour's ridge. Opposite the town, in the North Branch, is a long and beautiful island, called Lyon's Island. A fine bridge crosses the West Branch at its mouth, with the towing path for the Canal. At the western end of this bridge rises the high and precipitous sandstone of "Blue Hill," from which a magnificent prospect is enjoyed of the valleys of both rivers, whilst the town lies hundreds of feet beneath you, spread out like a map. The precipice of Blue Hill is several hundred feet in perpendicular height. The town is well laid out, with spacious streets, and to those who love quiet and seclusion, is a pleasant place to reside.

A traveller visiting this region a few years ago, thus describes a scene he beheld:—

"I ascended a hill called Mount Pleasant this morning, just as the sun was rising. The scene was enchanting—at my feet as it were, lay the borough (Sunbury) in quiet repose, embowered in shade and foliage, and surrounded on three sides with rich fields, pastures and herds. In front of the town was the river, which being raised by the Shamokin dam, looked like an immense mirror, or a glassy lake, more than like a river. On the opposite side of the river, the land rose abruptly into a craggy mountain: looking further up the stream, I saw two branches gradually approach each other, till they met and mingled their waters. Over each of these were long bridges leading to and from the village of Northumberland, back of which and between the two branches, the country rose gradually from the plain, till it became almost mountainous, yet covered to the very tops with fields, pastures, flocks and herds. Turning again to the left, and looking down the Susquehanna, a sort of vista was presented, bounded on each side with romantic hills, and finally appearing to end in the blue tops of the mountains. Never have I beheld a more varied or beautiful landscape than was here presented."

Travellers passing up the West Branch, on leaving Northumberland, will observe two small square buildings, or towers, on the edge of the high precipice of Blue Hill, overlooking the country for miles around. One of them leans over the precipice, apparently ready to fall and be dashed to pieces on the rocks below. A single breath of air would apparently blow it over. It inclines probably at an angle of 35°, and strange as it may seem, was built in that manner, by an eccentric individual named John Mason. The building is firmly fixed on a solid foundation, and fastened down with strong iron bolts, or it would have been precipitated over the rocks long ago. It had a railing around the top, and visitors could go up and view the prospect; but few had the nerve to approach the edge and gaze below. The other building stands a few yards from this one, and not so near the edge. It was finer, much higher, and had an observatory on the top, where visitors could go with perfect safety. It does not lean like the other. The view afforded from this height is superlatively grand, and no just conception of its beauty can be formed, without visiting the spot.

John Mason owned the land here, and had these buildings erected to gratify his peculiar whims, being quite eccentric. He was reputed wealthy, but would always travel to Philadelphia and other places on foot, and many anecdotes are related of him. Being an old bachelor, he lived hermit-like, on this high elevation; but the peculiar oddity of his buildings attracted large numbers of visitors. He had finely laid out grounds around them, and seemed to enjoy himself well. He died in 1849.—The buildings are neglected, and rapidly going to decay; one of them is quite dilapidated, and cannot be ascended with safety.

Immediately in rear of the *leaning* building, under the wide-spreading branches of a chestnut, is the grave of the eccentric John Mason. The hand of affection has fitted it up with care, and planted sweet-flowering shrubs. On visiting the spot in June last, I copied the following inscription from the neat tomb stone, placed at the head of the grave:

JOHN MASON
of Blue Hill
Born in Philada, Dec,
7th 1768
Departed this Life
At Long Reach Farm
Near Newberry
Lycoming Co. April 25th
1849
Aged 80 years, 4 mos.
and 18 days.

In 1833, a town was laid out at the end of the bridge opposite Lewisburg, and named Churchville, by an individual well known as Jerry Church. Respecting this town, Mr. Church, in his Autobiography, says:

"The next town we made our appearance (he was accompanied by his brother;) in was Lewisburg, formerly called Derrstown. We there made a purchase of one hundred and twenty-five acres of land, of General Green, at forty-five dollars per acre, lying on both sides of the cross-cut, from the end of the bridge to the Pennsylvania canal, opposite the town of Lewisburg. Having been in the habit of making towns, we concluded that we could make one most anywhere, and we thought we would try a small one in opposition to the one on the other side of the river—Lewisburg. However, we did not frighten them much as a rival, but we got their feelings raised and blood up, so that they bought of us at beautiful prices. There was one gentleman who purchased seventeen acres at one hundred dollars per acre, the next day after we had bought it at forty-five. We laid out the balance into streets, alleys and out-lots, and called it Churchville. We sold out the whole purchase in two weeks, and made some money, but not much of a town. It was a very pleasant place for a town, but there were no houses built in it but one, I believe, and that was a hotel; and in order to let the people know that that was the town of Churchville, the proprietor of the house had the name written on a large sign—'Churchville Hotel,' and I am very thankful to the gentleman for keeping up appearances."

The original plot of this town is now in the possession of James F. Linn, Esq., of Lewisburg.

East of this place, a mile or two, is a small straggling village called Sodom. It takes its name from an Irishman named Lot Carson, who lived here, and frequently imbibed large potations of whiskey. On one occasion he got intoxicated and tumbled into the well in the evening, where he remained till morning, when he was taken therefrom a corpse. The place was afterwards called Sodom; because *Lot* had resided there. There was probably a wide difference between the two men, however.

The following table will show the names of *all* the Sheriffs of Northumberland county, and the time elected, from its first organization down to the present day. The facts are obtained from the Prothonotary's Office in Sunbury, and are correct:

NAMES.	TIME ELECTED.	NAMES.	TIME ELECTED.
Geo. Nagel,* (from Ap'l to Oct.)	1772	Thomas Painter,	1812
William Cook,	1772	Walter Brady,	1815
William Scull,	1775	William Shannon,	1818
Jonathan Lodge,	1776	James R. Shannon,	1821
James Crawford,	1779	Martin Weaver,	1824
Henry Antes,	1782	Jacob McKinney,	1827
Thomas Grant,	1785	Peter Lazarus,	1830
Martin Withington,	1788	Henry Reeder,	1833
Flavel Roan,	1791	George W. Keihl,	1836
John Brady, Jr.	1794	Henry Gosler,	1839
Robert Irwin,	1797	Felix Maurer,	1842
Henry Vanderslice,	1800	T. A. Billington,	1845
Andrew Albright,	1803	James Covert,	1848
Jared Irwin,	1806	W. B. Kipp,	1851
Daniel Lebo,	1809	Henry Weise,	1854

According to the census of 1850, Northumberland county contained 23,272 inhabitants. Number of acres of improved land, 135,086; unimproved, 62,682. Cash value of farms, $5,766,803; total value of farming implements

* Nagel was Sheriff of Berks county when Northumberland was stricken off, but served in the latter, till the election of Cook.

and machinery, $242,407. The county also contained 525 horses, milch cows, 5,794, sheep, 9,980; total value of *all* live stock, $548,073. Bushels of wheat raised, 289,522, rye, 120,354, corn, 282,087. The county also contained 7 Baptist, 2 Episcopal, 11 German Reformed, 8 Lutheran, 9 Methodist, 13 Presbyterian, and 1 Roman Catholic, churches; the total value of which was estimated at $103,000, with a capacity for 17,910 auditors.

During the time of the construction of the canal, quite an amusing incident occurred on the farm of Mr. Nesbit, opposite Lewisburg, denominated the "Coffin fight." Mr. N. describes it as follows:

> "One foggy morning as I was plowing, and came to turn my horses on the side of the field next to the river, I espied a coffin lying in the middle of the road. I at once came to the conclusion that it had been lost by some of the Irish canal-laborers on their way to the Catholic burying ground in the neighborhood of Milton. Crossing the fence, I drew it aside out of the way of wagons, concluding that they would soon discover their loss and return for it. I had not waited long before I saw them on their way back; but unluckily at the same time, another company with a corpse in a cart, going to the same cemetery, met them nearly opposite the place where the *lost* coffin lay in the fence-corner! Without a "good morning," the losing party of disconsolate mourners accused the advancing party of having stolen *their* corpse—for the pleasure of acting the mourners and tasting the joy of grief and a little whiskey—and before I could make them hear my voice, the lie was given, and copious volleys of blows, kicks and curses were exchanged. It was for sometime in vain that I shouted—but having at length turned the attention of one of the females to the *lost* coffin, order was gradually restored—they shook hands—apologized for the mistake, took a friendly drink together, and marched on very amicably to perform the last rites for their dead!"

Many years ago, when Northumberland county embraced a great extent of territory, and when it was found necessary for our State Legislature to resolve that no member of their body should come to the House barefooted, nor be allowed to eat his bread and cheese on the State-House door-steps, there was sent, as a representative from this county, one Jacob Follmer, Esq., who faithfully represented a constituency possessed of more practical wisdom than book-learning. Jacob, however, thought himself, by virtue of his office, entitled to be critical upon occasions. He one day called at the lodging of one of his co-laborers for the public good, to look over some memorial relative to the building or incorporating of a church. As it was to be presented on that day, he was naturally anxious that the matter should be in good shape—so as to do no discredit to him—for he intended to support the application. Carefully scanning the paper, his critical eye fell on the barbarous word "*gurggh*," (meaning church.) "Ah!" cried he, "you must take better care of your spelling—you have put a double G, where there ought to be but one, this way—'*gurgh*,'—that's the way I spell it!"

During one of the winter's of his service, there were two or three lawyers—young men—who, a little vain of their learning, interlarded their speeches with long quotations from the Latin authors. This gave some offence to Jacob, who thought, and very justly, if he was to be reasoned with, it ought to be done in a language that he could understand. He, therefore, in his reply, commenced by remarking, that as it was the fashion to make speeches in unknown tongues, he must be excused if he spoke in the Delaware Indian dialect, for he could not pretend to anything so "*high larned*" as the Philadelphia lawyers spoke. He accordingly drew very liberally on his stores of savage *classicality*. The effect was quite decided—"the Latin fled and never was heard of more."

Once in a contest for the Legislature, he was opposed by a gentleman named Bull, whom he defeated. After serving out his term, and the time of election drawing near again, he was asked by one of his neighbors, if he intended to be a candidate again. He replied—

"Vell, I guess I'll have to kill another Bull dis fall!"

Mr. Follmer was a very honest and faithful representative, and discharged his duties in a satisfactory and efficient manner. His descendants are among the most respectable citizens of the West Branch Valley.

University, Lewisburg, Pa.

CHAPTER XLVIII.

EARLY HISTORY OF LEWISBURG—VALUABLE FACTS—RELIGIOUS DENOMINATIONS—HISTORY OF THE UNIVERSITY—DIVISION OF THE COUNTY—STATISTICS OF UNION COUNTY—A DEED THAT DATES BACK TO THE CREATION OF THE WORLD—SKETCH OF FLAVEL ROAN—ANECDOTES.

A PATENT for the land on which the borough of Lewisburg* is located, was granted to Richard Peters, August 11th, 1772, for 320 acres. On the 17th of November, 1773, Peters transferred it, by deed, to Ludwig Derr. In 1785, Derr laid out the plan for the town. It was then called Derr's town. Derr died in Philadelphia in November, 1785, where he had gone to sell lots, leaving an only son, George Derr. On the 20th of December, 1788, he transferred the town plot, embracing 128 acres, to Peter Borger, excepting seventeen lots, and all lots that his father had sold by deed, or written agreement. January 2d, 1789, Borger disposed of the same, with the same reserve, to Carl Ellinckhuysen, of Amsterdam, Holland. On the 8th of May, 1789, Ellinckhuysen, by letter of attorney, authorized Borger to sell lots for him; who, as attorney-in-fact, sold, mortgaged, and disposed of lots, for about eighteen months, when *he* was superseded by a letter of attorney to the Rev J. Charles Hil-

* For the facts in relation to the history of Lewisburg, both ancient and modern, I am indebted to James F. Linn, Esq., of that place.

burn, a Catholic Priest, dated September 30th, 1790. He also sold and mortgaged lots, so that in consequence of mistakes, or something else, many lots now have three or four distinct written titles.

About this time Carl Ellinckhuysen sent his son, Matthias Joseph Ellinckhuysen, to America, and put him under the surveillance of Hilburn, the Priest. Being dissipated, he ran his course rapidly, and died on the 17th of July, 1792, aged 38 years and 3 months. His widow, Clara Helena Ellinckhuysen, married John Thornburgh, who also soon died. They were both buried in the old grave yard on Market street; the tombstone of the latter is entirely gone; that of the former is broken in three pieces. It contains the following inscription, which I have copied as, perhaps, the only means of perpetuating it. Not a brick is left of the wall which formerly surrounded his grave. Surely THAT tomb-stone is worthy of preservation, for the honor of the town, as well as a relic of the olden time. But to the inscription:

Here Lieth
the body of
MATHIAS JOSEPH
ELLENKHUSEN
who departed this Life
July 17, 1792, aged 38
Years and 3 Months.
Since it is so we all must Die
& Death no one doth spare
So lot us all to Icsus Fly
& seek for refuge their

A large brick church now stands on the site of his grave. Mrs. Thornburgh married a man named Moore, and removed to Erie, where she died.

The proprietors thus dying, and removing away, and the lot owners living principally in Philadelphia, and not paying attention to their claims, the citizens fenced up the lots, with the view of holding them by possession right. In 1814, Robert E. Griffith, of Philadelphia, brought an ejectment for a large number of lots, which was defeated in the Supreme Court in 1823, on account of the defective proof of the execution of the letter of attorney to Peter Borger. The ejectments were renewed in 1824; and from 1827 to 1832, the cases were all compromised, by the defendants paying a small sum to the plaintiff for each of the lots. In 1841, George W. West, and others, brought an ejectment for one hundred lots against John Lawshe and Charles Beyer, neither of whom were in possession of any of the lots. The writ was set aside for informality, and never renewed, which was the last difficulty in lot titles, originating out of the Ellinckhuysen title.

In consequence of this defect of title, very few buildings were erected previous to 1830, which proved an advantage to the place, as by that time, those who built were able to erect much better edifices than they would have erected years before. Hence the reason of Lewisburg having such good buildings, and being such a cleanly town.

In 1826, there were two wooden church edifices; the Methodist Episcopal, which now constitutes a part of Geddes & Marsh's foundry, on the corner of Front and St. Lewis streets, and the Christian, near the north end of Fifth street.

In 1812, a M. E. Church was organized; Messrs. Dawson and Ross had preached occasionally in the place for some months before. In 1818, the Saints, with the assistance of other denominations, erected the house spoken of above. In 1832, they erected a brick chapel on Third street, which they took down in 1854, and rebuilt it. Rev. Mr. Dashalle is now the pastor.

In 1833, a colony from the old Buffalo Church, at Buffalo × Roads, was organized, by the name of the Lewisburg Presbyterian Church, and the same year erected a brick chapel on the N. W. corner of Front and St. Lewis streets. A few years ago, an old deed to trustees, for the use of a Presbyterian Church and grave yard, for the lots occupied by the English grave yard on Market street, was found among the old papers of William Wilson, late of Kelly township, deceased, on the grant of his son William of this place. The Presbyterians of Lewisburg and vicinity, during the summer of 1856, erected a magnificent brick church on the site of this old grave yard. The Rev. P. B. Marr was the first pastor, who was succeeded in the autumn of 1852 by the Rev. James Clark, D. D., who is the present pastor.

In 1834, the German Reformed and Lutherans erected a brick Union Chapel on the German grave yard, on the corner of South Third and St. Lewis streets. In 1847, the German Reformed seceded from the Union, and built a brick chapel on the corner of North Third and St. John's streets. The Rev. J. H. Fries was the first pastor, who had preached here many years before, 1834, in a log school house on the German grave yard, succeeded by the Rev. R. A. Fisher, and others, till 1844, when the Rev. Henry Harbaugh was installed pastor, who was succeeded, in 1850, by the Rev. D. T. Heisler, who was succeeded, in 1853, by the Rev. Benjamin Bousman, the present pastor.

The Lutherans having bought out the interest of the German Reformed, to the church on the grave yard lots, in 1852, took down the old church, and rebuilt a brick chapel on the same lot. The Rev. R. A. Fink is the present pastor.

The Christian Society was organized in 1820, under the auspices of the quite celebrated Elijah Bacon. While he was in the South, collecting funds to erect a meeting house, Messrs. Bussell and Badger took his place, changed the mode of worship from a room *without* seats, to that of one *with* seats, and in 1822 erected a wooden chapel on the north end of Fifth street. In 1854 the society purchased a lot on Third street, north of Market, and built thereon a brick church of very respectable appearance.

In January, 1844, the Baptists organized a church in this place, and in 1845, built a chapel on South Third street, in the cupola of which is placed the town clock. Rev. Isaac W. Hayhurst is the present pastor.

At a meeting of the Northumberland Baptist Association, held in Milton, August 1832, it was

"*Resolved*, That the exigencies of our denomination require that an effort be made to establish a Manual Labor Academy in the interior of this Commonwealth, for the education of our sons, and to furnish facilities for Literary and Theological improvement to brethren who may have been approbated to preach."

In October, 1834, however, the Association waived their plan, by passing a Resolution, highly approving of an effort then put forth by the Philadelphia Association, to establish a Literary and Theological Institution at Haddington, near Philadelphia. In 1835, a similar Resolution was again adopted.

The Philadelphia effort, however, proved an entire failure; and in August, 1845, the Northumberland Association resumed their original design. They Resolved, (through a committee for the purpose, composed of Rev. Charles Packer, Dr. W. H. Ludwig, Rev. Joel E. Bradley, Rev. J. Green Miles, and Dr. James Moore, Sr.,) in favor of establishing, "In Central Pennsylvania, a Literary Institution, embracing a High School for male pupils, another for females, a College, and also a Theological Institution, to be under the control of the Baptist denomination." Committees were appointed to carry out the object.

In the fall of 1845, Stephen W. Taylor, LL. D., a devoted and successful educator of Hamilton, N. Y., was employed as a General Agent, and drew up, and in the winter of 1846 obtained from the Legislature of Pennsylvania, a liberal charter for the "UNIVERSITY OF LEWISBURG."* Rev. Messrs. Eugenio Kincaid and William Shadrach, were subsequently appointed Canvassing Agents, and in 1849, had raised, by subscription, the sum of $100,000 as an endowment for the University; of which $20,000 were from the funds of the Association. Additional sums were subsequently secured for the endowment of Professorships, giving it a solid foundation and permanency of financial condition, hardly surpassed by any literary institution in the State. A large Academic building was afterwards erected at an expense of $8,000, and the west wing of the main edifice at an expense of $12,000.

The plan for the main University Edifice was kindly presented by Prof. Thos. U. Walker, Ph. D. The central edifice and the east wing will be erected this year. The buildings are of the best and most approved models.— Located in a native grove of unequaled beauty, on a

* I am indebted to O. N. Worden, Esq., for the history of the University, from the first inception of the design, to the present time.

gentle hill overlooking the boroughs of Lewisburg, Milton and other towns—on every hand fruitful fields, bounded by mountains in the distance—I know of no more attractive or delightful view from any "Hill of Science," than that to be furnished from the elevated dome of the University Buildings.

In the fall of 1846, Prof. Taylor commenced a High School, with a handfull of pupils, in the basement of a house of worship, and soon organized a Freshman class. Other instructors were engaged, and in 1851, President Taylor had the satisfaction of graduating the first class of six young men; when he resigned, having accepted the Presidency of Madison University, Hamilton, N. Y. He was succeeded by Howard Malcom. The Institution is now in successful operation, under the direction of a learned and substantial faculty, composed of the Rev. Howard Malcom, D. D., President, and the Rev. Geo. R. Bliss, D. Ph., Charles E. James, D. Ph., and Justin R. Loomis, D. Ph., as assistant Professors in the Collegiate Department. In 1855, Thomas F. Curtis, A. M., was appointed Professor of Theology. H. D. Walker, A. M., is Principal of the Academy. The University Female Institute, under the charge of Miss. A. Taylor, is located in town. There are three or four teachers in this department.

Between the town and the University ground proper, the flat is beautifully studded with the dwellings of the various Professors, and other private residences, constructed in a unique and attractive style of architecture.

There are several Literary and other Societies connected with the University and Institute. Also a superior Philosophical Apparatus, interesting Cabinets, and Museum—a Library of over 3000 volumes, a Manniken for physiological studies, and in fact, as large a store of advantages for acquiring a good education as at any other institution of a similar age. It has been blessed with a large share of prosperity, and promises lasting benefits to the favored country by which it is surrounded and nurtured.

The log cabin Academy, in Lewisburg, was built about the year 1805, by a joint stock company, on the corner of the English Graveyard, where it now stands a monument of olden times.

In the year 1839, a new joint stock company built the brick Academy on the corner of North Front and St. Mary streets. In September, 1845, it was sold to pay a debt, and purchased by six individuals, who have since sold out their interest, and it is now owned by the present Principal, Mr. John Randolph, who has in it a flourishing school. James McClure, Esq., Rev. Hugh Pollock, John Robinson, Esq., Rev. Samuel Shaffer, and Robert C. Ross, were successively the conductors of it previous to the present incumbent.

James Black, John Metzger, Henry Spyker, George Links, and Hugh Wilson, were among the earliest merchants of the place. In 1826, nearly all the business was done by William Hays and Alexander Graham.—Daniel Beyer and Jacob Bogar had small stores, but they both died that year, after which a number from a distance came in and erected stores. There are now nine dry goods stores, three drug stores, one hardware store, and a number of other establishments, in the town.

Union County was formed out of Northumberland by the act of 22d March, 1813. Seth Chapman was the first President Judge, and Hugh Wilson and —— Bolender were the first Associate Judges. Ellis Lewis succeeded Judge Chapman in 1832, and he was succeeded by Judge Wilson in 1842, who presides at the present time.

Under an act of Assembly, passed March 2d, 1855, Union County was divided. The division is called Snyder, in honor of the Governor, and embraces Middleburg, and the southern part of the old County of Union. The question of division occupied the minds of the people for several years, and was stoutly contested on both sides. The excitement engendered at the time will long be remembered by the people.

Lewisburg became the capital of Union County by ballot, and on the 3d of December, 1855, the records were removed to the new seat of justice. The first Court was held in the basement of the M. E. Church, commencing on the 17th of December, 1855.

By *private* subscription, a Court House and Jail are being erected in Lewisburg, and are expected to be completed in time for December term of Court, 1856. The building will be a model of neatness. It is one hundred feet front, and fifty feet back. The first story will contain the cells for prisoners—the second story the County Offices—the third story the Court and Jury rooms.

According to the census of 1850, Union County contained 132,049 acres of improved land, and 74,881 unimproved. The cash valuation of farms was $5,800,718. Value of farming implements, machinery, &c., $184,087. The County also contained 5,295 horses, 6,283 milch cows, 9,931 sheep, and 13,616 swine. Total aggregate value of all live stock $471,390. Bushels of wheat raised 353,095, rye 78,304, and corn 180,563. The

County also contained 1 Baptist, 1 Christian, 10 German Reformed, 13 Lutheran, 9 Methodist, 1 Moravian, 4 Presbyterian, and 1 Union, Churches, the aggregate value of which was $78,200, with accommodations for 17,800 people. The population of the County was 26,083. Lewisburg had 2,012, which is more than doubled at the present day.

The County having been divided, since the above census was taken, a great change has been effected in the figures, yet there has been a gradual increase.

Buffalo Valley is one of the best wheat-producing regions in Pennsylvania, and contains as fine farms as can be found anywhere. Lewisburg is the grand depot for the trade of this, as well as several other extensive valleys, and does an immense business. Thousands of bushels of wheat are annually shipped at this point.

The following indenture, which, upon examination, will be found to be a curious instrument, is a *bona fide* document, the original copy of which is still preserved in Lewisburg. The ground referred to is now part of the lot occupied by the Foundry of Messrs. Geddes & Marsh, which was formerly the Methodist House of worship.—It is certainly a rare curiosity in the conveyancing line. It is doubtful whether any other town has as clear a chronicle of possession from the original parents of mankind, downwards—and question if any borough in America has the "documents" to prove itself as venerable as Lewisburg:

This Indenture—Made the ninth day of October, in the year of our Lord one thousand seven hundred and ninety-three, Between Clara Helena Ellinkhuysen, of the town of Louisburg, in the township of Buffaloe, in the county of Northumberland and commonwealth of Pennsylvania, widow, of the one part, and Flavel Roan, of the town of Sunbury, in the county and commonwealth aforesaid, Esquire, of the other part. Whereas, the Creator of the earth, by parole and livery of seisin, did enfeoff the parents of mankind, to wit, Adam and Eve, of all that certain tract of land, called and known in the planetary system by the name of The Earth, together with all and singular the advantages, woods, waters, water-courses, easements, liberties, privileges, and all others the appurtenances whatsoever thereunto belonging, or in any wise appertaining to have and to hold to them the said Adam and Eve, and the heirs of their bodies lawfully to be begotten, in fee-tail general forever, as by the said feoffment recorded by Moses, in the first chapter of the first book of his records commonly called Genesis, more fully and at large appears on reference being thereunto had: And Whereas, the said Adam and Eve died seised of the premises aforesaid in fee-tail general, leaving issue, heirs of their bodies, to wit, sons and daughters, who entered into the same premises and became thereof seised as tenants in common by virtue of the donation aforesaid, and multiplied their seed upon the earth: And Whereas, in process of time, the heirs of the said Adam and Eve having become very numerous, and finding it to be inconvenient to remain in common as aforesaid, bethought themselves to make partition of the lands and tenements aforesaid to and amongst themselves, and they did accordingly make such partition: And Whereas, by virtue of the said partition made by the heirs of said Adam and Eve, all that certain tract of land called and known on the general plan of the said Earth by the name of America, parcel of the said large tract, was allotted and set over unto certain of the heirs aforesaid to them and to their heirs general in fee-simple, who entered into the same and became thereof seised as aforesaid in their demesne as of fee, and peopled the same allotted lands in severalty, and made partition thereof to and amongst their descendants: And Whereas, afterwards, (now deemed in time immemorial,) a certain united people called "The Six Nation of North America," heirs and descendants of the said grantees of America, became seised, and for a long time whereof the memory of man runneth not to the contrary, have been seised in their demesne as of fee, of and in a certain tract of country and land in the north division of America, called and known at present on the general plan of the said north division by the name of Pennsylvania: And Whereas, the said united nations, being so thereof seised, afterwards, to wit, in the year of our Lord one thousand seven hundred and sixty-eight, by their certain deed of Feoffment with livery of seisin did grant, bargain, sell, release, enfeoff, alien, and confirm unto Thomas Penn and Richard Penn, otherwise called The Proprietaries of Pennsylvania, (among other things) the county called Buffaloe-Valley, situate on the South side of the west branch of the river Susquehanna, parcel of said country called Pennsylvania, to hold to them the said Proprietaries, their heirs and assigns forever, in their demesne as of fee, as by the same Feoffment more fully appears; which last mentioned tract of country was afterwards, with other tracts of country, by the said Proprietaries by the advice and consent of their great council in general assembly met, erected into a county called Northumberland aforesaid, of which the said Buffaloe valley was and is parcel by the name of Buffaloe township: And Whereas, the said Proprietaries, by their letters patent bearing date the eleventh day of August, in the year of our Lord one thousand seven hundred and seventy-two, did grant and confirm unto a certain Richard Peters in fee-simple a certain parcel of the said township, called Prescott, situate at the mouth of Spring Run, adjoining and below the mouth of Buffaloe creek, on the south side of the west branch of Susquehanna aforesaid, in the township and county aforesaid, by metes and bounds in the said letters set forth, containing three hundred and twenty acres and allowance, &c., as by the same letters patent inrolled at Philadelphia in patent book AA., vol. 13, page 265, more fully and at large appears: And Whereas, the said Richard Peters, by his certain indenture bearing date the seventeenth day of November, in the year of our Lord 1773, did grant, bargain and sell the last mentioned tract and parcel of land, containing 320 acres and allowance, with the appurtenances, unto a certain Ludwig Derr in fee-simple, as by the same deed recorded in the office for recording of deeds in and for the county of Philadelphia, in deed-book No. 22, page 444, appears at large on reference thereunto had: And Whereas, the said Ludwig Derr, being so seised thereof, did lay out a town called and known by the name of *Lewisburg*, consisting of three hundred and fifty lots or parcels of land, with suitable and proper streets, lanes and alleys, containing about one hundred and twenty eight acres, parcel of the said tract last hereinbefore mentioned, as by the general plan of the said town appears: And Whereas, the said Ludwig Derr afterwards died intestate, (having previously disposed of divers of the said lots to divers persons,) leaving a widow (who is since deceased,) and issue, his only child George, his heir at law: By Virtue and reason whereof the lands, tenements and hereditaments aforesaid, whereof the said Ludwick was seised at the time of his death, and which he had not aliened, descended to and became vested in the said George Derr in fee-simple, who entered into the same and became seised in his demesne as of fee: And Whereas, the said George Derr being so thereoff seised, by his certain indenture bearing date the twentieth day of December, in the year of our Lord 1788, did grant, bargain and sell all his estate and interest in the town aforesaid, with the appurtenances, unto a certain Peter Borger in fee-simple, as by the same deed recorded in the office for recording of deeds in Philadelphia, in deed-book No. 22, page 442, and at Sunbury in Northumberland county aforesaid, in deed-book D, page 397, appears: And whereas, the said Peter Borger, and Florinda his wife, by their certain indenture bearing date the second day of January, in the year of our Lord 1789, did grant, bargain, sell and confirm the town, lots, lands, tenements and premises whereof they were so seised, unto a certain Carl Ellinkhuysen of the city of Rotterdam, in the province of Holland, in the United Netherlands of Europe, merchant, in fee-simple, as by the same deed recorded in the office for recording of deeds in and for the county of Northumberland, in book E, page 231, &c., appears: And Whereas, the said Carl Ellinkhuysen, being seised of the premises aforesaid by virtue thereof, by his certain deed in writing called a letter of attorney, sealed and delivered, bearing date the eighth day of May, in the year of our Lord 1789, did constitute, appoint, and authorize the said Peter Borger (among other acts and things) to sell, dispose of, and convey and assure to such persons as should agree for the same, all such lots of land in the said town as the said Peter Borger should deem expedient, as by the said letter of attorney recorded at Philadelphia in letter of attorney-book No. 3, page 84, reference being thereto had appears: And Whereas, the said Carl Ellinkhuysen (by his said attorney, Peter Borger, constituted as aforesaid, unrevoked,) by certain indenture bearing date the twenty-fifth day of June, in the year of our Lord 1790, did grant, bargain, and sell unto Matthias Joseph Ellinkhuysen, late husband of the said Clara Helena Ellinkhuysen, and to the said Clara Helena, wife of the said Matthias Joseph, All that certain lot or piece of land, (among other things,) parcel of the said town, not disposed of by the said Ludwig Derr, situate in the said town of Louisburg, and known on the general plan of the said town by the number 51, to wit, fifty-one, containing in breadth on Front street and Walnut alley sixty-six feet, and in depth on St. Louis street and lot No. 52, one hundred and fifty-seven feet and six inches, bounded on the south by Front street aforesaid, on the north by the said Walnut alley, and on the east by lot No. 52 aforesaid, To Hold to them the said Matthias Joseph Ellinkhuysen and Clara Helena his wife, their heirs and assigns forever: By Virtue whereof, the said Matthias Joseph Ellinkhuysen and Clara Helena his wife, became seised in their demesne as of fee of the lot of ground aforesaid, with the appurtenances in Joint Tenantcy, to wit, to them and to the survivor of them, his or her heirs and assigns for ever, as by the said deed recorded in the office for recording of deeds in and for Northumberland county, in book E, page 84, reference being thereunto had more fully and at large appears: And Whereas, afterwards, the said Matthias Joseph Ellinkhuysen died seised as aforesaid of the premises aforesaid, leaving the said Clara Helena his wife, By reason whereof, the said Clara Helena Ellinkhuysen became sole seised of the same premises in her own right and demesne as of fee: NOW, This Indenture Witnesseth, that the said Clara Helena Ellinkhuysen, for and in consideration of the sum of sixteen pounds and ten shillings, lawful money of Pennsylvania, to her in hand well and truly paid by the said Flavel Roan at the execution hereof, the receipt whereof is hereby acknowledged, Hath granted, bargained, sold, aliened, enfeoffed, released and confirmed, and by these presents, Doth grant, bargain, sell, alien, enfeoff, release and confirm unto the said Flavel Roan, his heirs and assigns, All that the aforesaid described lot of ground, Together with the appurtenances, rights, easements, liberties, privileges, and hereditaments whatsoever thereunto belonging, or in any wise appertaining, and the reversion and reversions, remainder and remainders, rents, issues and profits thereof, To Have and To Hold the aforesaid described lot or piece of ground numbered as aforesaid 51, hereby granted, or meant, mentioned or intended so to be, with the appurtenances, unto the said Flavel Roan, his heirs and assigns, to the only proper use, benefit and behoof of him the said Flavel Roan, his heirs and assigns forever. In Witness whereof, the said parties to these presents have hereunto set their hands and seals, interchangeably the day and year first above written.

CLARA HELENA ELLINKHUYSEN.
G. B. VAN CAPEL, [L. S.]

Sealed and delivered in the presence of
JNO. HAYES,
JNO. THORNBURGH.

[Purchase money received as above—acknowledged before Wm. Gray, J. P.—and recorded by J. Simpson, at Sunbury, Deed-book F, page 280, 3d Nov. 1793.]

The author of this curious "Indenture" was Flavel Roan, a witty and rather eccentric gentleman, the son of a clergyman in Lancaster. His education was good, and his penmanship superior. It is said that he kept a trading house near the mouth of Buffalo Creek, at a very early day. He was one of the first sheriffs of Northumberland County, and subsequently one of the original commissioners of Union County. He died among his kindred, the Clingans, and was buried at the Buffalo × Roads.

Many anecdotes are related concerning him, one of which I will give. He was travelling in Union County once in company with John Strubble, when the conversation turned upon making rhymes, and it was proposed that each should make a couplet, and submit it to the landlord, where they intended to stop that night, for his decision, and the one having the least merit, should pay the bill for both. Rising early the next morning, they proceeded to a large spring to perform the necessary ablutions, when Strubble commenced his rhyme thus:

"Our forefathers who were so wise,
First drank their bitters, *then* washed their eyes."

Whereupon Flavel Roan struck in as if by inspiration—

"But we, the younger race, *wiser* still,
First wash our eyes, then drink our fill!"

The landlord decided that Strubble lost the bet—the bill was paid, and they both departed.

CHAPTER XLIX.

INTERESTING HISTORY OF THE PRESBYTERIAN CHURCH AT BUFFALO × ROADS—NAMES OF PASTORS, ELDERS, &C.—THE RAINING ROCK—THE INDIAN GARDEN—SALT WORKS—AN OLD GRAVE YARD—CONCLUSION OF THE ANNALS OF UNION COUNTY, WITH A REMARKABLE CASE OF WITCHCRAFT IN 1825.

THE Presbyterian Church at Buffalo × Roads, is probably the oldest in the West Branch Valley, the history of which dates back before the Revolution. For the facts in the following interesting sketch of its history, I am indebted to an article published a few years ago, in the Family Presbyterian, by Rev. Isaac Grier.

On examining the records of Carlisle Presbytery, I find that it was organized by the Synod of N. Y. and Philadelphia, in 1786. It appears, on reference to the Minutes of that Synod for May 1765, that owing to difficulties in the Presbytery of Donegal, they determined to create the members living on the West Branch into a new Presbytery, to be called the Presbytery of Carlisle. We find there the following record: "The Synod having maturely considered the situation of affairs in the Presbytery of Donegal, agreed to erect the members of that Presbytery, that live on the western side of the Susquehanna, into a new Presbytery, together with the Rev. Andrew Bay, by the name of the

Presbytery of Carlisle, and appoint that their first meeting be at Philadelphia, the 23d of May, 1765; and the remaining members are hereby annexed to the Presbytery of New Castle." This caused considerable dissatisfaction among some of the members of the old Donegal Presbytery, and the next spring, 1766, a petition was presented to the Synod, requesting them to review their decision; and after various plans were proposed and debated, the Presbytery of Donegal was restored to its former state. So it appears that this Presbytery existed at that time for only one year, and was not again organized till the spring of 1786, when the Presbytery of Donegal was divided into two Presbyteries, one to be known by the name of the Presbytery of Baltimore, and the other the Presbytery of Carlisle. From this it appears that the congregation of Buffalo, if organized in 1773, must have been organized by Donegal Presbytery.

From the records of the various Synods, I find that as early as 1774, supplies were sent more than fifty miles higher up the West Branch. At the meeting of the Synod in May, 1774, "a petition was brought in and read from the Bald Eagle settlement, up the West Branch, earnestly praying for supplies to be sent to these parts. Mr. Latta is appointed to supply up the West Branch five Sabbaths in the months of October and November, and Mr. Samuel Dougal, a probationer under the care of New Castle Presbytery, seven Sabbaths in July and August." The earliest appointment of supplies for this part of Pennsylvania by the Synod, that I have been able to find, was in the spring of 1770, at a meeting in New York city, where it is stated, "Messrs. Elder, State, and Steel, are appointed to supply between Augusta Fort, and Juniata, and places adjacent, each two Sabbaths before next Synod." Any earlier supplies must have been under the appointments for the frontier settlements and Indians.

According to Mr. Hood's statement, Buffalo was organized in 1773, and James McClenahan and Samuel Allen were its first ruling elders; the former had been ordained in Derry, Dauphin county, and the latter in Silver Spring, then under the pastoral care of Mr. Waugh. These gentlemen continued to officiate as elders, and the congregation to receive supplies, until 1781, when it was broken up on account of the country being overrun by Indians.

In 1783, the people returned, and in the same year Mr. McClenahan died; and as Mr. Allen had died while the people were away, the congregation was without elders till 1785, when Matthew Laird, who had been a ruling elder in Big Spring, came to reside in the congregation.

In 1787, they were visited by Mr. Hugh Morrison, a probationer from Ireland, to whom they gave a call, and he appears to have been their first pastor. The names of the prominent pew holders at that time, were as follows: Robert Clark, Samuel Maclay, Christopher Johnson, James Forster, Andrew Forster, William Irwin, John Reynor, W. Marshall, Jonathan Holmes, Alexander Kennedy, Geo. Knox, John Linn, James Magee, Col. John Kelly, William McClenahan, James Fleming, Walter Clark, David Watson, Richard Shearer, Capt. W. Gray, W. Wilson, Matthew Laird, Robert Fruit, John and James Thompson, Joseph and James Roach, Christopher Baldy, Thomas Hutchinson, Flavel Roan, Andrew McClenahan, Paschal Lewis, Joseph Grier, William Linn, &c. The names of the following persons were pew holders at an earlier date: James McClelland, Col. W. Chamberlin, Robert Forster, Alexander Steele, Matthew Irwin, Robert Chambers, James Black, Hamilton Shaw, Roan McClure, Samuel Dale, Gideon Smith, Thos. Howard, Thos. Elder, Patrick Mecklin, Hugh Wilson, and Hugh Wilson, Jr., Nathaniel Strahan, Gabriel Morrison, &c.

In the records of the church for May 22d, 1788, is the following: "Carlisle Presbytery reported that they have ordained to the work of the gospel ministry, Mr. Samuel Wilson, in the pastoral charge of Big Spring congregation, and Mr. H. Morrison in the charge of Sunbury, Northumberland, and Buffalo Valley." As this report was made in May, 1788, it is probable that he was installed in the year '87, when he first visited them. Shortly after he came, there was an election for elders, and Walter Clark, John Linn, William Irwin, David Watson, John Reynor, and Joseph Allen, were chosen, and ordained ruling elders. Messrs. Clark and Allen, some years after, removed to the West, the others continued to act as elders till their death. About the year 1795, Mr. Clingan was added to the session. The Presbytery of Huntingdon was organized this year, and the congregations in this section of the State fell within its bounds.

Mr. Morrison continued pastor until 1801, when the relationship existing between him and the members was dissolved, on account of a difficulty that had existed for more than a year. Had temperance societies existed in those days, there would not have been so much drinking, probably, at weddings; and clergymen would not have been charged with taking too much!

In 1802 or 3, the congregations of Buffalo, and Washington, in White Deer Valley, were visited by Mr. James Magraw, a licentiate of the Presbytery of New Castle, to whom they gave a call, but he did not accept.

Mr. Morrison died in Sunbury, on the 15th of September, 1804, and was buried in the lower graveyard.

In the winter of the same year, Mr. Thomas Hood, a licentiate of the New Castle Presbytery, visited the two congregations, to whom they gave a call that summer, which he accepted at the fall meeting of the Presbytery, and was at that time dismissed to put himself under the care of the Huntingdon Presbytery, at Spring Creek, April 16, 1805, and was ordained and installed Oct. 2d, of the same year. Soon after Mr. Hood's settlement in Buffalo, Thomas Howard, Andrew McClenahan, James McClelland, and Samuel Templeton were elected and ordained ruling elders.

At the next election, some years after, Thomas Clingan, James Geddes, and Robert Forster, were chosen and ordained.

In 1816, the congregation erected a stone Chapel, the original house of worship being a small log building.

In 1832, Samuel Barber, William Forster, and Robert G. H. Hayes, were elected and ordained ruling elders.

In the spring of 1808, Mr. Hood commenced to preach one fourth of his time in Mifflinburg, leaving but one fourth to Washington. In 1812, he received a call from the church at Milton for one fourth of his time, the portion which he had given the four years previous to Mifflinburg, and he was installed in Milton, Oct. 1812. The people of Milton had made application to the Presbytery of Huntingdon, in the spring of 1811, to be organized into a Church, which was not granted at that time, and before the next meeting, the Presbytery of

Northumberland was organized, and the application was renewed at their first meeting in Oct. 1811.

As it may be satisfactory to the reader to see the Minute of the Synod, organizing the Northumberland Presbytery, I shall copy it. It reads as follows:

"By a resolution of the Synod of Philadelphia at their Sessions, May 16, 1811, the request of the Presbytery of Huntingdon, to be divided by the following line, was granted, viz.:—Beginning at the mouth of Mahantango Creek, proceeding a Northwesterly course so as to strike the West Branch at the line which divides Lycoming and Centre counties, so as to leave to the eastward the following members: The Rev. Messrs. Asa Dunham, John Bryson, Isaac Grier, John B. Patterson, and Thomas Hood, with their respective charges, together with the vacant congregations of Great Island, Pine Creek, and Lycoming. And it was further resolved, that the above named ministers and congregations be named the Presbytery of Northumberland, and meet at the Presbyterian Church in the town of Northumberland, on the first Tuesday of October next, ensuing the date of this resolution, at 11 o'clock, A. M."

Presbytery met in accordance with the above resolution, and was opened by the Rev. Asa Dunham with a sermon from Eph. 2: 14. The members that constituted that Presbytery, were the Rev. Messrs. Dunham, Bryson, Grier, Patterson, and Hood; with the elders, James Sheddan, James Hepburn, William Montgomery, and Thomas Howard. As the Presbytery of Huntingdon had not granted the request of the people of Milton, and a part of White Deer township, to be organized into a Church in Milton, at the first meeting of the Northumberland Presbytery, the application was renewed by Messrs. Bethuel Vincent and James P. Sanderson.—Presbytery agreed to meet in Milton on the first Tuesday in December, to take the matter into consideration, and hear the parties both pro and con. At that meeting,

Messrs. Vincent and Sanderson appeared again in behalf of the people desiring an organization, and Messrs. James Moodie and Joseph Kerr appeared in behalf of those opposed to it, and laid before Presbytery a remonstrance. The Presbytery granted the request, and a Church was organized in Milton. The next spring a call was made for one fourth of Mr. Hood's time, and he was installed. In 1819, he retired from the charge of the Washington congregation, and devoted the whole of his time between the congregations at Buffalo and Milton.

At the installment of Mr. Hood, there were sixty members in Buffalo Church; the largest number added at any one time, was thirty-five, in the fall of 1824. In the year 1828, there were two hundred and seventy-three members. At the time Mr. Hood left, the members were reduced to fifty-eight, owing to the organization of four or five other Churches, chiefly formed of members from Buffalo Church.

Mr. Hood retired from the pastoral charge of Buffalo Church in April, 1835, and died in Lewisburg, March 17th, 1848, at a good old age.

Rev. Isaac Grier supplied the pulpit from 1835 to the spring of 1853, when he left, and the Rev. Philip W. Malick supplied it one year, when he returned in the spring of 1854, was installed, and is officiating at the present time.

In 1846, the stone building was taken down and the present beautiful brick edifice erected in its stead. So ends the history of the Church at Buffalo × Road.

Dr. Robert Vanvalzah, of Buffalo × Roads, and Dr. Charles Beyer, of Lewisburg, were the first prominent physicians in Buffalo Valley. They both died at an advanced age: the former April 18, 1850, and the latter September 30, 1830.

The "Driesbach" German Reformed and Lutheran Churches, four miles west of Lewisburg, were organized about the close of the last century. A log building was first erected: in 1844, its place was supplied with a neat brick building. Rev. J. H. Fries, and Rev. Geo. Heim, preached there for many years. The Lewisburg German Reformed Church was a colony from it.

The oldest mill on Buffalo Creek is six miles from Lewisburg. It was built by a man named Bear at an early day, and is owned at the present time by the heirs of John A. Vandyke. It is supposed to be as old as Derr's mill.

A large Furnace was erected at the mouth of Turtle Creek in 1854–5, by Messrs. Beaver, Geddes, Marsh, & Co., and is doing a profitable business.

There is a place called the "Indian Garden," about an acre of cleared land, surrounded by thick woods, on Thomas Howard's farm, three miles above Lewisburg, on Buffalo Creek. Indian relics, such as darts, &c., have been found in great abundance. A few years ago, what was supposed to be the thigh bones of a Mastadon, were found on the same farm, in digging a ditch through a meadow.

On David Linn's farm there used to be what was called the "Raining Rock." A rock projected about six feet over the Creek, and about the same distance above the water, and about ten feet long, from the whole face of which—except in very dry weather—there flowed continued streams and drops of water. It was destroyed by the opening of a stone quarry a few years ago.

There is a remarkable "Sink Hole," three miles from town, on Dale's hill. It has been descended to a great depth without finding bottom, and a stone thrown in can be heard rumbling for a long time.

In quarrying limestone, near Winfield, in Dry Valley, a few years since, a large cave was discovered, filled with beautiful stalactites.

There is a graveyard on the banks of Turtle Creek, near Jenkins' Mill, that all recollection of who was buried there is lost, with the exception of a boy killed by the running away of a plow-team, some sixty years ago.

In 1822–3, there was a joint stock company raised to erect Salt Works, eight miles north-west of Lewisburg. They bored a hole into the earth some 600 feet, from which has run a constant stream of water ever since. It produced no salt, but has a strong sulphurous taste. I have no doubt its medicinal qualities are as wholesome as some of the far-famed watering places.

The parents of John Foster, Esq., of Buffalo × Roads, lived at an early day on Buffalo Creek, nearly opposite Vanvalzah's Mill. He remembers many incidents of Indian history, one of which is as follows:—One night the family were alarmed by Indians, and fled to a rye patch adjoining the house, where they passed the night. A small dog, that was usually very vociferous at night, stayed with them and made *no* noise. The family always considered it a special act of Providence. Next morning plenty of Indian tracks were found around the house. It was a log building, and is standing at the present day.

I might give many more interesting reminiscences of Buffalo Valley, as it is a fruitful field, but the limits of this work forbid it. I will, however, give a remarkable case of witchcraft, by way of concluding the annals of Union county.

About the year 1825, a remarkable farce of witchcraft

was played in the family of a man named Kern, in Beaver township. He had a wife and two daughters, and followed the occupation of farming. In his immediate vicinity lived a man named Romig, who, from some unknown cause, became a hypochondriac, and the impression got abroad that he was bewitched. Soon after this the milk in Kern's spring-house became sour, within a few hours after it was placed there. This occurred daily until the farce was concluded, which was in two or three weeks. The next act played was of a more remarkable character. Kern's tables, and kitchen furniture, were to be seen flying in all directions, thrown, it was *supposed*, by supernatural means. Knives, forks, spoons, ladles, &c., never remained more than five minutes on the dresser after having been placed there, but were thrown in various directions about the house; and, as the more *believing* portion of the neighbors asserted, it was no uncommon thing to see them thrown through the solid wall of the house without leaving any mark of their passage in the wall! A peddler, who stopped for the purpose of trading some of his notions to Kern, asserted that he had not been in the house ten minutes, before his hat and dog were thrown through the wall of the kitchen, into the adjoining yard! It is not to be presumed that he was influenced in propagating this story by the hope of assembling a crowd around his wagon.

During these transactions, Kern had a numerous crowd daily at his house; and on Sundays there was a gathering at his door, such as the most eloquent divine would have failed to assemble. Of these, the major part came prepared to believe *all* they saw and *all* they might hear; of course there was no lack of *true* stories. The unbelieving portion of the visitors—a very *small* number, for men of *sense* generally staid at home—kept their eyes open, and readily discovered that the old woman and the daughters were the witches, and threw the knives, forks, &c. A witch doctor was called, who proceeded, with great solemnity, to expel the evil spirit. Divers magical and mysterious rites were performed, exorcisms were chanted, and texts of scripture nailed to every door and window in the house. The witches, however, set the doctor at naught, and baffled all his schemes.

At length a party of young men, residing in New Berlin, resolved to try their skill at taking evil spirits. One of them having procured a mask, a huge flaxen wig, a pair of furred gloves, and other necessary apparatus, set out with the rest, in the afternoon, and arrived at Kern's early in the evening. At their request, the witches performed, to their great satisfaction, until a late hour. At length, when all the visitors, except the young witch doctors, had left the house, it was resolved to commence operations. They desired to see how the witches acted above stairs, and were accordingly conducted up the ladder, accompanied by the whole family. In the meantime, one of the party who had a remarkably hoarse and deep-toned voice, and who was to act the part of the Devil, was notified by a preconcerted signal—for he had not entered the house—to prepare for action. He accordingly put on his wig and mask, which he rubbed with phosphorus, and wrapped himself in a buffalo skin. The party up stairs were well provided with squibs. One of them had a piece of phosphorus, with which he wrote on the wall such words as "Devil," "Hell," &c., in a number of places. The signal being given, the candle was extinguished, the squibs distributed most copiously, and the horrid words on the wall shone out in liquid fire! The barrels and furniture in the room were trundled about the floor, and an astounding uproar was kept up for some minutes. Presently a terrific roar was heard from below; all parties ran to the stair-door, and saw at the foot of the ladder *his grim majesty* in all the terrors of flames, flax, fur and horns. Satan made an appropriate speech on the occasion, and then retired. His address was followed by a most edifying exhortation by the wag of the party on the sin of deceiving, and the danger of another visit from old Nick, if the present practices should be persisted in. The terrified witches made a full confession, and so ended the enchantment.

As the people became enlightened and refined, the belief in witchcraft declined. Ignorance and superstition go hand in hand.

CHAPTER L.

FIRST SETTLERS IN MILTON—NAMES OF THE FIRST BOROUGH OFFICERS—SCHOOLS—RELIGIOUS DENOMINATIONS—NAMES OF THE PASTORS—LITERARY ASSOCIATIONS—WHEN ORGANIZED—BENEVOLENT ASSOCIATIONS—CHRONOLOGICAL TABLE OF EVENTS—IMPROVEMENTS—POPULATION, &C.

For the information in this chapter, I am indebted to J. F. Wolfinger. Esq., who has kindly furnished it.

In 1772, the place where the town of Milton now stands was covered with a dense forest, and no sound was heard save that of the wild beast or bird, or that of the Indian as he roamed over the grounds in quest of prey, or paddled his light canoe over the rippling waters of the Otzinachson.

In 1775, Marcus Huling built a log cabin near the western curve of Limestone Run, and occupied it as a tavern stand. His son, Marcus Huling, Jr., also erected a similar cabin on the river bank, near Broadway, and occupied it as a blacksmith shop. These were the first buildings erected by the white man. When the British and Indians, under McDonald, captured Fort Freeland in 1779, they burned these buildings, and the Hulings took their canoes and fled to Duncan's Island.

In 1780, another and larger log house was erected on the site of Milton, and occupied as a fort, by a little band of soldiers stationed there to guard the slowly returning settlers. In 1790, Andrew Straub, millwright, from Lancaster county, and one Christian Yentzer, purchased at a Sheriff's sale, among other lands adjoining, all the ground forming that portion of Milton south of Broadway. It was sold as the property of Turbutt Francis, deceased, one of the early Associate Judges of Northumberland county Courts. In 1791, Yentzer conveyed all of his interest to Straub, who, in 1792, laid out the town of Milton, and built a small log grist-mill on Limestone Run, then diverted from its original course to the river, for the accommodation of the future town and people.

August 11th, 1795, all that portion of the town north of Broadway was laid out by its proprietor, James Black, of Sunbury. The town for some years continued to increase rapidly, and enterprising settlers from New Jersey, and the Counties of Chester, Delaware, York, Lancaster and Berks, in our own State, flocked in.— Bethuel Vincent was also one of the early settlers.

On the 26th of February, 1817, Milton was incorporated into a borough by the Legislature. The first borough officers elected in pursuance of this act, were as follows:

Chief Burgess, - - -	Arthur McGowan.
Assistant Burgess, - -	Robert McGuigan.
Supervisors of Roads, -	Jno. Jones, David Derrickson.
High Constable, - - -	James Sharp.
Constable, - - - -	Joseph Hartman.

Town Council—Joseph Rhoads, Daniel R. Bright, Samuel Hepburn, Daniel Scudder, Christopher Woods, George Eckbert and Thomas Comly.

The first settlement of the borough accounts was made on the 29th of April, 1818, from which it appears that the taxes levied and collected for the year 1817,

amounted to - - - - -	$739 04½
Expenses for same year - - -	691 56½
Leaving a balance in the Treasury of -	$ 47 48.

The taxes of 1817 were oppressively high, to raise funds in order to repair the heavy damage done by the great Limestone Run flood, which occurred on the 9th of August, 1817, and destroyed the Front street bridge, and washed out the great ravine now crossed by it.—The mill and several houses were swept off. The bursting of a water spout is supposed to have occasioned such an immense flow of water. The Legislature granted the borough $5000, and the County a larger sum, to aid in replacing the bridge.

The first educational institutions in Milton were an old log school house, erected on Lower Market street in 1796, and a frame building on Broadway in 1802.—Here most of the children of the first settlers obtained what little education they got. The first German settlers had a school for the instruction of their children in their own language, but it gradually dwindled away for the want of support.

About the year 1816, Joseph D. Biles began to instruct the sons of a few of the wealthier families, in the Latin and Greek languages, in the old Broadway school house, which thenceforward received the more dignified title of "The Milton Academy." The venerable log school house of Lower Milton was, in 1838, removed to Eckbert's mill and converted into a blacksmith shop; while its younger rival, the old frame Academy, was also removed from its site in 1849, by the colored people and converted into "The African Church." In place of these buildings, fine brick school houses were erected.

The higher and more successful Milton Academy was erected in 1823, on a rising ground, and still stands, where the Rev. David Kirkpatrick taught the classics with brilliant success to many, if not most, of the professional characters throughout the West Branch Valley. But the glory of this good old institution has departed never more to return, until another Kirkpatrick is found to take the youth by the hand and lead them gently up the rugged hill of science.

The Lancasterian school house was erected in 1830, and so called because it was designed to introduce the Lancasterian system of conducting schools, which was soon abandoned for want of support. The Prospect Hill school house was erected on a high and beautiful piece of ground near the northern limits of the town. The present schools are respectable, but fall far short of what they ought to be for such an enterprising town.

The Churches consist first of the English Protestant Episcopal church, called Christ Church. They had a log meeting house erected in 1795, in Morris Lane, but long since torn down and supplied by a new brick church of the same name, erected in upper Market street in 1849. The Methodist Episcopal Church, likewise a log building, was erected somewhere between the years 1802–15, and torn down about 1834, and a new brick edifice substituted.

The German Reformed, German Lutheran and English Presbyterian church, a union, styled "The Harmony Church," was commenced in 1817, and finished in 1819. It was considered a building of much splendor for that time. It is still standing on the eastern end of Mahoning street, where the three respective congregations worshipped till 1832, when the English Presbyterians withdrew, and in 1837–8, built themselves a new brick church on Front street, which was recently torn down and a magnificent edifice erected in its stead, during the summer of 1856.

After this, the German Reformed and Lutherans worshipped in the Harmony Church, on alternate Sabbaths, till 1850, when the Lutherans also withdrew and built themselves a new brick church.

In addition to these Churches, there is the Associate Reformed Presbyterian Church, erected in Church Lane in 1820, and afterwards called the Seceder, and then the Covenanter Church—but recently sold to the Sunbury and Erie Railroad Company, and supplied in 1854, by a new brick building in Walnut street, now styled The First Reformed Presbyterian Church.

The Baptist Church, a brick edifice,. was erected in 1829, in Church Lane, and is still standing. The Roman Catholic Church, likewise a brick building, was erected in 1844.

The Rev. Caleb Hopkins was the first and, indeed, only settled pastor of the old Episcopal Church, for his successors, the Revds. Elijah D. Plumb, —— Wiltberger, —— Smith, —— Carter, B. Eldridge, Wistar Morris, William Montgomery and John G. Furey, were only supplies for a short time. They have no pastor now.

The first regular pastor of the German Reformed Church, was the Rev. Justus Henry Fries, and his successors were, the Revds. Martin Bruner, Samuel Gutelius, Henry Wagoner, Daniel Gring, Henry Harbaugh, Ephraim Kieffer, Edwin M. Long and Albert G. Dole, the present pastor.

The first regular pastor of the German Lutheran Church, was the Rev. Philip Repass. His successors were the Revds. Frederick Waage, —— Garman, Chas. P. Miller, John George Anspach, Charles F. Stoever, Eli Swartz, Frederick Ruthrauff, John J. Reimensnyder, and Christopher C. Cullen, the present pastor.

The first regular pastor of the Presbyterian Church was the Rev. Thomas Hood. His successors were the Revds. James Williamson, David Longmore, D. D., and James C. Watson, D. D., the present pastor. All the other occasional preachers were supplies.

The first regular pastor of the Associate Reformed or Seceder Church, was the Rev. Geo. Junkin, D. D., his successors were the Revds. William Wilson, John McKinley, John Agnew Crawford, Matthew Smith, and William Theodore Wiley, the present pastor. All the others were supplies.

The first regular pastor of the Baptist Church was the Rev. Eugenio Kincaid, his successors were the Revds. Geo. Higgins, Thomas Brown, David C. Waite, Collins A. Hewit, J. E. Bradley, and Howard Malcom, D. D. the present pastor.

The names of the pastors of the M. E. Church cannot be given for the want of correct data. This is much regretted.

The first regular priest of the Catholic Church was John C. Flannigan, his successors were John Hannigan, —— O'Keefe, —— Kinney, Daniel Sheridan, Basil Shorb, and George Gostenschnigg, the present one in charge.

Among the early literary associations, may be named the Franklin Reciting and Debating Society, established about the year 1816, in which such spirits as Joseph B. Anthony, James Armstrong, William Cox Ellis, Elijah Babbitt, Daniel Scudder, William H. Wilson, and their youthful associates, measured their intellectual strength, and gave free scope to their wit, fancy and eloquence.—The Philomathean Society, was formed in 1821. The next was the Milton Book Society, formed in 1822, which gave rise, the same year, to the Milton Circulating Library. This was followed in 1828, by the Milton Library Association, the members of which contributed one dollar each annually to keep up a regular and fresh supply of the best library books for the benefit of themselves and families. The next was the Franklin Junto, a debating society, organized in 1832; and the Milton Lyceum, for lecturing purposes, formed in 1837. The Milton Literary Association, organized in 1840, was designed to purchase and encourage the reading of the standard literary periodicals of the day, by its members and their families. At a more recent date, the Franklin Institute of Milton was formed for the purpose of encouraging lawyers, physicians and literary men generally, to meet together to listen to lectures, participate in debates, &c.

The earliest known Benevolent Association was the Milton Bible Society, organized in 1815. The Auxiliary Missionary Society of Milton, was formed in 1824, and the Milton Tract Society in 1828. These Societies were designed to distribute the Bible and Tracts, and also aid in sending Missionaries from our land to preach the Gospel to the heathen. The Milton Temperance Society was organized in 1830—the Milton Reformed Temperance Society in 1835.

The Milton Sabbath Association was formed in 1844, in order to promote the better observance of the Sabbath; and the Milton Female Bible Society in 1845, still in active operation, for the distribution of the word of God.

The following larger, or more general, Societies have been located at this central point, to wit: The Susquehanna Bible Society, organized in 1815—the Northumberland Missionary Society in 1818—the Milton Sunday-school Union in 1827, and the Susquehanna Tract Society in 1828. These Societies were designed to aid in exploring and supplying the Bible throughout the Valley, and the adjoining counties of Union, Lycoming and Columbia, and to supply the destitute with preachers.

The various Sunday-schools of this wide region, including those of Milton, met in one harmonious Union for several years. Reports were received from each school, giving its name, number of scholars and teachers, supply of books, present condition and future prospects, &c., and then forwarded, in the shape of a general report, to the American Sunday-school Union, at Philadelphia.

The honor of originating, and giving life and energy to these noble institutions, belongs exclusively to the Presbyterians of this region, acting through their ecclesiastical court, styled The Presbytery of Northumberland, which then enrolled among its members such venerated names as those of the Rev. John Bryson, Rev. John B. Patterson, Rev. Thomas Hood, Rev. George Junkin, D. D., and Rev. Dr. Kirkpatrick. But of all these, the Rev. Dr. Junkin was evidently the master spirit, who set the wheels of Christian improvement and social reform in motion; and although he was at times severe, and perhaps extra strict, yet the citizens have reasons to rejoice at the results of his persevering labors.

The first Sunday-school was established by a little band of Presbyterian ladies, about the year 1815; and the first Infant Sunday-school established here in 1826, was a Presbyterian one. The Northern Temperance

Conventions, commencing with that held at Danville in 1841, and afterwards held at Milton, Lewisburg, New Berlin, Northumberland, Muncy, Williamsport and Lock Haven, were also of Presbyterian origin, originating out of a resolution offered by Mr. Wolfinger, before the Milton Temperance Society, in 1840.

The following chronological table will serve to show the dates of some of the leading events in Milton:

1815—George Eckbert's water power grist mill erected.
1816—The Northumberland, Union and Columbia Bank, commonly called the Old Milton Bank, established.
1816—Miltonian newspaper commenced by Gen. Frick.
1818—New bridge built on Front street by James Moore.
1820—Population of Milton 1015.
1822—Lightning strikes the Harmony Church, doing much damage.
1825—Great hailstorm.
1830—First Furnace or Foundry erected by Joseph Rhoads.
1830—West Branch Canal completed to Milton.
1830—John Deeter runs the first canal boat, named the West Branch, to Northumberland.
1830—Population 1352.
1832—Bridge across the river completed.
1835—Steam Grist Mill erected by F. W. Pollock.
1840—Population 1508.
1841—First Steam Saw Mill erected by Evans & McCleery.
1841—Bounds of Milton diminished.
1845—Second Foundry erected by White & Mervine.

The town of Milton is twelve miles from the junction of the two rivers, and has always transacted a large amount of business, especially in grain. The farmers of this region, at an early day, had to transport their grain during the winter on sleds to Reading. After the place had sufficiently increased in population to have boat-builders and boatmen, they commenced running it to Baltimore in boats on the river. After the completion of the canal, they preferred to send it to Philadelphia, which was a better market.

Since the completion of the Catawissa, and Sunbury and Erie Railroad to this point, the price of real estate has greatly advanced, and lands that could have previously been bought for $50 and $75 per acre, now readily bring $100 and upwards.

The country around Milton is very extensive as well as fertile—the principal commodity raised is wheat. The surrounding country is rolling, and contains beautiful and diversified scenery.

The town is rapidly improving, and numerous fine brick buildings are erected annually. It is well supplied with first class stores, and excellent hotels.

His Excellency, the Hon. James Pollock, Governor of the State, resides in Milton.

The population in 1850, was 1649, and at the present time it is considerably over 2000.

CHAPTER LI.

MODERN HISTORY OF MUNCY—EARLY TIMES OF WILLIAMSPORT—TRADE AND IMPROVEMENTS—IMMENSE LUMBER DEPOT—RAILROADS—LYCOMING CREEK—VILLAGES—LARRY'S CREEK—JERSEY SHORE—ITS HISTORY—NIPPENOSE VALLEY—TRUE ORIGIN OF THE NAME.

McEWENSVILLE, named after Alexander McEwen, is a flourishing village, on the main road to Muncy, three miles north of Milton, in a rich and well cultivated country. It does not improve much, being an old place, and contains about fifty dwellings, and several fine churches. It also contains several stores, and a good hotel. A very excellent and popular institution of learning is located here. The principal, at the present time, is C. Low Ryneirson.

New Columbia is a pleasant little village, one mile above Milton, on the Union county side of the river. It is said that an Indian town once stood here.

Watsontown, named after a Mr. Watson, is on the river, a short distance above the mouth of Warrior Run. It contains upwards of 40 dwellings, several stores, &c.

Uniontown is a smart village, on the west side of the river, in Lycoming county, on the road to Williamsport over the mountain. A fine bridge of recent construction, connects it with the other side of the river.

The town of Muncy is located in the rich and fertile

valley bearing the same name, about one mile from the river. It was first commenced in Penn's Manor, by Benjamin McCarty, in 1797, and called Pennsboro', which name it bore till its incorporation in 1826, when the title was changed. In 1832, the population was 479, in 1850, 910, and at the present time about 1500. It contains five licensed hotels, and fifteen stores.

The first building, for public worship, was put up in 1825, and dedicated by the name of the Union School House, denoting that it was for the use of all denominations, as well as for school purposes. In 1829, the first Methodist Episcopal Church was erected. It was a single story frame building, and was displaced in 1854 for the present elegant brick edifice. The Episcopal Church was erected in 1831, to which, in 1855, was added a neat and commodious parsonage; and preparations are now being made to substitute a new church for the old one.

In 1834, the Presbyterian, in 1841, the Baptist, and in 1851, the Lutheran, Churches were erected.

The Lycoming Mutual Insurance Company went into operation in 1840, and by their twelfth annual report it appears that they have property insured to the amount of $24,818,758 56, with a capital of $2,134,872 00.

The Muncy canal is a side cut from the West Branch Canal to the borough, about one mile in length, built by an incorporated company in 1848, at a cost of about $3000.

Penn's Plank Road connects Muncy with Hughesville, five miles distant. It was built in 1853.

The Muncy bridge, crossing the river, was erected in 1854, at a cost of $27,000.

Hughesville is an incorporated borough, located at the

point where Big Muncy Creek enters into the hill country, and contains several hotels and stores, and a Methodist and Lutheran Church. Considerable business is done in the lumber trade. John Lukins Wallis, claimed to be the first white male child born north of Muncy Hills, resides here. He is an old man.

Pennsville is situated about three miles north of Muncy, and has a store and one hotel. It is noted for being the centre of the Friends' settlement here, and their church stands at the west end of the village.

Muncy Creek, about three miles from its junction with the river, separates into two branches, called Big and Little Muncy. Both branches extend into some of the best timber lands of the State, where numerous saw mills have been erected; and it is estimated by those capable of judging, that from twelve to fifteen millions of feet of lumber are manufactured annually.

The hills on the north of Muncy are often regarded as the base of the Alleghany mountains, but really are of a different formation, and separated by a valley called Mill Creek, which is from one to two miles wide; on the north of which the Alleghanies rise up in majestic grandeur far above all other hills.

The geological formation of Muncy Valley, by Rogers' system, consists of stratas V. VI. VII. VIII. and IX., proceeding from the mouth of Muncy Creek northward, to the base of the Alleghany mountains; and east or south it is limited by passing the out crop of the same stratas to No. VIII., which is the formation of the Muncy Hills—and west, notwithstanding its elevation, the Bald Eagle mountain is found to be only No. III. This singular elevation of No. III., which comprises the Bald Eagle throughout its range to Hollidaysburg, commences opposite the mouth of Muncy Creek, and the consequence is, that each strata laps in a semi-circle round its east base, thereby making the rocks on the north-east and south dip in opposite directions. No. V. is principally covered by the bottoms and river, which probably conceals the corresponding locality of the valuable iron ore of Montour's ridge, which has only been discovered in small quantities. No. VII. composes the best farm land of the valley, and is as valuable as the limestone deposit. Lead, in small quantities, has been taken out at the Lime Bluffs, about three miles from Muncy. It was found in the white seams between the rocks. This fact gives strength and probability to a tradition from the Indians, that they knew a valuable mine of lead on Glade Run, within a short distance of the town. It was said that they visited Muncy to get supplies of the ore, but refused all knowledge of its location to the whites. The confidence reposed in its existence was so strong by the early settlers, that considerable time and expense was incurred in efforts to find it. If at any future time a discovery shall be made, it will no doubt be where formation No. VI. crosses said run, which is now known to be in the locality of this tradition.

A discovery has lately been made of what is believed to be valuable deposits of iron ore in Muncy township, about eight miles north of the town, in formation IX.; and in the same, on Big Muncy Creek. In Shrewsbury township, two or more locations of copper ore have been known for several years, from which small quantities of the metal have been manufactured.

It has been suspected strongly that coal exists in formation VIII., and examinations were made about twenty years since, in the shales at the base of Muncy Hills, on the south side of the valley, but only traces were found, and as no coal was known to exist in that formation by geologists, search has been abandoned.

Montoursville, on the banks of Loyal Sock Creek, has grown to be a very pleasant, enterprising village. The buildings are mostly of brick, and constructed in a neat and tasty manner, and show off to a fine advantage. It contains a population of about 350, and is well supplied with hotels, stores, churches, &c. The origin of the name has already been given.

Williamsport,* the county seat of Lycoming, is eligibly situated on the left bank of the river, forty miles above its confluence with the North Branch. It was laid out and selected as the seat of Justice, at the organization of the County, in 1795, under the auspices of Michael Ross, who was then proprietor. At that time it contained but a few houses, and trees were growing where the best part of the town now stands. Ross, at that time, owned about 600 acres.

The first innkeeper was named James Russell. A mistake has originated by supposing that he was the first settler. John Moore was the second innkeeper.

The town is well built, the streets are all wide, crossing each other at right angles, and the side-walks well paved and adorned with beautiful shade trees. The buildings exhibit a wide diversity of taste, but most of them are well arranged, and many are models of architectural beauty. The Court House, and public square on which it is built, reflect great credit upon the taste and enterprise of the citizens. It is a brick edifice, and was commenced in 1801, and completed in 1803. The

* For many items in the history of Williamsport, I am indebted to J. W. Barret, Esq.

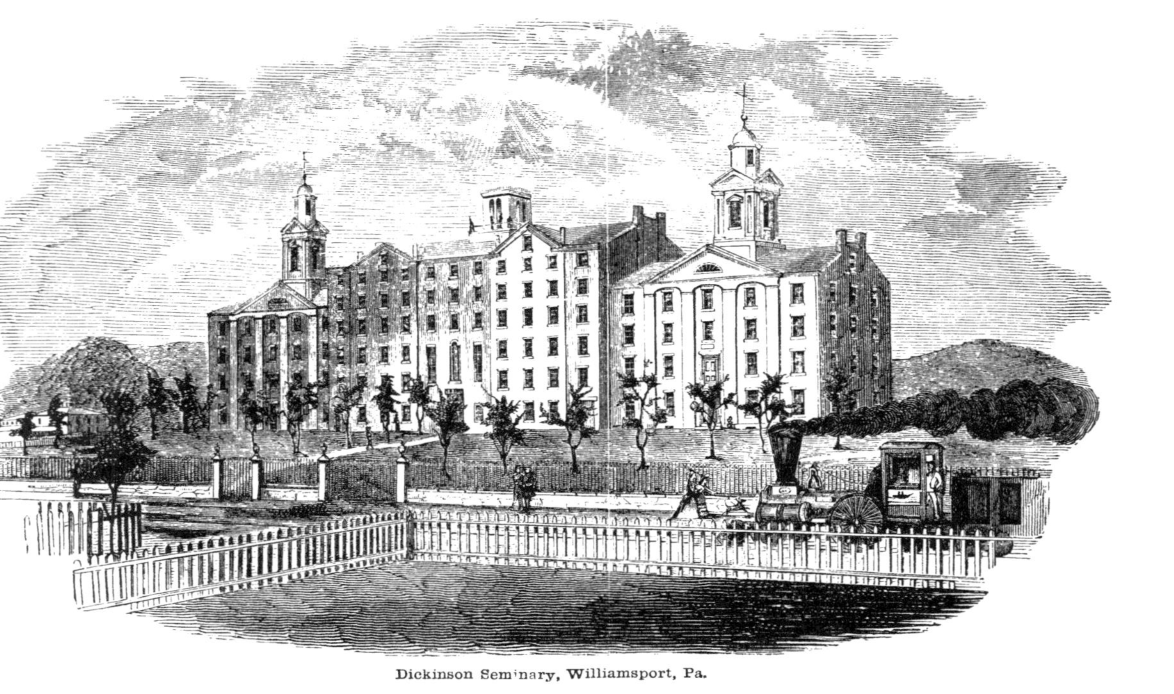

Dickinson Seminary, Williamsport, Pa.

area in front is covered with a substantial brick pavement, and adorned with handsome shade trees; while the Court yard is neatly laid out and surrounded with a beautiful iron railing, and the ground planted with trees and shrubbery in great variety.

The first Court was held in the house of John Winters, near the old Lycoming grave yard. Mr. Winters was one of the early sheriffs, and had a family of twenty-two children! The second Court was held in September, 1796—and for several years afterwards—in the old log building on the corner of the street opposite the residence of General Packer. It yet stands, in a good state of preservation. The first presiding Judge was William Hepburn, with Dr. James Davidson, Robert Fleming, and John Adlum, as Associates. Gov. McKean also presided in that venerable old building.

Williamsport has improved very rapidly during the last four or five years, and now contains four first class hotels, three taverns, eight eating saloons, six ice-cream saloons, and sixty-eight stores, including those of every style and variety, among which may be found some rivaling in size and splendor, as well as amount of trade, many of our city establishments.

There are located here three Foundries and Machine Shops, with appliances and facilities for manufacturing all kinds of machinery, steam engines, &c.; two steam Tanneries, a hot blast Anthracite Furnace,* with a capacity for making 140 tons of iron per week; two extensive steam Planing Mills, for the manufacturing of sash, blinds, doors, &c.; one Flouring Mill, with a capacity for making one hundred barrels of flour per day.

Besides these varied interests, Williamsport is the

* Since burned down and entirely destroyed.

centre of an extensive lumber trade, and the facilities for its manufacture in the vicinity are unrivaled. Within three miles of the borough are nine steam saw mills; and just above and within the borough limits, are two mammoth water-mills, one containing eighty-eight, and the other one hundred saws. The latter is capable of manufacturing 60,000 feet per day. Some idea of this heavy interest may be formed from the raw materials annually lodged in the boom, some three miles above town. It is estimated that over 200,000 logs were lodged therein at the last spring freshet, and that to convey the same to the several mills, manufacture and deposit it upon the bank of the canal ready for transportation, will give employment to 1000 men during the whole year. At the usual estimate of population, this would give support to 5000 persons, and produce from forty to fifty millions of feet of lumber for the market.

Williamsport enjoys admirable business facilities from its location upon the line of the Canal, and at the intersection of several lines of railroad. It may be regarded as the terminus of the Williamsport and Elmira Railroad, and the Catawissa, Williamsport and Erie Railroad, whilst the Sunbury and Erie Railroad, now in process of construction, passes through it; Williamsport being the only intermediate point made in the charter. These facilities have had their influence in promoting the growth and prosperity of the borough. In 1840, the population was about 1300; in 1850, 1615; June 1st 1855, 4043, and the present population is not less than 5000.

In 1833, Jeremiah Church purchased a farm adjoining Williamsport, containing about one hundred acres, and laid it out in town lots, and called it "Church's addition to Williamsport."

From the continuous advancement of every interest, it is probable that the time is not far distant when it will burst its present barriers and expand to the full proportions of an inland city.

Williamsport contains one Old School, and one New School Presbyterian Church, one Methodist, one Episcopal, one German Reformed, one English Lutheran, one Catholic, one Evangelical, and one African Church; whilst the Baptists and Unitarians have each their adherents, and hold regular services.

Due attention is also given to education, Dickinson Seminary is located at this place, and enjoys a liberal patronage. The last catalogue gives 419 students for the past academic year, and the institution holds a high rank among the Seminaries of the State.

The public Schools of Williamsport rank deservedly high. A large brick building is in course of construction, designed to accommodate all the schools of the borough; and the School System bids fair to be properly appreciated and rendered highly efficient.

The West Branch Bank, with a capital of $200,000, is located here. A. Updegraff, Esq., is President.

Supreme Court, for the Western District, sits in Williamsport a portion of the time.

A fine bridge is thrown across the river at this point. The railroad bridge is also a substantial structure.

Preparations are now making to have the town lighted with gas, and the necessary buildings are in course of construction. Arrangements have also been entered into for supplying it with water, to be conducted across the river in a pipe, from a mountain spring.

Williamsport is distant from Washington 220 miles, Philadelphia 197, Harrisburg 90, Elmira 78, Niagara

Falls 244, New York 287; all of which points can be reached by railroad.

What it is destined to be in the future, it is difficult to predict; but if energy, intelligence and moral worth do not prove unavailing, we may safely anticipate for it a high and proud pre-eminence.

Newberry is a small village two miles west of Williamsport. It contains Methodist and Presbyterian Churches; three hotels, several stores, and two very extensive flouring mills. It was laid out about the same time with Williamsport, and was a competitor with it for the honor of the County Seat. Jaysburg, a small village nearer the river, was also intended for the County Seat, and quite a strife existed among the various rivals till the location was definitely fixed on.

The commencement, at this point, of the old road to Painted Post, commonly known as the Block House road, gave to Newberry considerable importance at an early day. The road was laid out by Mr. Williamson, an agent of Sir William Pulteney, about the year 1795.

Lycoming Creek empties into the river near this point. Four furnaces, two forges, and one nail factory, are located on the Creek, and large quantities of iron are manufactured. Iron ore of a very superior quality, exists in great quantities in this region; and a few years ago, when the United States Government talked of establishing a National Foundry for the manufacturing of cannon, it was strongly argued that this iron was better adapted to such purposes than any other, and it was contended that the Foundry should be established at this point.—The project failed, however, or Lycoming would probably have been selected.

Bituminous coal is taken out in considerable quantities,

and salt is said to exist here also. Large quantities of lumber are manufactured annually, but iron is the great staple.

The Valley of Lycoming Creek is quite an important region, surrounded by rugged mountains, however, but possessing some of the most charming and diversified scenery in the country. It is traversed by the Elmira railroad, making it easy of access from the north or south.

Linden, a small village at the mouth of *Quenishach-shachki* Creek, contains two stores, two hotels, one church, and a number of dwellings. It is six miles from Jersey Shore.

Larry's Creek, emptying into the river two miles below Jersey Shore, is quite an important stream. An enterprising village, called Salladasburg, is located four miles up the Creek. It is supplied with stores, hotels, two churches, and a number of shops of various kinds. One of the largest Tanneries in the State is located here. It is owned by Messrs. John A., James, and Matthew Gamble, of Jersey Shore.

The Larry's Creek plank road, commencing at the mouth, and running through to Englishtown, on Little Pine Creek, passes through the village. It is eighteen miles in length, and cost $36,000.

A large amount of lumber is manufactured annually on this stream. The number of saw mills on the Creek, and its tributaries, amount to over thirty. Several of them are driven by steam. The first saw mill was erected by Capt. Isaac Seely, at the mouth of Seely's Run, in 1785. The first grist mill was erected on the site now occupied by Hillier's Woolen Factory, in 1788, by Andrew Stroub.

Iron ore also exists in considerable quantities on the Creek, and has been mined to some extent.

All the lumber is hauled to the Canal and piled there, where it is loaded into boats and conveyed to Baltimore, Philadelphia and Reading. It is estimated that from ten to fifteen millions of feet are manufactured annually.

Jersey Shore, fifteen miles west of Williamsport, is an enterprising village of near two thousand inhabitants.—The land on which the town stands was purchased, after the treaty of Fort Stanwix, by Jeremiah and Reuben Manning, who came from New Jersey—hence the name which it took in after years. They laid out the town and called it Waynesburg, but so accustomed were the people to calling it Jersey Shore, that the name was never eradicated, and in 1826, it was incorporated as the borough of Jersey Shore.

In 1800, the *town* consisted of four houses. The first public house was opened in that year by Gabriel Morrison. It improved slowly for a number of years. At the present time it contains three hotels, four eating saloons, fourteen stores, one iron foundry, two tanneries, and a large number of shops. The store rooms are, without exception, the most elegant to be found in any town in Northern Pennsylvania. Immense quantities of goods are annually disposed of.

Within a radius of six miles from Jersey Shore, there are six excellent flouring mills. Several of them were constructed at great expense, and furnished with all the modern improvements in machinery, for the manufacturing of flour.

The first Church was erected by the Methodists in 1830, where they continued to worship till 1845, when they erected a more elegant and imposing structure on

Main street. The old building is now occupied by the Africans, as a Church.

In 1832, the old brick Church, now occupied by the High School, was erected by the Presbyterians and Baptists, and called a "Union Church," where both congregations continued to worship till 1844, when the latter erected the fine frame edifice on Main street, now occupied by them.

The old building was occupied by the Presbyterians till 1850, when they also erected a more elegant brick Church, on Main street.

The first Presbyterian preacher in this part of the Valley, was Rev. Isaac Grier, who came in 1791, and took charge of the Pine Creek Station. He was the father of Judge Grier, of the Supreme Court, who was born near Jersey Shore. He was succeeded by John H. Grier, who took charge of the Pine Creek and Great Island Stations in 1814. He officiated as pastor, at the former place, for eleven years, and thirty-seven at the latter; Rev. D. M. Barber was a co-laborer with him for nine years. They both were succeeded by Rev. Joseph Stevens, the present pastor, in 1851.

These two persons, though of the same name, were not related. Rev. John H. Grier was born in Bucks County in 1788, and is a licentiate of the Presbytery of New Castle. He resides in Jersey Shore, much esteemed and respected by his numerous friends. The old gentleman has always been exceedingly popular with the young folks, and whenever the marriage ceremony is to be performed, his services are generally sought. Up to the 1st of September, 1856, he had married *four hundred and sixty couples!*

The first regular pastor of the Baptist Church was

Rev. George Higgins. His successors were the Revds. Charles Tucker, Cyrus Shuck, George W. Young, J. Green Miles, and Allan J. Hires, the present pastor.

The West Branch High School or Seminary for young ladies and gentlemen, is located at this point. This institution was founded by the Presbyterian Church of Jersey Shore, in 1852, and although its origin is of such recent date, and it has had to contend with the difficulties which usually beset the career of every young institution, yet it has made very commendable progress, and attained a high position among the schools of the higher order in this section of the country.

This school is designed to give pupils of both sexes an efficient education, in all the higher branches of the English language, with an especial aim at fitting them for respectably discharging the duties of practical life; and also to prepare young men for any of the advanced classes of College. The male and female departments are in organic connection; but each has its separate rooms, and intercourse is not allowed, except by special permission of the Principal. The course of instruction is complete and thorough. With regard to the efficiency of this school, I take the following from the Pennsylvania School Journal for November, 1853.

"We had the pleasure of attending the semi-annual examination of the Students of the West Branch Seminary on the 26th, 27th, and 28th days of September. This examination, in justice to the teachers and pupils, deserves more than a passing notice. It was continued a sufficient length of time to test the proficiency and accuracy of the students. The examinations were thorough. The pupils gave abundant evidence that they were well acquainted with the different studies to which they had given their attention during the Session. We have never attended an examination where the students answered more

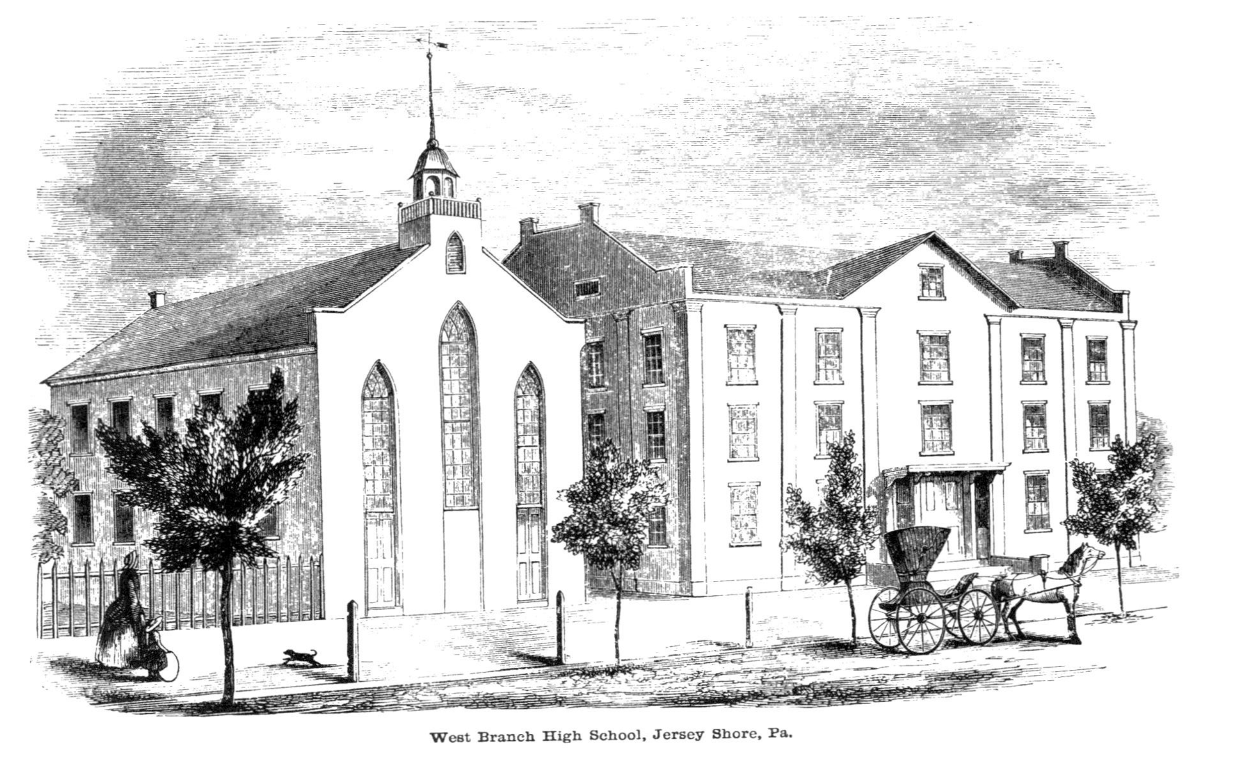

West Branch High School, Jersey Shore, Pa.

accurately or correctly. Time and space will not allow us to enter into details of the different classes examined. Among them we were particularly interested in the examination of the classes in practical Geometry, Physiology, and the classes in the Bible. We heard classes questioned for the space of an hour which did not miss a single question; be it said to the honor of the West Branch Seminary, this we never heard before."

The buildings of this school are correctly exhibited in the engraving given in this work. They consist of a Seminary building conveniently arranged for the purposes of instructing the pupils, hearing recitations, keeping the Library and apparatus, and public examinations, &c; and also a boarding house of fine appearance, well arranged, and capable of accommodating from eighty to one hundred pupils. This latter building has been recently erected by the liberality of the citizens of Jersey Shore and vicinity, and is highly creditable to their zeal in the cause of education, and to the town. The Boarding house is managed by a Board of Managers separate from the Directors of the School. The Principal and his assistants board in the establishment with the pupils, and have the constant supervision of them. The present Principal is the Rev. William W. Howard, a gentleman of fine abilities, and large experience in conducting such an institution; in every respect abundantly qualified for his position, and eminently successful in the business of educating youth.

The common schools of the borough are carefully attended to, and a large brick building was erected some years ago for school purposes. It embraces several rooms, with a commodious hall for town purposes.

A beautiful Cemetery, on a commanding eminence, to the west of the town, was laid out and arranged in 1854, by Mark Slonaker, Esq. It will soon make one of the handsomest in the country. Mr. S. deserves great credit, and the thanks of the people, for this much needed improvement.

Jersey Shore, at one time, bid fair to be an important place, and had opportunities, and enjoyed facilities, that, if embraced, would have tended to place her in a pre-eminent position. Being the central depot for the immense lumbering regions of Pine and Larry's Creeks, her trade was good, and if mills had been erected at this point, the town would rapidly have grown in wealth, population and importance. Her chances are excellent yet. Large deposits of iron ore are found to exist in the adjacent hills, with plenty of limestone, and companies have already commenced working them. They are contiguous to the Canal, and every opportunity desired for easy shipment, and favorable locations for the erection of furnaces are found here. In fact, advantages exist here, worthy of the careful consideration of capitalists and iron manufacturers.

Long Island, opposite Jersey Shore, was quite an important place with the Aborigines. It is a beautiful spot of ground, composed of rich alluvial soil, and highly productive. It makes a beautiful farm.—There is but little doubt that the island originally extended nearly, if not altogether, as far down as Stewart's Ripples. Then it was emphatically a *long* island.

A few miles south of Jersey Shore is a very peculiar valley, called Nippenose. It is an oval basin surrounded by a chain of high mountains, containing about 13,000 acres. The land is good, and produces heavy crops of wheat. Limestone abounds in great quantities, and the valley underneath is evidently filled with fissures and caverns to a great extent. The name is corrupted from an old Indian called Nippenucy, who had his wigwam there, and in the Bottom of the same name, where he lived and hunted alternately. This is the true origin of the present title.

The first improvement was made in 1776, by John Clark, on the farm now owned by David Shaw. He was driven off with his family during the war, but returned in 1784.

John and William Winlin lived in the Valley in 1790. They commenced to sink a well, and after digging some distance came to a flat rock that resisted all further progress. One of the workmen commenced striking on it with a sledge, when a hole was broken through, and there appeared to be a large cavern underneath. A plummet, thirty feet in length, was let down, without finding bottom. They became alarmed and filled it up again.

The Valley is very thickly populated, and contains several villages and hamlets, with stores, hotels, churches, mills, &c.

Most of the streams, running down from the mountains, sink and disappear under the Valley. There appears to be only one place of outlet, called Antes' Creek, through the Gap of the same name. It is a small stream, abundantly filled with trout, notwithstanding they are constantly fished for, and great numbers caught; yet the supply seems inexhaustible. It is supposed that they multiply in great numbers under the Valley, and come forth in the Creek. The theory, it must be admitted, looks plausible.

CHAPTER LII.

PHELPS' MILLS—LUMBER TRADE OF PINE CREEK—THE BIG ISLAND—EARLY HISTORY OF LOCK HAVEN—THE TOWN FOUNDED BY JERRY CHURCH—INTERESTING SKETCH—HIS FOLLY—POPULATION—THE LUMBERING BUSINESS—THE BOOM ERECTED—EXTRAORDINARY FACILITIES FOR LUMBERING—RAILROADS, CANALS, &c.—FUTURE PROSPECTS—STATISTICS—STEAMBOATS.

Two miles west of Jersey Shore, we come to Phelps' Mills on Pine Creek. Operations were commenced here in 1847, and the following year, a large saw mill was started. Within the last two or three years, quite a village has grown up, wearing a business aspect. In the spring of 1856, the company put in operation a large steam saw mill for manufacturing boards, shingles, lath, palings, &c. The two mills number, in the aggregate, sixty-four gang and English saws, with eight circulars. They are capable of making 8,000,000 feet of lumber per annum. The Company also erected a fine flouring mill, and two miles further up the Creek they have another. They have a fine store in the village, and a Church has been recently erected. A neat and substantial bridge has been thrown across the Creek, at an expense of nearly $5,000, which was borne exclusively by the Company, for their own, and the accommodation of the surrounding country, free of toll. All the buildings erected, are beautiful frame edifices. See engraving opposite title page.

This is the most extensive lumbering establishment on Pine Creek, and the site is one of the best in the country. They have excellent facilities for the harboring of their logs—have extensive booms; and, in fact, every natural and artificial advantage to be desired. A railroad has been built to the Canal, a distance of two miles, where their lumber is transported and deposited upon the wharf ready for shipping. Since the starting of their first mill in 1848, to the present time, they have sent 22,000,000 feet of lumber to market.

Mr. J. C. HOWARD, an eastern gentleman of much experience, has control of the sawing department.

The general agent and superintendent for this immense establishment, is E. B. CAMPBELL, ESQ., who is well fitted for the station. Few men, probably, could conduct the business as successfully and satisfactorily, as he does. He seems to be in his sphere.

The village is named after the late Anson G. Phelps, of New York, who is well remembered throughout the United States for his many acts of public and private benevolence. While living, he was the head of the firm. The present head is WILLIAM E. DODGE, ESQ., a very worthy man, and a philanthropist.

The Company have it in contemplation to make further improvements at this point. They are also interested in extensive operations in different parts of the United States, and in Europe. These works have been a material benefit to the country, and they give employment to upwards of seventy men.

One mile below this establishment is another large mill, owned by McEldry, Trump & Co., of Baltimore. They run about thirty-eight saws, with a capacity of about 4,000,000 feet per annum.

Pine Creek is a great lumbering region, and is dotted with saw-mills. The total number on the creek, and its various tributaries, is about one hundred and thirty-four; and not less than 60,000,000 feet of lumber, including boards and logs, are run out to market annually.

A few miles above the First Fork, is another extensive mill, owned by Stoddard, Magraw, & Co., with a run of thirty-eight saws, and a capacity of 4,000,000 feet per annum.

These three mills are the leading ones on the stream. There are other good ones of a less capacity, and I regret that I cannot notice them in detail.

At the Forks of Pine Creek, twelve miles from the mouth, is a pleasant and flourishing village named Waterville, containing two hotels, two stores, church, shops, &c. The location is very pleasant. The scenery along the creek is wild and diversified.

Charlton, on the road to Lock Haven, is a small village containing one store and a tavern.

New Liberty is a place of similar size, containing one store and tavern, and ten or twelve dwellings.

Dunnstown, near the Great Island, was laid out in 1794, by William Dunn, in the hope that it might become the county seat of Lycoming. He was disappointed, however, and the town never improved much. In later years, an effort was made to have the capital of Clinton located there, but it failed.

The Great Island was a very important place with the Indians one hundred years ago. It was to them a perfect Paradise—an elysian home—where they loved to dwell and offer up their orisons to the Great Spirit. No lovelier spot can be imagined—a luxuriant alluvial soil—wide-spreading trees—enchanting scenery—humble wigwams—the smoke gracefully curling on the breeze. Near this lovely spot, encircled by the crystal waves of the Otzinachson, on the opposite side, was a village where the Chief, Bald Eagle, frequently dwelt. The mountain range from Lock Haven to Muncy, takes its name from him.

The Great Island contains about three hundred acres of very fertile land, in a high state of cultivation. It is divided into two farms. The first settler was William Dunn, who purchased it, according to a tradition, from the Indians, for a barrel of whiskey, a rifle, and a hatchet! It would take a great many such articles to buy it now. It is also said that the Indians became dissatisfied with their sale, and frequently laid on the rocks on the north side of the river, watching an opportunity to shoot him. They never succeeded. One of the farms at the present day is owned by William Dunn, a grandson. Two fine bridges have recently been erected, connecting the island, on both sides, with the main land.

Lock Port is a small village on the river, directly opposite Lock Haven, containing two hotels, two stores, &c. It is an important point with the lumbermen during the spring freshets. A substantial bridge crosses the river to Lock Haven.

The flourishing town of Lock Haven is located on the south side of the river, on the beautiful undulating plain, at the mouth of the rich and fertile valley of Bald Eagle. It will be remembered that the land in this vicinity was embraced in the grant to Rev. Dr. Allison, by Richard Penn. Judge Fleming, and the McCormicks, were among the earliest settlers, and were heirs of Dr. Allison. William Reed had a cabin on the site of Lock Haven in 1778. His neighbors were Cooksey Long, 'Squire Fleming, and a man named McCormick.

The present enterprising town owes its paternity to Jerry Church, who seems to have a sort of mania for founding towns. Its early history is very interesting. I copy from Mr. Church's Autobiography, as follows:

"After I arrived at New Cumberland, where my brother Robert lived at that time, and had stayed a few days to rest myself, I left and went up to a place called Milton, on the West Branch. I there found a younger brother by the name of Willard Church, who had come down from the State of New York into the old Keystone State to try his fortune, and was ready for anything that presented itself that he could do without capital. He told me that he knew of a splendid place for a town, if we could get the land. He said it was located at the head of the West Branch Canal, on the pool of the Dunnstown dam, and they were working on the Spring Creek and Bald Eagle cross-cut that emptied into the pool, and run through the place or farm, that we must purchase. I asked him how much he thought it worth per acre. He said he thought it worth one hundred and fifty dollars an acre for as much as we would want for the town lots, and that would be about fifty acres. I told him that was a beautiful price to think of giving; and, in particular, when we had not much money. He said that if I would go with him and look at it and make the purchase, he would risk his capital at any rate. I concluded that I would go up and view the place. So we got aboard of the stage and went up to Williamsport, and from thence to Dunnstown, twenty-eight miles, crossed the river at that place, went up about one mile on the opposite shore, and put up with a man named Develin, who lived on the farm as a tenant. The farm belonged to Dr. John Henderson, of Huntingdon, and there were two hundred acres in the tract. We took a walk over the premises, and found it to be a delightful spot; two hundred acres of the best kind of ground, beautifully located between two rivers, the Susquehanna and the Bald Eagle, and the scenery nature had formed around it, could not be excelled in the State. I stood and looked at it with delight, and told my brother that we must have it in some way.

"We then left the place, and went down to Williamsport. There I met with a gentleman lawyer who I had been some time acquainted with, and I told him that I had been viewing up at or near the Big Island, and would like to purchase it if I knew where to get the money; and also told him the object: that I intended to lay out a town on it, if I could obtain it. He said he thought the money could be got, and he would be willing to be a private partner—what I would call a sleeping partner. He proposed to put one-third of the purchase money in, and give me a letter to Dr. Henderson to that effect. I then left Williamsport and went to Huntingdon to see the Old Doctor. When I arrived there I called on him, and introduced myself, and handed him the letter the lawyer had given me at Williamsport. That informed him what my business was. He replied, that it appeared by the letter that I wished to purchase his farm, near the Big Island, or a part of it. I told him that was my intention, if we could agree. He then said he would not sell a part. If he sold any it must be the whole farm, and he had his price set and could not be changed. I asked him what it was. He said $20,000, and not a dollar less. I told him it was a beautiful sum for one farm. However, I said I had made up my mind to give him $18,000, if I could make the payments to suit him. I told him also that I was not rich, and had not the money, even at that price, in hand. He then repeated that his mind was made up not to take anything less than he had above stated. I saw that there was no use to parley any longer, so I told him that I would close the bargain, if the payments I could make would suit him. He asked me how I wished to make them. I told him that I could pay $5,000 in hand, or when I took the property in possession, and the balance in two years. He said that would do, but he could not give me full possession until the 1st of April, 1834. This was in October, 1833. I gave the Old Doctor a fifty dollar bill to bind the bargain, and then went into a lawyer's office and had our bonds made by a gentleman by the name of Steel—a very honest man, considering all things.

"After we had all our writings finished, and took a few glasses of old rye, we got aboard of the stage and went to Bellefonte, and from there down to the river Susquehanna, on the property. The Dr. went with me in order to give the tenant notice that he must leave by the first of April—that the property was to pass into other hands, and was no longer his—that he had sold the farm to Jeremiah and Willard Church. I got permission of the Dr. and the tenant to plot out a town on paper, and make a sale, if we thought proper, immediately, and give our titles and possession on the first day of April. We did so, and called the town Lock Haven. We made a public sale on the 4th of November, 1833, and sold a number of lots, receiving ten per cent. on the purchase money, and the balance on the 1st of April.

That was the time we were bound to meet our old friend the Dr., and I knew by the cut of his jib, that he would be on the ground at the proper time.

"I then called on my sleeping partner for his share of the purchase money, but I could not wake him up for any part of it. He sent me his resignation in writing, stating that he had changed his mind on the subject, and could not put up the money, but wished to be excused from any further liability. A beautiful note to write at that stage of the game! However, I told my brother we must try and make the payment ourselves; we had gone so far with it, there was no backing out; that he must watch while I would pray. I said I would go to Williamsport and try to make a *raise* of money to meet the Dr. on the first day of April, which was then drawing very near, and I was very doubtful whether we could meet our engagements or not. Accordingly, I went down to Williamsport, and there met with a gentleman who had money. I told him that I wanted $3,000 for a few weeks, and that I would give him for the use of it, $500, and he let me have the money. I was very thankful for the accommodation, for it saved my credit, and that was worth more to me at that time than the $500 were. In that way we met our first payment. Then we made all the sales we possibly could in town lots, and the back land we sold to a gentleman from Chester County, by the name of James Jeffries. He paid us about $9,000 in cash at one time, and that saved us the second time with the Doctor.

"About that time my brother married a lady near Milton. His wife had an interest in a store with her brother, Robert Montgomery. Of course my brother became a partner in the store, in the town of Milton, as large as life. They concluded they would move their store to our new town of Lock Haven, and did so; but it did not last long. They had to break the first year. They all lived together, and too fast for their income; so the sheriff came on them to show cause why they did not pay for their goods. They could not show any reasonable excuse, only that they had not the money; so the sheriff seized the goods and sold them for what he could get, and turned them out to the mercy of the world. My brother had all his interest in the town of Lock Haven sold for his debts, together with his dear brother-in-law's, and both were left even with the world once more. My brother then left the new town and went to the west, to the state of Missouri, and settled down with his family.

"I then undertook to manage the town of Lock Haven myself. All my sleeping partners had left me, and I had to be all the society there was at that time in town. If there was any music to be played, I had to be a full band myself, having no person to assist me. I now undertook to divide the Counties of Lycoming and Centre, and make a new County to be called Clinton. I had petitions printed to that effect, and sent them to Harrisburg, to have them presented to the Legislature, and then went down myself to have the matter represented in good order. My friend John A. Gamble, was our member from Lycoming at that time, and he reported a bill. The people of the town of Williamsport, the County seat of Lycoming, and Bellefonte, the County seat of Centrė County, then had to be up and be doing something to prevent the division; and they commenced pouring in their remonstrances, and praying aloud to the Legislature not to have any part of either County taken off for the purpose of making a new one, for it was nothing more or less than some of Jerry Church's Yankee notions. However, I did not despair. I still kept asking every year, for three successive years, and attended the Legislature myself every winter. I then had a gentleman who had become a citizen, by the name of John Moorhead, who harped in with me—a very large portly looking man, and rather the best borer in town; and, by the by, a very clever man. We entered into the division together. We had to state a great number of facts to the members of the Legislature, and perhaps something more, in order to obtain full justice. We continued on for nearly three years longer, knocking at the mercy seat, and at last we received the law creating the County of Clinton. In the year 1839, the County was organized by the Hon. Judge Burnside.

"I then concluded that having a county seat and law and justice so handy, we could get judgment against our neighbors almost any time. However, I was mistaken about that, for when I went to law I could not obtain it, in consequence of not having just claims, as the lawyers told me. I then concluded I would change it, and have a suit on justice alone, which I could not obtain according to law. I soon found out that the less a person has to do with law and attending courts, the more money he can have in his pocket, and the happier man will he be.

"We had three Commissioners appointed to locate the County seat. Their names were Col. Cresswell, Maj. Colt and Joseph Brestel. These gentlemen met at Lock Haven, and viewed the different places that were offered for the County seat, but there was none to be compared to Lock Haven. So they made up their minds that Lock Haven should be the place, and selected the square for the public buildings. My friend Moorhead was displeased with the location, and had a special law passed allowing the Commissioners to alter the location, for his own interest and others, without my knowledge, and offered a bonus to the County to have it moved into another part of the town. But it would not do. The people sustained me; and the square I had located in the first place was retained. We went on and built the Court House, as good a one, perhaps, as any in Northern Pennsylvania. The inhabitants numbered about 700 at this time, viz., in 1844. Ten years ago there was but one house, and probably about a dozen inhabitants in the place, and now (1845) it is a beautiful village, and a place of considerable business. It has seven retail stores and groceries, one drug and two candy shops, three preachers, two meeting houses, (and one 'Jerry Church,') six lawyers, two doctors, and two justices of the peace, and the balance of the inhabitants are what I call a fair community."

The first County Commissioners were Col. Kleckner, Col. Hugh White, and Robert Bridgens. Mr. Church made a donation of the land for the public buildings. It was his design to remain here. He says:

"I stated in the commencement of this little book, (His Life,) 'that I intended to stop at Lock Haven for the present.' I will here further describe some of my works at that place. In order to carry out my originality, I built an office in the town, standing eight feet above the ground, on *thirteen* large posts, or pillars, to represent our thirteen Continental States. In the first place it is made by placing thirteen large pine trees, five feet in the ground, and thirty feet long, in their natural state, with the exception of taking the bark off, and painting them in imitation of marble, with a fourteen feet room formed inside of the posts, so as to form a balustrade all around it; and the roof projecting over so as to protect the building. I concluded when I was making it, that it was an odd looking office, and different from any one I had seen in this country. And as I was no lawyer, and could not expect any notice or business in that way, I concluded that I would build my office so that clients might look at it without any expense. If I am not very much mistaken, they would make as much at that, as they would if I had been a lawyer myself. I had a number of scientific gentlemen to view the little building, and they always asked what *order* I intended it to be. I told them I never did any thing according to *order*—it was all a matter of taste—that I never learned anything by note, and therefore, could not inform them any more, than that it was *my own* order, and that appeared to satisfy their inquiries always. I had always concluded that there was no chance for me to have any kind of a monument erected in remembrance of me, unless I should place some of my odd matters and things before the public myself, so that they could not all pass by without observing that some person had been there before.

"I had a summer seat built in the first place, at Lock Haven, so that if I got tired I could go up and take a rest. It was formed in a cluster of black walnut trees. It was twenty-five feet from the ground, forty feet long, and seven feet wide, placed so as to be supported by the trees, bannistered, and a seat running all around, and winding stairs up one of the trees. And I must say, that when I went up on to the upper seat I felt like a bird. I had it painted by a German painter, and I told him I would like to have it made like marble; but, as he did not understand English very well, he made it what I call *Dutch marble*, all full of white and black spots. The natives of that country thought it was a wonderful thing, that I should throw away my money so, to make a nice seat to sit on, and asked me why I did so. I told them that I sat far more comfortable on that seat, than I could on a bag of dollars. So they gave it up. It has ever since gone by the name of 'Church's folly.' However, all were willing to take a seat with me now and then."

Mr. Church did not remain long in Lock Haven; in 1846, he went to the west, and has already founded two or three different towns. Ten years have produced a great change in Lock Haven. His "summer seat" is gone, but the unique looking office yet stands, in a good state of preservation, near the Court-house. It is occupied by a family—is quite a curiosity, and goes by the name of "Jerry Church's folly."

The following sketch, of the history of Lock Haven since 1850, is from the pen of H. L. Dieffenbach, Esq.:

"In 1850, the population of Lock Haven did not exceed 800. At the present time it is estimated at from 2,500 to 3,000, not including the adjacent villages of Lock Port and Boyd's Hill. This fact sufficiently indicates the rapidity of its growth, which is progressing with more speed at the present time than at any former period. There are now four large steam saw-mills—exclusive of the one at Reed's Basin—in successful operation.

"There are also two large steam mills on the canal below Lock Haven, which depend upon the Boom, at the latter place, for their supplies, and are capable of manufacturing 5,000,000 feet per annum. But while the capacity of *all* the mills may safely be estimated at from fifty to sixty millions of feet annually, their actual work has not as yet much exceeded 30,000,000.

"A company of gentleman interested in the lumbering business, have made a fine basin, which is filled from the Bald Eagle Canal, immediately adjoining the town, and which covers several acres of ground, with high natural banks on both sides. It is estimated that this basin will hold 2,000,000 of feet of saw logs. The company are also authorized to connect their basin, by canal, with the boom and river, thus affording extraordinary facilities for lumbering operations. Another large basin, covering ten to twelve acres, could be constructed, at small cost, extending from the canal to the Bald Eagle Creek, about one mile above its confluence with the river.

"Clinton Harbor, the large basin below Lock Port, half a mile below Lock Haven, and directly on the West Branch Canal, from which it receives its water, will contain 1,500,000 feet of saw logs, and has abundant facilities for additional saw-mills or other manufacturing operations.

"For a hundred miles west of Lock Haven, there is but little tillable land along the West Branch, or its tributaries; but this mountainous district is well covered with a great variety of the finest timber, and abounds in excellent veins of bituminous coal, iron ore, and fire clay. The principal business of the lumbering and mining operations is transacted at Lock Haven; and from this point all supplies must necessarily be obtained. The valleys around the town abound in limestone, and hence all the facilities for the manufacture of iron may readily be obtained at this point.

"The principal cause of the rapid growth of Lock Haven heretofore, however, must be attributed, besides the proverbial energy of its citizens, to the manufacture of lumber, and the facilities it affords for that purpose. Immense quantities of timber are floated into the pool of the Dunnstown dam, on which the town is located, by every flood.

In consequence of the demand of rafting hands at such periods, and the comparative certainty of obtaining a market at or from this point, the rafts are usually tied up here until all or nearly all the lumber from above is brought down. Being at the head of the market, where such immense quantities are landed on every flood, lumber dealers could name no better place for making advantageous purchases.

"In the fall of 1848, Col. Johnson, of New Hampshire, who had purchased considerable quantities of timber land in Clinton county, suggested to some citizens of Lock Haven, that if they would obtain a charter for a company, a boom could be constructed in the river above the town, which would attract lumber manufacturers, and, besides proving a profitable investment, would give an impulse to the growth of the town, which would in time make it the principal town in this part of the State. The gentlemen to whom the suggestion was made, obtained the charter—not, however, without vigorous opposition on the part of some "old fogies," who could see nothing but private speculation in the effort—and soon afterwards transferred it, without price, to Peter Dickinson, Esq., one of the most enterprising and accomplished business men in Lock Haven, upon the sole condition that he would erect the boom within a given period. Faithful to his contract, Mr. Dickinson soon had the boom built and filled with logs. From this period the rapid growth of Lock Haven commenced—property doubled, trebled and quadrupled in value, and soon the fields around the town were dotted with houses, and the streets filled with an industrious, energetic and prosperous population. The boom was sold last spring to a stock company, and is now valued at $100,000. At some periods it contained nearly 200,000 saw logs—thirty-five to forty millions of feet of timber.

"The Lock Haven Bank, with a capital of $200,000 paid in, is in successful operation. L. A. Mackey, Esq., is President.

"One of the largest and finest hotels in the State—the FALLON HOUSE—is now being erected in Lock Haven, and is nearly completed. It is estimated to cost upwards of $26,000.

"There are two public halls in the place—one large three-story building erected by Clinton Lodge of Odd Fellows, at a cost of near $5,000—one large and elegant Presbyterian Church, and three other very fine ones in the course of erection—a large and commodious Court-house, and Academy, and a Common School building, two stories high, containing four large rooms, the ample grounds of which are

29

enclosed by a neat high fence. This school is conducted on the union graded plan, and has the reputation of being one of the best conducted schools in the State.

"There is also a large steam flouring mill, a large foundry, a planing mill in course of erection, and other manufactories usual in towns, in successful operation. The mercantile business is carried on with great success, and immense quantities of goods are annually sold. There are eighteen stores in the place. The various mechanical arts are also pursued with great energy and success.

"The Bald Eagle Canal, commencing at Milesburg, Centre county, intersects the West Branch Division of the Pennsylvania Canal at Lock Haven, and a steamboat plies regularly between the latter place and Queen's Run,* Farrandsville and Tangascootack, the principal points for lading boats with bituminous coal and fire brick. The Sunbury and Erie Rail-road will soon be finished to these points. Ample arrangements, too, have been made to construct the Lock Haven and Tyrone Rail-road, as soon as the Sunbury and Erie is finished to the former place. This will give Lock Haven an eastern, western, and north-western rail-road connection; and the Sunbury and Erie will traverse one of the richest mineral and agricultural valleys in the State. The principal depot of the Tyrone Rail-road will necessarily be at Lock Haven, as will probably that of the Sunbury and Erie road.

"The citizens of Lock Haven will not admit that there is another town in the State so favorably located in all respects for every variety of business, and especially for large business operations. Time alone can test the accuracy of this judgment; but, even the rival towns are free to admit, that Lock Haven, *at least*, possesses extraordinary facilities for business."

According to the census of 1850, Clinton county contained 11,207 inhabitants—44,982 acres of improved land, and 38,229 unimproved. Cash value of the farms $2,028,610—value of farming implements, machinery, &c., $73,555. The County also contained 1,795 horses, 2,413 milch cows, 6,116 sheep. Total value of *all* live

* The proper name of this stream is Quinn's Run. It was named after Samuel Quinn, a Surveyor, who had a camp on it in 1788.

stock $201,530. Bushels of wheat raised 191,065, rye 36,798, corn 115,760. The Churches were as follows: Two Baptist, 1 German Reformed, 2 Lutheran, 6 Methodist, 3 Presbyterian and 1 Union. Total value of church property $21,280—aggregate accommodations 4,700.

A steamboat named the Farrand, plied on the river between Farrandsville and Muncy in 1831–2. On her first trip in 1831, she brought up some sixty men, amongst whom was S. G. ALLEN, of Jersey Shore, on their way from the east, to commence operations at Farrandsville. Mr. Allen had charge of the company of workmen.

CHAPTER LIII.

HISTORY OF THE NEWSPAPERS OF SUNBURY, NORTHUMBERLAND, LEWISBURG, MILTON, M'EWENSVILLE, MUNCY, WILLIAMSPORT, JERSEY SHORE AND LOCK HAVEN; SHOWING THE TIME WHEN ESTABLISHED, BY WHOM, THEIR NAMES, HOW LONG CONTINUED, ETC.

[NOTE.—When this work was commenced, it was not designed to give a history of the newspapers; and the proposition has only been entertained for a few weeks, hence the facts have been hurriedly collected, and some errors may occur; but, it is believed that the history of the *leading* papers is correct.—Many papers published at an early period, and continued for a short time, have almost been forgotten, and in many instances the files have been lost. I am indebted mainly for the facts to publishers in the respective localities.]

The first newspaper published in Sunbury, was called the *Freyheitsvogel,* printed in the German language. It was established in 1800, by a gentleman named Breyvogel, during the exciting presidential contest between Jefferson and Adams, and continued but one year, when it was suspended.

The next paper was called *The Times,* and established by William F. Byers, in 1812. It was printed in English. The career of this paper was attended with many changes and vicissitudes. At the end of three years Byers retired from it, and it passed through a great many different hands. Samuel J. Packer was interested in it at one time, and W. F. Packer at another. The name was finally changed to the *Gazetteer*, by William Shannon. It expired in 1833.

The old Ramage press, and materials, remained for a long time as rubbish in an upper room of a building belonging to the Shannon family, and were finally bought by H. B. Masser, Esq. It is quite a curiosity, in comparison with the presses of the present period.

In 1812, about three months after the commencement of the *Times*, John G. Youngman—whose uncle, Gotleib Youngman, printed the first paper in the city of Reading—came from Baltimore, and established the second German paper, called the *Northumberlaad Republican*. This name was continued four years, when it was changed to the *North Western Post*, Sunbury being considered quite a north western town at that time.

This name was continued till the commencement of the construction of the Canal, when, to suit the feelings of the times, it was re-christened the *Canal Boat*. With this name the publication of the German paper was discontinued, and an English paper, called the *Workingmen's Advocate*, started in 1832. In 1838, it was enlarged and the name changed to the *Gazette*, which title it continues under at the present time.

From 1812, up to the present time, John G. Youngman has been connected with the Gazette printing office, under the the various names which the paper has underwent. In 1840, Geo. B. Youngman took charge of the editorial department of the paper, and was succeeded in 1855, by John Youngman, the present editor.

There were two other papers published in Sunbury, the dates of which I cannot ascertain. One was called the *Beacon*, by George Lathey, and the other by Ezra Grassman, called the *Emporium*. Mr. Grassman is now an extensive printer in New York.

In 1840, the *Sunbury American* was established by H. B. Masser and Joseph Eisely. Mr. Eisely went out of the establishment in 1849, and since then Mr. Masser has been sole editor and proprietor. The same gentleman is also publishing a *German American*, started about twelve years ago.

On the 1st of January, 1856, Bachman & Co., commenced printing the *German Democrat*. At the present time there are two German and two English papers published in Sunbury.

The first paper in Northumberland was called the *Northumberland Gazette*, and established in 1797 or 1798, by Andrew Kennedy, and continued till 1819 or 1820.

The *Republican Argus* was commenced by John Binns in 1803, and discontinued in 1816 or 1817. He is well known to the old people of the Valley. He afterwards published a paper in Philadelphia, where he is now living, at an advanced age.

The first paper established in Lewisburg was called the *News-Letter*, by William Carothers, in 1824–5. It continued about eighteen months. It was followed by the *Union Hickory*, by the same publisher, and continued from May 5, 1829, till April 13, 1830.

Next came the *Lewisburg Journal*, by Daniel Gotshall, who controlled it from May 1, 1830, till February 18, 1833, when it passed into the hands of Geo. M. Miller and Edward S. Bowen. It was discontinued February 22, 1834.

On the 20th of June, 1835, G. R. Barrett, Esq., started the *Lewisburg Democrat*, which lived till May 1836.

The next was the *Lewisburg Standard*, by D. G. Fitch, who published it till the 1st of September, 1839, when it passed into the hands of H. L. Dieffenbach, Esq., a forcible writer, who, at the end of three months, discontinued it and took charge of a paper in a neighboring county.

Jonas Kelchner soon after commenced the publication of the *People's Advocate*, which was discontinued April 12, 1841, "for reasons best known to ourselves," as Mr. K. remarked in his valedictory.

September 4th, 1841, *The Independent Press* made its appearance, edited for a time by S. K. Sweetman, and then Sweetman & Maize, and also Sweetman & Busch. Its career was terminated, Dec. 16, 1842.

After a vacancy of some months, W. B. Shriner & S. A. Burkenbine, started the *Lewisburg Chronicle*, September 23, 1843. March 16, 1844, Mr. Burkenbine retired discouraged. Mr. Shriner plucked up courage and continued the paper, which was printed a part of the time for him by Samuel Shriner, till December 25, 1847, when he sold out to O. N. Worden, who conducted it till January 1st, 1850, when H. C. Hickock became principal editor, and continued till 1855, when he was appointed Deputy Superintendent of Common Schools by Gov. Pollock.

Mr. John R. Cornelius, soon after, became associated with Mr. Worden in the publication of the paper, by whom it is continued at the present time, and seems established on a permanent basis.

In 1845, R. I. Nesbit & Co., published *The Humorist*, a small sheet devoted to fun. It had a "short but a merry life."

In January, 1850, Rev. Henry Harbaugh issued *The Guardian*, a monthly magazine, devoted to social, literary and religious interests of young men and ladies. It was printed in the Chronicle office by O. N. Worden, for one year, when Mr. Harbaugh removed to Lancaster, where he still continues its publication.

About September, 1850, the *Lewisburg Democrat* made its appearance. It was edited and published by Samuel Shriner. It was discontinued in 1854. In the summer of 1855, a few numbers were issued by Messrs. D. C. Kitchen and John Harbeson, when Mr. Harbeson retired. Mr. Kitchen continued the publication a few weeks longer, when he retired, and transferred his subscription list to the Argus, a rival paper.

In 1851, *The Union Weekly Whig* was started by R. I. Nesbit and Daniel Bower. Mr. Bower soon retired, when it was continued about a year by Mr. Nesbit alone.

July 31, 1855, *The Union Argus* was commenced by F. M. Ziebach and Peter Stout. At the end of two or three months Mr. Stout retired, and was succeeded by J. Merril Linn, who continued a few months, when he was succeeded by H. W. Crotzer, as associate editor. It is now published by Ziebach & Crotzer, and has entered on its second year.

In April, 1856, *The American Flag*, of New Berlin, was discontinued, after ten months' publication, transferring its subscription list to the Lewisburg Chronicle.

The first newspaper in Milton, was *The Miltonian*, established in 1816, by Gen. Frick. The following table will show its history at a glance:

September	21, 1816	to	April 21, 1827,	by	Henry Frick.
April	21, 1827	to	April 16, 1831,	by	Henry Frick & Montgomery Sweny.
April	16, 1831	to	April 20, 1833	by	Henry Frick, Robt. Bennett & Jno. W. Correy.
April	20, 1833	to	Oct. 18, 1834	by	H. Frick & R. Bennett,
Oct.	18, 1834	to	June 3, 1837	by	Henry Frick alone again.
June	3, 1837	to	June 3, 1840	by	H. Frick & Jno. H. Brown.
June	3, 1840	to	Jan. 1, 1842	by	John H. Brown.
Jan.	1, 1842	to	May 5, 1843	by	John Frick & Edward B. Hunter.
May	12, 1843	to	July 14, 1843	by	John Frick alone.
July	14, 1843	to	Dec. 31, 1852	by	John & Robert M. Frick.
Jan.	7, 1853	to	Aug. 26, 1853	by	Robert M. & Henry Frick, Jr.
Sep.	2, 1853	to	Jan. 1, 1854	by	Henry Frick, Jr.
Jan.	1, 1854	to	present time,	by	John Robins.

The next in order is *The States Advocate,* established in 1826. Its history is as follows:

February,	26, 1826	to Aug. 13, 1829	by	William Tweed & E. H. Kincaid.
August,	13, 1829	to Aug. 15, 1833	by	William Tweed alone.
August,	15, 1833	to Nov. 13, 1834	by	William Tweed & Jonas Kelchner.
November,	13, 1834	to Nov. —, 1838	by	Jonas Kelchner alone, when he removed the press to Lewisburg.

The *West Branch Farmer and True Democrat,* was commenced September 3, 1834, by Montgomery Sweny, and continued two or three years.

The Northumbrian was established, Nov. 20, 1837, by Hamlet A. Kerr, and discontinued in a short time. It was a very neat paper.

Tho Milton Ledger was established in the summer of 1838, by McGee & Wilson. In 1839, Wilson retired, and was succeeded by Mr. Collings. They were succeeded by H. L. Dieffenbach in Dec. 1839, who left it in March 1843. John M. Porter then became publisher, and was followed by Brewer & Armstrong in 1844. They were succeeded a short time by a man named Frank, when the paper ceased to exist.

December, 1844, *The Advocate and Day-Spring,* a temperance paper, was started by Rev. W. H. T. Barnes, who continued it about two years, when he went to Mexico, during the war, and died at Vera Cruz.

April 17, 1852, the first number of *The Milton Democrat* was issued by John R. Eck, by whom it is continued at the present time.

About 1849 or 1850, a paper called the *West Branch Intelligencer* was started in McEwensville by a gentleman named Case. It lived about eight months and then expired.

The first paper established in Muncy was called *The*

Muncy Telegraph. It was commenced the 9th of October, 1831, by J. Potter Patterson, and continued by him till the 7th of April, 1835, (the time of his death,) when J. K. Shoemaker took the establishment, and continued the paper till 1841.

The *Muncy Luminary* was commenced April 10, 1841, by W. P. I. & G. L. I. Painter, who continued together till 1846, when the former withdrew. It has been continued to the present time by G. L. I. Painter.

During the summer of 1844, a paper called *The Olive Branch*, was started by J. M. Newson. It was discontinued at the end of a year.

Next in order we come to notice the papers of Williamsport. The *Lycoming Gazette* is the oldest existing paper in the valley, having been published for over half a century, without change of name or suspension. Many other papers have been established in Williamsport, but after living for a brief period, they ceased to exist, and have been forgotten, whilst the Gazette continues on in the even tenor of its way.

The early history of the Gazette is involved in much mystery, as no regular files, from the commencement, are to be found. After 1821, the exact dates and changes can be given accurately, as the files are preserved from that time. After much research and inquiry, I have obtained the following account, which is believed to be very nearly correct:

The *Lycoming Gazette* was established in 1802, by William F. Buyers, who continued alone till about 1808, when William Brindle became associated with him as a partner. Buyers then appears to have retired, and I. K. Torbert took his place, and the publication of the paper was continued for some time under the firm of

Brindle and Torbert. Brindle having retired, Torbert continued alone till 1819, when Ellis Lewis—now Judge of the Supreme Court—became a partner with him. How long they continued together is not known, but Torbert appears to have retired in the meantime, and Lewis conducted the paper alone till July 1821, when he disposed of the establishment to T. Coryell, who continued it alone till the 1st of August, 1823, when it was purchased by Henry Miller and John Brandon. It was continued by them till the 1st of August, 1827, when Miller retired, and James Cameron became associated with Brandon. This firm dissolved on the 19th of December, 1827, when W. F. Packer purchased Cameron's interest, and the paper was published by Brandon and Packer till the 17th of August, 1829, when Packer became sole owner and publisher. He continued alone till December 19, 1832, when John R. Eck became a partner with him, and they continued together till May 11, 1836, when Packer retired, and Eck conducted it till the 21st June, 1837, when it was consolidated with the *Chronicle*—a rival paper—and continued by John R. Eck and C. D. Eldred, under the title of the *Gazette and Chronicle*, till May 9, 1838, when Eck again became sole editor, and continued till the 20th of June, 1838, when Eldred became the owner, and it was published by him under the title of the *Lycoming Gazette*, till the 13th of August, 1840. At this time, C. W. Fitch purchased the establishment, and published the paper till February 10, 1842, when John F. Carter became associated with him, and they continued it till May 7, 1842, when Fitch retired and Carter became sole publisher. He continued the paper till February 11, 1843, when John B. Beck became a partner with him. This firm lasted till the

4th of March, 1843, when Beck became publisher, and Carter editor, which arrangement continued till November 18, 1843, when Carter retired, succeeded by Hamlet A. Kerr, (Beck still publisher,) who edited the paper till August 17, 1844, when he retired, and the firm changed to Beck & Co. On the 24th of June, 1846, C. D. Eldred, (who formed the Co. with Beck,) became editor and publisher, and continued till February 17, 1850, when P. T. Wright became associated with him, and continued till February 17, 1851, when Eldred retired, and Wright continued the paper till February 17, 1855, when J. W. Clark became a partner. This firm lasted till August 17, 1855, when Wright retired. Clark continued the paper till February 17, 1856, when he was succeeded by Atwood and Wilson. The latter retired on the 18th of August, 1856, and it is continued at the present time by N. L. Atwood alone.

This is a correct history of this old paper since 1821—previous to that time the periods when changes took place had to be guessed at, but the names of the publishers are correct.

The Lycoming Advertiser was commenced in 1815, by Simpson and Gale, and continued about six months.

The Lycoming Chronicle was started September 26, 1829, by A. Boyd Cummings, and continued till January 9, 1833, when he was succeeded by Alexander Cummings, Jr., now of the Philadelphia Bulletin, and published by him till September 7, 1836, when C. D. Eldred became a partner. This firm continued till April 12, 1837, when Cummings retired, and Eldred conducted the paper till it was consolidated with the Gazette, June 21, 1837.

I have been unable to find complete files of the following papers which had but an ephemeral existence, and the information had to be obtained from the old citizens, and the dates guessed at.

The Free Press was commenced in July, 1836, by R. F. Middleton, who published it about one year, when it went into the hands of Cramer and Reed. It was also published by Loehr and Middleton. Discontinued about 1838.

The publication of *The Freeman* was commenced about 1839, by John R. Eck, and continued till 1840, when W. P. and James R. Coulter, purchased the materials and commenced the publication of the *West Branch Republican,* which lived till about 1842. About this time the materials were purchased by John Sloan, who started the *Lycoming Sentinel.* It lived about one year, when *The North Pennsylvanian* was established by John F. Carter, who let it die in about six months.

The Jackson Democrat was started in 1845, by J. M. Newson and G. W. Armstrong. It was afterwards published for a short time by S. S. Seely, and by G. W. Armstrong. It lived about a year.

The Lycoming Democrat was started June 4, 1851, by John F. Carter. June 28, 1851, John R. Eck became a partner, but retired November 29, 1851, when it was continued by Carter till the fall of 1852, when it was discontinued, aged a year and a half.

The Independent Press was established out of the materials of the Democrat, in 1852, by J. W. Barrett. In the fall of 1855, he disposed of the concern to a company, and F. A. Van Cleve became the editor, who discontinued it after issuing a few numbers. No paper was issued till the spring of 1856, when the publication was resumed by Barrett and Butt. Barrett retired, Oct. 18, 1856, and was succeeded by Jesse Fullmer.

The first paper in Jersey Shore was started on the 8th of January, 1827, by Daniel Gotshall. It was called the *West Branch Courier*, and continued till about 1830.

In 1828, a little sheet, called *The Nose*, was commenced by William Piatt, Jr. It was printed in the office of the Courier, and continued but a short time.

Alexander Hamilton commenced the publication of *The Anti-Masonic Advocate*, about 1830, and continued it till the winter of 1834, when he was succeeded by Loehr and Middleton, who discontinued it in 1835.

No paper was then published till January 1846, when *The Jersey Shore Republican* was established by S. S. Seely, who continued it till October, 1850, when the office was destroyed by the big fire of that year. The town was again without a paper till June, 1851, when the Republican, in an enlarged form, was revived by its old publisher. In September, 1851, R. Baker became associated with Seely in the publication of the paper, and it was continued by them till June 9, 1852, when Seely disposed of his interest to Jacob Sallada, Jr., and it was published under the firm of Baker and Sallada, till June 9, 1854, edited by J. F. Meginness; when both Sallada and Meginness retired, the former having disposed of his interest to R. Baker, who became sole owner. On the 9th of June, 1855, R. Baker associated with him his son, F. A. Baker, as a partner in the establishment, and it is continued at the present time under the firm of R. &. F. A. Baker.

On the 29th of June, 1854, the first number of *The News Letter* was issued by Seely & Meginness, by whom it was continued till the 30th of August, 1855, when Meginness retired, and Seely became sole publisher.— On the 6th of December, 1855, James Jones became associated with him as a partner. Jones retired from the firm on the 18th of September, 1856. Seely continues it alone.

The National Vidette was commenced on the 15th of May, 1855, by H. J. B. & L. J. Cummings, by whom it was continued for a period of six months, when H. J. B. Cummings retired. A few numbers were issued by L. J. Cummings, when he retired also, and the paper ceased to exist. On the 25th of September, it was resuscitated by James Jones.

The first paper started in Lock Haven was called *The Eagle*, by William A. Kinsloe. This was in August, 1838. It advocated the formation of a new county to be called "Eagle." When the county of Clinton was formed in 1839, the name was changed to *The Clintonian*. At the close of the campaign of 1840, it was suspended. In a short time it was resuscitated, however, by Robert McCormick and J. B. G. Kinsloe—brother of the former—and the name changed to *Clinton County Whig*. Kinsloe soon went out, and was succeeded by I. B. Gara, who remained with McCormick for a short time. In 1843, W. P. Coulter and John W. Ross became the publishers. In the spring of 1845, Ross was alone, Coulter having retired. About the 1st of May, 1845, I. B. Gara took the paper again and continued it until the 6th of November, when he retired, and H. E. Shoemaker became the publisher, and continued till the 17th of October, 1847, when the press and materials were taken to Jersey Shore. In December, 1849, Adam J. Greer brought on a new establishment, and on the 26th of the same month issued the first number of a new paper, entitled *The Clinton Tribune*. He was assisted in its publication by H. E. Shoemaker. At the close of a year, Greer sold out to R. W. Rothrock, who continued the paper till the 6th of April, 1852, when Col. W. T. Wilson became a partner. On the 1st of September following, Rothrock retired, having disposed of his interest to his brother, W. P. Rothrock. Wilson conducted the paper till the 15th of February, 1853, when he sold out to C. Cather Flint, and his brother H. M. Flint, but the name of the former only appeared at the head of the paper. On the 18th of July, 1853, C. Cather Flint retired, and was succeeded by his brother, who continued the paper till the 10th of October, 1854, when he retired, followed by Daniel Bower, who continued a short time, when Thomas Martin came, and changed the name to *The Watchman*. Mr. Martin retired from the paper on the 3d of October, and was succeeded by D. S. Dunham.

The Clinton County Democrat was started by Wilbur & Shriner, in 1839 or '40, and continued a year or two. In 1843, it was revived by John R. Eck.

The Clinton Democrat was published till the fall of 1844, by S. S. Seely. In December of that year it passed into the hands of H. L. Dieffenbach, who, in June, 1845, united the two rival papers. On the first of January, 1850, he sold out to Geo. A. Crawford, who, at the end of one year, received Lyons Mussina as a partner. At the end of two years Crawford & Mussina were succeeded by Henry Frysinger, who continued two years, and then gave way to Atwood & Wilson, who also continued two years, and were succeeded on the 1st of January, 1856, by James W. McEwen, the present editor.

APPENDIX.

HISTORY

OF THE

NORTHUMBERLAND BAPTIST ASSOCIATION.

BY O. N. WORDEN.

It is believed there were some members of the Baptist denomination in the West Branch Valley, before the Revolution, emigrants from New Jersey, and the lower counties. In the Minutes of the Philadelphia Association for the year 1774, it is stated that "letters from well disposed persons in Tolbert, in Northumberland in the Province of Pennsylvania," were read, and it was "voted that Brothers David Sutton, William Worth and Elkana Holmes, are to visit the inhabitants of *Tolbert* township, at times to be fixed upon by themselves." In 1775, "supplies were granted to *Tolbert* township, Baltimore town, Oyster Bay," and other places.

We observe no further notice of Baptist labor in this region until 1792, when the same Association recommended that "Elders Patten, Clingan, and Vaughn, agree to travel for three months in the ensuing year, about Juniata and the West Branch of Susquehanna, to preach the Gospel to the destitute; and this Association recommend that a sufficient sum be subscribed by the Church, and paid immediately into the hands of Colonel Samuel Miles, to bear their expenses."

In 1794, the Association record that "A letter was received and read from the Church in Buffalo Valley, in Northumberland county, Pennsylvania, requesting to be received into this Association. Postponed, no messenger appearing to receive the right hand of fellowship."

In 1796, "a Church newly constituted at Shemokin (in 1794,) was received into the Association, and the Churches recommended to aid them in building a meeting house." That year, the Church reports 34 baptized, 8 received by letter, 1 deceased, 50 whole number—John Patten, pastor. In 1799, the Churches of the Association contributed $60 02 to "aid the Shemokin Church;" and the same year, 46 baptisms were reported, and a membership of 101, under Elder Patten's pastoral care.

It is supposed that "Tolbert," or "Talbert," and Turbut, are the same names, and that scattered through the then large township of Turbut, were several persons of Baptist sentiments. Some of them, it is known, were driven from the present township of Shamokin, back into "the Jersies" during the Revolution.

There were also a few Baptists, and preaching stations, in Buffalo Valley, after the Revolution, but whether a church was really formed there, (as would appear from the foregoing extract,) or whether those composing it were the same as immediately afterward organized in Shamokin, is not clear from the record. There is no knowledge of any Baptist church in what is now called

Buffalo Valley, until the formation of the Lewisburg church, in 1844.

The Shamokin church is the fruitful mother of most of the churches from Milton eastward, in Northumberland County.

In 1808, Elder Thomas Smiley, originally a Seceder from Virginia, organized some scattered Baptists into a church in White Deer Valley, Lycoming County, where he served for twenty-three years, until his death in 1832. His remains lie unmarked in the grave yard in front of the third meeting house built by this church. The church-book kept by Elder Smiley, is a repository of ecclesiastical and personal history, local and general, and from this source a considerable portion of the information contained in this article has been derived.

About 1817, a church was formed on the head waters of Little Muncy Creek, of which Elder Henry Clark, late of White Deer, was pastor, reporting 8 baptized, and 14 members in all. This church, with the White Deer, joined the Chemung Association, extending up the head waters of the Chemung river in New York State.

In 1820, the *Northumberland Baptist Association* was formed, comprising the Shamokin, White Deer, and Little Muncy churches, which had obtained letters of permission from their respective Associations for that purpose. They convened in a meeting-house in Moreland township, Lycoming County, and for the benefit of those who are curious in such matters, as well as for future reference, we have thought proper to subjoin the following table, giving the names of the churches, and the delegates or messengers from each church present at the organization of the Association:

Churches.	Messengers.	Baptized.	Rec. by Let.	Dis. by Let.	Excluded.	Deceased.	Total.
Shamokin.	John Woolverton,	3	0	3	2	0	84
	John Moore.						
	Charles Saxton.						
	Isaac Woolverton.						
	David Kelly.						
	Gideon Chamberlain.						
White Deer.	Thomas Smiley,	0	0	0	0	1	14
	John Lewis.						
	John Oakes.						
	Philip Gibbon.						
Little Muncy.	Henry Clark,	3	3	0	0	0	26
	Silas E. Shepard.						
	James Moore.						
	Richard Demutt.						
	James Halit.						
	Powel Bird.						
		6	3	3	2	1	124

The progress of the Association, since its organization thirty-six years ago, in that then wild part of the country, may be inferred from the following condensed tabular summary, which has been carefully compiled from its Annual Minutes, and which may be relied upon for correctness. The table, upon examination, will be found to embody much valuable information, and may be interesting to those members of the Baptist persuasion who are anxious to post themselves up in the statistics of their Church:

YEAR.	Where held.	Preacher Introductory Sermon.	Moderator.	Stated Clerk.	New Churches.	Whole No. Churches.	Baptized.	Whole No. Members.
1821	Moreland,	Thomas Smiley,	Thomas Smiley,	Thomas Smiley,	....	3	6	124
1822	Shamokin,	Silas E. Shepard,	Do.	Do.	....	3	9	125
1823	White Deer,	Thomas Smiley,	Do.	Do.	....	3	14	128
1824	Moreland,	Silas E. Shepard,	Do.	Do.	....	3	6	120
1825	Shamokin,	Thomas Smiley,	Do.	Do.	Loyal Sock,..............	4	4	133
1826	White Deer,	John Miller,	Do.	Do.	....	4	3	120
1827	Washingtonville,	(None.)	Eugenio Kincaid,	Do.	Milton,..................	5	8	135
1828	Shamokin,	Thomas Smiley,	Isaac Woolverton,	Do.	....	5	3	132
1829	White Deer,	Joseph Mathias,	Emanuel Rogers,	Do.	....	5	29	154
1830	Washingtonville,	Thomas Smiley,	Thomas Smiley,	Do.	Clinton,.................	5	26	172
1831	Shamokin,	Do.	Zophar D. Pasco,	Do.	....	6	41	221
1832	Milton,	Dr. Geo. Spratt,	James Moore, Sr.,	Do.	Jersey Shore,............	7	22	267
1833	White Deer,	J. G. Collom,	Samuel Rogers,	Samuel Rogers,	....	7	39	294
1834	Clinton,	E. M. Barker,	Do.	Do.	....	7	74	350
1835	Madison,	Geo. Higgins,	Geo. Higgins,	Geo. Higgins,	....	7	51	374
1836	Jersey Shore,	Thos. B. Brown,	Do.	Do.	....	7	75	449
1837	Shamokin,	Geo. Higgins,	Do.	Do.	....	7	48	477
1838	Milton,	Geo. M. Spratt,	Daniel C. Wait,	Robert Dunbar,	Lock Haven,..............	8	139	622
1839	White Deer,	Geo. Higgins,	Geo. M. Spratt,	Geo. M. Spratt,	Rush,....................	9	84	677
1840	Clinton,	Daniel C. Wait,	Charles Tucker,	Do.	Minersville,.............	10	173	850
1841	Madison,	Collins A. Hewitt,	Daniel C. Wait,	James Moore, Jr.,	Union—Muncy,.............	12	82	899
1842	Jersey Shore,	Wm. S. Hall,	Charles Tucker,	Do.	North'd—Sunbury—Danville—Berwick,......	13	242	1092
1843	Rush,	Charles Tucker,	Collins A. Hewitt,	Do.	....	16	438	1483
1844	Muncy,	John S. Miller,	Eugenio Kincaid,	Wm. S. Hall,	Augusta—Lewisburg,.......	18	195	1637
1845	Shamokin,	Joel E. Bradley,	Joseph Moore,	John Budd,	....	18	110	1564
1846	Madison,	John Edminster,	Dr. Wm. H. Ludwig,	Joel E. Bradley,	Derry—Moreland,..........	20	135	1560
1847	White Deer,	A. A. Anderson,	Eugenio Kincaid,	Do.	....	20	71	1526
1848	Moreland.	John H. Worrell,	Wm. S. Hall,	Do.	....	20	102	1522
1849	Jersey Shore,	Wm. T. Bunker,	John H. Worrell,	Geo. W. Young,	Hughesville—Youngwomanstown,...........	22	100	1588
1850	Danville,	J. Green Miles,	J Green Miles,	Do.	....	22	193	1675
1851	Derry,	Geo. W. Young,	Wm. T. Bunker,	O. N. Worden,	Briar Creek,.............	23	97	1715
1852	Berwick,	E. W. Dickinson,	A. J. Collins,	Do.	....	23	224	1886
1853	Milton,	A. J. Collins,	Howard Malcom,	Do.	McEwensville,............	24	145	1961
1854	Lewisburg,	H. Essick,	James Moore, Jr.,	Do.	Laporte,.................	25	126	2028
1855	White Deer,	Geo. R. Bliss,	H. Essick,	Do.	Williamsport,............	26	129	2023
1856	Jersey Shore,	J. W. Hayhurst,	Joseph Moore,	Do.	Benton,..................	27	95	2078
							3338	

The Summary of Changes among the Membership for thirty-six years, is as follows:

Received	by Baptism,	3338
Do.	by Letter,	847
Do.	by Restoration,	113
Dismissed	by Letter,	1579
Excluded	or Erased,	651
Deceased,		318

The Association was an early and active advocate of special efforts for Revivals—of Temperance—of Foreign and Home Missionary enterprises—and of all means calculated to benefit the human family. The churches are nearly all supplied with houses of worship, yet have rarely been blessed with a "stated ministry" of long continuance. The instability of the pastoral relation, (from whatever cause,) and the constant losses by emigration to the westward, have caused the churches to be less efficient than the large numbers from time to time added to them by baptism, would seem to promise. No church formed within the bounds of the Association has become utterly extinct, although several are very feeble, and nearly half of them are without pastors.

SUMMARY HISTORY

OF THE

METHODIST EPISCOPAL CHURCH

IN THE

WEST BRANCH VALLEY.

By A. H. McHENRY.

At the close of the war of the Revolution, in which the West Branch Valley had become almost entirely depopulated, the people, upon receiving the joyful news of peace, began to make preparations to return, and re-possess the territory from which they had been driven by the Indians in 1777–8–9. They began to return in the autumn of 1784, and established themselves permanently in the West Branch, Bald Eagle, and Penn's Valleys; and subsequently in Nittany Valley.

At that early period, but little information is to be had respecting the formation of any church, or ministerial effort, amongst the people, in these respective valleys. I remember, some ten years since, of seeing the original manuscript of a subscription, dated 1784, the funds of which were—as set forth—for the support of a Presbyterian minister, to preach at Mahoning, (now Danville,) Warrior Run and Muncy. It was among the papers of Gen. William Montgomery, dec'd, and appeared to have been carried into effect. But as regards the Methodist Church, the first authentic information of their efforts to promote the Gospel in this region, is from the Minutes of the Conference held at Baltimore, May 6, 1791.* A new Circuit—with others in different parts—called Northumberland, was formed, and two preachers appointed, viz:—Richard Parriott and Lewis Browning. The county had previously been explored by the former without receiving or asking any compensation for his services or expenses. This Circuit, from the time of its formation, till 1806, extended over the following territory: From Wilkesbarre down the Valley of the North Branch to Northumberland—then up the West Branch, including White Deer Hole Valley, and up the Bald Eagle about four miles above Milesburg, and the same distance up Spring Creek from Bellefonte, to Penn's Valley, near, and south of Potter's Fort—thence by the old horse path to Buffalo Valley and Northumberland.

Each preacher traveled around this Circuit in four weeks, preaching every day except when the distance was too great, as from Penn's to Buffalo Valleys, thus supplying each appointment once in two weeks. During the first part of the year 1791, there was no regular preaching place from Northumberland to Lycoming Creek, which was at the house of Arad Sutton. This house, or a part of it, is yet standing on the east bank of Lycoming Creek, on the main road from Williamsport to Jersey Shore, and is now owned by Oliver Watson,

* This year was distinguished by the death of that eminent man of God, and founder of Methodism, the Rev. John Wesley—also, by the establishing of Methodism in Canada.

Esq., of the former place. At this place was formed the *first* society above Northumberland. After a lapse of sixty-five years, it would not be expected to find many of the members of that society living; yet two still survive, viz: Letitia Williams, of Montoursville, aged 82 years 1 month, and Rebecca Smith, of Lycoming township, aged 94½ years. She came to Lycoming in 1774. Mrs. Williams did not join the society till about 1795.

The names of the members of the first class are given entire, as follows:

James Bailey—Leader.	Eve Updegraff.
Rhoda Bailey.	Susanna Updegraff.
Amariah Sutton.	Hannah Sutton.*
Martha Sutton.	Rebecca Smith, (living.)
John Sutton.	Alexander Smith.
Dorothy Sutton.	Ebenezer Still.
Harman Updegraff.	Lois Still.

Letitia Williams, (living.)

Soon after the organization of this class, societies were formed at various other points. At Larry's Creek was one of the earliest above, or perhaps at a yet earlier time, Antes' on Bald Eagle.

In the month of August, 1806, a Camp Meeting was held on Chilisquaque Creek, half a mile from the river. This was the *first* Camp Meeting held in this section of the State.

I herewith give the names of the Preachers appointed from time to time, on the several Circuits and Stations, embracing the West Branch Valley.

* Died April, 1855, in Indiana, aged 94 years 4 months.

YEAR.	No. of Members. White.	Colored.
1791—Baltimore District, Northumberland Circuit—Richard Parriott, Lewis Browning, - -		
1791—Baltimore District—Nelson Reed, P. E. Northumberland Circuit—Richard Parriott, Lewis Browning, - - - - - - - -	250	
1792—Baltimore District—Nelson Reed, P. E. Northumberland Circuit—James Campbell, William Colbert, - - - - - - - - - -	170	1
1793—Wyoming District—Valentine Cook, P. E. Northumberland Circuit—James Campbell, James Paynter, - - - - - - - -	310	1
1794—Another change this year. The District was composed of Bristol, Chester, Lancaster, Northumberland and Wyoming. Valentine Cooke, P. E. Northumberland Circuit—Robert Manley, John Broadhead, - - - - - - - - -	310	3
1795—Wyoming, Tioga and Seneca District—Valentine Cook, P. E. Northumberland Circuit—James Ward, Stephen Timmons, - - - - -	260	1
1796—Philadelphia District—Thomas Ware, P. E. Northumberland Circuit—John Seward, Richard Sneath, - - - - - - - - -	264	2
1797—Philadelphia District—Thomas Ware, P. E. Northumberland Circuit—John Lackey, Daniel Higby, - - - - - - - - -	231	1
1798—Philadelphia District—Thomas Ware, P. E. Northumberland Circuit—John Lackey, John Leach, - - - - - - -	229	
1799—This year they were connected with Albany District—Wm. McLenahan, P. E. Wyoming and Northumberland connected, and three preachers formed a six weeks' circuit, viz.: James Moore, Benjamin Bidlack and Daniel Stevens. Northumberland 244 members, Wyoming 193.		
1800—Connected with Philadelphia, &c.—Joseph Everett, P. E. Northumberland and Wyoming, Ephraim Chambers, Edward Larkins and Asa Smith. Northumberland 215, Wyoming, - - -	190	

YEAR.	No. of Members. White.	Colored.
1801—This year, for the first time, the field was divided into regular and fixed districts.		
Philadelphia District—Joseph Everett, P. E.		
Northumberland Circuit—Johnson Dunham, Gilbert Carpenter, - - - - - - -	175	
1802—Philadelphia Conference, Philadelphia District, Northumberland Circuit—Anning Owen, Jas. Aikens, - - - - - - - - -	251	2
1803—Philadelphia Conference, Susquehanna District, Northumberland Circuit—Daniel Ryan, James Ridgeway, - - - - - - - - -	430	3
1804—Baltimore Conference, Susquehanna District—James Smith, P. E.		
Northumberland Circuit—Thomas Adams, Gideon Draper, - - - - - - - - -	400	2
1805—Baltimore Conference, Susquehanna District—Anning Owen, P. E.		
Northumberland Circuit—Christopher Fry, James Saunders, - - - - - - - - -	518	5
1806—Susquehanna District—Anning Owen, P. E.		
Northumberland Circuit—Robert Burch and John Swartzwelder, - - - - - - -	341	1
Lycoming—Timothy Lee, Jesse Pinnel, - -	522	8
1807—Baltimore Conference, Susquehanna District—Anning Owen, P. E.		
Northumberland Circuit—Nicholas Willis, Joel Smith, - - - - - - - -	430	1
Lycoming—James Charles, William Wolfe, -	530	10
1808—Philadelphia Conference, Susquehanna District—James Herron, P. E.		
Northumberland Circuit—Thomas Curren, John Rhodes, - - - - - - - -	532	
Lycoming—Anning Owen, Daniel Stansbury, -	553	14
1809—Philadelphia Conference, Susquehanna District—Gideon Draper, P. E.		
Northumberland District—Timothy Lee, Loring Grant, - - - - - - - - - -	586	
Lycoming—John Rhodes, Jacob Barnhart, -	557	14

YEAR.	No. of Members. White.	Colored.
1810—Genesee Conference, Susquehanna District—Gideon Draper, P. E.		
Northumberland District—Abraham Dawson, Isaac Puffer, - - - - - - -	622	
Lycoming—Timothy Lee, Samuel Ross, - -	428	
1811—Genesee Conference, Susquehanna District—Gideon Draper, P. E.		
Lycoming—George Thomas, Abraham Dawson,	472	2
Northumberland—B. G. Paddock, J. H. Baker, R. Lanning, - - - - - - -	588	1
1812—Genesee Conference, Susquehanna District—Geo. Harman, P. E.		
Lycoming—John Hazzard, James S. Lent, -	481	1
Shamokin—James H. Baker, James Hickcox,	189	
Northumberland—George Thomas, Ebenezer Doolittle, - - - - - - - - .	588	
1813—Genesee Conference, Susquehanna District—Geo. Harman, P. E.		
Lycoming—George Thomas, Israel Cook, -	480	
Shamokin—Abra. Dawson, Nathaniel Reeder,	183	
Northumberland–Joseph Kinkead, Israel Chamberlin, - - - - - - - - -	483	6
1814—Genesee Conference, Susquehanna District—Geo. Harman, P. E.		
Lycoming—Peter Jones, James Bennett, -	824	4
Shamokin—Marmaduke Pearce, - - -	152	
Northumberland—John Hazzard, Abraham Dawson, - - - - - . . -	467	2
1815—Genesee Conference, Susquehanna District—Marmaduke Pearce, P. E.		
Lycoming—John Thomas, Wyatt Chamberlain,	429	
Shamokin—Benjamin Bidlack, - - - -	159	
Northumberland—Renaldo M. Everetts, Israel Cook, - - - - - - - - - -	416	
1816—Susquehanna District—Marmaduke Pearce, P. E.		
Lycoming—Israel Chamberlain, Renaldo M. Everetts, - - - - - - -	420	1

YEAR.		No. of Members. White.	Colored.
	Shamokin—Benjamin Bidlack, - - - -	170	
	Northumberland—John Thomas, Alpheus Davis,	501	
1817—	Susquehanna District—Marmaduke Pearce, P. E.		
	Lycoming—John Thomas, John Rhodes, - -	407	10
	Shamokin—Abraham Dawson, - - - -	166	
	Northumberland—Benj. Bidlack, Peter Baker,	456	
1818—	Susquehanna District—Marmaduke Pearce, P. E.		
	Lycoming—John Rhodes, Benjamin Bidlack, -	413	6
	Shamokin—Israel Cook, - - - -	131	
	Northumberland — Gideon Lanning, Abraham Dawson, - - - - - - - -	422	
1819—	Susquehanna District—George Lane, P. E.		
	Lycoming—Israel Cook, Thomas McGee, -	413	6
	Shamokin—Elisha Bibins, - - - -	138	
	Northumberland—J. Rhodes, Darius Williams,	470	
1820—	Northumberland—John Rhodes, Israel Cook, -	551	
	Lycoming—John Thomas, Robert Menshall, -	481	
	Shamokin—Marmaduke Pearce, - - -	217	
1821—	Northumberland District, Baltimore Conference—Henry Smith, P. E.		
	Northumberland—Ma. Pearce, J. Thomas, -	551	
	Shamokin—John Rhodes, - - - -	280	
	Lycoming—Robt. Menshall, Jacob R. Shepperd,		
1822—	Northumberland District—Henry Smith, P. E.		
	Northumberland—J. Thomas, Mordecai Barry,	682	2
	Shamokin—John Rhodes, - - - -	300	
	Lycoming—Robert Caddon, William McDowell,	471	10
1823—	Northumberland District—Henry Smith, P. E.		
	Lycoming—Robert Cadden, Nathaniel Mills, Jno. Thomas, Sup., - - - - -	477	8
	Northumberland—Jacob R. Shepperd, Mordecai Barry, - - - - - - - -	600	1
	Shamokin—David Steel, - - - -	306	
1824—	Northumberland District—Henry Smith, P. E.		
	Lycoming—John Thomas, Thomas McGee, -	576	10
	Northumberland—R. Caddon, F. McCartney, R. Bond, - - - - - - - -	675	3
	Shamokin—Jacob R. Shepperd, - - -	307	

YEAR.	No. of Members. White.	Colored.
1825—Northumberland Dist.—Marmaduke Pearce, P. E.		
Bald Eagle—John Rhodes, (this year extended to Great Island.) - - - - - -	343	10
Lycoming—Thomas McGee, Francis McCartney, - - - - - - - - - -	644	13
Northumberland—Robt. Cadden, Rich'd Bond,	683	
Shamokin—John Thomas, - - - - -	287	
1826—Northumberland Dist.—Marmaduke Pearce, P. E.		
Shamokin—John Taneyhill, - - - -	266	
Northumberland—John Thomas, Geo. Hildt, -	691	3
Lycoming—Amos Smith, John Bowen, - -	580	12
(Bald Eagle changed to Bellefonte)—John Roads, - - - - - - - - -	346	6
1827—Northumberland Dist.—Marmaduke Pearce, P. E.		
Shamokin—Jonathan Munroe, - - - -	287	3
Northumberland—John Thomas, David Shaver,	657	3
Lycoming—John Bowen, Henry Tarring, -	706	8
Bellefonte—Amos Smith, Edward E. Allen -	364	11
1828—Northumberland Dist.—Marmaduke Pearce, P. E.		
Shamokin—Henry Tarring, - - - - -	316	3
Northumberland—Chas. Kalbus, Wm. James,	660	2
Lycoming—Edward E. Allen, Robt. Kemp, -	708	10
Bellefonte—Amos Smith, David Shaver, -	402	16
1829—Northumberland District—David Steele, P. E.		
Shamokin—Edward E. Allen, - - - -	340	3
Northumberland—James W. Dunahay, Josiah Forest, - - - - - - - - -	820	
Lycoming—William Prettyman, Charles Kalbus, - - - - - - - - -	692	7
Bellefonte—S. Ellis, James H. Brown, - -	450	6
1830—Northumberland District—David Steel, P. E.		
(Shamokin changed to Sunbury,) Josiah Forest, - - - - - - - - - - -	423	5
Northumberland—James W. Dunahay, Alfred B. Eskridge, - - - - - - -	1030	
Lycoming—William Prettyman, James H. Brown, - - - - - - - - -	776	17
Bellefonte—Isaac Collins, Oliver Ega, - -	549	9

YEAR.		No. of Members. White.	Colored.
1831	Northumberland District—David Steel, P. E.		
	Sunbury—Oliver Ega, James H. Brown,	455	2
	Northumberland—David Shaver,	273	
	Lycoming—James W. Dunahay, William Evans,	676	20
	Bellefonte—Samuel Bryson, A. Brittain,	566	9
	[A new circuit taken off Northumberland this year, and called Berwick.]		
1832	Northumberland District—David Steel, P. E.		
	Sunbury—Wesley Howe, J. Clark,	530	3
	Northumberland—M. Pearce, Josiah Forest,	611	
	Lycoming—D. Shaver, John R. Tallentyre,	521	10
	Bellefonte—S. Ellis, James Sanks,	656	7
1833	Northumberland District—William Prettyman, P. E.		
	Sunbury—Thomas Taneyhill, John R. Tallentyre,	530	3
	Northumberland—Josiah Forest, J. Reed, jr.,	611	
	Lycoming—S. Ellis, Oliver Ega,	521	10
	Bellefonte—R. Barnes, James Sanks,	656	7
1834	Northumberland District—William Prettyman, P. E.		
	Sunbury—Thomas Taneyhill, John Guyer,	473	
	Northumberland—Henry Tarring, Oliver Ega,	624	
	Lycoming—James Sanks, Joseph S. Lee,	587	15
	Bellefonte—David Shaw, J. Forest,	715	3
1835	Northumberland District—William Prettyman, P. E.		
	Sunbury—Oliver Ega, J. Anderson,	436	
	Northumberland—Henry Tarring, John Guyer, R. Beers, T. Myers,	627	
	Lycoming—James Sanks, S. Ellis,	518	16
	Bellefonte—J. Forest, A. G. Chenowith,	558	4
1836	Northumberland District—William Prettyman, P. E.		
	Sunbury—Oliver Ega, G. C. Gibbons	536	3
	Northumberland—Charles Kalbus, J. T. Chaney,	644	

YEAR.	No. of Members. White.	Colored.
Lycoming—Thomas Taneyhill, Isaac T. Stratton,	589	17
Bellefonte—John Rhodes, Thomas Myers,	560	3
1837—Northumberland District—John Miller, P. E.		
Sunbury—Henry G. Dill, Charles E. Brown,	531	3
Northumberland—Charles Kalbus, John Hall,	460	
Lycoming—Thomas Taneyhill, Isaac T. Stratton,	590	11
Bellefonte—John Rhodes, R. W. H. Brent,	581	1
1838—Northumberland District—John Miller, P. E.		
Sunbury—Henry G. Dill, John W. Haughawaut,	494	
Northumberland—James Sanks, Isaac T. Stratton,	531	
Lycoming—James Ewing, George L. Brown	647	11
Bellefonte—Thomas Taneyhill, George Guyer,	540	1
1839—Northumberland District—John Miller, P. E.		
Sunbury—John Rhodes, William Hirst,		
Northumberland—James Sanks, Isaac T. Stratton,	580	
Lycoming—James Ewing, George Guyer,	694	12
Bellefonte—Thomas Taneyhill, George Bergstresser,	552	
1840—Northumberland District—John Miller, P. E.		
Sunbury—John Rhodes, John Ball,	554	
Northumberland—Thomas Taneyhill, William Hirst,	611	2
Lycoming—Charles Kalbus, John W. Haughawaut,	794	10
Bellefonte—William Butler, S. V. Blake,	723	2
1841—Northumberland District—George Hildt, P. E.		
Sunbury—John Ball, Gideon H. Day,	550	
Northumberland—Thomas Taneyhill, James W. Miles,*	411	5

*James W. Miles remained but a short time. About the month of July, Northumberland and Milton were again united, and were supplied the balance of this year, (1842,) by Taneyhill, Brown, and Hirst.

YEAR.		No. of Members. White.	Colored.
	Lycoming—Robert T. Nixen,* John W. Haughawaut - - - - - - -	915	10
	Bellefonte—William Butler, Elisha D. Owen,	829	10
	Milton—John Bowen, William Hirst,		
1842—	Northumberland District—George Hildt, P. E.		
	Sunbury—George Bergstresser, Wm. S. Baird,	640	
	Northumberland—James Ewing, William R. Mills, - - - - - - - - -	564	1
	Lycoming—George Guyer, Ephraim McCollom,	574	9
	[March of this year, the Lycoming circuit was divided at *Quenishachshachki* creek, (near Linden,) and the new circuit called West Branch. It took in Nippenose valley, Wayne township, Dunnsburg, and up Pine creek to the First Fork. In 1843, it was extended up this Fork as far as English Centre.]		
	West Branch—William Hirst, I. H. Torrence,	713	
	Bellefonte—Francis M. Mills, W. T. D. Clemm,	794	3
	Milton—John Bowen, Thomas M. Reese, -	527	5
1843—	Northumberland District—George Hildt, P. E.		
	Sunbury—Alem Brittan, Jacob Montgomery,	626	1
	Northumberland—James Ewing, W. T. D. Clemm, - - - - - - - - -	515	
	Milton—George Guyer, George A. Coffey, -	515	
	West Branch—William Hirst, James Guyer, -	647	
	Bellefonte—F. M. Mills, Ephraim McCollom,	772	2
	Lycoming—John Bowen, W. R. Mills, - -	612	9
1844—	Northumberland District—George Hildt, P. E.		
	Sunbury—Alem Brittan, John W. Tongue, -	609	
	Northumberland—B. H. Crever, James Guyer,	482	3
	Milton—George Guyer, Alfred Wiles, - -	517	
	[March, 1844, Lycoming Circuit was again divided at Loyal Sock, and the new circuit called Williamsport. It extended westward as far as Newberry, and northward as far as Ralston, on Lycoming Creek, and southward to Bald Eagle Mountain.]		

* In July of this year, R. T. Nixen left the circuit, on account of ill health, and George Guyer was appointed to supply his place.

YEAR.		No. of Members. White.	Colored.
	Williamsport—John Bowen, - - - -	280	
	Lycoming—J. A. Ross, John J. Pearce, -	430	
	West Branch*—Thomas Tancyhill, S. G. Hare,	580	
	[March, 1844, Bellefonte Circuit was divided at a point in Nittany Valley, about three miles below Washington Furnace, and at Mill Hall, in Bald Eagle Valley, and the new circuit called Lock Haven. It included the east part of Nittany and Bald Eagle Valleys to the mouth of Bald Eagle Creek, and the West Branch Valley from Lock Port on the east, and westward to and including Cook's Run; also including Kettle Creek Valley.]		
	Lock Haven—W. R. Mills, John W. Elliott,	274	1
1845	—Northumberland District—Samuel Bryson, P. E.		
	Sunbury—John W. Haughawaut, Jacob S. McMurray, - - - - . - -	555	1
	Northumberland—B. H. Crever, N. S. Buckingham, - - - - - - -	414	
	Milton—Alem Brittan, E. F. Busey, - -	518	
	Williamsport—Mayberry Goheen, - - -	281	2
	Lycoming—J. A. Ross, John W. Elliott, -	475	
	Jersey Shore—Thomas Taneyhill, J. W. Tongue,	580	
	Lock Haven—P. B. Reese, (no report.)		
1846	—Northumberland District—Samuel Bryson, P. E.		
	Sunbury—J. W. Haughawaut, Thos. Barnhart,	510	1
	Northumberland—P. B. Reese, J. J. Pearce, -	440	1
	Milton—Alem Brittan, J. W. Tongue, - -	520	
	Williamsport—Mayberry Goheen, - - -	310	2
	Lycoming—James Ewing, W. L. Murphy, -	440	
	Jersey Shore—Joseph A. Ross, Chas. Maclay,	855	
	Lock Haven—John Stine, - - - -	350	
1847	—Northumberland District—Samuel Bryson, P. E.		
	Sunbury—Peter McEnally, H. Huffman, -	458	1
	Northumberland—W. R. Mills, J. W. Elliott,	440	
	Milton—H. G. Dill, J. J. Pearce, - - -	456	
	Williamsport—John Guyer, Charles Maclay, -	410	
	Jersey Shore—Joseph A. Ross, N. S. Buckingham, - - - - - - -	795	

* On the 19th of August, 1844, the name was changed to Jersey Shore.

YEAR.		No. of Members. White.	Colored
	Lock Haven—J. W. Haughawaut, - -	345	3
	Lycoming—James Ewing, - - - -	492	
1848—	Northumberland District—Samuel Bryson, P. E.		
	Sunbury—James Ewing, J. P. Simpson, -	491	
	Northumberland—J. S. Lee, S. A. Wilson, -	446	
	Milton—H. G. Dill, B. B. Hamline, - -	447	
	Lycoming—John Stine, Thomas Barnhart, -	359	
	Williamsport—John Guyer, Charles Maclay, -	430	
	Jersey Shore—S. L. M. Conser, I. H. Torrence,	667	
	Lock Haven—J. W. Haughawaut, - - -	334	
1849—	Northumberland District—John A. Gere, P. E.		
	Sunbury—James Ewing, William Gwynn, -	705	
	Northumberland—J. S. Lee, B. B. Hamline, -	452	
	Milton—M. G. Hamilton, David Castleman, -	552	1
	Lycoming—John Stine, - - - -	366	
	Williamsport—H. G. Dill, Samuel Wilson, -	385	2
	Jersey Shore—John Guyer, Thomas Barnhart,	616	
	Lock Haven—I. H. Torrence, - - -	423	
1850—	Northumberland District—John A. Gere, P. E.		
	Sunbury—John Stine, William Gwynn, - -	683	
	Northumberland—S. L. M. Conser, H. W. Bellman, - - - - - - - -	341	2
	Milton—M. G. Hamilton, (Station,)* - -	160	
	Lewisburg—John Guyer, (Station,)* - -		
	Lycoming—Thomas Taneyhill, Justus A. Melick, - - - - - - - -	460	
	Williamsport—H. G. Dill, A. M. Barnitz, -	436	2
	Milton—John Moorhead, - - - -	300	
	Jersey Shore—G. H. Day, Thomas Barnhart, -	687	
	Pine Creek—W. E. Buckingham, - - -	220	
	Lock Haven—I. H. Torrence, A. T. Ewing, -	416	

* This year, these two Stations were connected with Huntingdon District, of which T. H. W. Monroe was Presiding Elder.

YEAR.	Members.	Prob.
1851—Northumberland District—John A. Gere, P. E.		
Sunbury—John Stine, Albert Hartman, -	450	100
Northumberland—S. L. M. Conser, - -	299	81
Lewisburg Station—John Guyer, - - -	159	66
Milton Station—P. B. Reese, - - -	175	92
Milton Circuit—John Moorhead, W. E. Clark,	342	43
Lycoming—Name changed to Muncy.		
Muncy—Thomas Taneyhill, F. M. Slusser, -	327	43
Williamsport—Thompson Mitchell, B. B. Hamline, - - - - - - - - -	378	54
Jersey Shore—G. H. Day,* B. H. Crever, -	511	43
Pine Creek—John H. C. Dosh, W. E. Buckingham, - - - - - - - - -	149	47
Lock Haven—Joseph G. McKeehan, H. W. Bellman, - - - - - - - -	406	73
1852—Northumberland District—John A. Gere, P. E.		
Sunbury—Jos. A. Ross, T. M. Goodfellow, -	346	112
Northumberland—John Moorhead, F. M. Slusser,	319	
Lewisburg Station—S. L. M. Conser - -	190	90
Milton Circuit—John Stine, Joshua Kelly, -	331	95
Milton Station—P. B. Reese, - - -	214	16
Muncy Circuit—Jos. S. Lee, J. Y. Rothrock,	320	80
Williamsport Station—Thompson Mitchell, B. B. Hamline, - - - - - - -	392	37
Jersey Shore—B. H. Crever, J. J. Pearce, -	494	119
Pine Creek—J. H. C. Dosh, W. C. Gantt, -	180	60
Lock Haven—I. G. McKeehan, A. G. Murlatt,	377	66
1853—Northumberland Dist.—Thos. B. Sargent, P. E.		
Sunbury—Jos. A. Ross, - - - -	500	42
Northumberland—Thos. Barnhart, J. Y. Rothrock, - - - - - - - -	287	191
Lewisburg Station—S. L. M. Conser, - -	239	60
Milton Station—J. S. McMurray, - - -	203	5
Milton Circuit—John Stine, S. Barnes, - -	371	55

* About the 1st of May, Mr. Day was appointed General Agent for Dickinson Seminary, at Williamsport, and immediately entered upon the duties of his appointment; and B. H. Crever became preacher in charge, and J. J. Pearce preacher of the Jersey Shore Circuit.

YEAR.		Members.	Prob.
	Muncy—T. H. Switzer, E. Eakle, - - .	350	30
	Williamsport Station—J. France,* - - -	237	6
	Newberry—Jos. S. Lee, Thos. Sherlock, - -	330	39
	Jersey Shore Station—P. B. Reese, - -	204	38
	New Liberty—John H. C. Dosh, - - -	172	23
	Pine Creek—I. G. McKeehan, - - -	107	3
	Lock Haven—J. J. Pearce, W. C. Gantt, -	404	15
	[In March, a new District was formed, called Bellefonte, taken from Northumberland and Huntingdon Districts. There were included within this District, three Circuits, and one Station, that were nearly all within the West Branch Valley, viz.:—Pine Creek, Lock Haven, Great Island, or New Liberty, and Jersey Shore Station.]		
1854—	Northumberland Dist.—Thos. B. Sargent P. E.		
	Northumberland—Thos. Barnhart, - - -	371	48
	Sunbury—J. G. McKeehan, James Curns, -	450	9
	Lewisburg Station—Benjamin B. Hamline, -	230	30
	Milton Station—J. S. McMurray, - - -	181	3
	Milton Circuit—Thos. Taneyhill, C. C. Maybee,	345	45
	Muncy—T. H. Switzer, Samuel Barnes, - -	314	30
	Williamsport Station—John Stine, - - -	260	40
	Newberry— J. S. Lee, J. Y. Rothrock, - -	359	36
1854—	Bellefonte Dist.—John Poisal, P. E.		
	Jersey Shore—John W. Elliott, - - -	208	14
	Great Island—George Warren, - - -	172	38
	Lock Haven—Justus A. Melick, - - -	365	78
1855—	Northumberland Dist.—T. B. Sargent, P. E.		
	Sunbury—J. G. McKeehan, B. P. King, -	424	79
	Northumberland—Joseph A. Ross, . -	130	90
	Lewisburg—B. B. Hamline, - - - -	229	19
	Milton Station—Franklin Dyson, - - -	155	25
	Milton Circuit—Thos. Taneyhill, - - -	335	24
	Muncy—Joshua Kelly, Thos. Sherlock, - -	340	48
	Williamsport Station—John Stine, - -	275	12
	Newberry—J. S. McMurray, C. C. Maybee, -	342	62

*In the month of September, of this year, the health of Mr. France failed, and his place was filled the balance of the year by Edward E. Allen.

YEAR.	Members.	Prob.
1855—Bellefonte Dist.—John Poisal, P. E.		
Jersey Shore—John W. Elliott, - - -	178	12
Pine Creek—Albert Hartman, W. M. Showalter, - - - - - - - - -	91	24
Great Island—George Warren, - - -	181	34
Lock Haven—J. Melick, T. A. Gotwalt, -	344	18

BOUNDARIES OF SOME OF THE OLD CIRCUITS, &c.

In 1806, Lycoming Circuit embraced all of that part of Northumberland Circuit west, and south, of the town of Northumberland.

In 1812, Shamokin Circuit embraced all the territory east of the Susquehanna to the Broad Mountains, south to Mahantongo Creek, and north to Nescopeck Creek.

In 1815, Bald Eagle Circuit was formed out of the Lycoming Circuit west of Beech Creek, and in 1825 it was extended east to the Great Island.

About 1827, Northumberland Circuit was extended west, taking from Lycoming Circuit all the territory to Muncy Hills, north of the river, and all that south to the mouth of White Deer Creek.

About the close of the year 1831, another part was taken from Lycoming, and added to Northumberland, taking in Washington and Clinton townships, Lycoming County.

Having pursued the progress of the Church for a period of sixty-five years,—from May 1791, the time of the organization of the Northumberland Circuit, with two preachers—we find in March, 1856, the same territory divided into twenty-five Charges, viz:—18 Circuits, 6

Stations, and 1 Mission, with a membership of 7170 in full connection, 1063 on probation, and 11 colored members, making a grand total of 8244, with 43 travelling or stationed preachers.

The membership, in what is denominated the West Branch Valley, from Sunbury to Lock Haven, in March, 1856, was as follows: 3223 members, 21 preachers, including 1 Presiding Elder, with 37 Churches.

The Indian Hunter of the Susquehanna.

The following interesting sketch, of some of the adventures of Capt. Brady, was originally published in the *Blairsville Appalachian*. The manuscript was found among the papers of a near relative of Brady, and is the narrative of Peter Grove, an ancient hunter and ranger of the Susquehanna, detailing a series of thrilling enterprises against the Indians by Brady, in which he participated. Their adventures extended through the present counties of Huntingdon, Clearfield, Centre, Lycoming, Clinton, and Union.

The incidents are related in so probable and likely a manner, that there can be but little doubt of their actual occurrence. No dates are given, but it is quite likely that the year following Broadhead's expedition up the Alleghany river may be assumed.

It will be observed that Peter is fond of repeating the name "Sam," and uses it with unnecessary frequency. But the person who copied the manuscript for the press, did not feel at liberty to alter or vary from the original, except in the arrangement of paragraphs, (the original consists of one,) correction of errors in spelling, and, in a few instances, supplying a word where it was evidently required to perfect the sense, and had been omitted through mistake.

ADVENTURES OF CAPT. SAMUEL BRADY.

A Story as related by Peter Grove, a man well known for his bravery as a Warrior and Hunter, on the Susquehanna, at an early day.

The old gentleman says, at one time when Grove called at my house for refreshment, after four weeks' hunt up the river, I persuaded him to remain over night, which he did with a good deal of reluctance. His character was to be moving to nightfall, then it made no difference to Grove where he was.

In that evening's conversation, I inquired of him if he had ever seen Captain Samuel Brady, of the Rangers. He rose from his seat; his eyes glistened with pleasure. His countenance evinced to me I had struck a string on which he liked to dwell. He replied, "Oh, yes!—Poor Sam is dead, so they tell me," and seated himself, his countenance changing to a cast or two past its natural gravity, to gloom and deep thoughtfulness.

After meditating for a short time, he cast his eyes around the room, with quickness, arose, put up his rifle, which was standing in the corner, placed it on the hooks, walked to the door, called up his dogs, gave them some food, and bade them go back to the canoe, which command they promptly obeyed. He then returned to the fire, then stirring it up, got his blanket and spread it upon the floor, and rested upon it with peculiar composure. "Yes," said he, "Mr. Porter, I *have* seen Sam, (so I always called him, except in the presence of strange officers.) I could tell you many of Sam's exploits, but one or two will suffice for the present evening. It gives me great pleasure to relate these things to a man that appears to take interest in our welfare.

The day was, when we were all as brothers along these waters. I see a change, but I shall not long have to witness these unfriendly habits.

"I was well acquainted with John Brady, who was killed at Wolf Run—the father of Sam. Also with all the boys. John, the brother of Sam, was wounded at Brandywine, fighting by the side of his father, at the age of sixteen. James was killed by the Indians, and after the murder of Sam's father and brother, there was ugly play between the Bradys and their friends, and the Indians.

"There was an uncle of Capt. Sam's whose name was also Sam Brady; and to distinguish them we called him 'Uncle Sam.' He was a man of the largest size, and of great activity; a great friend to liberty, and he proved it, for many a red coat he gave a deeper dye; and many a lowering savage he laid low.

"It was him that taught the boys in their youth, to run, jump, swim, shoot, and all exercises that he thought would be of use, in case the storm would burst that was then gathering over our country. It *did burst*, and Uncle Sam's country was rewarded for his pains, in the service of his nephews.

"Brave Uncle Sam!—long may you live! for you were a protector to the unprotected!

"I had been up through Pennsylvania on a hunt and lookout, and I discovered Indian signs; and, from what I saw, was convinced that there were Indians between the West Branch (of the Susquehanna) and the Juniata river. I returned with all speed to Buffalo, (valley we presume,) to communicate to Captain J. Foster and others, my suspicions, that the Indians were working around us.

"On my way down I had discovered a man's track, at different times, which astonished me, for I had taken a route I thought no man would have travelled, red or white, except *one*, and he was far distant west of Alleghany.

"I observed the size of the track, and the length of the step—a thought struck me. But it could not be!

"I found after I got into the valley, and on the path, that the traveller ahead had deviated from his path, which gave me great uneasiness, and caused me to quit the path and take another route through the woods.

"I called on Capt. John Foster, and informed him of the discovery I had made. His countenance was fired in an instant. He was a brave, strong, and active man, ever ready to perform his duty. His rifle was a fatal one to the enemies of his country. I have seen it so in many instances.

"The Captain observed to me, 'Peter! Peter! I fear there has been sad work west of the mountains. The tracks you saw on the path coming down, must have been the tracks of one of Brady's Rangers.' 'No, Captain,' I replied, 'there is no man living who would have taken the route I did, but Sam, himself.' 'They could have travelled it by his direction,' said the Captain. 'No, never,' I replied. 'Well, well, Peter! we will not differ long; to-morrow we will know. So go to the top of the ridge, and discharge your rifle three times. They (i. e. Foster's spies) will collect in a short time.'

'I did as I was directed; and in a short time twenty of our men made their appearance. The Captain informed them of the discovery I had made, so far as related to the Indian signs, but nothing in relation to his apprehensions about the West. After he had given them their orders to keep strict watch about their houses, for the night, and to be ready to march in the morning, at a moment's warning, he dismissed them for the night.

"When they were gone, the Captain observed to me, 'Peter, we must go to the Widow Brady's, and I think we will there find one of the brave fellows from the Allleghany river.

"When we approached the house, our path was crossed by a man, whom the Captain hailed in a low tone of voice. The man advanced to us—but what was our surprise to find in him the brave Sam Brady.

"Our surprise I have not language to tell you. He accoutred as a hunter—his blanket on his back. He had just arrived; having been detained by avoiding the path, and hearing the shots I had fired so soon after my arrival at Foster's.

"He and the Captain walked aside, and after a moment's absence, returned, and we made the best of our way back.

"I observed to Sam, 'will you go to see your mother and children?' 'No, Peter,' said he, 'I understand they are well yet, and for their preservation I must be off.' This brought tears to my eyes, and I cannot now relate it without weeping. To think of the hardships he had undergone, of his long absence, and widowed mother—her little, fatherless flock, who had been made so by the merciless savages, during his absence. Yes, sir, these scenes are now forgotten by many, but they are yet fresh in my memory; and while my heart beats, I cannot forget them.

"We travelled back in silence, save that our brave Captain Foster's feelings gave way, and he moaned aloud. When we got into the house, 'Weep not, brethren,' observed Sam to us, 'It is better that my mother and the family should be ignorant of my being in this part of the country, for by to-morrow's dawn we must be off, at least I, and one man, with your permission, Captain.' 'Give us the news, first, from the West,' replied Captain Foster, stepping up to Sam, and laying his hand on his shoulder. 'And tell me,' says I, 'how old Uncle Sam is—or is he yet alive?' 'Yes, Peter,' said Sam, 'and spoiling a great many countenances in that part of the country.' 'We seldom hear of him,' I said, 'since you got a command.' 'You know, Peter,' said Sam, 'he always goes in a gang by himself, and picks those whom he knows to be leaders. You wish to have news. I have none, but that we are fighting whenever we meet, and we generally beat them.'

"The Indians have disappeared of late to the number of one hundred and fifty. They have some grand project in view; and my opinion is, it is a descent on this part of the country. This is a conjecture of my own, and has caused me to cross the mountains at this time.—They have been informed of men having been drawn off from this section of the country; and, by quitting the Alleghany in small parties, they expect to surprise you, and disappoint us. I crossed the trail of thirty west of the Mountains; I crossed it again near the Standing Stone, and on this side of the Juniata. I am convinced of their leading to the 'Bald Eagle's Nest,' but they must now be on the waters of the Juniata, hunting, and refreshing themselves.

"The party I trailed is headed by two brothers—young warriors of uncommon skill and bravery. I believe they were both present at the murder of my friends, and they have sworn vengeance against me and my kindred. Since I was here, Uncle Sam and I have caused their nation to bleed in its most vital parts.

"The Panther and the Blacksnake, who are the leaders of the party nearest us, are men of uncommon strength and action—first-rate rifle shots, that seldom fail at two hundred yards. The Panther and the Blacksnake *shall never taste the waters of the Alleghany again!*

"Two weeks before my departure for this part of the country, I was dogging them, and lay so close to their fires as to witness them go through the tragic scenes of my father's and brother's death. This induced me to think they were engaged in those murders. On the night I mentioned, I had determined to send the Panther to another world, but a squaw placed herself by his side with a papoose in her arms, and in such a position that I should have sent them along as company. But no blood but that of a warrior shall ever stain my skirts. It was hard to let them slip, for he boasted in his dance that the day would come when he would dance the death of Uncle Sam and I. So I determined he should fall by my hand. The Blacksnake danced the Susquehanna murders, and vaunted the exploits he would perform on his next visit. The death of my mother and children was threatened; after which I would weep through the woods, and he would take me prisoner; and how he would triumph over me.

"Blacksnake!—the day is not far distant when you shall coil around the pit of your own stomach, and vomit blood for the wolf and panther to roll upon!"

"Sam cast his eyes upward, and with devotion I never before witnessed, called upon God who had preserved his kindred and neighbors, to look down with an eye of mercy upon our devoted country. 'My brethren,' said he, 'it is in Him alone I confide for the preservation of our country. It appears to me Government has given us up as unworthy of its protection.'

"'No, Captain,' replied Foster, 'Gen. Potter says that in a conversation he had with Gen. Washington, respecting the frontiers; Gen. Washington remarked 'you have *an army* in Captain Sam Brady and his Rangers.'"

"'I hope,' replied Sam, 'they have a devotion not excelled by any now combating for the rights of man. Oh! may Liberty blossom! Her roots shall be watered by crimson streams! Her branches may yet flourish in the wilderness! Future generations may enjoy the fruits of our labors, and our names live in the memory of our countrymen. We have a warfare never before witnessed. Degenerate Britons! why do you excite a savage people to acts that must draw upon them the vengeance of the living God!'

"We made the necessary preparations that night; Sam and I were to march as soon as he thought best.

"Before we lay down, he asked me for my rifle. 'Is she good, Peter?' 'Yes—no better.' 'Who owns the gun I heard the reports of, this evening?' 'You have her in your hand.' 'She will do,' says Sam, handing her back to me.

"We lay down, and Sam soon fell into a sound sleep, but I could not rest.

"About two hours before day, Sam sprang to his feet with the nimbleness of a cat, crying 'Arise, Peter, we must be off.'

"Captain Foster bounced from his bed, with the force of a horse. 'You come down heavy, Captain,' says I. 'It is the way I awake my family,' says he. And it was not long till we had a proof of their early rising.—Our breakfast was on the table in a crack; and a part of our treat was a cup of coffee—a thing which Sam had not tasted for six months. It made him speak; he had been silent from the time he bade me arise, till we had placed ourselves around the hospitable board of our humane and gallant Captain Foster.

"I observed Sam's countenance had a smile upon it. 'You look pleased,' said I. 'And I am pleased,' said he, 'that you have yet some of the comforts of life with you in this country.

"'They are few,' observed Foster, 'but while we have them, we will not deny ourselves. I hope the day is not far distant when comforts will abound in this land; and though we may not live to see it, I trust in God our children will. Then, with the fullest confidence in His Providential care, let us thank him for what we have.'

"After we rose from the table, the Captains laid their plans. They were to be secret with us. Sam and I were to go and kill some meat, and have it collected for the party, at a run in Penn's Valley, called Elk run; also at Spruce-Creek, or a place called 'The Clear Fountains.'

"Foster was to start, after two days, with fifteen men, and send the remainder up the river as far as the mouth of the Bald Eagle.

"Our arrangements being completed, we bade the little flock farewell. I observed that when Sam bade the lady of the house to be kind to his mother, he wept. And he wept not alone, for our hearts sympathized with his, and we all with one voice called on God to be a husband to the widow, and a father to the fatherless.

"I bounced out of the door, and got into the path.—

Sam sprang from the door to the middle of the enclosure, and from thence over the fences into the path before me. I do believe the fence was eight feet high. He could spring like a panther, and run like a buck.

"We got to Elk Run in time to dress a deer apiece. The next morning we killed five, and moved off in time to reach the Fountains that day. Here we hung up some meat, after which we took the scout.

"We soon found 'signs' after we got to the Juniata hills. We were to return to the Fountains and let Foster know, as soon as we had discovered the lurking places of the Indians.

"When at our fire at night, Sam related to me some astonishing feats performed by him and his men. It was seldom he would speak of himself—he left that for others. He took great pleasure in relating the hair-breadth escapes of his brave companions.

"One evening while at rest, we were disturbed by the screams of a panther. I wanted to go and kill it, but Sam told me, 'Peter, beware of that fellow—*I have heard his screams west of the mountains!*'

"He covered what little fire we had, and told me to follow him. We slipped through the woods in a different direction from where the panther was, and on the top of the ridge lay down. Sam slept sound until his usual time of awaking, which was about the time I generally fell asleep. But sleep was far from my eyes, which he discovered. 'Peter,' said he, 'you are alarmed at the hints I gave you yesterday and last night.' (We had found some meat of a very fat deer, and I wanted to take a piece to cook for supper; but he forbid me, saying, never touch *their* meat.) 'If you had eaten their meat, you never would have seen this morning's sun rise. I lost two brave fellows—young men who had come on, voluntarily, to join us; they were from Virginia. In my precautions to them, I neglected to charge them respecting the danger in eating the meat hung up by the Indians. It is a contrivance of the warrior Wamp, who is with this party. It would have proved a fatal thing to us, had I not discovered its effects on one of their own dogs, and two wild cats that I found lying dead by the meat that they had hung up.'

"'Blast me,' said I, 'but I will Wamp him to the d—l, if ever I get my eyes on him.' 'We will see, then, to-night,' said he. 'This day we must travel with the greatest precaution.'

"We struck into a run that led into the river, in a winding direction, through the hills. We had not advanced far when we discovered meat hung up; we examined it, and found that it had been killed the day before.

"We then concealed ourselves in the laurel, and while in the laurel, says Sam—'I thought I was not mistaken in the Panther; he and some of his party have been to Sinnemahoning, and are now just returning. They are in this neighborhood, and they will be here for this meat to-day. We must dog them to their camp, and ascertain their numbers.'

"I asked Sam why these devils delighted in murdering their old neighbors? 'They are encouraged by wicked men,' he replied, 'in the service of the King of England.' 'That can't be, Sam,' said I; 'the Indians have got to be devils in human shape. Oh, God! Little did I think, when Wamp lay sick with the small-pox, that he would be so wicked. Your brother James and I killed his winter meat, for he was not able to hunt. We divided with his family, Logan and his squaw; also, the Eagle and his people; and now he would poison me with what I gave him to keep him alive. Logan is true, but the Eagle is off. 'Yes,' said Sam, 'he is out of sight, but not without marking uncle Sam, by shooting off the lower part of his ear. They were watching each other, and as uncle Sam peeped round a tree, Eagle fired, but it was his last shot. The next moment he was wallowing in his own blood—his head cleft with the force of the tomahawk.'

"'I am determined to kill Wamp. You must kill the man I point out. And when with me in ambush, you must watch my motions.' Which I did. His countenance would tell me, without an order, when he desired to strike a fatal stroke.

"We espied three Indians coming; two squaws, and an old man, who was a camp-keeper. They had not got to the meat before I discovered that Wamp's squaw was with them; which I told Sam. He told me there were twenty choice warriors he knew. 'There must be about thirty. Their spies must be Wamp, Hawk, Muncy, Snow, and Greatshot. They must fall first, and before they form a junction with the Sinnemahoning party, they will be but few.'

"We watched their movements, and in the evening discovered their fire. They thought themselves in perfect safety; their fires were brisk, which is a thing uncommon.

"After looking at them from the top of a hill, Sam observed—'Providence is smiling upon us—a good light for us, but bad for them.'

"While they were yet moving about the fire, Sam told me to 'come on.' 'Won't you wait till they lie down?' said I. 'No, now is the time,' said he, 'follow me.'

"We advanced to a tree-top, and there we stayed till we had counted every man, and Sam told me the name of every one. The Panther he particularly pointed out. Also the Blacksnake. We saw them step to the fire together; and two better-proportioned men never stepped the earth. 'Now,' says Sam, 'we could drop them.' 'Well,' said I, 'let us do it. Give me the right hand fellow, and I'll insure him bounce into the air ten feet.' With that they wheeled off. 'Their time is not yet,' said Sam. 'There comes the Panther, with his rifle. Peter, draw on that warrior that is resting his arm on his gun; *that is Wamp.* Hold, Peter, that old man will save the Panther once more. I will let him go; it would be too nice work, through the blaze of that fire, to graze the old man and kill the Panther. Make ready, and *fire!*'

"I saw them both bound, and light in the fire. In an instant the war-whoop was ringing through the hills. Sam held me by the arm for the space of a minute, then dropped down; I did the same, and twenty bullets whistled over us.

"We bounced to our feet; they were all in a bustle. 'Now, Peter, follow me, and load as you run.'

"We had not gone a hundred yards, when Sam stopped and bade me run in a line with the North Star. I went a short distance and halted. In a few minutes, Sam rushed by me with the speed of a frightened deer. I took after him, but soon found my error in not obeying his order. He was out of hearing in a crack, and the warriors at my heels. I thought I could run with any man, but that night I was convinced how inferior I was to my savage pursuers and my brave leader. They were coming up fast, when I heard a whoop ahead, (not like Sam's,) which induced me to believe I was surrounded. There was no reply to the whoop; and this created in me strange thoughts. I turned from the course, and lay down by the side of a large tree that had fallen out of root. I had just got placed, when four warriors bounded over the body of the tree, within a few feet of my place of concealment. They rushed through with the force of elks and the swiftness of arrows. Soon after they left me, I heard the report of a rifle, which I feared had laid my brave leader low. But soon after I heard the strange whoop, at a greater distance, and I was induced to believe that Sam whooped in that strange way to deceive the Indians in his race; to let me know that he was safe, and that he considered me so. The shot they fired was to lead him to think they had killed me, and by that means get him to risk his life for his companion.

"In an hour they returned from the chase, and passed within fifty yards of where I lay. I understood their talk, and heard them say they thought we were from the mouth of the Juniata; that we had some place appointed to meet in the night, and would then take the right course for home.

"When they got by me a little, they halted. The talk then was as to which course I had taken. They concluded it was the swiftest runner they had neared so fast, and that I only then laid out my strength at that place.

"After they had disappeared, I got up and steered the course Sam had directed; but had not gone far before I met Sam. He complained of my not obeying his orders. I told him I had thought I could run as fast as him, or the Indians, but I was convinced that I couldn't. 'No,' said Sam, 'neither is there a man living that can beat me running through the woods. Peter, I would be doubtful of your speed in daylight.' 'Fear not, Sam, I will obey you after this; and would like to try them fellows to-morrow night again.' 'We will let them rest to-night,' said he; 'to-morrow we will try them again.'

"We then went to hunt a place to rest ourselves, and prepare for to-morrow's work. We had not travelled far until we found a place every way calculated for our purpose.

"We then examined our arms. I repaired my moccasins, and, after refreshing ourselves, we returned to where we had a view of the enemy.

"'I think, Peter, I sent the *Hawk* after the *Eagle.*' 'Yes, Sam, and *Wamp* has accompanied him.' 'They fell in the fire, which was in our favor. I knew they would do so, from the positions they stood in. You should never attempt to load or run when you fire upon them as we did to-night. The first thing they do, after the report of the gun, is to give the war-whoop; there is then a few minutes meditation with them; they then direct their pieces for where the flash was. Therefore it is better, after night, to stand in ambush and shoot. You can have a better view of them and who they are; you can discover when they raise their rifles, and then, as we did to-night, drop to the earth, and you are safe from that round. The instant the report of the guns is heard, bounce and be off. You then have the advantage of the smoke between you and them; and also the confusion of re-loading their guns, which will be heard above the sound of your feet. By observing these rules, I have picked out five choice shots in one night. We got through well, to-night; but I was determined the Panther's earthly career should be at an end to-night, if he joined pursuit, which he did. I passed you without observing where you stood, and that ruined my calculations. I thought you were ahead, until I ran as far as I thought you could have reached, taking your speed into consideration. The whoop I gave to let you know I was ahead and safe. You say it is a strange one to you. It is the way they mimic our young warriors, and was such as they would not take for mine. They will think I was a young hand, and the other they will take for you, when they see your tracks where we crossed the run.'

"We both fell asleep, but before day Sam waked me up. We moved to a more favorable position to watch their motions, and at daylight we saw them packing their things for a move.

"My heart was wrung to tears with the cries of Wamp's squaw. But after considering that we had always treated Wamp as a brother, and that he would conduct a party to destroy his old neighbors and best friends, the companions of his youth, (for we had often hunted with Wamp,) I did not regret his death. I well knew she would soon forget poor Wamp, and find a companion in the person of some other warrior.

"They moved off, as we expected, in a direction for the Eagle's Nest.

"After they had got out of view, we took a circuitous route, and got to a spring which we expected they would refresh at. After we had got ourselves fixed, Sam inquired of me how far I thought we were from the Clear Springs. I told him, 'not more than eight or ten miles.'

"After sitting silent for a short time, Sam observed to me, 'If you are willing, Peter, we will take a shot at them here, win or lose.' I told him I was. He then gave me his commands, pointed out the course I was to run, and stated what he thought the distance would be, which was one hundred and fifty yards.

"'Now, Peter, this will be quick work. They have but two guns that can hurt us above one hundred and fifty yards, so you may see we have twenty-five yards to gain before we are safe from their shortest shots. We will drop the Panther and the Blacksnake, but you must shoot the man I point out, be he whom he may.' I told him I would be particular.

"They soon made their appearance, descending the hill to the spring.

"The Panther led the way—terrible in appearance. Their step was hurried and unsteady, which proved their uneasiness of mind, and anxiety to join their brethren.

"We heard the Blacksnake say, as he came up, 'We will not delay long here; to-morrow night we must be with —— Jacket's party.'

"'You see that man that is talking?' 'Yes, I do.' 'That is your mark. The signal will be the pressing of my foot against yours; when it stops, the trigger must go. Hold, Peter! The Panther is preserved again, the papoose is on his lap, and the squaw holds his gun. He must again slip. I have his brother,' and with that, off goes our rifles, and we to our heels.

"I led the way, which raised my pride. I was determined Sam should not pass me. I never looked behind until I had made not only twenty-five yards, but five hundred, good measure. I then looked down the hill and saw Sam coming, bounding over the bushes with the ease of a buck, and at least two hundred yards behind me.

"I could not help but laugh, to see Sam coming.

But my laugh was soon changed by the appearance of the whole party, (excepting the two squaws and an old man, who remained with the children.) They came like as many wild horses.

"One was advanced far ahead of the rest, and I thought it was best to be off, if I wanted to keep the lead, and save my credit. When I got to the top of the hill, I turned round and discovered that they were coming up with me, fast. I heard them holla, 'Petey, Petey, Petey,' which was the name they had for me. I dashed down the other side of the hill from where they were; and when I thought I had made my distance again, I halted. I looked back, and, to my surprise, spied the Panther on the ridge, not three hundred yards from me, and Sam was out of view.

"The first thought that struck me was, that Sam had met his fate; and I had just determined to await mine, and avenge his, by the death of the Panther, when I heard the report of Sam's rifle. I saw the Panther bounce into the air, and behold Sam run up to him and speaking for a moment. Then he snatched up his rifle, and with the speed of the eagle's flight he passed me. The Indians in an instant sent a volley of balls after us, and in an instant after, it was returned by the brave Capt. Foster and his party, who rushed by like hungry wolves. Then it went helter skelter; crack after crack we had it from behind the trees. But the Indians had to turn out and receive the messengers of death; for Sam, ever ready and thoughtful, had connected a fire round and got between them and their baggage. It was then the Indians gave way to despair, and rushed through the woods for life.

"We found ten on the ground, besides Blacksnake and Greatshot, whom Sam and I had shot at the spring.

"We found the Panther dead, but the Blacksnake was yet alive, and *vomiting blood.* We took the old man and squaws prisoners, whom Captain Foster released. We made all dead shots that day.

"The Indians were buried as well as we could bury them. Our men all escaped with sound hides.

"I shall always think Foster and Sam had laid the plan to meet at the spring. But Sam told me, after the battle, that the Captain had got uneasy about us. He had heard the reports of our guns the night before.

"The men told me the Captain had been absent the night before. As it was, we had defeated the Indians, which was all we desired.

"I well remember the looks of the Blacksnake, and old man. When Sam stepped to them, the Chief looked with astonishment; with a sullen composure, he named 'Sam Brady,' and departed.

"'He is gone,' said Sam, 'to appear before that bar where his brethren and I will have to be judged for the deeds done in the body.'

"Sam examined the prisoners' stock of provisions, which he did not consider sufficient to last them to where they could be provided for. He added of ours to their stock until he thought the supply amply sufficient. He then told them if they would go to one of the forts and remain until a treaty was made, they would be well treated; but if they did not, they must expect great difficulties before they again found their people. He gave the old man a rifle and plenty of ammunition, and bade him travel for Chinklecamoose. We then marched for the Nest, (Bald Eagle's,) and reached it by ten o'clock at night.

* * * * * * * *

"The Indians were far ahead of us, and our rest was

but short; we were kept on the move by that industrious warrior, Sam. By ten o'clock the next day, we were on the waters of Panther Run—now called Beech Creek.

"After we had crossed the creek, Sam, Bob Lyon, and myself started on; we went at a quick pace, and found, by signs, that we were coming up with the Indians.

"At nightfall, we went to the highest peak near us; from thence we could see the fire of our party far behind us, and that of the enemy before us about three miles. We saw another light in the direction for the Sinnemahoning. Also, a glimmering light, on the ground, about a mile from the furthest light, and to the left of our line of march. Sam appeared to observe the small light particularly. He was silent for a long time. At length he arose and told us we would go nearer the first Indian light.

"'There are,' said he, 'two Indian lights before us; the small light has disappeared; I suppose it was a star.'

"We went within half a mile of the Indians' fire, and to where we had a fair view of them. There were but five of them, and they were all standing up. 'It would be hard to get a shot at them to-night,' said Sam; 'they are keeping a sharp watch, and will soon be off to the bush.'

"We lay down. I looked in an hour afterwards—there was a large fire, but the Indians had disappeared.

"Lyon observed this and awakened Sam, and told him we had better go down to the fire, it would be more comfortable.

"'If we do,' says Sam, 'we will perhaps find ourselves placed alongside of a fire before morning that would not feel any better than these cold rocks.'

"In the morning we started by sunrise, and had not advanced far when we discovered a man descending a hill in front of us. Sam asked me who would be the spies from the other party. I told him I thought Peter Vincent would be the only man out from that party, and that must be him. We soon met. He was much surprised to meet Sam, as all the party were, the day before.

"He informed us that the Indians were collecting at Upper Youngwoman's Creek; that there were some hunting on the Sinnemahoning, and up Kettle Creek; that their party were waiting at Muncytown until they could hear from us.

"'You have had a brush with them, I think, from their movements,' said Vincent, 'I saw ten this morning who appeared to be limber in their joints; they walked slowly and in silence, as if they thought the race over, and they were mourning their departed friends.'

"Vincent hated them beyond my power of expression.

"We were soon led off by Sam, at a smart gait, and in a different direction. In about two hours we reached a run that formed a gap in one of the many mountains in that part of the country. We climbed up the side of the mountain next the run. We had but just placed ourselves to take a view, when Vincent spied them—told us he saw them, and pointed to the direction in which he saw them coming.

"Sam led off and descended the mountain to where he thought they would pass. We then got our orders, and placed ourselves in ambush.

"The direction we were to run, if there were more than twelve, was down a descent, and along a deer path which wound around the side of the mountain. If there were twelve or any number below it, we were to take trees which we had picked out—every man knowing his tree. After the second fire we were to close with the Indians.

"I noticed Lyon looking at the stock of his rifle, very attentively. Says I, 'Bob, is there any thing wrong with your gun?' He had fell that morning, and I thought he had cracked it. 'No,' said he, 'I am looking to see how it will do to club with. I have had two hard races, in consequence of breaking my gun in these d——d closing scrapes.'

"We took our stations, and they soon came; but, to our surprise they were fifteen in number. They moved in the utmost silence within seventy yards of us. Vincent was next to Sam, and I was next to Vincent, consequently Lyon was to take the ninth man. The pressure of the foot was from Sam; it continued for the space of a minute, when off goes our rifles, and we to our heels.

"I was again in the lead, and before I heard a shot from the enemy I was two hundred yards around the side of the mountain. I looked around and saw Lyon at my heels, bounding like a Conestoga horse. Vincent was a short distance behind him, and Sam was hid from me by the mountain, as I supposed; he always would be hindmost, and generally stayed till he saw what they would do.

"By turning my head to look, it caused Lyon to look around also and brought me so close to the body of a tree which lay across the path, that when I jumped, the toe of my moccasin touched a knot on the body of the tree, and I fell across the path, and out of Lyon's sight.

When he turned his head I was gone. He sprung over the log, and lit fair on my shoulders; he lost his balance, and fell with his head against the root of a tree.

"In the meantime Vincent came on; he cleared me, but Bob in his struggle, threw up his leg, which Vincent's foot took and he went cantering down the mountain like a bear, on all fours.

"I was not able to rise for some time, and when I did rise to my seat, I saw Bob getting up and rubbing his head with both hands, and with a rueful countenance he says, 'Grove, what made you lie across the path?' With this Vincent came up in a terrible rage, saying, 'And what the plague did you trip me for? I saw you laughing as I ran by you.'

"'You are d—dably mistaken, Vincent,' said Bob.—(They were both hard swearers, and Vincent was a man of quick and violent passion.) 'Come,' says I, 'this is no time to wrangle; let us be off, or the Indians will be upon us.' 'Darn them, let them come,' says Lyon, 'they will find the work half done with me, for verily I believe my skull is cracked.' 'It was darn thin,' said Vincent, 'ever since I knew you.'

"At this, Sam bursted out laughing. I thought he would never get over it. He had seen Vincent take the pitch, and concealed himself,—knowing Vincent's temper.

"'It must have been Bob's grinning with the pain in his head you took for laughing, Peter,' said he to Vincent. 'I don't know,' said Vincent, 'but one thing I do know; I took a darned hard fall from his foot.' We were soon reconciled.

"The Indians took off—leaving their dead—four in number. We laughed about an hour; and I have often laughed out when by myself, when this came into my mind.

"We returned, but had not travelled far before we met our party, which had been fired upon by one of their spies, but no harm was done. Capt. Foster would not let our men pursue, for fear of being ambushed.

"We encamped and set our watches. This was the first night Sam and I had the benefit of a good fire, since we left the Clear Fountains.

"Sam was a great quiz, and therefore, we had made him promise not to tell our tumbling scrape to the party. But it was too good for him to keep. Vincent could not stand it so well as Lyon and I, which made Sam more severe on him. Vincent told Sam that he thought him a better warrior since he had been over the mountains —'But,' said he, 'the older you grow, the darned sight bigger fool you are.'

"In the morning the watch told us they had seen lights on the river hill, and one that appeared at a great distance, and was soon out of sight. Vincent said he had observed that light the two preceding nights. There were many remarks about that light from the men; but I noticed that Sam and Foster said nothing about it.

"Sam, Vincent, Lyon, and I, started for the river.— After travelling for an hour together, we parted; Vincent and Lyon steered for Youngwomanstown, and Sam and I for the Sinnemahoning.

"As we parted, Sam said, 'Vincent, try and keep your feet.' 'I'll take care,' said Vincent, 'that Lyon don't take them if it comes to running.' Bob hallooed— 'This darned critter will tomahawk me to-night.'

"We struck the river between the mouth of the Sinnemahoning and Kettle Creek. The mountain is high. We sat down and took a view of the country, which is mountainous and broken. The mountains butt in close to the water's edge, with here and there a small bottom. The Indian path runs along the opposite side of the river from where we were seated. The country had a dreary aspect, beyond anything I ever saw.

"We sat in silence for some time. Sam says, after we had taken a view of things, 'Peter, it seems hard we can never leave the savages in peaceful possession of this country, which appears so rough and terrible to us, but so well adapted to their habits of life. It appears to me as if the Great Creator of the Universe, who provideth for all creatures, had formed this for their particular use; those small bottoms to raise their corn, the river their fish, and the mountains their deer.' 'Yes, Sam, and if they would quit murdering our families and friends, and stand by us in obtaining the object for which we are now fighting, they would find us brothers, and they might roam in safety through the land.'

"'Now, Grove,' observed Sam, 'we will soon be within the range of some as brave warriors as ever stepped. We must proceed with the utmost care, and if we are surprised do as you see me do; and my orders obey.—If you are shot, I will stand by you till you die, or die in your defence. But I will not cross that river until you promise me that if I fall by a bullet, you will leave me to my fate and risk nothing for me. Bear to my friends the tidings of my death; tell them I fell fighting for the rights of my oppressed country, and in defence of the unprotected inhabitants of Pennsylvania.' 'This is hard for me to do,' said I, 'I would rather stick to you to the last.' Sam replied, 'I will not cross on any other condition.' I made the promise, determined to stick to it, as I knew Sam was determined to stick to his to me.

"He then opened his wallet, from which he drew a bundle that he opened and spread upon a stone. He then painted my face and hands, and after he was done he handed me a small looking-glass to see myself. There I was, a complete Indian, painted for war, with the mark of my tribe.

"I gave him the glass, and as quick as a cat could wash herself, Sam was painted. His mark was different from mine; he told me the meaning of the marks. We now ate some jerk, and prepared for a move.

"Sam looked down the mountain—'Peter,' said he, 'here is the Rubicon'—he then looked up and down the river—'and, as Cæsar said, 'the die is cast.'

"We crossed the river at a ripple near the mouth of the run, and on the path, and along the beach, we saw 'signs.' We rushed into the bushes, and put to the top of the mountain, to where we had a view of the surrounding country far up the run. Sam told me he had a camp far up this run. * * * * *

"We avoided the path, and all soft ground. Sam was in the lead, as usual, when four bullets went whistling past our heads, and rattled in the leaves far beyond us. Sam bounced into the air and fell as if to rise no more until the day of the resurrection—from what cause I know not. I was by his side and ready for the enemy. They came bounding like panthers, two abreast. *I got the touch of the foot.* Whang goes our rifles. The first two dropped—giving the death scream; in a crack we were engaged with the other two, whom we soon laid dead at our feet, and we were off for the Sinnemahoning.

"We had not run far when we heard whooping, which Sam answered, and made motions to these Indians which way their enemy ran. They took us for their own people.

We continued our own course for a short time, till we were hailed again; we made no answer, but altered our course and travelled at a slower pace.

"Says Sam, 'this shirt that Mr. Foster gave me, had nearly cost us our lives. The collar is too clean, which I saw when I looked in the glass; I intended to color it, but forgot to do so.'

"I lookod at tho shirt, and saw that it was bloody. 'Sam,' says I, 'you are wounded, let me look,' which I did. He was grazed by a ball, but would not let me say it was a wound. Many a deep scratch Sam got, but would never acknowledge he was wounded, while I was with him.

"We struck the Sinnemahoning at the lead mines or 'copperas works,' ascended the highest mountain in the neighborhood, and stopped for the night. We had shot a deer and cut out the rounds of it, and, by making a low fire among the rocks, we feasted well. After our feast, we put out our fire, and moved away from where it was. Then we climbed into a tree, for the purpose of watching for lights.

"We saw lights descending the Sinnemahoning, and reflections of lights on the river, (Susquehanna,) up against the clouds. Also, one light over on the run where we had the last skirmish. And north of that light we saw the faint glimmer, for a minute, when it disappeared, and we saw it no more.

"Sam heaved a sigh when the small light flashed; it appeared to me to be far above the earth, and caused me to think strange thoughts; but I trusted in Sam's spirit, and was not afraid. I asked Sam what he thought they were about. He said they would now collect in a body, and descend the river to murder and ravage the country, or re-cross the mountains to the Alleghany river.

"Sam named to me a chief, (whom I will not now name,) who he said was the deepest villain amongst them. He was cowardly, avaricious, and cruel. He was well known as one of the murderers of his brother James. Had taken his scalp, and owing to his cowardice, had lived to this day. Said Sam, 'many of the whites believe he is friendly inclined. He wears the mantle of peace before them; but I have seen his cloven foot. And if he ever dares to stand in battle where I am, he shall bite the dust, and know who caused him to do it. But he ever keeps a strong party of his warriors around him. He is more afraid of me than he is of the bad spirit. He knows if he ventures from safety, uncle Sam or I has him. Then he is lost to his people, though they should suffer famine.' We descended the tree and lay down to rest. Before day we were off, and soon came to the run where the Indians had fired on us the day before. We found they had started in the night. We kept west and north of their trail. We crossed the Kettle (creek) about three miles above the mouth, and by four o'clock we were on the highest land between Kettle Creek and Youngwoman's Creek. We pushed on with speed; also in different directions. We slipped through the bushes until we got to where we could count their number, which was one hundred and twenty-five.

"'This is a fearful odds,' says Sam, 'what will be the number from Fort Augusta?' I told him about fifteen. Vincent told us Captain Coler was on Pine Creek when he left the party, for the first scout; that Reed had killed two of their spies up the creek; and that the party would remain there until we sent them word.

"Sam and I then lay down. About the middle of the night we got up, and all the fires were out. 'Now, Peter,' said he, 'they are for the other side of the mountains.' I told him I thought not. 'We will soon see,' said he.

"We travelled so as to intercept them or cross their trail by daylight, if they had steered for the Alleghany.

"At daylight we spied them. Sam told me we must get in front of them, which would be fast travelling. They went on at a quick pace. We put off, and soon got even with them. We were hailed by one of them that was on the scout. Sam stopped and looked at him, telling me to keep moving on. He soon came up to me. 'That fellow is deceived,' said Sam. With that we heard the crack of a rifle—another, and all was silent for the space of a few moments.

"We stepped by the side of two trees that stood close together. We saw the Indian running to join his companions that had hailed us. I told Sam I could drop that lad. 'He will stop presently,' which he did, by a tree.

"We now heard the firing of rifles in the rear of the Indians. Sam took off, and I after him. We were hailed three times, which we both answered, without ever turning our heads. We stopped behind trees in line with the Indians, and in front. We waited until they were within one hundred yards, when I got the signal from Sam. We fired and kept our station. We heard two rifles go off on their left, and three on their right. The Indians halted; we re-loaded and fired again. The Indians gave the war-whoop, and the bark of the trees behind which we stood whistled round our ears. We wheeled to run, when we spied two Indians running for life. We made for them; they stopped, and in an instant they were laid low, but not by us. We wheeled again, and just in time to have a chance for our lives—three Indians, of uncommon size, were in the act of tomahawking us. I punched the muzzle of my rifle in the stomach off one, which caused him to bend forward, and with my tomahawk I laid him. One of the others bounded against me with the force of a wounded buck, which knocked me off my feet, and I lit on my knees. He was shot through the heart. Sam and a mighty warrior were standing with their tomahawks hooked, and * * * * *

[The manuscript is here mutilated. Three inches, or about twelve lines, are lost. At the top of the next page, the narrative thus proceeds:]

"'Devil'—with that he tore the scalp off. I looked at Sam; his whole frame shuddered.

"In the meantime, up comes Vincent holding up his arm with his hand full, saying, 'here, Sam;' with that Sam takes off, and Lyon tells Vincent, 'you're a darned hog.' The latter replied, 'hold your tongue, or by thunder I'll skin them every one, and send their skins to the fort.' 'If you do,' says Lyon, 'I'll shoot you the first time you come down to the Point.' (Northumberland.)

"Uncle Sam and Vincent were great friends, and hated the Indians about equally.

"We now went to the river. We found the Indians' canoes, which they had not destroyed. We remained four days. The second day, Sam disappeared, and I never saw him again till after the war.

"I was walking down the street in Carlisle. I heard he was there. I spied a number of gentlemen coming up street. I knew Sam by his walk; he was walking alongside of the brave and humane General Potter.

As Grove spoke it, (saith the MSS.) I will give it to you:

"'I thought Sam youm darned brout. I see he look on the side of his het to me. I hat mine hundin shirt on, and rifle gun on my sholder. All the shentlemens but Sam and General Botter look on the odder side of their hets. Sam look pig—I get tam mat. I go to durn up anoder street, Sam say, 'ma, ma,' I does shtop and say 'ma.' Sam jumb to me in doo jumb. Well, it dook all but Botter a long dime to walk. Sam and de General dake me to a dabren, where we had one d—d hard frolic on wine—*de General bay for all!*"

[It was now nearly day—my wife and children gathered around him while he related these expeditions.]

"I told Grove, if he would call, I would write this down; it might be of use in a future day. He called at different times, and I continued the subject until I got it all, which I *reserved*, believing the day would come when it would be wanted."

Grove related to me his massacreing the Indians on the * * * You shall also have it if you give * * * *

[And here it ends—the lower end of the page being off, as before observed.]

THE END.

www.ingramcontent.com/pod-product-compliance
Lightning Source LLC
LaVergne TN
LVHW021257110826
845150LV00003B/410

9781425560706